HOW TO Restore Your CORVETTE 1963-1967

Chris Petris

CarTech®

CarTech®

CarTech®, Inc.
838 Lake Street South
Forest Lake, MN 55025
Phone: 651-277-1200 or 800-551-4754
Fax: 651-277-1203
www.cartechbooks.com

© 2012 by Chris Petris

All rights reserved. No part of this publication may be reproduced or utilized in any form or by any means, electronic or mechanical, including photocopying, recording, or by any information storage and retrieval system, without prior permission from the Author. All text, photographs, and artwork are the property of the Author unless otherwise noted or credited.

The information in this work is true and complete to the best of our knowledge. However, all information is presented without any guarantee on the part of the Author or Publisher, who also disclaim any liability incurred in connection with the use of the information.

All trademarks, trade names, model names and numbers, and other product designations referred to herein are the property of their respective owners and are used solely for identification purposes. This work is a publication of CarTech, Inc., and has not been licensed, approved, sponsored, or endorsed by any other person or entity.

Edit by Paul Johnson
Layout by Monica Seiberlich

ISBN 978-1-934709-76-4
Item No. SA223

Library of Congress Cataloging-in-Publication Data

Petris, Chris.
  How to restore your Corvette 1963/1967 / By Chris Petris.
       pages cm
   ISBN 978-1-934709-76-4
1. Corvette automobile--Conservation and restoration--Handbooks, manuals, etc. I. Title.

  TL215.C6P395 2012
  629.28,722--dc23

                2012000640

Printed in USA
10 9 8 7 6 5 4 3 2 1

Title Page:
For a complete and thorough restoration, the body needs to be separated from the chassis. Keep an eye on the rear fenders as the body rises because they tend to come very close to the rearmost body mount stanchions. Look frequently to make sure there are no wires, cables, or hoses that should have been disconnected.

Back Cover Photos

Top Left:
Now the front end with the inner fenders installed can be set in place. The side fenders need to be pulled outward to go around the cowl at the doors. You need to plan out the procedures before the adhesive is mixed. There is no backing off now; the front end must be placed back in the same position it was fitted in as soon as possible.

Top Right:
The cylinder heads have seventeen 5/8-inch bolts on each side. The outer cylinder head bolts can be difficult to get a socket onto fully. These special Snap-On sockets help get into the tight spots. Use a short 5/8-inch socket and extension in lieu of the special socket. The cylinder heads have dowels to hold them in place until you are ready to remove them.

Middle Left:
Applying an even coat at the corners and edges is very critical. The spray gun can be adjusted to limit material flow and fan pattern to avoid puddles of base coat. Pay careful attention at enclosed areas because the paint may spray back at you. Usually the spray back also ends up with sags.

Middle Right:
Slip the bearing on after first gear, and then install the blocker ring. We apply heat to the bearing to prevent the use of the hammer, but you may have to give the bearing a little help with a small hammer and punch to get it in place.

Bottom Left:
This front disc brake assembly is in need of a complete reconditioning. The rotor will be replaced and the caliper will be disassembled and new seals and components will be installed.

Bottom Right:
Each front floorboard carpet section is installed after Thermo-Tec and jute insulation is installed. This is where you have to be extra careful and ensure the carpet is fully seated into the floorboard recesses. If the carpeting is not sitting tightly to the floorboard when trimming it can end up too short at the console.

CONTENTS

About the Author 5
Acknowledgments 5
Introduction 6

Chapter 1: Choose Your Corvette 7
   Fiberglass Bodies 7
   Handling 8
   NCRS and Bloomington Gold 9
   Collector Values 10
   Exterior/Interior Differences 11
   Options 11
   Skills and Capabilities 13

Chapter 2: A Corvette by the Numbers:
   What to Look For 15
   Codes, Codes, Codes 16
   Inspection Results 24
   Analyzing a Potential Project 27

Chapter 3: Getting Started 28
   Types of Restoration 28
   Shop/Garage Requirements 29
   Parts Cleaning 30
   Paint Preparation 30
   Equipment Needs 31
   Sourcing Parts 32
   Disassembly 33
   Body Lifting 40

Chapter 4: Bodywork 41
   Components to Consider 42
   Inspection 42
   Fiberglass Repair 45
   Fiberglass Panel Replacement 51
   Fiberglass Panel Removal 52
   Frame Repair 55
   Prepping to Paint 56

Chapter 5: Paint 59
   Safety Concerns 59
   Choose a Shop 60
   Should You Do It Yourself? 61
   Paint Types 62
   NCRS or Bloomington Gold Paint Refinishing 63
   Practice Applying Paint 63
   Paint Facilities 64
   Body Prep 65
   Post-Paint Work 72
   Body Reinstallation 72

Chapter 6: Engines 74
   Other Factors to Consider 75
   Engine Disassembly 75
   Machine Shop Service 78
   Short Block Assembly 81
   Top End Assembly 85
   Valve Adjustment 86
   Alternative Engine Options 86
   Bloomington Gold/NCRS Requirements 89

Chapter 7: Transmissions 90
   Identification 91
   Disassembly 94
   Inspection 97
   Assembly 99
   Transmission Options 104

Chapter 8: Driveline 106
   Clutch Linkage 106
   Bellhousing 110
   Differential 111
   Driveshaft/Axleshaft Installation 118

Chapter 9: Brakes 120
   1963–1965 Drum Brakes 125
   Drum Brake Options 127
   Hydraulic System 127
   Master Cylinders 128
   Brake Lines, Fittings, Hardware 128
   Power or Manual Brakes? 129
   Brake Fluid 130
   Parking Brakes 130

Chapter 10: Suspension 133
   Design Innovations 133
   Alignment Terms 135
   Suspension Restoration 137
   Rear Wheel Bearing Service 138

CONTENTS

Make a Plan of Attack 141
Chassis Disassembly 142
Subassembly Disassembly 144
Rear Trailing Arm Installation 145
Steering System Installation 145
Subassembly Installation 147
Component Installation 149

Chapter 11: Electrical and Wiring 151
Electrical System Inspection 152
Wiring Advances 153
Component Restoration 154
Alternators 155
Using a Multi-Meter 156
Starter Motors 156
Ignition Distributors 158
Electric Motors 160
Gauge Clusters 162

Chapter 12: Interior 164
Seat Covers 165
Headliner and Insulation 167
Cowl Vents 167

Dash Assembly 168
Carpet 170
Window Trim 171
Seats 171
Door Panels 171
Convertible Top 171
Hardtop 176

Chapter 13: Other Components 178
Fuel System 178
Mechanical Fuel Injection 180
Cooling System 181
Air Conditioning 183
Sound System 184
Ignition Shielding 184
Wheels and Tires 185
Power Steering 186
Power Windows 188
Exhaust System 189
Windshield and Glass 189

Source Guide 191

ABOUT THE AUTHOR

Chris Petris owns Petris Enterprises, a Corvette restoration and repair shop. He gravitated toward the Corvette service industry after spending many years involved in drag racing, restoring, and modifying Chevrolets. His involvement with Corvettes began at Greenwood Corvettes where he performed tuning and built performance transmissions and differentials. Eventually, he went on to manage Eckler's Corvette Service Center, and during that time Paul Zazarine, editor of Corvette Fever magazine, asked if he would provide tech material for the magazine. Later on, Petris' own tech articles and tech columns were published in Corvette Fever and Corvette Enthusiast magazines.

Chris has been presenting seminars at Bloomington Gold, Mid America Fun Fest, and Corvettes at Carlisle for several years. He also provides tech material and annual seminars for the National Corvette Owners Association. Chris is a SEMA member and avid motorsports fan who enjoys driving his own collection of early Chevrolets and Corvettes as often as possible.

ACKNOWLEDGMENTS

Many thanks go out to the Corvette community for working with me through the book. Sometimes things just seem to fall in place without even trying. For instance, Jerry and Scott Kohn of Corvette Central had been talking about possibly restoring a 1963 Corvette split-window coupe. The conversation took place just a few weeks before I was approached about writing this 1963-1967 restoration book. The timing was right and having an iconic 1963 split-window as the lead restoration Corvette could not have been scripted better.

Many thanks go to Jerry Kohn, Scott Kohn, and Mike Coleman at Corvette Central. Jerry spent countless hours discussing the project and helping to find the right parts. Scott kept the parts coming while Mike, Corvette Central's shop guru, helped with many of the date-coded and stamping photos.

John Ferguson of Market Street Performance deserves a special thanks for allowing me to photograph the entire engine component machining process at his shop. The majority of the restoration took place in our shop with the exception of the bodywork and painting.

Seth Wood, owner of Lucky's Customs, spent many hours making the 1963 look good while I took notes and photographed the process.

Many other Corvette suppliers listed in the source guide deserve credit for the fine components they provided.

Writing this book has been quite a ride from beginning to end. I was fortunate enough to have the support and help of family so this project could be completed. In the final analysis, I think I have created a unique, instructional, and immensely helpful guide for restoring a Midyear Corvette, and I hope you agree.

The project started out strong, then my wife, who has been by my side through many of my 40-plus years in the automotive industry, suffered a medical issue. Our daughters, Stacy and Stephanie, stepped in and helped us get through that rough time. I also got a dose of just how hard my wife works to keep up with everything around the business and household. I was able to write a good portion of the text while she convalesced and it made me realize just how much my family means to me. The tough part was trying to keep our Corvette restoration shop going while shuttling back and forth from writing to our business/family matters. Somehow as a family we made it. Many heartfelt thanks go to my daughters who have backed me in all the automotive endeavors I have pursued.

I would like to thank the many people who helped in the process of writing this book. My daughter Stephanie critiqued the text and photo captions as each chapter was completed, which it sorely needed. Mike Uruquart created computerized illustrations and helped in

ACKNOWLEDGMENTS

the shop as the restoration progressed. I truly appreciate the support and friendship of both Michael McKenzie and Sean Hotaling over the years. Austin Weddington, a very good friend, performed the bulk of the mechanical work and put up with me as I took hundreds of photos. I greatly appreciate Austin's contributions and his willingness to keep working near midnight and beyond on many occasions. Andy Bolig of *Auto Enthusiast* magazine and Ed Hartnett of Ed Hartnett Standard Transmission Service, thank you for helping me with some of those difficult-to-find photographs; I could not have done it without you. The hard work and professionalism of so many dedicated individuals helped this book to be completed in true team spirit. I must also say many thanks to my editor Paul Johnson who worked with us through the ups and downs to make this restoration book something we could all be proud of.

INTRODUCTION

Midyear Corvettes have been restored, modified, and kept in survivor status for many years. Plenty of books about how to restore them have also been written, with the majority covering the correct numbers-matching aspect. We have plenty of nearly perfect specimens representing the Midyears' rich history in cocoons protecting them from the harsh environment. Of the approximately 125,000 Midyears built, why not drive a few? This restoration book covers the importance of the numbers-matching angle and how it can affect the value of your finished project, but the main focus is to help you restore a fun, drivable Midyear without lessening its ultimate resale value. No Midyear Corvettes were harmed during the writing of this complete restoration book, and in fact, all modifications are reversible.

This book gives you an idea of which cars to look for or avoid and, more importantly, which to modify or leave factory original. Once you find a candidate for purchase, a rigorous pre-purchase inspection is detailed so you avoid buying a car that has major mechanical or body problems that will cost you big money. As you progress through the book, it explains the correct flow of work to keep you on track, which saves valuable shop space while managing your time efficiently. I also cover where to locate parts so you have them on hand when needed for a particular procedure.

In-depth restoration procedures, including plenty of photos and explanations, are presented in an easy-to-understand format. The mystique of correctly repairing damaged Midyear Corvettes fiberglass body panels is shown in great detail. Painting and preparation tricks and techniques are shown to create a Midyear you may just want to drive or make a top-dollar show car.

Owning a Midyear to show is one thing, but setting one up for driving on today's public roads requires real seat time. Detailed explanations of upgrading components for better overall performance and adding creature comforts are provided. The Midyear braking system, for example, went through a number of changes throughout its existence. I explain how to choose the pieces for the best possible braking system without devaluing your early Corvette. The upgrades make the car safer and more enjoyable to drive, whether it's a daily driver or a weekend cruiser.

The procedures covered are gleaned from many years of hands-on experience and from a true Corvette shop perspective. Insight into what the savvy mechanic should and should not do is covered in detail. If outside restoration help is required, and in most cases at least one or two phases necessitate it, this book helps show you whether the procedures have been performed correctly. I have performed and written the procedures, not translated and then put into words by someone else. The one exception is the overall exterior paint itself. Although we do not do overall paint in our shop, we have been involved in many paint restorations. My number-one goal is to make novice restorers feel comfortable with the work and decisions made as they restore their first Midyear Corvette.

CHAPTER 1

CHOOSE YOUR CORVETTE

Let me start with the "lingo" that the Corvette crowd uses so you are on the inside track. The 1963 to 1967 Corvettes are called "Midyears" and anyone engaged in the hobby immediately knows the Corvette generation we are talking about: the cars built during the middle years of the decade. Based on my conversations with well-versed Corvette historians, no one seems to know for sure who dubbed the '63 to '67s Midyears, but it stuck. I will be referring to the entire second-generation Corvettes as "Midyears" throughout the book.

"Solid axles" are the 1953 to 1962 Corvettes equipped with a conventional-style solid differential.

Because of their long, low, shark-like bodies, the 1968–1982 Corvettes have been nicknamed "sharks."

Fiberglass Bodies

Corvette fiberglass bodies have changed throughout their existence. The 1963–1967 bodies were heavier than the early solid-axle cars, not much, but just enough to take care of some inherent flex issues. There are no bolt-on panels except for the rear lower valance. The body assembly is comprised of numerous fiberglass panels bonded together. The front end consists of an upper surround that goes from the front bumper to the windshield frame. Lower side fenders are attached to the upper surround to complete the front end. The rear has the roof and deck panel with rear fenders. The front and rear fender split line meets the upper panels about an inch below the surround panel. Bonding strips are used to connect and reinforce the panels at the front fenders and rear areas. Factory-supplied Midyear body panels are press-molded fiberglass, meaning both the inner and outer surfaces are smooth.

The main body panels are bonded to the "birdcage," as most Corvette restorers call the steel enclosure for the driver/passenger cockpit area. The windshield frame and door-pillar posts compose the

This is a beautiful example of a Bloomington Gold Certified 1963 coupe. The washboards on the unique '63 hood really set it apart. Many painstaking hours were put into this correct restoration. Is this the path you are interested in taking? This museum piece keeps the Corvette heritage alive. It is not very likely that this Coupe will be driven much, if at all.

Convertibles with hardtops have a smooth look that is timeless; the best of both worlds allowing you to drive your Corvette in just about any weather. The owner of this '64 told me he has fun attending car shows within a 100- to 200-mile radius.

front section of the birdcage. C-channels connect the front and rear sections. Rear pillar latch posts connect to the roof frame on coupes. Coupes have the added strength of the windshield frame connection to the roof frame.

Handling

You need to familiarize yourself with the many changes that occurred in the short span of the Midyear's existence, especially if you plan on aggressively driving the restored car such as driving a couple hundred miles to a major Corvette show or maybe even entering a Gymkhana track event.

The 1963–1964 model years have drum brakes, which work okay, but we are all spoiled now with disc brakes. Sliding behind the wheel of an original '63 or '64 after driving your late-model car can get you into trouble. The fading brakes can turn your stomach in knots during high-speed stops. All the pieces are readily available to convert to disc brakes at all four corners.

The 1965 Corvettes dropped front drums for four-piston-calipered disc brakes as standard equipment. You could also order rear disc brakes, if you were so inclined on the '65s. Even with the rear drum brakes, the '65 is much more drivable at highway speeds.

The 1966 and 1967 model years had four-wheel disc brakes to counter the ever-increasing horsepower. Transmission options were plentiful and the minor mechanical annoyances of the first model years were fixed. These early Corvettes were on the cutting edge for their time, in spite of their idiosyncrasies. Mechanical fuel injection units available on the 1963 through 1965 Midyears had their issues. Many of the early fuelie units were removed in favor of carburetors, to eliminate the constant need for tuning and adjustments. Three-speed, fully-synchronized manual transmissions were standard. Manhandling a Midyear without any power accessories meant just that.

The point is, you have many things to consider when choosing the correct Midyear for you. Drive it, show it, or a combination of both can work depending on how comfortable you want to be on the road.

Another path you may take is finding a desirable Midyear to restore, then hit the show circuit attaining National Corvette Restorers Society (NCRS) status. Many of these projects are eventually sold as an investment, but market trends are hard to project, sometimes turning an investor car profit into a deep downward spiral.

This is what an award-winning Midyear looks like from the bottom. The original raw fiberglass floors are spotless. This beautiful example of a '66 convertible has been flawlessly maintained for many years.

These spring tags and shock absorber stickers were part of the assembly build. Every Midyear received multiple markings to denote what pieces should be installed. NCRS and Bloomington Gold Judges look for the correct placement of these stickers and correct finishes.

CHOOSE YOUR CORVETTE

A team of NCRS judges checks out an original '63 from all angles. The first order of business is to verify the VIN and trim tag under the glove box. It's not a quick process, and many items are checked from front to back then scored on tally sheets. It takes a lot of stamina to have someone scrutinize every aspect of your vehicle. You are competing with yourself as to how well the restoration was done.

The judges are conferring on their findings on this 1967 Midyear convertible with "Stinger" hood. Marina Blue 427-ci convertibles, such as this one, are highly sought after. The knock-off look-alike wheels were available only in 1967. These wheels bolted on in the traditional fashion eliminating the possibility of loose wheels, which was commonplace with knock-offs. Expect to have some items removed as the judging takes place, such as the ignition shielding and air cleaner on the ground in front of the car.

These are the many considerations you should put into the equation before heading out to find your project.

NCRS and Bloomington Gold

What is the NCRS? The National Corvette Restorers Society has taken on the challenge of keeping Corvettes in their original state. The NCRS prides itself on preserving the history of the American sports car. Thankfully, many 1963 to 1967 Midyear Corvettes have been restored to off-the-assembly-line status and judged by NCRS to ensure authenticity. Each component, nut, bolt, and assembly is carefully inspected for correct fit and finish, which is great for preservation of the Corvette heritage for future Corvette owners.

Many Corvettes have been over-restored using many differing standards than off-the-assembly-line status. This is a concern to the NCRS because they want the fit and finish to look as it did when the factory assembled each Midyear. Restoring a Midyear to NCRS standards is in a class by itself. You need to consider every piece on the Midyear, and each one you purchase. Is it going to pass the judge's inspection?

Bloomington Gold Certification is another highly recognized standard for the Corvette restorer to achieve. Bloomington Gold Certification was conceived to encourage Corvette owners to preserve or restore their cars to factory-authentic condition. Within their process to restore and preserve the Corvette's heritage, they recognize the owner's efforts. Achieving Gold status requires an off-the-assembly-line finished vehicle standard.

There is no competition among Corvettes at Bloomington Gold events. Any Corvette that meets the Bloomington Gold standard receives the award. Corvettes awarded Survivor status are "Worn in, but not worn out" as quoted from

CHAPTER 1

So you say your '63 convertible was in rough condition? This partial '63 convertible was seen at a local Corvette show with a sale price of $6,900 with title. This gives you an idea of the great lengths Corvette restorers go to have their own Midyear. Restoring this for a first-time project really puts you to the test. I say spend a little more and get a Midyear in one piece.

the Bloomington Gold Quick Guide. The ultimate award for a factory-original Corvette is the Benchmark. These Corvettes must also be able to pass a 40-mile road test. Neither the Benchmark nor Survivor categories pertain to our project, but they do play a part in how an original restoration should look.

Concerns you may run into are finding someone who understands all the correct original Corvette component finishes. This is an important part of Bloomington Gold and NCRS judging guidelines. General Motors used a number of different cadmium coatings on driveline components, requiring the help of specialty shops for proper plating. This all means more cost to do an NCRS or Bloomington Gold restoration. To find all the pertinent data for correct pieces you need to consult other publications.

Date codes are on almost every casting: engine blocks, transmissions, water pumps, fuel pumps, carburetors, and alternators for instance. These date codes are carefully scrutinized along with casting codes and part numbers during judging.

Finding the correct original GM fasteners is another time-consuming part of the restoration. General Motors had specific stampings on the heads of the screws and bolts that must be in place. Most of the major Corvette suppliers have many date-coded components available to help ease some of the anguish in locating the correct parts. Invariably there are a few pieces that cannot be found easily. You know what that means; more money due to limited supply.

The NCRS or Bloomington Gold path may be the way for you to go and is certainly worth investigating. They both have great websites that explain their heritages and missions. The wealth of information provided is worth the membership. These organizations have technical information, manuals, and judging guides that cover Corvettes from 1953 to 1996. All the manuals provide excellent, up-to-date information on part numbers, casting numbers, date codes, and detailed descriptions. We need to have those correct Corvettes out there to show our pride in the great accomplishments of so many people who made the Corvette a reality.

Restoring any Corvette to NCRS or Bloomington Gold standards means resale value may be higher than the typical Corvette. Keep in mind that the knowledgeable buyer carefully scrutinizes every component as if it were being judged for correct casting, date coding, and part numbers. Many things affect resale price, making it impossible to say with any certainty that certified NCRS or Bloomington Gold Midyears have better value. On the other hand there are many Corvette owners who want to customize and personalize their Corvette. The numbers-correct and the personalized crowd generally put up with each other, in spite of their differing opinions. It makes sense to enjoy both sides of this hobby.

We need to preserve the heritage, but also enjoy driving the Midyear Corvette. History shows that certifications and awards do help, but do not bank on those alone. It comes under the heading, "There is a seat for everyone's backside, you just have to find the right backside for your seat."

Collector Values

Chances are the '63 split-window coupe and any '67 Corvette coupe or convertible with excellent documentation costs the most upfront. There is usually a premium on the aforementioned cars due to their popularity. The '63 split-window has legendary status, making it more costly. There are few people who restore a low-production-run 1967 427-ci convertible for use as an everyday driver. Likewise, the 1963 to 1965 Corvettes with mechanical fuel-injected 327-ci engines are rarely driven. The 1965 one-year-only big-block 396-ci Midyear is in the same category.

The pinnacle of power in the Midyears occurred in 1967 with the 435-hp Tri-Power engine, or so it may seem. General Motors built what many believe to be a very underrated option L88 427-ci engine with aluminum cylinder heads. Historians say early L88s had iron cylinder heads. The single Holley 4-barrel-equipped L88 was rated at 430 hp and could approach nearly 600 in the right tuner's hands. With only 20 known L88 Midyears produced, they are the costliest to purchase. Many Corvette purists feel that no matter how rough or how few

Assembly-line workers placed two red and one green slash frame markings to denote how many shims were required. Shims are used at the radiator core support for correct fiberglass front-end position.

Paint dots were placed on many components to signal that a procedure was completed on the assembly line, or possibly to let the assembler know that this particular steering box was ready for installation. This information is from various sources, and no one can definitively answer as to why they were used. However, you must have them if you want to be awarded.

pieces you may have, fuel-injected and big-block cars must be put back together as original. This keeps their value in the stratosphere for the most part.

Less desirable are the 1964 Corvettes with drum brakes all around. Low-horsepower '63 to '65s with minimal options are easier on the wallet in comparison to the big-blocks. General Motors produced few Midyears equipped with 3-speed manual transmissions; but a few of these command big dollars. Those equipped with Powerglide automatic transmission are also few in number, but are more desirable than those with 3-speed manual transmissions.

Purchasing any '64 to '65 Corvette can make sense if you are not hung up on the look of the '63 coupe, '66, or '67. General Motors upped the low-horsepower version of the '66 to 300, increasing its value over the earlier years. Something you need to consider is that the money saved on purchasing a less desirable Midyear can be more than consumed during the restoration phase. No matter how you look at it, you will be in a Midyear Corvette, and that is never a bad thing.

Exterior/Interior Differences

What makes a '63 Corvette different from a '64? The '63 coupe has the unmistakable split rear window with "washboard" inserts in the hood. The 1964 brought about some cleaning up of the exterior. No more washboards on the hood, although the recesses for them remained. The '65s and '66s had smooth hoods with redesigned gills. The 1967 received a completely different looking gill treatment with functional airflow. Standard equipment back-up lights were added to the rear valance in 1967, as well. Big-block-equipped Midyears had hood bulges to accommodate the taller big-block engines.

Interior differences from year to year were minor. The '63s had a turn signal switch mounted on the outside of the column with a cable operating it. The '63 and '64 instrument clusters have unique-looking gauges with recessed centers. The '66 and '67 had optional headrests available; must have been to keep your head on your shoulders when the 427-ci engine Midyears were drag raced. General Motors put an all-new parking brake lever in the middle of the car for 1967 that worked so much easier than the earlier Midyear under-dash release. Why is the '67 Corvette possibly the most sought after? Like so many car lines, the last model year in a generation is best. The '67 was the culmination of all the hard work for this generation.

Options

What should you look for? The 1963 coupe or convertibles were available with air conditioning and leather seats (saddle was the only color available) for the first time. Signal-seeking radios dubbed the "Wonderbar" appeared in the '63s. Larger metallic brake linings with finned brake drums were offered for 1963 and 1964. The 1964 brought knock-off wheels into the picture and leather seats in all colors. More goodies came about in '65: side-mounted exhaust, goldwall tires, and telescopic columns with teakwood steering wheels. Shoulder harnesses and headrests were added to the option list in 1966. Back-up lamps became standard equipment in '66s; the last year for knock-off wheels.

CHAPTER 1

Brake calipers with dots and more shock absorber stickers. We all know that these markings and paper stickers are often destroyed or ripped off during service. Major Corvette suppliers have the stickers and paint to reproduce the markings.

More shim slash markings here where there are no shims. Quanta Reproductions has kits available with all the stencils, crayons, and correct color paint for the ultimate restoration. Quanta Restorations has paint daubs and instructions on where and how to place these markings.

The '66s had a push-button AM/FM radio available for the first time.

The 1967 Corvettes were all about race-related options, and there were plenty of engine and transmission possibilities. Bolt-on knock-off look-alike aluminum wheels were available with red-stripe tires. A speed-warning indicator was also offered on the '67 to warn you that you were on the throttle. Most likely, the big-block '67s kept the speed-warning indicator active all the time! Differential options were plentiful from 3.08:1 to 4.56:1 for those who wanted to visit the local race track.

Special performance equipment option Z06 was available in early 1963 and included a 36-gallon fuel tank and knock-off wheels. There were other mandatory options that had to be ordered with option Z06, including fuel injection, 4-speed transmission, and Positraction differential. Z06s got big, sintered metallic brake linings, finned brake drums, and vented backing plates. These Z06 brakes were not the same as the J65 offered as the metallic brake option; these were true race braking systems that took getting used to. Later, during the '63 production run around January 1, the Z06 option was modified to include convertibles, but excluding the big tank.

Knock-off wheel availability for '63 is questionable; there is no verification that any customer ever received them on a car. Rim porosity problems caused leakage concerns, which held up their availability until '64. General Motors dropped the Z06 moniker in '63, although the big tank Midyears could be ordered through 1967.

Midyear "tanker cars" as we call them today, are essentially road race coupes, plus the one convertible that was produced for 1963. Sure, there were some tankers that did not see race use or the standard equipment, but they are even more rare. Tankers are a rare find and very valuable, no matter what year you may find. With only two tanker '67s made, you can imagine their values. Six figures is the going price for any one of these rare big tank road race examples.

Power steering, power brakes, and air conditioning were available in all the Midyears, with a few exceptions. General Motors mandated that engines equipped with solid lifter camshafts not have air conditioning, nor do Z06s, of course. General Motors added another Tri-Power carburetor engine rated at 400 hp with a hydraulic camshaft (and oval intake ports) to comply with A/C requirements. This meant you could have plenty of ponies and enjoy A/C in southern climates.

Transistorized ignitions were available in 1964 and were required with special high-performance engine packages. Hardtops, tinted glass, and other creature comforts made the Midyear at home on the track or cruising the highways.

Deleted equipment can sometimes equate to more value than highly optioned cruisers. General Motors gave you a credit for deleting the heater and defroster. Out of 117,966 Corvettes produced, only 312 had the heater/defroster delete package. You know what use these Corvettes were destined for. Finding any Midyear with the heater/defroster delete is a great find. On the other hand, a non-Positraction-equipped Midyear detracts from its value. Not many non-Positraction Midyears left the factory, but they are of no help on the bottom line at resale.

Missing original driveline components are a major concern if you plan on seeking any NCRS or Bloomington Gold certification. Finding the dated and casting coded pieces with correct part numbers can be a daunting task. Some Corvette suppliers specialize in providing correct-coded engines and transmissions. They have typically spent time locating and storing engine blocks and

Stencils were used on the canister oil filters of the day. I found a blue oil pan gasket on this '66. The gasket was cork for an original factory-built Midyear. At this stage, you need to decide if you want all of these beauty marks on your chassis or if you want to drive it. You can rest assured any water under this '66 is unintended and discolors the paper tags.

The RPO Z06 was an awesome factory-built race car for the time. The $1,293.35 option was a really big price to pay for a $4,250 base-price Corvette. Today, this Z06-optioned coupe is highly sought after, and the price tag reflects it. This particular Z06 never made it to the racetrack back in the day and has actually accrued more than 50,000 miles. That is a big deal if the original race-bred brakes are still in place. The brake shoes had to be good and hot before they were predictable.

transmissions, waiting for the opportunity to sell one. You pay plenty for all those correct numbers and date codes, even if the components are not that rare. The supply is limited and they understand that. So will you, when it comes time to pay.

Many Midyear pieces have been reproduced by now. The positive side is that every day, more and more parts are being reproduced. High sales volume pieces get top priority, so there will always be some difficult items left to find. Exterior stainless-steel trim around the doors, for example, is really tough to find. No one is reproducing the stainless-steel pieces and that could cost a bundle if they are missing.

There are some birdcage and windshield frame pieces available new, but not enough to build a complete assembly. If you find a severely rotted birdcage, you had better be able to do the required metal fabrication and welding. Remember: someone else is always trying to build a Midyear from pieces. They, too, may be on the hunt for what may seem to be insignificant parts, at the same time that you are looking for yours.

Missing original seat frames can be tough to locate, especially good, restorable assemblies. Interior trim items around the rear window or windshield are made of "unobtainium." The restoration business has coined the term "unobtainium" for pieces that are hard to find and are therefore just about priceless. Instrument cluster restoration is going to cost considerably more if gauges are broken or missing. If the original radio is missing, they are available, but expensive.

Hot cars are another thing to watch for. No, not stolen cars (although you should be aware of those also). I'm talking about toasty cars that have been on fire. Personally, I would rather restore a burned car than a severely wrecked car. Either way, tread lightly if you consider getting involved with any wrecked or burned Midyear. There are limits: for instance, a small underhood fire that destroys the hood or maybe some inner/outer fender damage is not so bad. If the firewall has been badly burned, I say, "Run!" These pieces require many hours of meticulous hand fabrication. This is extremely costly, and most likely the birdcage has heat damage also. Collision work is tough, and you need to be able to measure properly and then pull to square things up. This takes expensive equipment and expertise to make sure the job is done correctly.

Skills and Capabilities

My objective, as I mentioned earlier, is to find a Midyear intact with possibly only the drivetrain missing. I have the tools and resources to handle just about any project that comes into the shop. Major labor operations like lifting the body can be difficult at home. For example, restoring the rear suspension trailing arms requires special tools and preferably a sturdy bench to work on. The engine and transmission can be removed easily enough, then sent out for repair or restoration. Rebuilding an engine or transmission can be a major concern for someone doing a project at home. Tools are expensive, especially if you are only going to use them once.

Before you go out and look at the first Corvette, consider just how much of the

CHAPTER 1

This ultimate barn find has all documentation and 99 percent of the original pieces intact. This '67 435-hp engine and close-ratio Muncie 4-speed require a complete restoration. This would be a great restoration project for someone starting out except for the price tag. Many hours of research are saved when the Midyear has all its pieces in the right place. The finished product commands high dollars, as do the parts and labor to restore it.

project you can do yourself. It is easy to get caught up in the moment thinking, "That really should not be that tough to do." Then you get home and realize just how hard it will be to complete your Corvette. Many unfinished projects are sold for just this reason. Lack of interest can stop even the most determined restorer when things go wrong.

Some areas of a restoration require higher skill levels than others. Equipment and special tools play heavily into the equation; hard work sometimes just does not suffice. Engine restoration requires precision machinery to bring the components back to factory specifications. Transmissions require more specialized training than tools, making them easier for the first-time restorer to accomplish. Differentials that require a bearing and seal change require more experience than special tools. Changing a differential ring and pinion, on the other hand, requires special set-up tools. Send the engine out for machining and send the differential out if you plan on a ring-and-pinion change.

The bodywork and paint is a tough call (see Chapter 4). Paint and body shops usually do not like it when you bring in a car "ready for paint." Painters do not like to paint cars that were at other professional body shops. They know that no matter what the outcome, they are responsible for what it looks like. If the paint looks bad due to poorly performed bodywork, no one will say "look at that atrocious bodywork." The bad rap will be on the painter. You either need to find someone to paint after the bodywork is done, or do both.

The interior seems easy enough, and for the most part it is. The trick is knowing how and where each fastener is installed. The dash electrical systems for the Midyears are relatively simple, if you use new harnesses. The connectors are not fool-proof, so recording how things come apart plays heavily into the outcome here. By far the windows and doors can be the most perplexing.

My plan is to make you feel comfortable with each area of the restoration, whether you plan on attacking it yourself or not. Knowing what the finished product should look like is a powerful bargaining chip. The same goes for how all the systems should operate. The upside is that there are few special interior tools that need to be purchased; patience is the main tool to have.

Before you take the plunge, check with local experts and Corvette owners for reputable local shops. Take the time to visit the recommended shop and see what it looks like and the attitude of the workers. If you find someone you feel comfortable with, explain that you are looking for a Corvette to restore. Whether you plan on doing the bodywork/mechanical restoration yourself or not, shop owners can give you an idea of what costs are involved. This gives you an idea of what areas you should consider doing yourself. Many times the cost of the equipment or tools outweighs the cost of doing it yourself. At the very least, try asking two shops for information and some insight on their costs.

You should expect to pay them a reasonable fee to look over a potential project. This can save plenty of money in the long run, avoiding the "bad penny," so to speak. If the relationship is good, it can be well worth the money spent having them consult on the project. No offense to the brother-in-law who spent the last 20 years working on Honda Civics, but there is a good chance he most likely does not have the expertise required. It takes years of experience to know the in and outs of any mechanical device and this is no different.

You can waste a lot of hard-earned money listening to the wrong person. Opinions are everywhere and certainly there are people who restore Corvettes as a hobby that are well-versed. This is who you need for help—as long as he really has hands-on experience. One last thought on the subject: Yes, there are people who tell you what you want to hear. Accepting their advice after others have cautioned you to stay away, is usually very costly!

CHAPTER 2

A CORVETTE BY THE NUMBERS: WHAT TO LOOK FOR

General Motors, like all the other car manufacturers of the time, did not put much valuable information on the vehicle identification number (VIN) plate. Starting in 1963, the VIN denoted coupe or convertible and build sequence. The fourth VIN digit is a 3 for a coupe or a 6 for a convertible for all of the Midyears built. The serial number followed the coupe or convertible code, to give you an idea when the Corvette was built. The serial number is where the date codes on the engine and other components come into play. All date-coded driveline components could be cast weeks, if not months, before the vehicle assembly took place. Finding an early production VIN Midyear with an engine date coded later than when the Midyear rolled off the assembly line is not correct.

A thorough inspection begins on bright sunny day which will allow you to see all the possible problems that you may encounter. Times like this can get you fired up and in trouble and restraint needs to be exercised. Put together a plan before talking any numbers. Bring a flashlight, note pad to record numbers, and possibly a floor jack to have a quick look underneath. If you feel that the project has possibilities set up a date when you can have a professional come by to look at the candidate.

To the left of the VIN tag, General Motors placed a trim tag with some helpful information. Unfortunately though, no drivetrain data is included. Assembly and body build dates help to decipher correct component date coding. There are Corvette numbers fanatics who can tell you that on the fourth week of May only "x" number of bodies were built because there was a shortage of resin. This is somewhat exaggerated, but they do analyze every number carefully. Many of the original assembly line workers are no longer with us, so it is difficult to really pin down some of the things that slowed or sped up production. Research is the only way to find out as much data as possible. I urge you to be very cautious concerning any date or casting codes. Part numbers also should be researched very carefully to ascertain validity if an NCRS or Bloomington Gold restoration is in your future.

Once you determine whether the engine VIN matches the vehicle VIN, paperwork concerning the validity of the Midyear increases the value. As hard as this may seem to believe, valid paperwork can mean an increase of 50 percent or more in a Midyear's value. General Motors started using Protecto-Plates in

CHAPTER 2

This VIN plate is riveted onto the lower dash support brace where the glove box door is attached. The second and third digits (08) tell you it is a 1963 or 1964 Corvette. The fourth digit (3) tells you it is a coupe. "S" identifies the St. Louis assembly plant. The last six digits (112xxx) tell you it was built about two thirds through the model year.

You can see whether the VIN and this trim tag information coincide. The "H2" is the build date; "2" is the second week of "H," April. That makes sense with the later VIN production number with the final Midyear being built in the last week of August. The style information on the left should match the VIN: '63 for 1963 and 837 for coupe. Trim "490J" denotes dark blue vinyl. Body 6909 is the actual body production run making it right for the number of coupes built that year. Paint "916A" is the Daytona Blue exterior color of the coupe.

1965 for their warranty records, which denoted specific engine, transmission, and axle codes. The Protecto-Plate was affixed to the owner's manual, but all too often, the manual was lost or was not given to the next owner. Protect-O-Plates also had the original purchaser's name, along with the other data. This could be immensely helpful, if the original owner is still available to verify the information on the Midyear.

In 1967, the factory used a "build sheet," containing all the pertinent data for the build as the Corvette moved down the assembly line. This is the most sought after document because it validates the complete drivetrain and all options and accessories. The build sheet, also known as the tank sticker, was affixed to the top of the fuel tank. Unfortunately, many of these tank stickers have been damaged with time and the elements. Since 1967 Corvettes are such a hot commodity, convincingly forged tank stickers have been found. Some forgers have created weathered reproduction tank stickers to look like the original item, so beware.

Codes, Codes, Codes

General Motors stamped the engine block with the last six digits of the VIN. Letters and numbers were used to denote horsepower, and the transmission to which it was to be coupled, as well as the month and day built. "F" or "T" was used to denote Flint, Michigan, or Tonawanda, New York, as the foundry supplier. An anomaly occurred during the 1965 model year run during a foundry shutdown: A limited number of 327-ci engines with casting number 3858180 were supplied by Tonawanda. The Flint foundry manufactured all other small-blocks, which were 327-ci engines. The Tonawanda foundry supplied all of the big-block 396- and 427-ci engines.

Engines

All major castings and many other parts received a part number permanently cast into the component. This part number is referred to as the casting number. Engine blocks (or "cases" as General Motors called them) have foundry casting codes denoting the time and day it was built. This is what judges and perspective buyers are looking for. The engine pad stamping must coincide with the casting number and date codes for a true "numbers matching" engine case.

For example, deciphering the 1966 engine code F0219HP goes like this: F is for Flint, Michigan; 02 is the month of February; 19 is the day built; HP identifies it as a 327-ci 350 HP engine with 11.0:1 compression ratio, 4-barrel carburetor,

This is not a Corvette Protect-O-Plate; it is from the 1965 GM car line. Beginning in 1965 the Protect-O-Plate was imprinted with engine, axle, and transmission code information. The imprinted plate was sent with the vehicle documents. After purchase, the owner's information was imprinted. It was then sent to the new owner to be affixed in the warranty booklet. When a warranty repair was required, the service writer ran the plate through a credit-card-like swipe machine transferring the data to the repair order. Reproductions are out there, so having an original Protect-O-Plate is a very valuable piece of documentation.

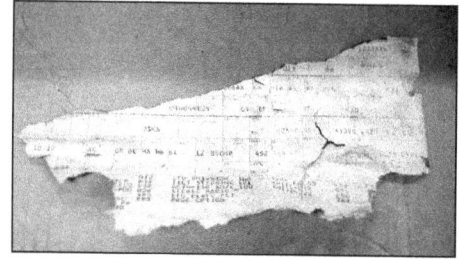

General Motors began attaching a tank build sheet/sticker in 1967. Finding an intact tank sheet or sticker is rare. I found the remnants of this one on top of the fuel tank. The elements are tough on the paper over the years. The few Corvette purchasers who retrieved these highly sought after documents were paid dividends later.

A CORVETTE BY THE NUMBERS: WHAT TO LOOK FOR

Engine Identification

Checking for the correct engine ID requires looking for a corresponding VIN, casting codes, and proper date codes. This engine ID code chart will point you in the right direction while giving you an idea of how to check for casting and date codes.

1963 Corvette Engine Codes

Code	Number of Cylinders	Displacement (ci)	HP	Ratio	Carburetor	Transmission
RC	8	327	250	10.50:1	4-barrel	Manual
RD	8	327	300	10.50:1	4-barrel	Manual
RE	8	327	340	11.25:1	4-barrel	Manual/SHP
RF	8	327	360	11.25:1	Fuel Injection	Manual
SC	8	327	250	10.50:1	4-barrel	Automatic
SD	8	327	300	10.50:1	4-barrel	Automatic

1964 Corvette Engine Codes

Code	Cylinders	Displacement (ci)	HP	Ratio	Carburetor	Transmission
RC	8	327	250	10.5:1	4-barrel	Manual
RD	8	327	300	10.5:1	4-barrel	Manual/HP
RE	8	327	365	11.0:1	4-barrel	Manual/SHP
RF	8	327	375	11.0:1	Fuel Injection	Manual
RP	8	327	250	10.5:1	4-barrel	Manual/A/C
RQ	8	327	300	10.5:1	4-barrel	Manual/A/C
RR	8	327	365	11.0:1	4-barrel	Manual/SHP/A/C
RT	8	327	365	11.0:1	4-barrel	Manual
RU	8	327	365	11.0:1	4-barrel	Manual/A/C
RX	8	327	375	11.0:1	Fuel Injection	Manual
SC	8	327	250	10.5:1	4-barrel	Automatic
SD	8	327	300	10.5:1	4-barrel	Automatic
SK	8	327	250	10.5:1	4-barrel	Automatic/A/C
SL	8	327	300	10.5:1	4-barrel	Automatic/A/C

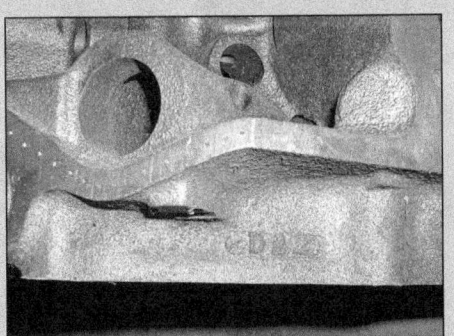

GM used engine block casting number 3782870 from 1962 to 1965. A few 3858180 casting number blocks were used in 1965. Two different 327-ci blocks were used with casting numbers 3858174 and 3892657 during the 1966 build year. The 3892657 casting carried over into the 1967 production run. The 1965 big-block 396-ci engines used casting number 3855962. The 1966 and early 1967 427-ci production run used casting number 3869942. You could find two other 427-ci casting numbers during the 1967 model year, 3904351 and 3916321.

This D22 cast into the engine block denotes the casting date. "A" for January and so on. "I" was used for September and "L" was December. "D" is April with the "2" representing the second day of the month. Digits 1 through 31 are used for day built. The last digit "2" denotes the year 1962. Since the production run starts before the end of the previous year "September," the engine block could possibly be found in an early 1963 Corvette. This would only be possible if there were a problem with the engine block during machining that required it to be pulled from production. The problem was solved, and then the block was put back into a production run. This is not the typical scenario, though date codes should be within a week or so of the final vehicle build date.

Engine Identification CONTINUED

1965 Corvette Engine Codes

Code	Cylinders	Displacement (ci)	HP	Ratio	Carburetor	Transmission
HE	8	327	250	10.50:1	4-barrel	Manual
HF	8	327	300	10.50:1	4-barrel	Manual
HG	8	327	375	11.00:1	Fuel Injection	Manual
HH	8	327	365	11.00:1	4-barrel	Manual/SHP
HI	8	327	250	10.50:1	4-barrel	Manual/A/C
HJ	8	327	300	10.50:1	4-barrel	Manual/A/C
HK	8	327	365	11.00:1	4-barrel	Manual/SHP
HL	8	327	365	11.00:1	4-barrel	Manual
HM	8	327	365	11.00:1	4-barrel	Manual/A/C
HN	8	327	375	11.00:1	Fuel Injection	Manual
HO	8	327	250	10.50:1	4-barrel	Automatic
HP	8	327	300	10.50:1	4-barrel	Automatic
HQ	8	327	250	10.50:1	4-barrel	Automatic/A/C
HR	8	327	300	10.50:1	4-barrel	Automatic/A/C
HT	8	327	350	11.00:1	4-barrel	Manual/SHP
HU	8	327	350	11.00:1	4-barrel	Manual/SHP/A/C
HV	8	327	350	11.00:1	4-barrel	Manual/SHP
HW	8	327	350	11.00:1	4-barrel	Manual/SHP/A/C
IF	8	396	425	11.00:1	4-barrel	Manual/SHP

1966 Corvette Engine Codes

Code	Cylinders	Displacement (ci)	HP	Ratio	Carburetor	Transmission
HE	8	327	300	10.50:1	4-barrel	Manual
HH	8	327	300	10.50:1	4-barrel	Manual/AIR*
HR	8	327	300	10.50:1	4-barrel	Automatic/AIR*
HD	8	327	350	11.00:1	4-barrel	Manual/SHP/AIR*
HO	8	327	300	10.50:1	4-barrel	Automatic
HT	8	327	350	11.00:1	4-barrel	Manual/SHP
HP	8	327	350	11.00:1	4-barrel	Manual/PS
KH	8	327	350	11.00:1	4-barrel	Manual/SHP/AIR*
IK	8	427	425	11.00:1	4-barrel	Manual/SHP
IL	8	427	390	10.25:1	4-barrel	Manual/HP
IM	8	427	390	10.25:1	4-barrel	Manual/AIR*
IP	8	427	425	11.00:1	4-barrel	Manual/SHP
IQ	8	427	390	10.25:1	4-barrel	Automatic
IR	8	427	390	10.25:1	4-barrel	Automatic/AIR*

* RPO K19 Air Injection Reactor system.

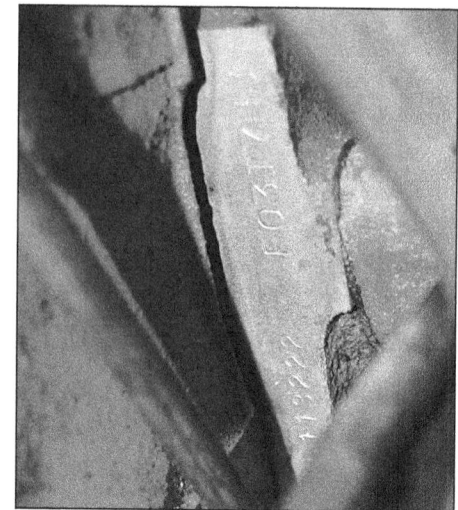

On A/C-equipped cars, such as this one, it is usually difficult to read the engine deck stamping on the block, which is in front of the passenger-side cylinder head. On F03I7HJ, "F" denotes Flint, casting "03" is for month built (March), and the day built is "17." The engine data code "HJ" tells you the 327-ci engine produced 300 hp and had a Carter AFB 4-barrel carburetor. The suffix letters also tell you it was in front of a manual transmission, and the 1965 had air conditioning. The serial number below it coincides with the VIN plate.

manual transmission, and power steering. General Motors used this same HP code in 1965, and it is quite different from the 1966. Still, it was a lower compression 300-hp 327-ci engine coupled to an automatic transmission. This is why matching the date codes to the engine pad stamping is important.

Cylinder Heads

Casting and date codes are also on each major component and many ancillary pieces. Cylinder heads have casting numbers with date coding like the engine block. Unfortunately, the valve covers hide all the numbers and codes. Intake manifolds have a date code along with a casting number. Aluminum cylinder heads and intake manifolds usually have a "W" stamp within a snowflake design

Engine Identification CONTINUED

1967 Corvette Engine Codes

Code	Cylinders	Displacement (ci)	HP	Ratio	Carburetor	Transmission
HE	8	327	300	10.25:1	4-barrel	Manual
HH	8	327	300	10.25:1	4-barrel	Manual/AIR*
HR	8	327	300	10.25:1	4-barrel	Automatic/AIR*
HD	8	327	350	11.25:1	4-barrel	Manual/SHP/AIR*
HO	8	327	300	10.25:1	4-barrel	Automatic
HT	8	327	350	11.00:1	4-barrel	Manual/SHP
HP	8	327	300	10.25:1	4-barrel	Manual/SHP
KH	8	327	350	11.00:1	4-barrel	Manual/SHP/AIR*/AC**
IL	8	427	390	10.25:1	4-barrel	Manual
JC	8	427	400	10.25:1	3X2	Manual
JE	8	427	435	11.00:1	3X2	Manual/SHP
IT	8	427	430	11.00:1	4-barrel	Manual/L88
IU	8	427	435	11.00:1	3X2	Manual/Aluminum Heads
IM	8	427	390	10.25:1	4-barrel	Manual/AIR*
JF	8	427	400	10.25:1	3X2	Manual/AIR*
JH	8	427	435	11.00:1	3X2	Manual/AIR*/Aluminum Heads
IQ	8	427	390	10.25:1	4-barrel	Automatic
JD	8	427	400	10.25:1	3X2	Automatic
IR	8	427	390	10.25:1	4-barrel	Automatic/AIR*
JG	8	427	400	10.25:1	3X2	Automatic/AIR*
JA	8	427	400	10.25:1	3X2	Manual/AIR*

* RPO K19 Air Injection Reactor system.
** RPO C60 Air Conditioning.

Cast-iron cylinder head casting number 3782461 was widely used from 1962 through 1966 on small-blocks. Casting "461" (as most people in the business call it) was available on optional engines in 1963 and 1964. Then in 1965 and 1966, it was used on all 327-ci engines. The 1967 Corvettes had a new casting (3890462) for the 327-ci engine.

The 396 engines in 1965 used the 3856208 casting. The 1966 through 1967 big-block engines had six different casting numbers. The big-block 396-ci engine had rectangular-port, closed-chamber heads (casting number 3856208). The 1966 had two casting numbers: 3872702 represented the oval-port, closed-chamber head for the 390-hp version, while 3873858 specified the 427-hp version with closed chambers and rectangular ports. The 1967 had early and late versions of both the rectangular- and oval-port heads. The early 3904390 and late 3909802 castings had oval-port, closed-chamber heads. The 3904391 and 3919840 casting had rectangular ports with closed chambers. The only aluminum cylinder head available for 1967 was casting 3904392 for the L88 and L89 427. All of the casting numbers are in the same location on big- or small-block—between valves.

indicating Winter's Aluminum Foundry Company.

Exhaust manifolds have casting numbers, but they may not have date codes. If the exhaust manifold has a date code, it may not be visible with the manifold bolted onto the cylinder head. General Motors used exhaust heat flowing through a tube connected to the passenger-side exhaust manifold for choke operation. The 1963 to 1965 fuel-injected exhaust manifolds do not have this machined hole for the hot air tube on the passenger side. The driver-side manifold received the machined hole for the fuelie's choke heat.

Transmissions

Midyears are often found with incorrect engines and transmissions because of the hard life that many early Corvettes had. Service replacement engine blocks were installed, and in some cases, engine blocks were "decked" (the cylinder head surface was machined, due to warping or

CHAPTER 2

Winter's Foundry cast this snowflake-and-W logo into GM factory aluminum intake manifolds. Aluminum cylinder heads typically have the same "snowflake" cast on them. This is the position to find the snowflake on valuable three-deuce intakes. The 1967 was the first year for limited availability of aluminum cylinder heads on big-block engines.

damage). When the surface is decked, the factory stamping is eliminated.

There are people who provide correct engine block stamping with all the anomalies that occurred when the factory did the stamping. The decking or machining also must match the finish that left the factory. Done properly with the correct matching date and casting codes, it is possible to pass NCRS judging. Companies, such as Paragon and Crane's Corvette Parts, have a stockpile of early Corvette engine blocks and other components. They are the first stop to find a correct engine block if that is the direction you are headed.

General Motors offered one automatic transmission for the Midyear: an aluminum Powerglide 2-speed unit. Manual transmissions were widely used, with Muncie-built 4-speeds being the predominant choice for buyers. General Motors' Saginaw 3-speed transmissions were offered as the base transmission.

This 1967 Muncie case (casting number 3885010) is in excellent condition. The letters and numbers on the vertical seam at the left side tell you that it is indeed a 1967 case. "P" stands for Muncie plant while "7" stands for the year cast. "D27" is the month of April on day 24. Letters began appearing in the 1967 model year using the engine block month designation system.

This Warner T10 has been through it all. The 12-28-62 side cover denoted it could have been in a 1963. The vertical clean spot (or kind of clean) has two of what should be letters telling you what gear ratio set it came with. QQ were 2.54:1 first-, 1.89:1 second-, 1.51:1 third-gear ratios. RR, SS, and TT were 2.20:1 first-, 1.64:1 second-, and 1.31:1 third-gear ratios.

Warner Gear was used to supply early 1963s with their 4-speed transmission.

For example, P01221 is a typical stamping found on a correct transmission for 1965: P for 4-speed Muncie Plant; 01 January month built; 22 for day built; and 1 for day shift.

Four prefix codes were used for transmissions with the exception of 1963, which had an additional "W" alpha for the Warner 4-speed. C represented Cleveland-built Powerglides, T for Toledo-built Powerglides, P for Muncie, and S for Saginaw-built 3-speeds.

Records say shift code 1 for day shift or 2 for night shift were used on 4-speed transmissions. Reportedly, day shift transmissions may not have the shift code suffix. Powerglide automatic transmissions were stamped D for day and N for night.

Finding incorrect casting and date-coded transmissions is commonplace. In many instances, cases were replaced or complete assemblies installed. There are vendors supplying correctly coded transmission assemblies for those who want to pay the price.

Axles

Rear axles were also stamped with rear axle codes and dates, but these can be very hard to see clearly. Stampings are found on the bottom rail of the differential housing where the cover meets the housing. The 1963 and 1964 rear axle coding identified the gear ratio, build month, and day. Rear axle code CJ0728 is: CJ, 3.08 Positraction; 07, July month built; and 28, the 28th day.

The 1965 to 1967 rear axle stampings were changed slightly to include build plant codes. Stamping AO0518W would tell us: AO, 3.70 ratio; 05, built in the month of May; 18, built on the 18th day; W, at the Warren plant. Buffalo would be "B" and Chevrolet gear and axle is "G" for their respective plants.

Axle Identification

GM used the same Eaton differentials from 1963-1979 and with so many identical-looking differentials out there, identifying them can be difficult. One major advantage is the lack of VIN coding with the ID codes making it easier to substitute differentials. This Axle ID chart will help verify the correct differential for your project if numbers-matching is your intent.

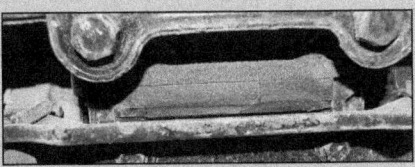

Rear axle codes are on the outer edge of the differential, visible between the rear spring plate and strut rod bracket. This stamping is a pretty good one. Many of these have been damaged over the years. This differential housing is in a 1964 coupe. Let us see how correct it is. AQ stands for a 4:56 Positraction gear ratio available only in 1965 with this designation. Then things get fuzzy because the 47 should stand for the month built and the 65 should be day of month built. There also should be a W suffix at the end for the Warren build plant. I believe this is a 4:56 Positraction differential built April 7, 1965.

1963 Corvette Axle Codes

Code	Description	Ratio	Code	Description	Ratio
CA	3-Speed	3.36:1	CD	Positraction	3.70:1
CJ	Positraction	3.08:1	CF	Positraction	4.56:1
CB	Positraction	3.36:1	CZ	4-Speed	3.08:1
CC	Positraction	3.55:1	CX	4-Speed	3.70:1

1964 Corvette Axle Codes

Code	Description	Ratio	Code	Description	Ratio
CA	3-Speed	3.36:1	CD	Positraction	3.70:1
CJ	Positraction	3.08:1	CE	Positraction	4.11:1
CB	Positraction	3.36:1	CF	Positraction	4.56:1
CC	Positraction	3.55:1	CZ	4-Speed	3.08:1
			CX	4-Speed	3.70:1

1965 Corvette Axle Codes

Code	Description	Ratio	Code	Description	Ratio	Code	Description	Ratio
AK	Open	3.36:1	AP	Positraction	4.11:1	AU	Positraction	3.36:1 396
AL	Positraction	3.08:1	AQ	Positraction	4.56:1	AZ	Positraction	3.55:1 396
AM	Positraction	3.36:1	AR	Open	3.08:1	FA	Positraction	3.70:1
AN	Positraction	3.55:1	AS	4-Speed	3.70:1	FB	Positraction	4.11:1 396
AO	Positraction	3.70:1	AT	Positraction	3.08:1 396	FC	Positraction	4.56:1 396

1966 Corvette Axle Codes

Code	Description	Ratio	Code	Description	Ratio	Code	Description	Ratio
AK	Open	3.36:1	AP	Positraction	4.11:1	AZ	Positraction	3.55:1 427
AL	Positraction	3.08:1	AR	Open	3.08:1	FA	Positraction	3.70:1
AM	Positraction	3.36:1	AS	4-Speed	3.70:1	FB	Positraction	4.11:1 427
AN	Positraction	3.55:1	AT	Positraction	3.08:1 427	FC	Positraction	4.56:1 427
AO	Positraction	3.70:1	AU	Positraction	3.36:1 427			

1967 Corvette Axle Codes

Code	Description	Ratio	Code	Description	Ratio	Code	Description	Ratio
AK	Open	3.36:1	AO	Positraction	3.70:1	AU	Positraction	3.36:1 427
AL	Positraction	3.08:1	AP	Positraction	4.11:1	AZ	Positraction	3.55:1 427
AM	Positraction	3.36:1	AS	4-Speed	3.70:1	FA	Positraction	3.70:1 427
AN	Positraction	3.55:1	AT	Positraction	3.08:1 427	FB	Positraction	4.11:1 427
						FC	Positraction	4.56:1 427

Documentation

Smaller ancillary items, such as the carburetor, starter, and alternator, were stamped with build and date codes. This is where you need to pull out your NCRS pocket guide and start crunching the numbers. No matter what direction you take, correct casting and date-coded pieces are valuable. For instance, if you find that the numbers do not show up in your NCRS pocket guide. They may be very valuable to someone with a factory-correct Camaro, Chevelle, Impala, or early Chevy truck. This can help offset the cost of replacing incorrect casting or date-coded pieces.

Be cautious with a really well-documented Midyear. Check all date and casting codes carefully. The stakes are high if you find a really great restoration project that has provenance; chances are you may invest more into the build. If the project is so valuable, why would someone sell it?

Alternator codes have an obvious placement at the alternator brace, which is typically on top of the alternator. The stampings should coincide with the engine options. This 1100694 unit is correct for my 1965 A/C-equipped coupe. The 5A14 build date is correct: "5" for the year 1965, "A" for January like the engine date coding, "14" for the day. The 42- to 61-amp-output alternators are found on big-block, A/C, and transistorized ignition Midyears.

Carter supplied all the carburetors for 1963 250- and 300-hp engines in 1964. The 1965 also used a Carter carburetor. The 250-hp engines used the Carter WCFB; 300-plus-hp engines received the AFB (Aluminum Four Barrel). The NCRS judges are looking for the stamped aluminum tag under the top cover screw at the right rear corner on this 300-hp 327-ci engine.

Holley carburetors were first used on the '64 365-hp 327-ci engine. The 1965 350-hp and 365-hp small-blocks, and the 396-ci big-blocks used Holley 4-barrel carburetors. In 1966 and 1967, Holley supplied all the small- and big-block carburetors, including the Tri-Power setup shown. Casting and part numbers were stamped into the right side of the air horn. This center carb (PN 3902355) has the correct number, but it is a new Holley replacement.

Even starter numbers are important. This casting number 1107365 starter field housing was for a 1966–1967 427-ci engine. "6H8" is the sixth day of August 1968. Starters and alternators were often changed after the vehicles were out of warranty. When I worked with General Motors, we rebuilt all alternators, starters, and wiper motors at the dealerships. In hindsight, that may have saved a whole bunch of trouble for many Corvette restorers.

A CORVETTE BY THE NUMBERS: WHAT TO LOOK FOR

Here is a case in point. I had a very nice 1967 Midyear convertible with a 435-hp 427 in the shop for some repairs. There were some concerns with engine performance. The new owner recently purchased the restored Midyear as an investment. While the car was in the shop, the owner wanted to know if I could verify the VIN engine codes and the trim tag. The block stamping looked peculiar. Mainly, the deck surface looked rougher than it should be. The trim tag designated a different exterior paint code than the paint on the Midyear. The interior color was also incorrect per the trim tag. I called the owner to see what documentation he might have.

The following day he brought a notebook in filled with photos and other paperwork. There was no tank sticker or buyer's order, just some parts receipts from previous owners. The photos had no VIN documentation, only pictures of someone restoring a multi-colored 1967 convertible Corvette. There really was no way to tell if the photos were even of this car. Not good!

There was a sick feeling in my stomach, knowing that the only thing I could verify was that the trim tag showed incorrect interior and exterior color codes. The next step was contacting a friend who sells Midyears regularly to see what he thought. Ouch! The incorrect exterior paint and lack of documentation meant the owner paid twice what he should have paid for this Midyear.

You need to understand that many of the early Corvettes are not going to have documentation available. This is where a decision has to be made, "Should I try to make it something it is not, or just drive it?" Without the proper documentation, the actual collector value is seriously eroded, and a high-end restoration for an undocumented car usually is not a wise investment. Because of the lower resale price it makes more sense to be frugal with the restoration and then drive the wheels off of it to get the most out of your money.

Every once in a great while, an unrestored Corvette comes along that has all the right stuff. I found an unbelievable Midyear in a barn at a major Corvette show with all the right documentation down to the original buyer's order. You know that unpleasant part of the new vehicle transaction when the numbers are laid out in front of you? The base vehicle is listed, then options are spelled out, and you had better make sure everything you are paying for is there. For example, the 435-hp 427-ci Tri-Power engine with transistorized ignition. Those who had the foresight to save the buyer's order, window sticker, and Protect-O-Plate warranty booklet have added substantial value to their Corvette.

Remember, window stickers are not reliable documents because they can be reproduced and then weathered to make you believe they are original. Sure, there are owners who held onto and preserved their window sticker, but that should not be the only document you put stock in. At best, without GM records showing exactly what came on any particular Midyear Corvette, you have to trust people. This is no reason to shy away; just do your homework. Do not get caught up in all the craziness surrounding the correct numbers.

Car theft has not been a major problem in the hobby because so many Midyears have history. The theft aspect is not so difficult, but covering it up after the fact is tough to do. It is kind of hard to keep secrets because when a Midyear is sold the word usually gets out in the tight-knit Corvette community. You do need to be aware that over the years original frames may have been swapped out when they rotted away. The replacement frame may or may not have the VIN stamped into it like it should. To play it safe, always get a signed and notarized receipt, and check the VIN with what is on the title. You would be surprised to learn that from time to time the VINs are not correct on the title. As I mentioned earlier, if there is no documentation, beware. Play it safe and do some research before becoming an unhappy owner of someone else's Midyear.

While this may not seem like a major concern, many early Corvettes could have a questionable past. After a certain number of years, some states drop the

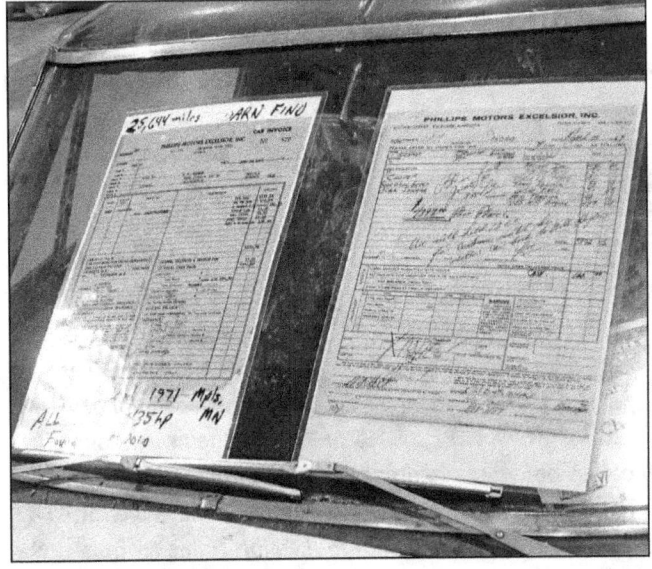

This is one of the many sought-after documents. This buyer's order spells out what options and trim level this 1967 had from the factory. This is a great piece of documentation that is very difficult to find. Be advised that there are artists out there who fake this document. If the dealership that sold the car is still open, you may be able to do further research.

GM stamped the last six digits of the serial number along with "S" for St. Louis. In spite of the typical corrosion found in this area, the VIN is legible on this Midyear chassis. The stamping is close to the outside edge of the frame rail directly above the driver-side rear tire. This number should coincide with the VIN. Bring a wire brush and flashlight to help find this stamping. Of course, it is a good idea to ask the Corvette owner before you go scraping and brushing on the car.

title requirement opting for registrations only. Someone who knows the rules of the system can obtain a registration in one state and then go to another to get a title.

A friend of mine called me frantically telling me that his early Corvette had a possible title problem. Someone had made claim to the Corvette, and it was their responsibility to prove it belonged to them. The officer said that if they had all the paperwork from the seller along with proper VIN verification everything should be okay. You guessed it; they wanted to see the chassis VIN along with the VIN plate. Luckily, all went well; the numbers matched and the paperwork was verified.

The point here is to make sure the paperwork is correct and all the VINs are in place before you pay for the vehicle. Go one step further and get the license tag and title or registration completed before investing in the project. If you find out that the paperwork is not right, you cannot register the car, or worse yet, have to hand the keys over to the legal owner.

It is important that you understand how documentation works and the value it adds. Many people are well versed in this segment of the hobby, so there's plenty of insight and knowledge available out there. *The Illustrated Corvette Series* by Scott Teeters has some really great Corvette facts and figures. *Fuelies: Fuel Injected Corvettes 1957–1965* by Robert Genat has excellent focused information on these revered Corvettes. *Corvette Sting Ray Gold Portfolio 1963–1967* has data, history, and plenty of specifications to assure you are looking at a correctly-numbered Midyear. *The Corvette Black Book* by Mike Antonick is a must for quick data on all years of Corvettes. NCRS has plenty of pocket-sized publications to get the skinny on all the numbers you could imagine. My goal is to help you feel comfortable with the knowledge to restore your project.

Inspection Results

Corvette frames have particular spots that corrode, and they can be easily seen unless they have been masked to cover damage. You guessed it; someone might actually improperly repair a corroded frame with body filler to save money. The most common corrosion area is at the rear frame rail kick-ups where the trailing arms pivot. The recessed area below the trailing arm pivot fills with dirt, salt, and water keeping the area ripe for corrosion. Over many years, this area can turn to rusty flakes and in extreme cases the entire corner of the frame can have huge holes. The same water/salt slurry attacks the frame behind the front wheels causing corrosion.

Front lower crossmembers can tell a tale of how the Corvette in question has been treated. The lower crossmember is the lowest and first point of impact. Any off-road activities bend this vulnerable area. Years of using floor jacks to lift the front end also takes a toll on the crossmember, eventually dinging it up even if there was never a substantial hit. Today, you can buy this lower crossmember panel to really clean up this often rough looking area. Cracks occur around the front spring pockets and steering box mount area. These cracks are not easy to spot until the grease is cleaned up in the area.

Midyear frame flex commonly occurs at the steering box, and over time

You need to carefully inspect Corvettes. This 1966 big-block coupe with off-road exhaust (not for use on public roads) has some serious frame rot. Both rear frame rails were eaten away with corrosion, which requires new rails to properly repair them. The C-channels and birdcage are also suspect for severe rot. The owner asked if I could just put some patch panels on the rotted areas. This is a structural issue and patching is not the answer. The body needs to be lifted to properly remove the rotted pieces and install new rails. Bottom line: Lots of money makes this frame rot go away.

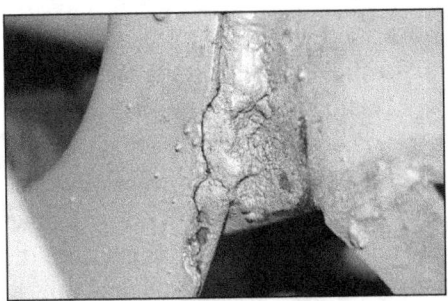

Look closely—this cracking occurs on many Midyear frames around the steering box and spring pocket area. This is not necessarily from accident damage or a hard life. Welding heat can weaken areas, especially at the outside edge of the weld, as the steel is pulled and thinner in that area. I would repair this and not be concerned about future problems. The crack has a V ground along the entire length and beyond for at least another inch. I then MIG weld the ground out V going past the V slightly, letting the steel cool naturally. Once completed a thorough inspection with a magnifying glass is required to make sure I didn't bring out another suspect weld in the area of repair.

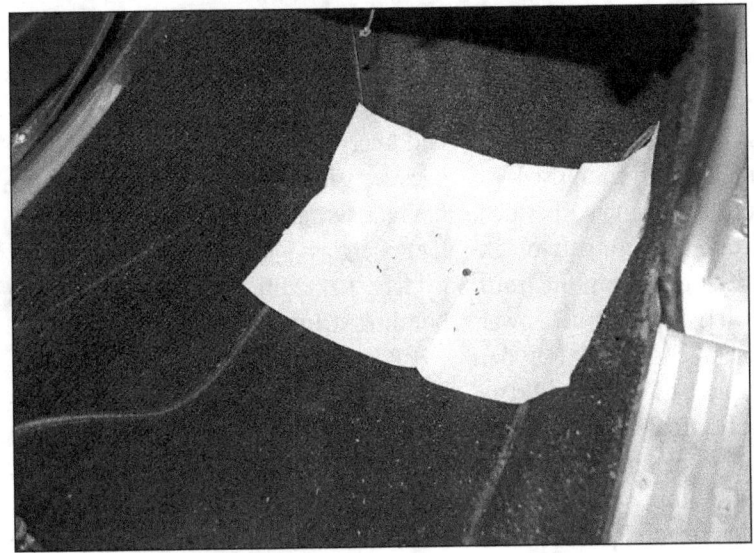

When gingerly closing the door, any corrosion pieces land on the white towel. Slamming the door may upset the seller, so keep that in mind. If you find flakes of corrosion you need to investigate further. You may conclude there is significant rust damage and pass on the car, as major corrosion damage to the birdcage and windshield frame is likely.

the flexing causes cracks around the box. Severe cracks can be seen while the steering wheel is turned from one lock to the other when the engine is running. Look closely around the steering box as the steering load is applied. The best procedure is to remove all crud and paint from the area for a thorough inspection. Check carefully around the front spring pocket where multiple pieces of frame are welded together.

Birdcages can be subjected to all the elements: water, salt, dirt, and anything that could possibly cause corrosion. Water/salt gets slung onto the bottom side of the C-channels causing them to corrode slowly. Windshield leaks are common, letting the water and corrosives work slowly over time. Water leaks between the windshield rubber seal at the glass or the frame itself. The trapped water eventually causes corrosion to form, and corrosion means rust. General Motors uses the word rust in warranty information. Corrosion is considered scaling of the metal surfaces. Perforation is when there are holes in the metal surface. Unfortunately, the birdcage is not visible without removing interior panels or the windshield trim. If you look carefully around the windshield frame you may spot some tell-tale signs of corrosion. Placing white paper towels on the floor around the lower dash area may help find corrosion. If there is major corrosion it falls onto the white paper towels when the doors are closed.

Canadian or northern coastal cars can be horrible to work on. Everything can be difficult to take apart due to corrosion. When it comes to disassembly, you often need two parts rust penetrant and one part heat to remove just about any bolt or nut. Some of the most difficult Corvettes I have ever worked on were Canadian cars. Literally every bolt and nut had to be heated in order to remove it. For the most part, many pieces were junk because they could not be removed without inflicting some major damage. Buying a severely corroded Corvette can really hurt your budget and ego. All costs are higher, from the disassembly to the parts list. Not many novices want to tackle major body reconstruction resulting from hidden corrosion

Green zinc-chromate primer was applied on the C-channels at the factory. If you see flaking rust-red C-channels, you are looking for trouble. These C-channels are rough, but there are no perforations, which is a very good thing. Another indicator that the C-channels are badly corroded is sill plate screws that do not tighten because they are stripped. This is why it makes sense to do a body-off restoration. There is no way to access these potentially corroded C-channels to preserve them.

damage. Birdcage repairs are costly in all ways, and hard to justify unless you have plenty of experience doing major reconstructive repairs.

Corvette bodies are comprised of numerous fiberglass panels bonded together. The front end consists of an upper surround that goes from the front bumper to the windshield frame. Lower side fenders are attached to the upper surround to complete the front end. The rear has the roof and deck panel with rear fenders. The front and rear fender split line meets the upper panels about an inch below the surround panel. Bonding strips are used to connect and reinforce the panels at the front fenders and rear areas.

Factory Midyear body panels are press-molded fiberglass, which means that both the inner and outer surfaces are smooth. Body panels are typically gray, but early 1963s may be white or pink. GM-supplied replacement panels were the same gray, white, or pink.

Press-molded fiberglass costs quite a bit more to manufacture so hand-laid is popular for replacement panels. Hand-laid fiberglass is obvious from the inside because the panels are rougher and the fiberglass strands are noticeable. Hand-laid fiberglass panels are easy to spot just by feel. In addition, broken or missing bonding strips are easy to spot.

Poorly performed or incorrect repairs are often found. We find fiberglass cloth (sometimes used for boat hulls) instead of stranded fiberglass mat that should be used for repairs. Pieces of cardboard stuck to the repair are another dead giveaway that a patch was used. Wadded up pieces of fiberglass cloth sticking out from the underside of a repair that never got saturated with resin are common. Spliced or patch panels are used in an effort to save money and many of these spell trouble. If you see a major body panel overlap with bonding adhesive oozing out there is a concern. Someone used a broken piece from another car and attached it hastily to the broken panel on the car.

Frames are easily tweaked in minor accidents causing the "diamond effect." The right or left front corner gets bumped and the rail is pushed back. Many times the frame damage is not caught until the alignment tech finds it. Look carefully at the tire and wheel's position in the fender opening. If you see one wheel back or forward noticeably farther than the other, it is often an indication of collision damage. The frame has been tweaked or the body was reassembled incorrectly after an accident.

I have way too many Midyear Corvettes come into the shop after major bodywork and paint with assembly problems. I find that the bumper brackets do not line up or that the exterior grilles are out of position. Worse yet, major body panels were replaced on tweaked frames and nothing fits properly, such as hoods, doors, etc.

One of the worst cases I have seen was a 1966 that arrived in baskets for

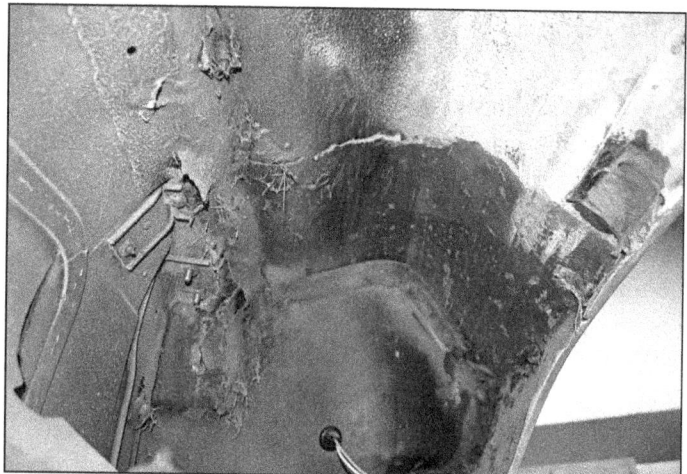

Wow! From the underside of this 1964, the incorrect repair is obvious. Someone took a right front fender corner and hacked it onto the original fender. It looks like the repair piece was chopped off the donor vehicle with a machete. This is bad, really bad. The bumper fits poorly and I cannot repair these existing pieces to make it close to right. The left side has a similar repair. The front end needs to be replaced to correct the frontend bodywork, and replacing the front end costs a minimum $3,000 with a hand-laid assembly.

Another suspect repair found on the rear of the same 1964, but at least they were consistent. Leaving the cardboard back-up for the repair then using the fiberglass woven cloth tells you that fiberglass repair was not their forte. Like the front end, damage repair was evident on both sides at the rear. The bonding strip to the left is in excellent condition with original bonding adhesive oozing out.

assembly. Of course, the body was painted very nicely. However, when the body was lowered onto the frame, it was obvious something was seriously wrong. The rear bumper brackets were almost 2 inches below the body's bumper bracket holes.

The only thing to do was call the owner and find out more about the body restoration. As it turned out, the body was restored on a dolly off the frame. The rear floor had been repaired after a hard rear-end crash. Unfortunately, the floor sat lower than its original height so the rear of the body sat higher on the frame. To resolve the problem, the floor needed to be removed and glued back together correctly, which was a major reconstruction project.

But that was not the only problem I encountered: When I had the body sitting on the frame correctly, I checked the front fender wheel well openings. The passenger-side tire and wheel was back so far that I could not turn the steering wheel. I found two problems: A side fender had been replaced without proper fitting procedures, and the frame was tweaked back just a bit. This is one of those typical things that you can run into when basket cases (aptly named) are involved.

Maybe the shop that had the project found these issues and gave up on it. When Corvettes come in baskets, you never know what you may find.

Analyzing a Potential Project

I found three possible Midyears that I wanted to investigate further. I had in my mind that I wanted to find a drivable Midyear that I could modify or personalize during a restoration. I desired the exterior look of the Midyear with some late-model amenities.

My first candidate was a rough-looking 327-ci fuel-injected 1963 split-window coupe with limited power options. A quick look under the '63 revealed a severely rotted frame that required major reconstruction or replacement. The original engine and transmission were gone. The well-worn interior was, for the most part, intact. I knew immediately that I needed a frame and almost every attaching piece. The crazy thing is that with all the chassis rust, the windshield frame and birdcage looked pretty good. Do not get me wrong: Chassis replacement is a big deal, but I would much rather do the chassis replacement than do major birdcage repairs. I needed to go look at other Midyears just to be smart.

My second candidate was a 1964 convertible in decent condition with a matching-number engine. My first thought was that I should not take the time to even look at this car. The matching numbers and decent condition made the car sound expensive. This could turn out to be a "stay at home in the garage and look at me" situation, not a drivable Midyear after restoration. Of course, I went to look at it because you never know what "decent looking" means to someone else, and it is a Corvette after all!

It turned out to be a good, solid car with matching-numbers engine, transmission, and differential. However, most of the ancillary pieces had been changed and had incorrect numbers. It would take some time to hunt for the right pieces. The paint and interior were dated and could use some TLC to get it back on track. The underside had some minor rust, but no obvious major problems.

This was probably not the car for me because it was too nice and should be put back together for NCRS showing or a nice, fun weekend show car. For the first-time restorer, it would make a great project. The majority of pieces were in place and working. An overall cleaning, painting, and freshening up of the drivetrain would make this one fine Midyear. The cost is higher upfront than the first project car I looked at, but it requires less work and parts to complete the restoration. Always remember: in many cases, it makes sense to spend more up front to get a better car. We sometimes equate that our time is not a monetary concern; after all, we are working on this as a hobby. Then as years drag by, it becomes apparent that a lot of money has been spent and you are not enjoying the fruits of your labor. All too often, a "for sale" sign is next.

My third candidate was a 1967 in need of everything: paint, interior, and complete chassis restoration. As I dug deeper into what I had in front of me, I found a completely original, numbers-matching 1967, right down to the carburetor. The Goodwood Green 300-hp 327-ci convertible had very few options. What makes sense: NCRS restoration, or personalize this relatively high-production Corvette? When I say "high production," I mean paint color of the 14,436 convertibles built that year. This was a tough call. With all the correct pieces, it would be a shame to not utilize them on an NCRS restoration.

After looking at the three Midyear possibilities, the 1963 was my first choice. I wanted to make an offer because this could be the perfect car for my project if the money was right. I could do all the modifications I wanted and really enjoy the car out cruising and on long runs.

The smartest tool to use right now is restraint. Go home and think it out. Consider what it takes to put this 1963 back together in decent shape. How in-depth can you go with the restoration? How much of the major work can you do? Is this beyond the scope of your capabilities? And do you have the space to pull off this major restoration? If the price is right, can you afford to have someone do the major work if you do not feel comfortable doing it? This is when patience is key to avoid paying way too much for a rough Midyear project.

CHAPTER 3

Getting Started

Your plan should begin with considering what skills, tools, and equipment you have available. You need to decide if you will buy, rent equipment, or send the work out. Do you have a paint and body shop that you feel comfortable with? Will you be doing your own bodywork and paint?

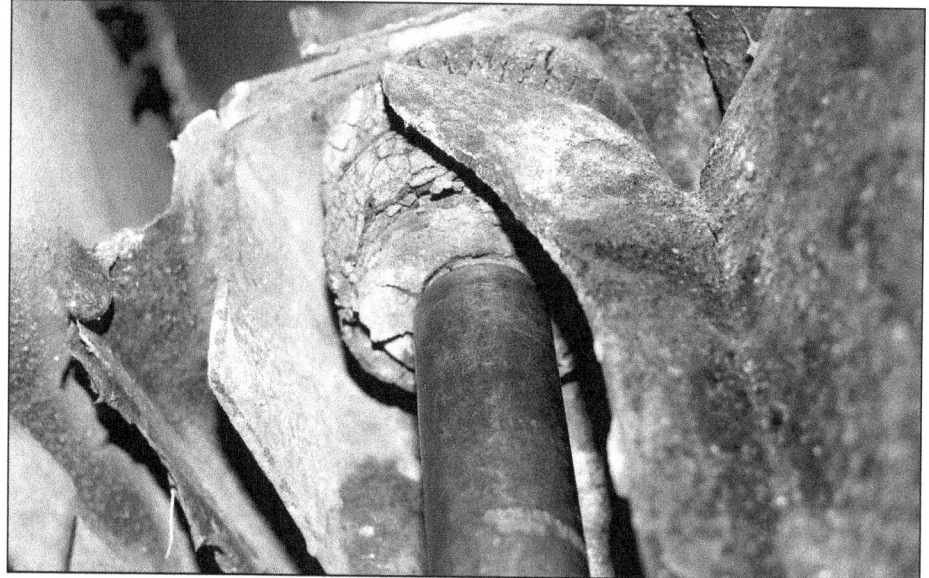

This is a great example of why most Midyear restorations usually end up as body-off projects. The deteriorated rubber of body-mount cushions is commonplace after 20 years. At 50 years steel crumbles and the cushions in general are junk. These unsightly cushions will be seen by anyone who peers under your finished project. Chances are the cushions will require replacement, and it's a lot of work to replace them with the body on; bite the bullet and lift the body if at all possible.

Types of Restoration

You also need to determine whether you will do a body-on or body-off restoration. If you are on a tight budget, you should consider doing a body-on restoration. Although you may have the skills to do a body-off restoration, you need to consider this cost before taking the plunge. Body-off restorations are at higher level altogether and usually leave no area untouched. When finished, the entire project is brought back to like-new condition.

The problem with doing a body-on restoration is that a very important part is left out of the project: properly inspecting the top of the chassis frame rails and the birdcage C-channels; to clean and preserve the frame and C-channels, you must remove the body.

Savvy potential buyers can spot a body-on restoration, and the value can be diminished. Many vehicles are body-on restored to save money and labor, which I can appreciate. The task does not seem nearly as daunting as a body-off project. Choosing a body-off option and taking the entire Midyear down to the last nut and bolt can sound so good. Be prepared, though, as there is no turning back once you start a body-off restoration. The reward will be great, however, when the final phases are completed and you can show off all your hard work.

Also, the 1964 to 1967 Corvettes have body-to-frame cushions made of rubber with steel sleeves. This makes a strong case for lifting the body to replace the deteriorated rubber cushions. Rubber dries out and deteriorates over time, no matter how well it is treated. As the rubber cushions age, they lose their shape and become compressed. Steel sleeves that back up the rubber cushions corrode and further deform the rubber, causing the body to sag in places. Body cushions can be replaced without removing the body, although the labor is considerable, requiring some body lifting for cushion access.

Another consideration is that your Midyear Corvette project may be clean enough to do a body-on restoration if it has been restored in the recent past. A thorough inspection of the frame and body underside determines if this is feasible. Decent body mounts with minimal to no corrosion should allow you to perform a body-on restoration (and avoid a body-off restoration). Remember that down the road, a potential buyer will easily spot deteriorated body cushions. This could negatively affect the resale value, considering the labor cost to replace the cushions.

Once the project is at your work place, a proper plan provides goals and milestones to keep things going smoothly. While you are putting the plan together, you should order a GM factory service manual and assembly manual. Have a dedicated clipboard with legal pad handy to write notes as you scrutinize the project requirements. At the end of the week, it is a good idea to transcribe your lists to a computer document. Be sure to back up photos, parts lists, and labor operations on a DVD for your records.

Before any parts are removed, take photos of each assembly at multiple angles. No matter how good your recall is you'll need a refresher when it comes time to put it all back together. Also photograph the work as you progress through each phase of disassembly, for future reference.

Remember to take photos of all the casting and date codes. This can save plenty of effort down the road for many purposes. Photos are good insurance verification and if you decide to sell you can show them to potential buyers. Keeping records of any new-old-stock (NOS) or original pieces installed can also add value.

One absolutely essential piece of advice: Do not discard any part until you are finished with the project. Even then, carefully consider whether or not it is worth saving.

Shop/Garage Requirements

If you do a body-off restoration, you really need three garage spaces: one is for enough room to do the actual work, one is where you put the body after you remove it, and one is for parts storage and paint preparation. Even then, the area is tight, but the project is doable within that space. Careful planning is the key.

Parts Storage

As you remove parts and pieces, safely store them. Care needs to be taken to preserve them. Whether you use the parts again or sell them, these need to be stored safely away. If you do not take the proper steps, mistakes happen and pieces can be easily damaged by weather

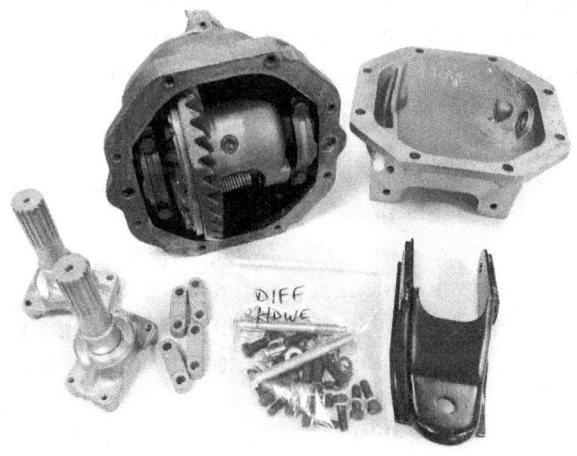

A good practice is to keep each sub-assembly together with all of the pieces and fasteners in one place. This method lessens the chance of missing small parts necessary for reassembly and spending hours trying to figure out what components go with each sub-assembly. Follow through with this practice as you clean the components. Once cleaned and painted they should be put into separate containers until it is time for assembly.

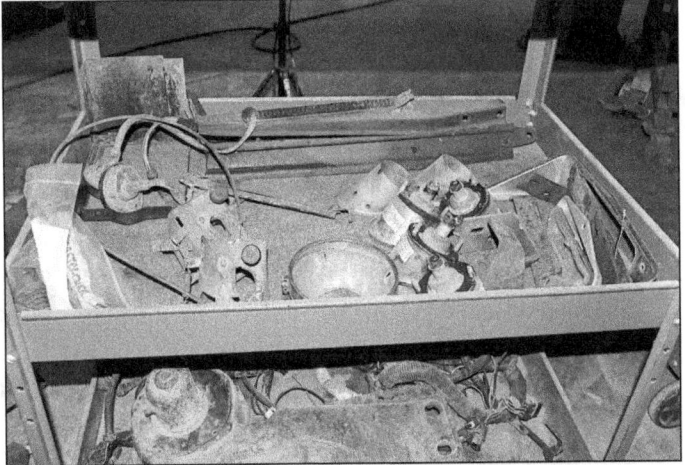

This large four-shelf cart allows me to separate the different areas. I designate each shelf for a certain area during the disassembly. This shelf has the exterior and underhood parts which were removed. The idea is these parts may be used again after the cleaning and refinishing processes. All parts are inspected to determine their value and whether it makes sense spending the time cleaning and refinishing them.

or improper handling. In many cases, these parts are valuable as good reference material, so treat them with care. In other words, do not lay engine cylinder heads on the door panels out in the driveway even if you plan on replacing them. Surprisingly, people do this frequently without even thinking about it. Likewise, trim pieces are very delicate and in some cases irreplaceable. They should be put in a safe place as soon as they are removed.

Designate an area for small and large pieces. For large pieces, 2-foot-deep shelves 4 feet wide by 24 inches high will hold most of the pieces as they are removed. I designate a category for each shelf: front suspension, rear suspension, and interior for example. Organization saves money and time and minimizes the stress of keeping track of so many pieces.

I designate two areas during disassembly for restorable pieces and pieces to be replaced. Once all the pieces have been separated, I can carefully make a list of replacement pieces I require. Few things are worse than getting started on restoring a sub-assembly to find out that the parts were not ordered and work grinds to a halt. Sub-assemblies are considered the carburetor, power steering pump, alternator, etc.

When parts arrive, unpack them carefully then check them for accuracy and quality as soon as possible. Notify the supplier immediately of any problems and keep a log of any pending issues that need to be resolved. Once the parts have been verified, place them with the sub-assembly to be restored. Fasteners and small hardware should be placed in good-quality plastic bags with notes on each bag indicating where they came from. You can go one step further and place each bag with that particular assembly.

If you're modifying your Corvette (which is outside the scope of this book), you need to take appropriate steps for parts storage. You need to safely store many pieces, if you plan on being able to transform your custom project back to original-equipment standards in the future. Storing parts for an indefinite time is much more difficult than you may think because each one must be carefully wrapped to prevent corrosion or breakage.

Parts Cleaning

Greasy, rusty parts require cleaning for any restoration project. Properly cleaning pieces takes time and it's a dirty job. You should clean as many parts as possible during disassembly with mineral spirits. All the oil and grease needs to be completely removed for best results. When bead blasting, grease and oil contaminate the blasting agent, plus it forces the contamination into the pieces. I use older mineral-spirits-based wash tanks with recycling capabilities.

You need a variety of cleaning brushes. Nylon-bristle brushes work well to loosen grease and built-up dirt. Then the correct metal-bristle brush does the final corrosion removal and cleaning. Stainless-steel brushes work great on aluminum surfaces to remove corrosion and baked-on grease. Carbon-steel brushes work well on iron castings and all internal iron engine pieces, such as engine blocks, cylinder heads, connecting rods, etc. Brass brushes work best on bronze or brass fittings. (Note that brass brushes transfer brass from the bristles to aluminum and iron when scrubbing pieces.)

Paint Preparation

Once the parts have been cleaned, you should have a dedicated area to hang each piece after prepping. Your painting area should be large enough that you can prep enough parts to do one phase of the assembly at a time. The goal may be to clean, prep, and paint the components for the chassis assembly in one batch. This is a tough proposition because of the amount of pieces in multiple colors. Plan to paint as many pieces as possible in one particular color that you plan on assembling first. This is the frame and major suspension components, for example. The painted pieces are setup for assembly out of the first batch. While you are assembling the major components, another batch of pieces is in the next paint phase. Pieces like the brake backing plates and other silver items are the next paint batch. Jumping from one area to another doing a little assembly on each usually leaves bolts, nuts, or screws loose. Plus, the painted pieces have less chance of finish damage if they are bolted in place rather than being laid down on any surface.

You need a clean area and some time to do the prep work. You need to wear nitrile or latex gloves to keep the parts as clean as possible. Folding tables or plywood on sawhorses works well for paint prep areas. You need to keep contaminants off the prepped pieces. You have one chance to do the prep correctly. If the parts are contaminated, the paint may come off or "fisheye." Fisheyes go down to the undercoat and occur from contamination (usually oil) that prevents the paint from sticking.

After the pieces have been prepped, the parts need to be painted. We prefer to use professional paint spray equipment for a durable smooth finish on all parts. Potential buyers and judges can usually detect the use of spray can applied paints. This could possibly hurt the value of the car and receiving a higher status certificate. A spay gun allows quicker, smoother, and heavier paint application than a rattle-can paint. In addition, gloss finishes are much deeper, uniform, and durable than any rattle can paint. Also, professional paint spray equipment is available at very reasonable costs. Imported paint spray equipment does a decent job, especially for component refinishing.

Rattle-can spray paint can produce good results, but it isn't the best method. Seymour, Krylon, and Plasti-coat are very good durable spray paint products. Cast-iron and semi-flat finishes work best when using rattle paints. Uniform high-gloss finishes are tough to apply unless the ambient temperature is around 75 degrees F and humidity is low. The rattle paint tends to dry too quickly in high temperatures, leaving orange peel or tiger stripes. Cold, humid days usually leave cloudy or hazy areas on large flat pieces. Spray-can etch prime and primer are available to ensure good top-coat adhesion and one of these should always be used. Cast-iron, aluminum, and stainless-steel coat spray paint products are used for factory look-alike finishes. These spray-can specialty coatings can be used for NCRS or Bloomington Gold restoration projects. Clear coat is available in spray cans and should be applied as the final top coat for good durability. You may want to consider the cost of the rattle paint because it adds up quickly. If done properly, you need quite a few cans to apply enough paint to give all the pieces a good even coating.

Equipment Needs

An air compressor is necessary for many phases of the project when using air-powered tools for disassembly/assembly, cleaning tools, and painting. You need air to sand components or to use cut-off saws that make the tasks much easier. Air compressors are rated in standard cubic feet per minute (SCFM). You can get away with a low-SCFM model if you use it primarily for air impact tools. Air-powered cut-off tools, sanders, and bead blast cabinets, however, use a considerable amount of air per minute.

A popular home workshop compressor with 5 peak hp and a 20-gallon tank requires 120 volts at 15 amps for proper power input. The minimum amount of air required to use multiple high-volume air tools at the same time is 10 SCFM. You need 230 volts at 15 amps to power the larger 5-hp model, but it works much less. Upright compressors take up much less room and make the most sense in tight work areas.

A high-quality set of hand tools (more on this below) and a 5-hp 20-gallon-tank air compressor are necessary to take apart all the major assemblies. Removing the body requires either a sling or lift to get it off the chassis. You can get all your buddies over for the body removal but when it comes time to install the body, you may want to consider another plan to slowly ease the body into position.

I have used an engine lift ("cherry picker") to remove and install bodies. You can rent one; or, if you want to own one, Harbor Freight collapsible models are good to free up garage floor space.

I prefer to remove the body then the engine and transmission as an assembly. The engine lift comes in handy a number of times during the project, so it may pay to own one.

Good Tools Versus Cheap Tools

I am an advocate of buying good hand tools, especially wrenches and sockets. Over a lifetime, they are used numerous times. Cheap wrenches and sockets can break or create extra work when the bolts you want to remove round off.

Ratchets and extensions of low quality may break, and they hurt you, not the fasteners. You should have a full assortment of 1/2-, 3/8-, and 1/4-inch sockets, ratchets, and extensions from Craftsman, Husky, Rigid, Snap-On, Mac, or others. The set should include combination wrenches from 5/16 to 1 inch.

You need a few extra large wrenches for A/C-equipped cars: 1 1/16, 1 1/8, 1 1/4 inch. These large wrenches work best in open end offset for the tight areas they are used in.

Specialty wrenches in 3/8, 7/16, 1/2, 9/16, and 5/8 inch take care of all the brake and fuel steel lines. There is no substitution for line wrenches if you want to properly tighten and loosen hard lines. Some of the interior switches require special wrenches to remove them without damaging them. Corvette Central has all the specialty wrenches to easily remove the switch nuts.

Propane torches should be considered for your tool box. They can help remove stubborn fasteners and possibly prevent the need for component replacement.

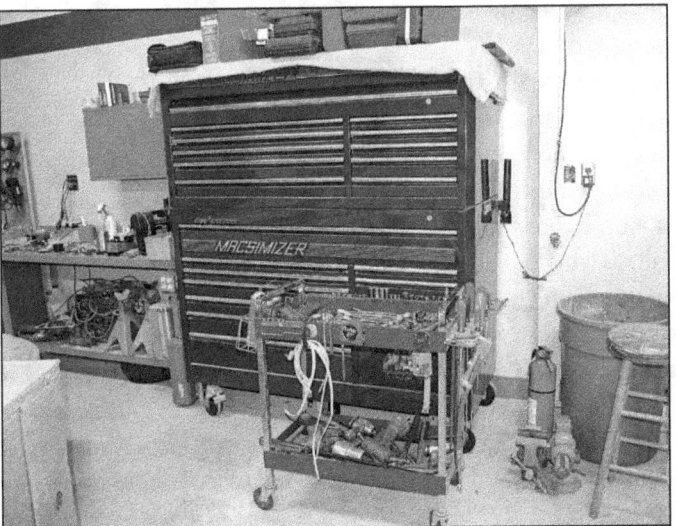

This fairly large tool box holds plenty of tools. The crazy thing is the tool cart beside it has just about any tool I need for a complete restoration. The large box has specialty tools that are not used very often. Using the tool cart is convenient and brings my tools to the job site.

Sourcing Parts

As I mentioned earlier, it is best to order the GM service and assembly manual before you remove the first bolt or nut. You also need to think about finding a GM parts manual, preferably an early-edition 1953–1982 version. As General Motors revised its parts manual, early parts tended to disappear along with the illustrations. Finding a 1953–1970s GM parts manual yields the best part number and photographic details for a Midyear project. This allows you to figure out what the original GM part numbers were and the illustrations are sometimes good enough to help with assembly. Companies, such as Corvette Central, have a part number conversion service that cross references the GM part to its number, which is helpful when you are having a hard time finding an obscure, small part.

When shopping for parts, find a supplier that understands Corvettes. Corvette Central, for example, has a great catalog with exploded views. Many times, cheap parts may save you a few bucks initially but are likely to fail quickly. If you are lucky enough to get the project completed before the discount parts fail, they may leave you stranded by the side of the road in the future.

Restoring Corvettes has become a cottage industry because of all the components that require specialized attention. Corvette suppliers, such as Stainless Steel Brakes Corporation and Vette Brakes and Products, sell specialized products. These same products are available through Corvette Central, Mid America, and Zip Products, making these large Corvette parts retailers a true one-stop shopping experience. You can spend plenty of extra time hunting the parts from individual suppliers. Either way, keep a journal to document where and when to expect the parts.

OEM Versus Reproduction Parts

Many reproduction parts are available for Midyear Corvettes. Many of the components are good quality, but some are not. Many NCRS and Bloomington Gold restorers avoid reproduction parts if at all possible. Using original parts costs more because of limited availability, but the resale value is often greater. Use a reputable and established Corvette parts vendor.

Corvette Central not only sells parts, but researches and checks as many as possible. Zip Products, Mid-America, and Eckler's are household names in the Corvette parts industry. Corvette Central, Crane Corvette Supply, Paragon, and Zip Products have a limited supply of NOS, original, and good used pieces for the NCRS or Bloomington Gold restorer. Also, Long Island Corvette Supply has been around almost 30 years and has dedicated an entire parts line to the Midyear Corvette.

Ebay, Craigslist, and swap meets are other sources for the pieces you need. Be wary, though because purchasing Corvette parts via the Internet can be risky. What "excellent," "good," and "poor" quality means to one person may not be the same to another. Ask for plenty of photos, especially of casting and part numbers because if you buy it from a private party often you cannot return it.

You can source parts from some Corvette events. Corvettes at Carlisle is a three-day event that starts on Friday for attendees. You can find anything Corvette related that your heart desires. Bloomington Gold is another must-attend event. Swap meet vendors are plentiful with all the major Corvette suppliers in one place. Many of the suppliers offer special deals for event attendees, including free shipping. Depending on the scope of your project, free shipping could add up to big savings. Local events may also have swap meet vendors who could have that difficult-to-find part.

Building an NCRS-judged car requires finding original parts from whatever source you can find. When you find a highly sought after part, you need to act quickly. In the time it takes to research whether the deal is good or not, someone else has scooped it up. Waiting until the last day of an event to purchase a tough-to-find part is not smart.

Do your homework and know what numbers to look for and the typical selling price before you leave home. Make a cheat sheet that you can refer to while you are on the hunt. This can be an enjoyable part of the project if you are well prepared. Happy hunting!

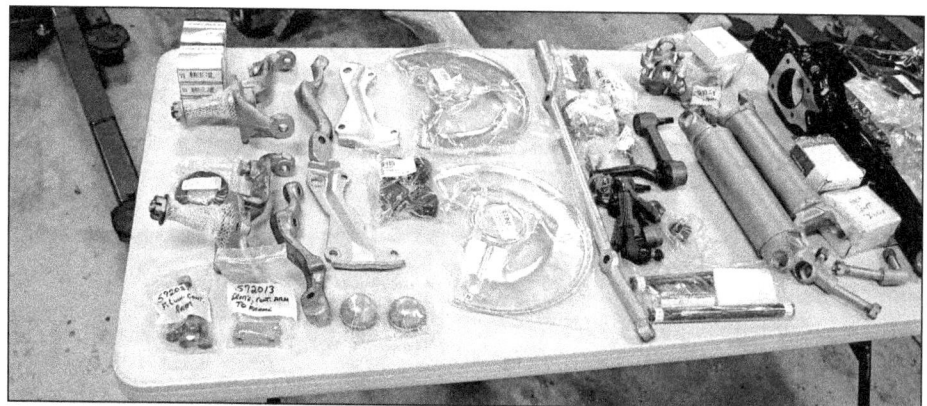

The table is loaded with my chassis assembly parts from Corvette Central. Organization is the key to a safe working environment for you and the project. If I have all the parts laid out that I need for a particular phase of the assembly it makes the task easier. Plus there is less chance of leaving something out of an assembly.

GETTING STARTED

Disassembly

Disassembly can begin once you have your secure storage area and documentation essentials ready. For this project, I am performing a body-off restoration and installing a new frame. I soak all the fasteners with rust penetrant before turning the first wrench. The longer you wait, the better; let the penetrant do its job. Many applications of rust penetrant are best. While the rust penetrant is at work, I strip the interior.

My project had no engine or transmission, which does not affect the body lift. I prefer to remove the engine and transmission after the body is lifted because you have easier access. I treat the frame, engine, transmission, and driveline as an assembly, calling it the "chassis assembly." It is much easier to disassemble the chassis once the body has been lifted. (Remember to use jack stands or sturdy ramps and always be

Inspection Techniques

Here's the tale of how I located and inspected my Midyear project.

The 1963 coupe had been sitting on the side of a garage partially covered for 20 years. Finding any Midyear project in this condition is unusual, as most have been restored or are in the process. I would rather find any project before a restoration was attempted and problems were covered up. Certainly, there will be surprises, but they will be minimal with so much of this coupe's underpinnings exposed.

I spotted severe rot at multiple locations, so the chassis was the most noticeable concern. I soon discovered whether the rest of the metal components were sound. No matter how bad it is, this is a '63 split-window coupe, after all, and should be restored.

I found that the front fiberglass had collision damage and replacement pieces had been spliced into the original front surround. The headlight assembly support area also had crash damage that was repaired poorly. Both of the inner fenders were broken from years of abuse. I could either repair the rough-looking front-end fiberglass or replace the entire front end.

I also need to consider the appearance of the repairs. If a myriad of repairs were made to the front end, most likely these repairs are visible from the underside. Repairing this front end makes sense for a daily driver, but if I enter the car at a show, then repairing the front end isn't suitable. I prefer that the underside look correct if I have the '63 judged.

I felt that an NCRS restoration was out of the question because of the extensive damage and many missing and incorrect original pieces. I had no documentation to verify the history. I set out to find a Midyear to drive and I found it. This is the perfect Corvette to modify with late-model running gear.

It appeared that years ago someone had removed the rocker molding and uncovered this serious rot. Many chassis are rough in this area, so this was not a surprise, but it is by far one of the worst I have ever seen. If this was the worst of the rot, I could have the original frame repaired. This frame had the same severe corrosion at the right rear and more corrosion at the front.

This pink fiberglass panel is an original GM part (not for this car originally). The lapped pieces of gray with blue overspray and pink fiberglass tell you that the front end was spliced near the firewall. The drill hole in the rib is where the spliced piece had a screw placed to hold it together while the bonding adhesive was drying.

CHAPTER 3

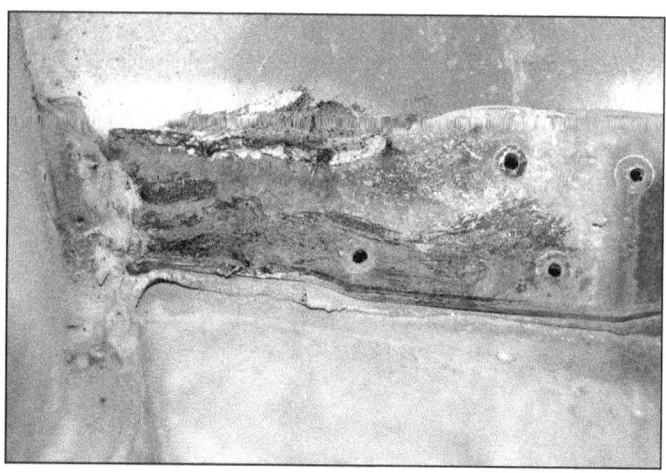

This front inner fender bonding strip has holes for an original "Fuel Injection" emblem. Could it be our 1963 project was a factory Fuelie? There was no evidence of filled holes in the bonding strip which would lead someone to believe the '63 was a Fuelie. The radiator core support had a factory opening for the air cleaner which furthered the possibility that we had an original Fuelie. However, further investigation showed that someone had replaced front end fiberglass pieces suggesting instead that an attempt was made to clone a Fuelie.

extremely careful when working under the car.)

You may be wondering why I just dove in and disassembled the entire car or almost the entire car. Preservation is the best reason. When the bodywork begins, dust, debris, and stuff that does not wash off can end up on just about every piece. Removing pieces and properly storing them provides essential protection and keeps them cleaner. You would be surprised how much extra time can be spent cleaning what was left behind from the clean-up and bodywork. "Work smarter, not harder," says Austin, my friend who has helped throughout the project, and it really makes good sense.

Dash Removal

I remove the interior first because it lightens the load for the body lift and allows me to store the pieces safely. The first interior pieces to remove are the door panels because these are easy to damage during disassembly. Seats can easily tear up the door panels, so I leave the seats in place and cover them for protection as I disassemble the dash.

The glove box door/liner assembly comes out next, and then the steering column. The "rag joint" or steering shaft coupler must be unbolted from under the hood. A few 1/2-inch hex-head bolts, along with the lower trim Phillips-head screws, and the column is ready to come out. Properly store the column because teak steering wheels can be easily damaged. I always have a designated place for the column to be stored. The steering wheel is removed and boxed up.

The original seats look fairly decent and the frames are in good shape with everything intact. Reproduction center armrest covers or the entire assembly is available. The carpeting was original, and I will hold onto it to make sure I trim the new pieces correctly.

Remove Steering Column

1 First, remove a couple of Phillips head screws holding the column trim, and take off four 1/2-inch hex bolts and nuts. Then the column comes out. I did go out under the hood first and remove the 7/16-inch 12-point bolt holding the steering coupler to the steering shaft. This gives me plenty of room to work in the interior.

GETTING STARTED

Disconnect Gauge Cables

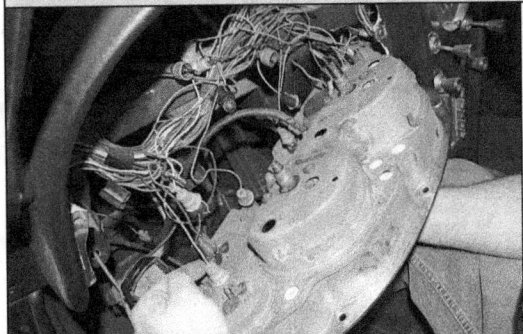

2 To help the removal of the dash cluster, disconnect the speedometer cable, tachometer cable, and oil pressure copper hard line from under the hood first. This allows the dash cluster to come out farther for bulb removal. I usually remove the wiper switch from the cluster, rather than removing the wiring connector. Invariably, if you tug on the wiper switch connector, it pulls the switch apart. The dash cluster in all Midyears is old-school, and therefore it has multiple plug-in bulbs with separate connectors for each gauge. The main dash harness has two plastic retaining clips with tabs that spring outward when they are pushed into the back of the cluster. If you plan on using the original dash harness, handle the clips with care. Cut the harness tape holding the clips into the harness, then the clips can be easily removed when the dash cluster is disassembled. The clips keep the harness from lying on the top of the speedometer and tachometer cables.

Remove Stereo Speaker

3 Take off the 3/8-inch hex nuts to remove the speaker grille and speaker. I commonly see the speaker grille pulled away from the top of the dash slightly because some are unaware that the hex nuts must be removed. Most likely a screwdriver was used in an attempt to pry the grille out. The speaker grille can be tweaked back into shape so that it fits tightly against the dash again. I caution you, though, because the outer circumference of the grille is made of pot-metal that can break easily if pushed too far.

Remove Pot-Metal Speaker Grille

4 The reason to make a big deal about this grille is late-model dashes have plastic speaker grilles snapped in place. Prying this fragile metal grille up distorts it. If you do this, you have a difficult time making it lay flat against the dash. The speaker grille frame is made from pot-metal, meaning they break if you try to modify their shape. There is some shaping (very little, though) or snap.

Remove Radio Head Unit

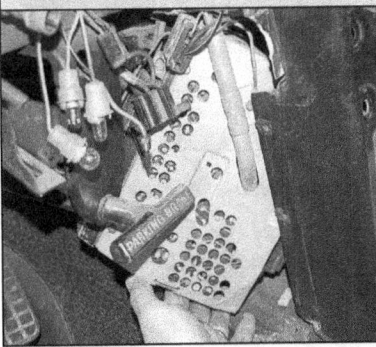

5 When the dash is installed, radio removal is cramped and difficult. For A/C-equipped cars, it's very tight and particularly difficult to remove the head unit. Try not to bang up the face or radio shafts during the removal. The head unit is valuable, so whether you use it or not someone most likely would like to have it. Radio removal begins with complete console plate removal. The rear of the radio is moved to the driver's side with the bottom of the radio coming out first. Carefully work the radio out past the parking brake handle; it is tight but it is possible to do without damaging it.

Remove Clock

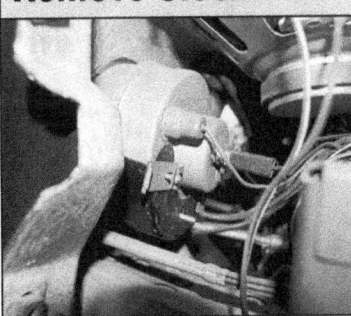

6 Clocks are held in place with these retaining clips that require a downward push near the retainer stud. Pull outward on the retainer clip while pushing downward. The electrical connectors and lamps can be removed once the clock has been removed from the dash.

Remove Dash Control Knobs

7 Old school knob removal requires a small flathead screwdriver to loosen the set screw. Once the set screw has been loosened, turn the knob counterclockwise to unscrew. Most of the knobs have these set screws at the bottom of the knob when the switch is turned off. If there is no screw present the knob twists off counterclockwise. A pair of pliers is sometimes required to hold onto the cable's shaft.

Remove Retaining Nuts for Headlight and Wiper Switch

8 This Corvette Central special tool (PN 251004) makes removing and tightening the special cable retaining nuts easy, and it works on the headlight and wiper switches. Two ignition-switch nut wrenches are available (PN 251003 for 1960 to 1965 Corvettes and PN 252001 for 1966-1967 Corvettes). I see ignition switch bezel nuts scarred up all the time from "Mr Goodpliers" at work.

Remove Pedal Assembly

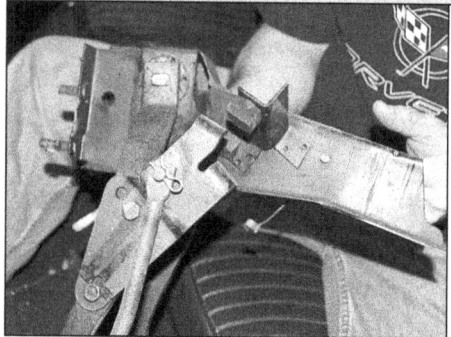

9 The pedal assembly has been removed for restoration. All too often, this assembly is left in place and cleaned as well as possible. Both the clutch and brake pedal pivots ride on plastic bushings that wear out. Clutch pedals wear from the extreme pressures, and many times crack near the pivot point. Remove the pedal assembly and put it in your sub-assembly restoration pile. The pedal assembly has two 5/16-inch screws holding it to the dash support. Two studs on the pedal assembly pass through the firewall that mount the brake booster or master cylinder to the firewall. The other two studs are held on the firewall with two 3/8 nuts.

Drain Radiator and Remove Hoses

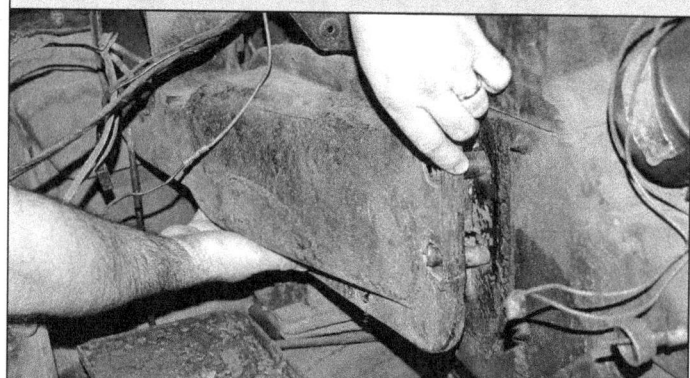

10 You need to drain the cooling system at the radiator and then go under the hood to remove the heater core. Next, carefully remove the heater hoses to avoid heater core damage. I usually slice the hoses along the heater core tube and peel it away. You should never tug on any heater hose at the core to remove it. Once the hoses are taken off, remove the 7/16-inch hex nuts from around the perimeter of the outside plenum cover.

Remove Inner Assembly

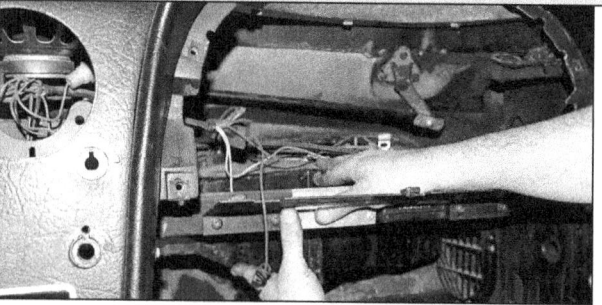

11 Once the cover has been removed, the inner assembly is ready to come down and out. The inner plenum has the defroster, heater, and temperature control cables attached to the controls. I remove the cables at the plenum assembly and the blower resistor wiring connector for the removal of the assembly out of the dash. Each control cable has a push-on retaining clip that goes on easily. Taking them off requires a pair of needle-nose pliers to grasp the clip and wiggle it upward. With careful removal the clips can be used again.

Door Glass Removal

I completely disassemble the doors and all hardware for the door glass. Locks and latches are also removed. Removing and replacing all the door glass sealing pieces is very important for like-new window operation. Additionally, the paint job is so much nicer when the edges of the doors do not have paint buildup. Coupe door glass removal is not too difficult, but convertible door glass is easier.

Both require the same procedure: The glass rides in a rear vertical glass run to control tilt position; this rear vertical glass run has to be removed to free up the glass for removal. Two large Phillips-head screws at the top and bottom of the latch side of the door hold the glass run in place. Two 7/16-inch nuts (one at the front; one at the rear) hold the glass on the horizontal regulator track. At that point, the convertible glass can be removed.

On coupes, the vent window frame screws are removed to allow the frame to be moved out of the way. It is common to find that the glass has come loose from the lift bracket because the glass is held in a rubberized-cloth like strip. When you pull the window, make sure the lift bracket is tight on the glass to avoid having to take things apart again.

Once the glass is out of the way, all the remaining hardware can be removed from the doors. Just remove the nuts and screws holding everything in place. Protect the power window regulator during disassembly. The power window motor keeps the window regulator in control. Once the motor has been removed from the regulator, unleash the lift-assist spring. There is a provision to install a bolt into the regulator to capture the regulator arms, so make sure you install the bolt. Manual window regulators are not a problem due to the fact that the lift-assist spring is captured at all times.

The Midyear's door-lock latch assembly wears and the door becomes harder and harder to open until it finally does not open. Zip Products sells door-lock latch rebuild kits, and you should rebuild both lock latches.

Early wax-based lubricants leave behind a waxy residue, which makes the linkages difficult to operate. Remove all of the lock-latch hardware for cleaning and lubing to restore like-new operation.

Remove Door Latch Linkage

1 Use a small screwdriver to release the retainer clip as you remove the door latch linkages from the latch assembly. The clip has a tab that must be pried out of the hole then pushed toward the linkage. The linkage then easily comes out, and it doesn't require prying on everything in the door to get the linkage out.

Remove Screws Under Weatherstripping

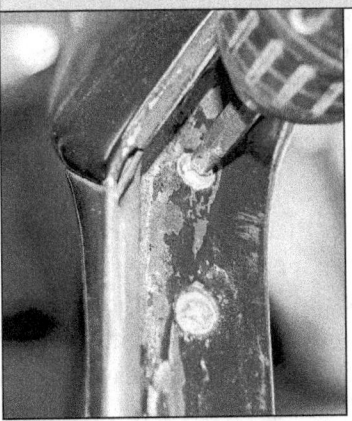

2 When you are ready to remove the vent glass assemblies, use a screwdriver to loosen and remove the screws, which are hidden under the weatherstrip at the door pillar. You can see the remnants of the weatherstrip adhesive near the screw heads. Dig out the adhesive so you get a good bite in the screw head before trying to remove them.

Remove Door Glass

3 You need to correctly position the front door glass so you are able use the access hole for fastener removal. To remove the front 7/16 hex nut that retains the door glass, move the glass to the correct height then a socket can be used for removal.

CHAPTER 3

Remove Door Glass (Continued)

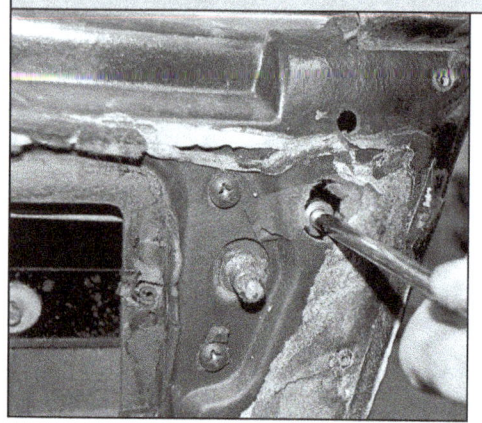

4 The rear door glass retaining 7/16-inch hex nut is accessed in the same way. You can see there is some tape and caulking over the hole that must be removed.

Check Door Glass Bracket

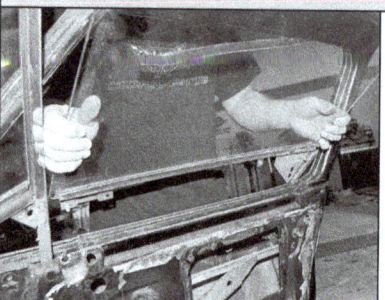

5 The door glass rear vertical run track has been removed, and the vent window is out of the way for door glass removal. Check the bond on the door glass to the lift channel bracket. I often find the brackets loose on the glass, as the factory used a rubberized cloth tape to install them. Corroded tracks often break the bond so check them and replace the tape if there is any doubt.

Remove Glass Adjuster Screws

6 The vent window has the door glass vertical run channel attached to it with an adjuster screw to control glass in and out angle. It takes some twisting and finagling to remove the vertical run channel with the adjuster screw in place from the door, but it is well worth the additional effort. Typically the adjuster screw is corroded to the run channel making it much smarter to take the assembly out and free up the adjuster screw while it is on the bench to avoid breaking pieces.

Exterior Disassembly

I detach the rear valance panel first, to ease rear bumper bracket removal. Once the bumpers are off, only the bumper brackets and braces remain. Front bumper brackets are adjustable, while the rear brackets use shims to adjust the fit to the body.

Bumper bracket shim position and quantity should be recorded to aid later installation. Knowing where they should be placed during assembly can save your freshly painted fiberglass. Keep in mind that replacing the frame or major body reconstruction can change the shim requirements.

One side of my rocker moldings was gone and the other rough, so I put them on my parts list.

The emblems are all dated and looking faded, requiring replacement.

Emergency brake cables and master cylinder brake lines require removal while working on the underside and underhood areas. I usually remove the master cylinder and let it hang on the lines to avoid brake fluid spillage. Drain pans can be placed in the proper locations when the body is out of the way for brake line removal.

Ground cables are placed at the driver-side rear frame, near the antenna and at the driver-side number-one body mount. All of the grounds, which are easy to miss during preparation, must be removed. Preserving pieces needs to be a top priority, and in many situations, the pieces get damaged from improper handling more so than from multiple years of use.

The engine harness temperature and ignition wiring is disconnected from the engine. You do not have to remove any of the wiring from the firewall bulkhead. The alternator wiring must be disconnected and tucked out of the way. I remove the throttle linkage and ground cable at the lever on the firewall so that it's out of the way for the body lift. There is no need to remove any of the other cooling system hoses.

I take one last, comprehensive look at everything for any missed wires or cables that should be disconnected and then the body mount bolts can be removed.

Removing body mount bolts can be difficult unless you find a Midyear that has been in a dry environment and never driven in wet weather. At this stage, you can become very frustrated. Remember that the less damage you do now saves more time and expense in the long run. Torching the bolts is an option, but the fiberglass can be easily damaged. Hopefully you have soaked the body mount bolts with rust penetrant for days or weeks.

GETTING STARTED

Remove Valance Panel

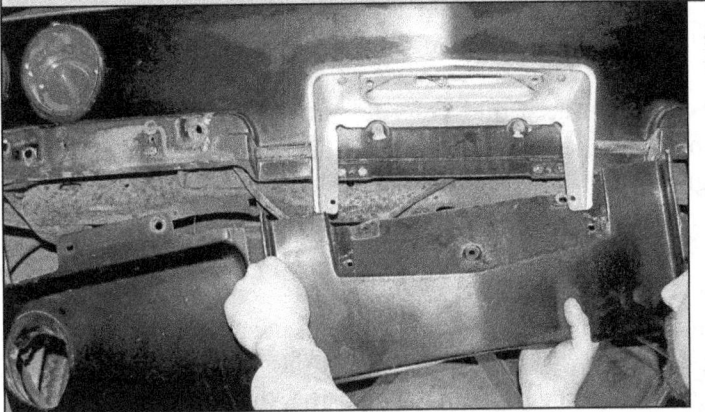

1 The rear valance panel must be removed for the body lift. The license plate frame has nuts on the screws holding the lamp assembly in place. It is easier to access the license plate frame upper nuts after the valance panel is removed. The valance panel is removed first after the 7/16 inch hex screws are removed. The upper license plate frame screws have 3/8 inch hex nuts that the Phillips-head screw into. A small box-end wrench holds the nuts while a Phillips-head screwdriver removes the screws.

Remove Bumper Bolts

2 Use an air impact wrench when removing stubborn bumper bolts. Original head marking bumper bolts are available, so it's not worth it to save the old ones. Use a propane torch to heat them if necessary, but be careful around the fiberglass.

Remove Corrosion-Damaged Bolt Head

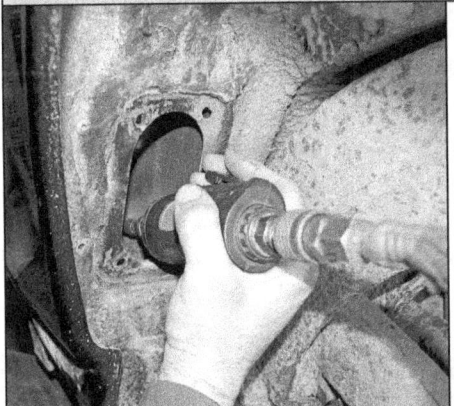

3 The bolt head was corroded so badly no socket could grab it. Rather than use a cutting torch to remove the remaining bolt head in a tight fiberglass pocket, I used a high-speed grinder to grind off the remaining bolt head. You may run into the same situation at the front when it comes time to remove the radiator core support bolts. There are two 5/8 hex bolts that retain the core support to the radiator. Make sure you remove them.

Remove Number-2 Body Bolt

4 On the 1963 coupe, the number-2 body mount is hidden under the sill plate. To my amazement the 5/8-inch hex head bolt came out easily, which happens every once in a while. The impact wrench can apply a hammering action to loosen stubborn bolts. It's best to let the impact hammer on the bolts for a few seconds at low speed. Holding the impacts trigger wide open could break the bolt or round off the bolt's head.

Remove Rear Body Mount Bolts

5 Remove the body mount bolts at the rear of the interior. These caged body mount nuts are in the back corner on both sides. General Motors used a light-gauge metal cage riveted to the fiberglass to keep the nut in check during body bolt installation. After years of water and dirt exposure, the caged nut is impossible to remove easily. With a helper on the underside, I held the nut and luckily the bolt snapped. Both sides were nice enough to break like this one did.

HOW TO RESTORE YOUR CORVETTE: 1963–1967

Body Lifting

I had to think about my situation before proceeding because my plan was to have Lucky's Customs do my bodywork and paint. Once the body is off the frame, it must be properly supported or severe fiberglass damage can occur. Should I lift the body at my shop and try to set it up for transport? Another option was to head over to Lucky's Customs for a body dolly, but that was a three-hour drive. My decision was to have the body ready for the lift and then carefully strap the body and chassis down for the ride to Lucky's Customs.

To lift the body, I recommend using one of three options. Option one: Convince your buddies that they need to be a part of this monumental occasion, so that they can manhandle the body off the chassis.

Option two: Use a specific sling assembly that grabs the Midyear's C-channel in the front and rear. A cherry-picker or chain fall can then be used to pick up the body with the sling in place.

Option three (the preferred method): Use a two-post automotive lift to pick up the body at the C-channel. The lift allows for a smooth, equal lift at a slow enough speed to make sure nothing gets damaged.

If something was missed during preparation for the lift, you can identify the issue and remove the fastener before body damage occurs. No matter how careful you are, it is possible to forget a cable or wire that could damage a lot more than just the cable or wire.

It is hard for people to manually lift a body off any chassis and avoid damaging it. Using a sling to lift the body is fine, as long as there are three or more helpers to keep the body level as it lifts upward. No matter how you choose to make the lift happen, everyone has to diligently keep watch as it progresses. The corners of the body can catch on the rear body mounts, damaging the fiberglass in seconds.

I use a simple fixture to keep the body supported properly. My body dolly uses each of the original body mounting points to rest on. The dolly is carefully positioned under the body, then the body is lowered onto the mounting points.

Even with careful planning, there is sure to be surprises. Inspect the condition of the C-channels and the birdcage. You can see hidden areas of the fiberglass panels and possibly any patchwork. Do not be in a hurry to move forward because this is a critical stage. You need to make notes on any obvious body damage that might have been missed. Using paint or a marker, indicate any suspect areas where damage may be present. Whether you do the body work or send it out, identifying potential problems saves wasted effort. If you plan to do the bodywork yourself, this is a good time to bring in your expert to consult with you on the best plan of attack.

Lift Body Off Frame

1 *Body lifting with this two-post lift is easy and you have plenty of control. Keep an eye on the rear fenders as the body rises because they tend to come very close to the rearmost body mount stanchions. Look frequently to make sure there are no wires, cables, or hoses that should have been disconnected.*

Inspect for Damage and Previous Repairs

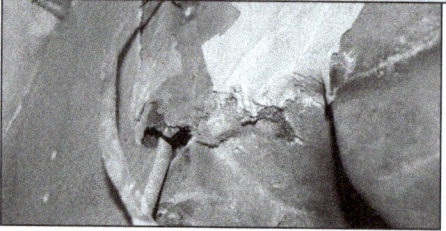

2 *After the body had been lifted off, I found one of the worst problems. Look at this patch at the rear body mount. Instead of repairing the fiberglass, this filler was smeared onto the broken fiberglass area.*

Evaluate C-Channel Damage

3 *After the body was lifted, I found the worst of the C-channel damage. A fabricated steel plate is welded into the driver-side number-3 body mount to reinforce the channel. This corrosion damage is very minor, especially considering the condition of the chassis it was sitting on.*

CHAPTER 4

BODYWORK

You need to be realistic about completing the bodywork yourself. Ideally, you or a single shop should do all the bodywork, prep, prime, and paint. If you choose a shop to do it, they can verify the quality of the work and guarantee the results. Completing the bodywork at one shop and having an owner participate in painting at a paint shop are two scenarios that rarely work out well. Bringing a completed, ready-to-paint vehicle to someone for paint is a tough proposition. No painter wants to take a chance on whether someone else has done bodywork and prep work correctly. It does not matter if you or a professional shop has done the work. Even if you tell the painter that there will be no responsibility on his part whatsoever, and that the outcome of the paint job is solely your concern, many paint shops are still reluctant because there are no guarantees.

Let's face it, bodywork is an art that requires patience and feel. You either have patience or not, and "feel" is something that's developed over time. Experienced body repairers have a touch or feel for straight panels. They can feel a rise or dip in what should be a flat surface. They can also feel when body filler has a noticeable transition edge from the repair to the panel surrounding it. Some of us can quickly grasp this acquired talent, while others take years to fully master, if at all.

If you have trouble with feeling the wavy panels, blocking shows you where the spots are. Blocking refers to taking a long straight wooden or plastic block, applying sandpaper to it, then using it to sand panels. This finds any high and low spots in the panels. The unfortunate part is that you may spend plenty of extra time and body filler taking the waves out until you get the "feel." Experience really pays off here, and this is why professional body repairers have a distinct advantage.

Professional body repairers also invest continually in the latest products, tools, and equipment to hone their craft. This gives them another advantage

The vent window has the door glass vertical run channel attached to it with an adjuster screw to control glass in and out angle. It takes some twisting and finagling to remove the vertical run channel with the adjuster screw in place from the door, but it is well worth the additional effort. Typically the adjuster screw is corroded to the run channel making it much smarter to take the assembly out and free up the adjuster screw while it is on the bench to avoid breaking pieces.

in using the latest technology in tools and repair techniques. The Environmental Protection Agency restricts the use of many of the early chemicals and products, and this is another reason why the cost of owning and running paint and body shops is so high. Cheap estimates equal low-quality work, and there is no way to do the job correctly without paying a reasonable price for it. Low-balling an estimate to get work in when every other shop is considerably higher, means the work will either be lower quality, or you will be hit with a supplemental estimate.

Be sure you are comfortable with your decision of how much you farm out and how much you do yourself.

Components to Consider

Let's begin with the birdcage, which is the steel cage that surrounds the passenger compartment. It is where the Midyear fiberglass body panels are attached. Coupe and convertible birdcages integrate the windshield frame into the assembly. Coupe birdcages are stiffer than convertible cages because the roof structure connects the windshield frame to the rear section. Major fiberglass body panels comprise the exterior to avoid as many visible seams as possible. The roof (coupes), upper rear surround panel (convertible), and front surround panel comprise the majority of the body.

Fenders and upper surrounds are bonded together with bonding strips to reinforce the body and seam. Fender break points start about an inch below the upper surround, following the crown.

Doors have steel framework with fiberglass skins. Working with the Corvette fiberglass bonded panels is quite different than repairing metal panels. You don't unbolt fenders for replacement, which many do-it-yourselfers are familiar with.

Inspection

You need a good idea of what repairs were done over the years and this is why all the paint was removed. A detailed inspection gives you a good indication. Make a plan of attack and stick to it. Once you know which structural parts of the body need to be repaired, you can proceed with the restoration.

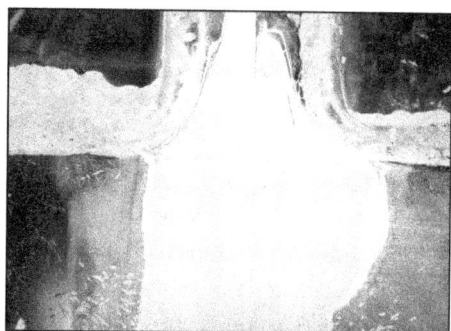

From the preliminary inspection, I found a distorted body line so I immediately removed the paint to identify the problem. Once the paint had been removed, I discovered previous major collision repair. With this Midyear, an amateurish body repair or Bondo body filler repair techniques were destined to show up again. Fiberglass should have been used to fill the splice joint and reconstruct the peaked line.

After finding the splice in the center, I knew there had to be another seam. To find it, I rubbed my hand across the rear deck area. This was not a factory seam, and it became very obvious as the repair shrank.

Underside

With the chassis out from under the 1963, I raised the body up on the lift to do a thorough inspection of the underside. I found some hidden, unknown fiberglass patchwork had been done at the rear of the car. It appeared that years ago, someone had spliced a rear section of another car to the upper roof panel. The center repair seam was located over a frame crossmember, and it would have been difficult to find with the chassis in place. That is, of course, until the paint stripping phase began.

I also uncovered this splice seam on the passenger side, going down into the side fender. Butt splices like this require specific repair procedures or they haunt you until the repair is correctly done. Cracks develop along the splice seam from road vibrations. The edges of the butted fiberglass panels become visible as body filler shrinkage occurs. In all cases the body filler shrinks in the space between the fiberglass edges, causing a noticeable line. Fiberglass must bridge the splice seams to prevent noticeable lines as the body filler shrinks. This area needs major fiberglass work.

The underside inspection revealed another area of concern: the passenger compartment tub had broken loose from the upper surround. I had not noticed the compartment tub bond issue from the interior, so removing the body was the right choice because it was very obvious with the body lifted. This is significant because road noise would be heard and air would flow unchecked through the passenger compartment.

I also found what appeared to be all-metal body filler used for bonding the body panels together. With this type of problem, you need someone with experience to help make the right decisions. Does all-metal body filler suffice for panel bonding? All-metal body filler was devised to strengthen the plastic filler

BODYWORK

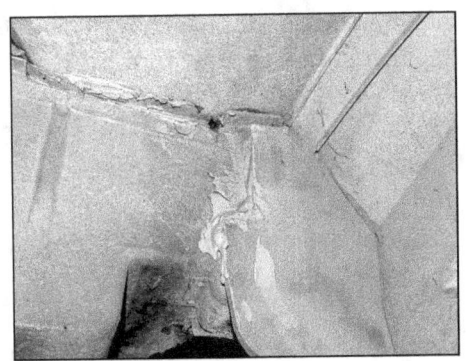

This all-metal body filler is an oozing mess that's coming out of the rear inner fender reinforcement panel. I found all-metal filler used as adhesive on all the panels that had been replaced or repaired at the back end. A technician was able to grab this reinforcement panel and pull it off easily without damaging it. The upper left corner shows the gap between the upper surround and tub.

commonly used and to inhibit water intrusion. I am concerned with the bonding strength of the all-metal filler. Does it perform as well as the prescribed fiberglass panel bonding adhesives?

Although I've been in this business for years, this was something I had never seen. I consulted with Al Sowash, who ran the body shop at Eckler's Corvette Service Center in the '90s. Al inspected the Midyear to determine the best solution to this problem. This Midyear had multiple experts discussing its fate. My next call was to Seth at Lucky's Customs to let him know that Al would be coming by to take a look at the project in the coming weeks. After a through inspection it was determined that someone had indeed used all-metal filler. To be safe all of the suspect filler was ground out to be replaced with fresh bonding adhesive. By now you are probably wondering, why are they going on and on about this bonding adhesive and filler that was used?

This body filler issue is important because body fillers shrink over time. Also, fiberglass bodies show more of the effects of body filler shrinkage than do metal bodies. When a fiberglass seam or hole repair has been incorrectly repaired, it eventually shows up and is noticeable through the paint. Even when performed properly, there is a possibility that the seam or hole will show up after a long period of time.

You may have seen minor imperfections while looking at really nice Corvettes at car shows. Then you may have wondered, "Why is there a divot here and there, or a sunken line running alongside the fender where the upper surround meets the side fender?" This shrinkage phenomenon is seen more often in the South because heat certainly brings out the worst in any questionable repairs.

You don't want to smooth a body and eventually have it show every repair that was made. Cracking occurs when a fender or inner support panel comes loose due to poor adhesion. The best possible techniques must be used to minimize shrinkage and fix loose panels. General Motors and AO Smith supplied bodies that used a specific bonding adhesive, but not "bondo," to adhere the panels to the birdcage.

The story is that asbestos-reinforced resin bonding adhesive was used in the early years of Corvette panel assembly. No one can verify when this lethal mix was used, or if it was used for sure. Multiple sources have said that Midyears have been assembled with this bonding adhesive. In addition, no one seems to know for sure whether all of the 1963–1967 Corvettes were done this way.

The use of asbestos also has not been absolutely verified, but it makes sense to be very careful during sanding or grinding. Wear breathing protection and contain and dispose of materials properly.

Paint

Next, I need to find out how many other repaired areas are lurking under my '63's aged paint. I cannot stress enough how important it is to remove all the paint down to the raw fiberglass because the best surface for primer and paint adhesion is raw fiberglass.

I once had a Corvette painted for a customer, and the body shop insisted that they had the perfect primer-sealer that allowed them to keep the old, underlying paint in place with minimal sanding. I urged them to rethink the job and quote it with complete paint removal.

After it had been painted and before I finished assembling the exterior pieces, door handles, etc., the paint was lifting. What made a bad situation worse was that the new "silly putty" paint took nearly 40 hours to remove. In some areas (not near enough) where the urethane and underlying paint were compatible, it came off easily in with a razor blade. Consider yourself warned; don't make a similar mistake.

You can use abrasives or chemicals to strip the paint. First, you don't want to cut into the fiberglass panels. But some

This 1965 Nassau Blue coupe with original paint shows seam distortion. The bonding adhesive has shrunk at the left rear upper surround and side fender. You might say it is a badge of honor having the original seam showing because it means this Corvette has withstood the test of time. After 44-plus years, all of the original untouched fender-to-upper-surround seams should look like this.

won't chemically strip the paint because they fear chemicals will leach into the fiberglass and prevent proper paint bonding. Done properly by the directions, chemical stripping yields good results. With media blasting, plastic bead or baking soda are most popular for fiberglass bodies. The plastic bead process removes most of the paint without damaging the fiberglass, but I had to sand quite a bit to remove all the remaining paint. The blaster said that they could remove all the paint, but they were hesitant because fiberglass damage could result. Soda blasting is less abrasive on the fiberglass, but sanding is required to get all the paint off.

Steel

Many people are not aware of how important the steel birdcage that supports all the fiberglass panels really is. Water leaks are inevitable and cause the birdcage to rot away slowly. With the birdcage hidden away under fiberglass panels, extensive metal damage can occur unknowingly. Rotted birdcages cause body panel flex and eventual cracks. A dead giveaway would be corroded rain gutters that direct water away from the door sills. The deteriorating gutters let more water intrude into the birdcage damaging the metal components underneath the rain gutters. If you find severely corroded rain gutters you should remove the door sill fiberglass panel to check the extent of the damage. Fiberglass panel removal is shown in the front end servicing portion on page 52.

Our project was typical with one severely rotted rain gutter with some minor underlying birdcage damage due to water intrusion. Reproduction rain gutters are available to avoid the need to fabricate an elaborate metal object. The majority of underlying birdcage steel pieces are not available and require custom fabrication. Fortunately, the birdcage pieces are relatively simple to fabricate. Next we move on the windshield area for additional metal structure inspection.

Windshield

My next area of concern is removing the windshield, to check its frame. Old-school windshield sealing techniques were used on the Midyears, making them susceptible to leaks. The use of metal windshield trim clips on the metal frame allowed corrosion to start almost immediately. When the stainless-steel trim was installed, it often scratched the painted metal surfaces, causing corrosion to form. As the corrosion worsened, perforations allowed water to get inside the windshield frame and posts and caused unseen damage. My project had some damage, but not much in comparison to corrosion damage I have seen on other Midyears.

Chances are good that there is some windshield frame rust/corrosion and perforations to repair on even the nicest of Midyears that require restoration. Complete sections of the windshield frame may require replacement, or you may get lucky and just need a metal patch here and there.

I have seen plenty of Southern cars with severely rusted windshield frames and no chassis rust whatsoever. The '63's chassis was ready to fall apart as a result of corrosion, yet the birdcage and windshield frame were in very good condition.

Removing the bubbling paint on this Corvette is no problem. I was able to remove the majority of paint with this razor blade scraper. While it was nice, the paint came off so easily I need to be sure the new paint sticks. All of the suspect primer is removed and carefully sanded right down to the raw fiberglass.

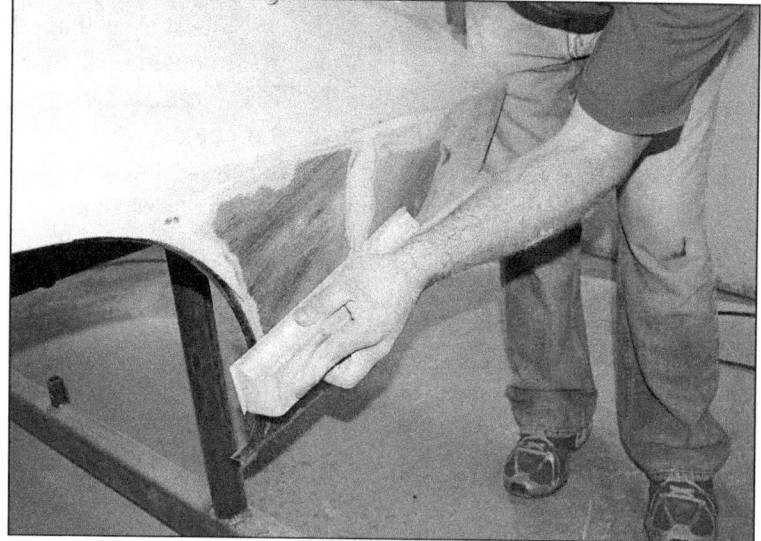
Use a long sanding block with 80-grit sandpaper to remove the paint. The bonding adhesive has distorted the side fender at the vertical spot in the center where the paint has been removed. This occurs at every bonding area on the body that is visible.

BODYWORK

The birdcage and C-channels are in remarkable condition considering the frame was just about cut into two pieces from corrosion. There is a corroded rain gutter at the rear of the driver door frame. The gutter sits on top of the birdcage where the rust eventually finds it way internally. Finding corrosion in the birdcage is common so I was lucky that this is all I found.

Do not expect that all Midyears from the North have the same rust/corrosion concerns. Many have much more extensive rust damage that requires far greater repair work, and it's difficult work to complete.

Personally, I would much rather change the chassis than delve deeply into the birdcage or windshield frame. Complete windshield frame or section replacements require extensive work and major fiberglass panel removal. Planning for this saves time and money. If the windshield frame is severely corroded, you should work on that while the front end is off the body.

Fiberglass Repair

Never use resin that has passed its "best if used by" date because older resin tends to gel and doesn't flow as well as fresh resin. It's also easier to work out the air bubbles during application. You need to precisely mix the hardener with the resin or you may run out of hardener. When the fiberglass resin and hardener mix, a chemical reaction takes place creating heat—a lot of heat. You want the finished fiberglass sandable within two hours. Any sooner and chances are you will not be able to lay the fiberglass matting down and remove the air bubbles completely. Longer set-up times can leave you with weak fiberglass that never fully cures. The best policy is to contact a body and paint supplier to purchase fresh, high-quality materials.

Consistency is essential when mixing the prescribed ratios of hardener to resin. Stick to the manufacturer's recommended mix ratio, application temperature range, and cure time. Another concern is careful preparation. Strong, dependable fiberglass panels require using 36-grit sandpaper to roughen the bonded surfaces. You need to have your materials ready to mix, matting to install, and tools ready. Do not forget to wear gloves and have some clean-up solvents nearby.

This is the typical windshield frame seen in the South; rusty and corroded with perforations, or holes. The entire perimeter of the frame is corroded with other holes requiring minor work. Rather than weld in the small patches I used Vette panel adhesive and milled fibers to fill the small holes.

Evercoat Vette Panel Adhesive/Filler is used as top coat after matting and resin is applied. The panel adhesive keeps the fiberglass strands from coming up through the finished bodywork.

Here are pro fiberglass resin, 1.5 mil fiberglass mat, and the hardener dispenser. The hardener dispenser forces the required amount into the upper cup to ensure consistent measurements. When the "best if used by" date has passed, get rid of it.

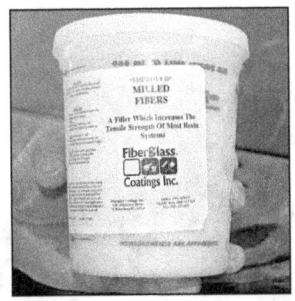

Milled fibers from Fiberglass Coatings are used to reinforce the fiberglass repairs.

Before application, the milled fibers (balls of fiberglass) are added to the Evercoat Vette Panel Adhesive/Filler. There is no prescribed amount to add, just add enough to thicken the filler slightly.

HOW TO RESTORE YOUR CORVETTE: 1963–1967

Seam Repair

With materials nearby, you are ready to tackle seam repairs. The goal is to bond two separate panels of fiberglass, making them one piece. The repair procedure illustrated here should be used anywhere two pieces of fiberglass are spliced together. If done properly, the repair remains undetectable for the duration of the Midyear's life. Time is the crucial factor, and you have to apply a few layers of fiberglass mat before the fiberglass resin kicks off. Fiberglass resin takes about 15 to 20 minutes to start to thicken. Once the resin activates, it's set and you cannot make changes. You have to grind out any areas that are suspect and start again.

Grind Fiberglass for Repair

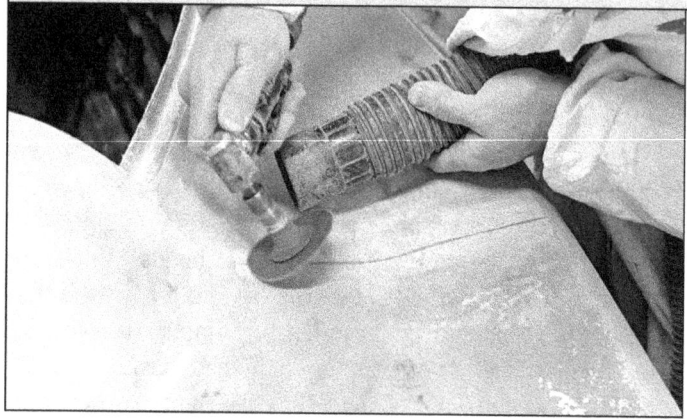

1 A 3-inch-diameter disc is used first to remove the majority of material at the center of the seam. You want the edges of each panel to be thin and then tapered upward. The aggressive 36-grit disc is mounted on a flexible backer to allow the disc to follow the panel's curvature. The paint suit and shop vacuum help keep some of the irritating fiberglass off during this messy part of the task.

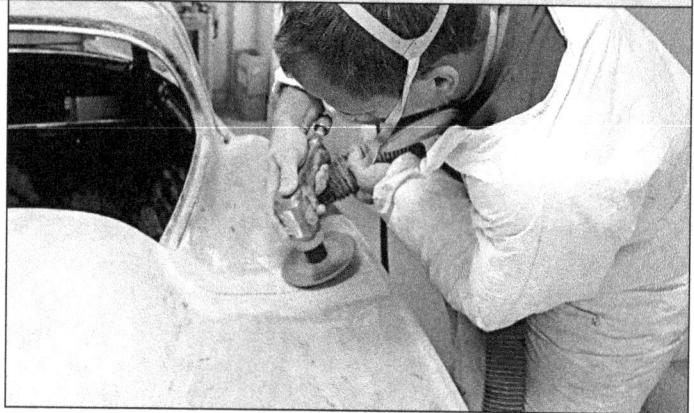

2 An 80-grit disc on a larger-diameter air grinder roughens up the area surrounding the seam. The taper is pronounced a bit more outward, hopefully without grinding through surfaces. Coarse-grit grinding discs ensure that the resin has good bite during the fiberglass work. Be cautious, though, because the aggressive-grit discs chew up material quickly.

Cut Fiberglass Mat

3 You must cut your fiberglass mat before you even think about mixing any resin. There are two sheets of mat thinner than the final top sheet to taper the repair. The fiberglass mat goes over the crown of the fender because the panel repair seam goes into the factory side-fender seam.

Apply Resin and Mat to Repair Area

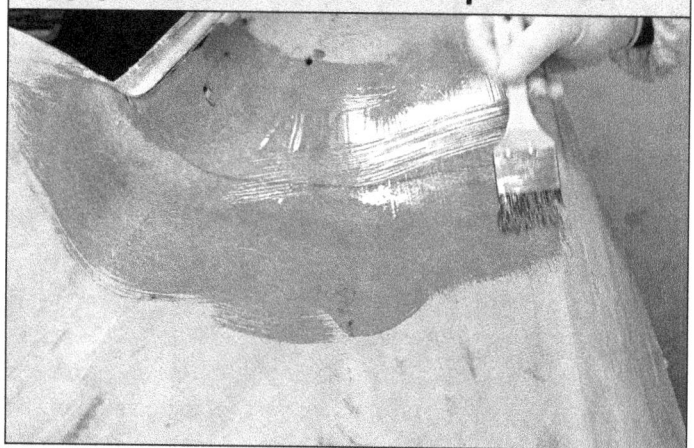

4 An ample coating of resin is applied beyond the area of fiberglass mat. Do not try to save resin here. A healthy dose of resin is required because it soaks in quickly. Make a couple of passes over the area, filling the brush each time.

Lay Mat on Repair Area

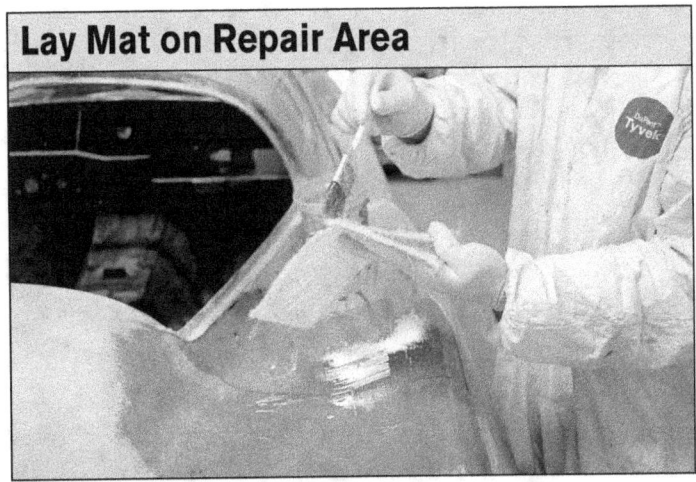

5 Timing is important when the first layer of fiberglass mat is soaked with resin. Apply resin to the mat until it is saturated. Then lay it onto the seam, splitting it down the middle.

Fine-Tune Application Technique

6 Use an inexpensive, throwaway application brush to push down the fiberglass mat and soak any dry areas. You want the entire area to be wet with resin for the next application of mat.

Squeeze Out Air Bubbles

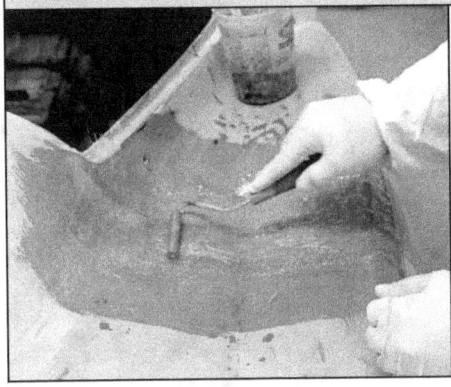

7 Between each application of fiberglass mat use a job-specific roller to force out any air bubbles. This should be done over the entire mat area with wet resin.

Forcing out the air bubbles is very important to prevent delamination of the subsequent layers of mat.

Avoid Air Pockets

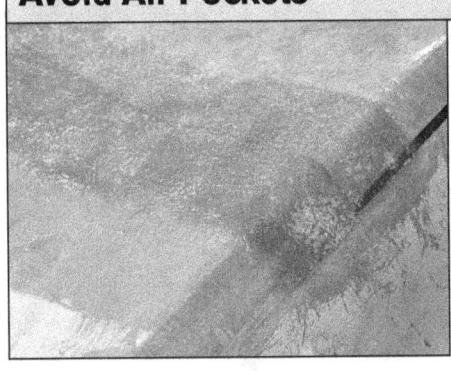

8 An air pocket is underneath the fiberglass matting that was placed over the top edge of the fender. When the matting changes directions it has a tendency to develop air pockets. This can be seen as the light-colored circular area in the center of the vertical area. The light-colored area is more prominent on the left side of the splice seam.

Saturate Repair Area with Resin

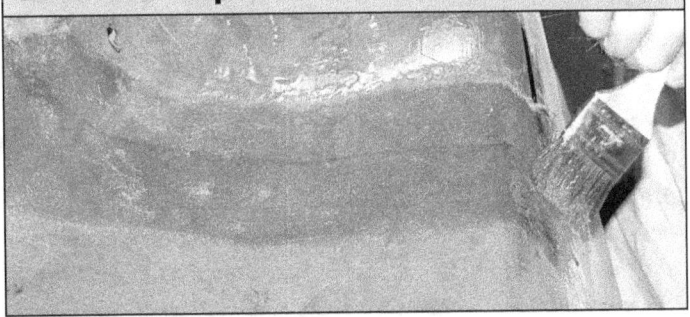

9 The best policy is to saturate the vertical area with another application of resin to remove the air pocket. An air pocket is disastrous to the integrity of the body panel, especially if it lays down just enough that the sander does not break into it. Days, months, or even years later a major bubble may be noticeable when it finally comes loose from the resin.

Apply Final Coat of Resin and Mat

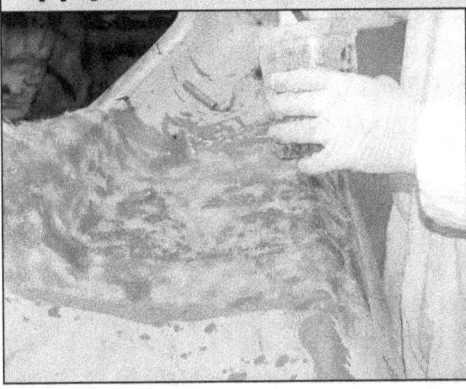

10 The final, wide layer of resin-soaked fiberglass mat is laid down. Note the wide fiberglass mat is going into the rear window glass area to prevent a ragged edge on the corner of the body where the stainless-steel trim sits against it. Keep in mind that this entire three-layer procedure has been accomplished within a 20-minute window. Each layer should go on top of wet resin for best results.

Work in Resin with Roller

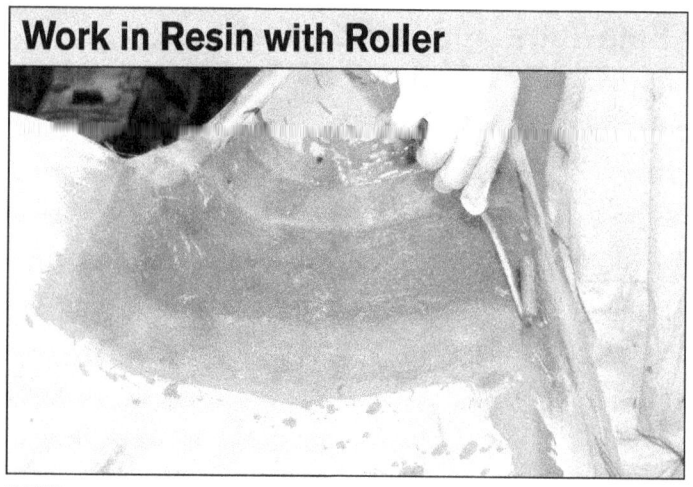

11 Starting at the center and working outward, make one more pass with the roller over the entire area to force any remaining bubbles out. The edges need to be rolled well to prevent them from curling upward.

Properly Position Mat

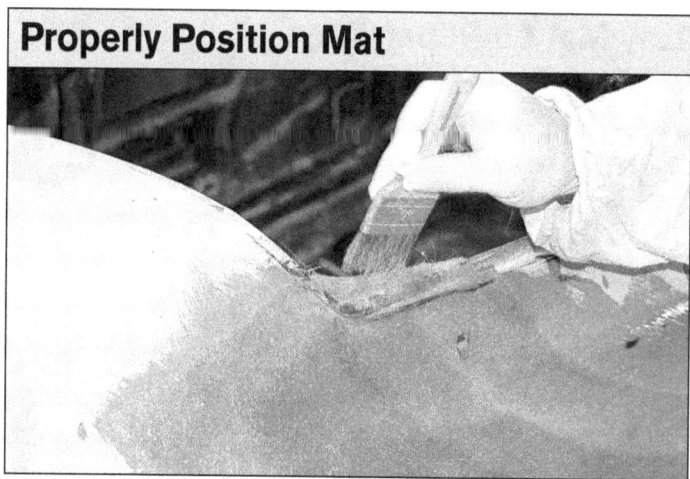

12 You must force the fiberglass mat into the corner while applying resin to make sure it sticks well. Carefully watch this area for a few minutes. Make sure it does not come up and away from the window channel as it cures.

Apply Heat to Repair Area

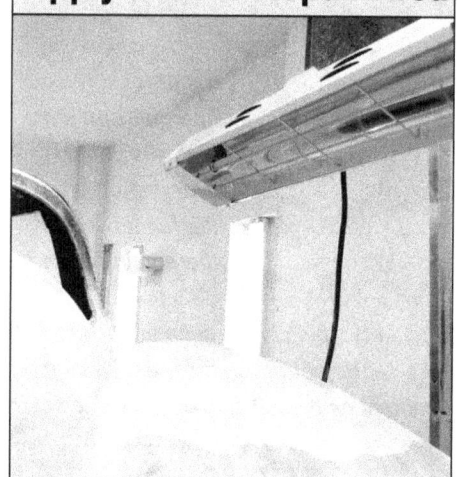

13 You should wait approximately two hours for the repair to cure before shaping the area. Apply heat to the entire area to confirm the integrity of the repair and verify that that the repair has not been compromised. To speed up the curing process, professionals use infrared heat lamps to cook the repaired area and check for lamination defects. You can buy a home infrared lamp or find a deal on a pro model. An alternative to the heat lamp is to let the Midyear sit outside for a week on sunny days to see if any surprises occur. Better to know before the top coat is on for sure.

Shape Rough Repair Area

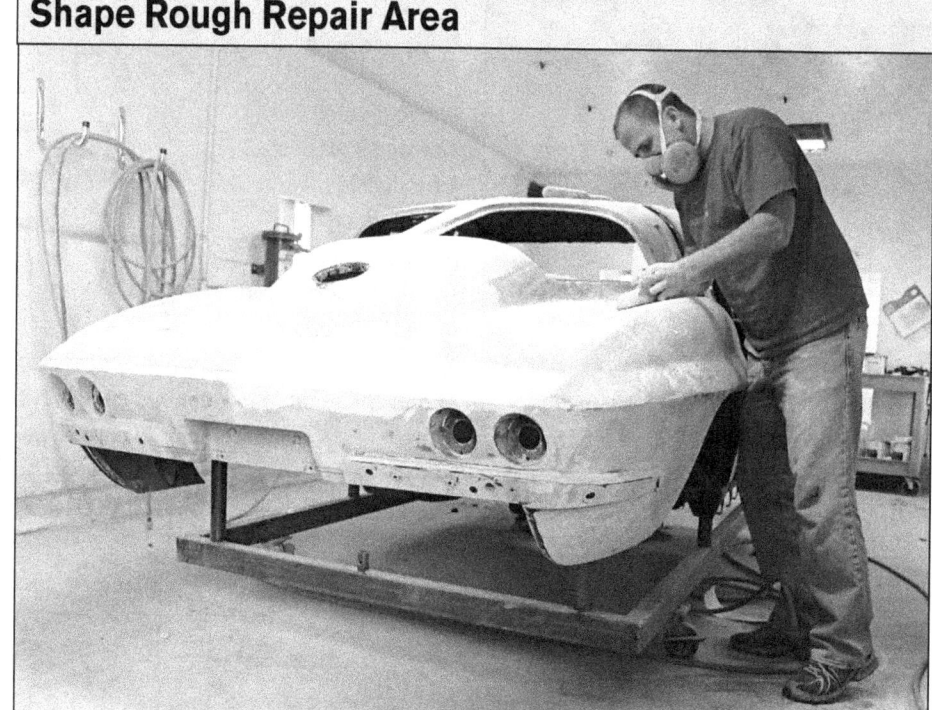

14 The raw fiberglass repair is rough sanded to get it close to its correct contours. Repaired areas should be shaped before a coat of filler is applied to keep the consistency of the body filler uniform. Additionally, when the filler is applied, the 36-grit paper gives the surface bite. Smooth surfaces allow the next application to peel off easily or, worse yet, bubbles to form and show up later. Note the respirator. Our body worker not use his paint suit to avoid the fiberglass dust. Some people can tolerate the fiberglass dust and minute pieces of glass and others cannot. If you do happen to get these painful flecks on you, cold water works best to rinse them off. Hot water opens the pores and draws in the itchy fibers.

BODYWORK

Clean Repair Area

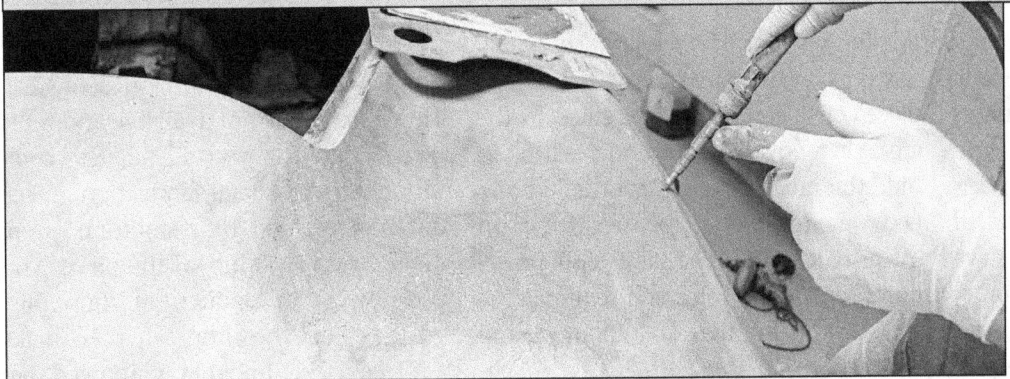

15 The area is roughed in and looks almost ready for primer. Blowing away any stray fiberglass debris ensures a good bond for the next coat. Blow out any pin holes with extra caution. If they are not cleared of all debris, tiny bubbles may show later.

Apply Adhesive Filler

16 Apply Evercoat Vette Panel Adhesive/Filler to seal the fiberglass strands and add strength to the area. During mixing, milled fibers are dispursed throughout the panel's adhesive/filler to add reinforcement. The idea is to achieve the final contour with just one coat. This milled fiber reinforced filler is difficult to sand and requires extra work to smooth out. Carefully applying the filler can save you plenty of elbow grease.

Sand and Shape Repair Area

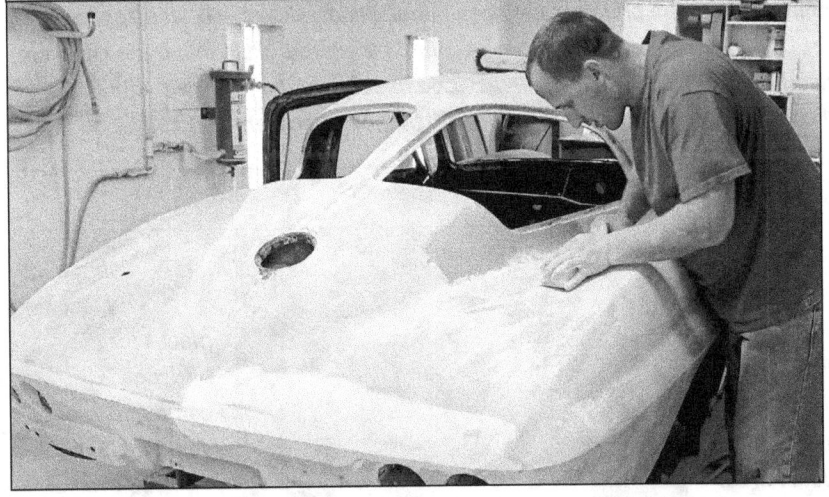

17 Use 80-grit sandpaper with the block sander and take long deliberate strokes to shape and smooth the area. Remember to avoid pushing down too hard as you sand. The repair area flexes and can cause unexplained low spots. In this area, a long sanding block works best to keep the surfaces flat. Do not be disappointed if it takes multiple applications to get the panel contour correct.

18 Use a piece of round steel tubing with 80-grit sandpaper to smooth out the inner contour at the rear deck. Like the sanding block, this tubing keeps the sanded area spread out to prevent low spots and dips.

Left Fender Repair

Next to be addressed is a really tough fiberglass repair under the left rear fender. Working horizontal and vertical surfaces out in the open are good places to learn. Repairing major broken structural fiberglass can be difficult because of impaired accessibility. In this particular case, I have a complete blow-out at the left rear inner fender. No one ever gets to see the work put into the area, but it is very important structurally. I could spend the better part of an afternoon properly repairing this section of broken fiberglass. Back-up molding panels (which take considerable time to fabricate) are required to form the missing sections of fiberglass. The previous repair was done quickly with some pieces of fiberglass quickly glued to the area, then covered with undercoating to hide the mess. An area like the left rear body mount has to be repaired with integrity in mind. The same basic procedures are used to form and reinforce the area. That is my next area to attack and conquer.

Earlier, I exposed some corrosion damage at the driver door latch area in the jamb. I removed the door jamb fiberglass panel at the latch area to see how extensive the corrosion was. Luckily, the damage was minor and required only one small piece of fabricated steel. These pieces are not available and must be fabricated. If you do not feel comfortable trying metal fabrication, check out a street rod or restoration shop. Make sure you bring all the pieces you possibly can and understand how they go together. The shop can then make a piece close to what you need per your sample. This is the only area that requires any welding, so you shouldn't need to go out and buy a welder. The next few photos show you how I handled the birdcage repair.

Inspect Body

1 This damage appeared to be minor until all the grime and undercoating was removed from the wheelhouse. Most likely, this damage was left behind from the rear partial upper surround repair work. The area was cleaned, ground out, and prepared for fiberglass mat installation. The trick is having the fiberglass mat follow the original contour.

Position Fiberglass Backing Material

2 I backed up the missing piece of the wheel house and body support from inside the passenger compartment. A piece of cardboard was conformed to mimic the original fiberglass panel. Mold-release wax was applied to the cardboard back-up mold then fiberglass mat and resin were applied to the area. Good to see that the major structural corner has been repaired correctly, not just covered up as I found it.

Fabricate Replacement Body Pieces

3 The extent of the birdcage damage is shown at the driver-side door latch area. The replacement piece must be fabricated from a sheet of steel. The area will be cleaned up and rust inhibitor applied before the newly fabricated piece is installed.

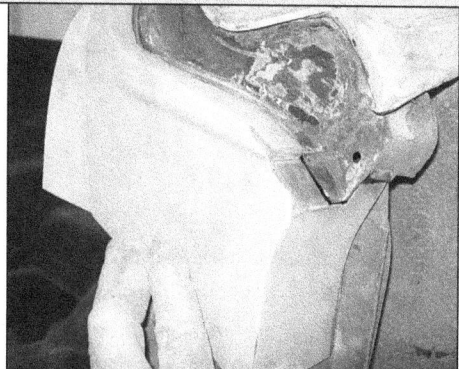

4 Fabricating replacement pieces for the birdcage is commonplace, so some metal work is involved even on fiberglass-bodied cars. The piece is welded in place then coated with primer to prevent the same occurrence. Once the fabricated metal piece has been welded into place the original fiberglass sill cover can be installed.

Fiberglass Panel Replacement

Fiberglass replacement panels come in two forms: press-molded, and hand-laid. Press molding requires an inner and outer mold form. The inner and outer molds are pressed together under high pressure, resulting in smooth surfaces on both sides of the fiberglass panel. The press-molded process is extremely time consuming, which in turn raises the cost. Hand-laid panels are pretty much self-explanatory: Fiberglass matting is laid into the mold, then fiberglass resin is applied. Of course, you can smooth the inside of a hand-laid panel to look like the press-molded pieces, but it takes a considerable amount of time to do it. NCRS Corvettes are required to have press-molded panels; however, hand-laid panels with the bonding strips installed are fine for fun driver cars.

My '63 needs major front end panels or possibly a one-piece front end assembly. The 1963–1967 Corvette front end consists of three pieces: an upper surround and the two side fenders. Bonding strips were used to put all three pieces together. To make assembly easier, a one-piece front-end, hand-laid mold was devised. Bonding strips should be installed to strengthen the one-piece front-end assembly. I mentioned earlier that the side fender-to-upper surround bonding seam distorts over time. One advantage of using the one-piece front end is that there are no seams to worry about down the road. Another advantage is that the installation of the one-piece front end takes less time.

In my case, I am using a hand-laid, one-piece front end to save money and time. Hand-laid fiberglass has noticeable chopped fiberglass strands on the inner surfaces. I will install the correct bonding strips to prevent wheel lip cracking. At first glance, the front end looks correct, even with the hand-laid fiberglass strands. The bonding strips are really there for reinforcement and should be used on whatever front end you decide to install. If your front end is fine, but the wheel lip is damaged, you should replace or repair the bonding strips. While I am working on the front end, I need to install inner fenders, since mine were in rough shape, with pieces missing from crucial areas. Take a good look around the hood hinge and hood prop area, which become damaged from even a light frontal impact. Repairing the inner fender in this area is possible, but it may come back to haunt you. Since the hood hinge and prop area of the inner fenders are under high stress loads, repaired cracks almost always return with a vengeance, far surpassing the original cracked area. At this point, it may sound like I cannot make up my mind. I am going to use press-molded inner fenders instead of hand-laid

Sermersheim's (Lee Bumb Composites, Inc.) sells press-molded front-end pieces in a variety of ways for a correct look inside and out. You can buy the pieces for assembly or as an assembly ready to install with all the correct bonding strips in place.

Sermersheim assembles the front end on a precise jig with the correct bonding strips and inner fenders in place ready for installation. Another alternative is using one Sermersheim's one-piece press-molded front ends and installing the bonding strips. Seth mentioned that he likes to use the Sermersheimer complete front-end assembly without the side fenders on. This allows him to fit the fenders to the doors easier.

This aftermarket hood from Eckler's shows the dramatic difference between hand-laid and press-molded fiberglass. The rough hand-laid fiberglass is easy to spot. GM did not use any hand-laid fiberglass on production Corvettes. All OEM pieces or panels were smooth press-molded fiberglass. To reduce cost, some body repairers smooth the inner panels themselves. This is a lot of work and tricky if you plan on putting a high-gloss finish on the completed panel.

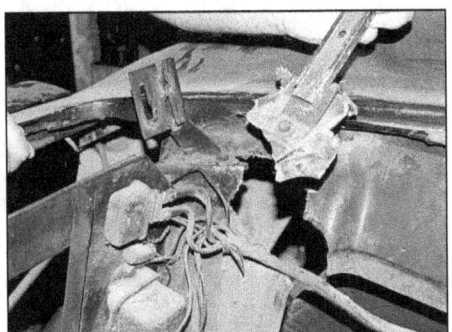

This worst-case scenario can be fixed, but at what cost? Repairs are difficult when both the hinge area and the hood prop mount are broken out. The inner fenders are not that costly and look very nice compared to the junk in place now.

The one-piece front end is on the ground and ready to receive the inner fenders and bonding strips. The bonding strips are glued in place, and then the inner fenders are installed. All the pieces are then installed with bonding adhesive just like all the other body panels.

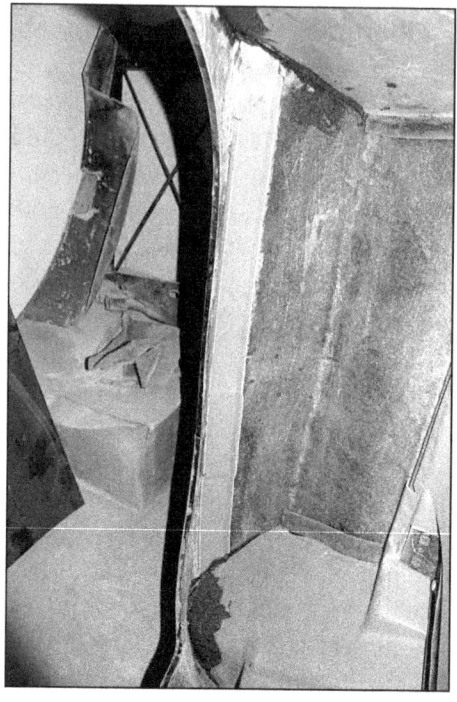

The hand-laid one-piece front end is sitting upright and ready for installation. The tan vertical bonding strip is in place right above the wheel opening. The lap joint is where the front and rear strips come together.

pieces. The press-molded pieces are easier to install and the price is close to the hand-laid pieces. Both the inner and outer surfaces of the inner fenders are actually highly visible, unlike the unfinished interior of the front end itself.

Fiberglass Panel Removal

Removing any fiberglass panel is not for the weak-hearted:

You must break loose the bonding adhesive from the panels. Hearing the crunch of fiberglass as you break each seam loose can be unnerving. To make matters more challenging, you must remove the piece to be replaced without breaking the bonding flange. Professionals use a variety of specially shaped scrapers and knives to access the bonding areas. The idea is to avoid damaging the fiberglass panels' mounting flange.

If you can apply heat to the bonding adhesive, it does break loose more easily. But it makes more sense to break or cut the damaged panel near the bonding area first. Heat can then be applied to ease the removal of each panel. As you apply heat, a large, stiff scraper works nicely to separate the bond.

Once the complete panel to be replaced is out of the way, flange cleanup begins. The idea is to remove just the old bonding adhesive, then roughen the flange for the new adhesive. Remember the fiberglass goes away quickly when using a high-speed grinder.

Once all the flanges have been cleaned up, it is time to fit the panel. Most fiberglass manufacturers leave material at each end of the panel to allow proper fitting. They usually have notes on the panel that state "FIT PRIOR TO PAINTING." That absolutely means you own the panel if it has paint on it.

Since I am installing a major fiberglass assembly, I need to consider what other body panels are affected. I should check the door gaps to door frame before installing the front end. My resto expert, Seth, likes to center the doors on the hinges first. Then he checks the fit of the door at the front where the front end meets the vertical door seam. The goal is to avoid doing any major reconstruction of the door gap at the front. Seth explained that, if necessary, he could build up the rear of the fender for a nice, tight, even door gap.

Always think about what other panels come into play before bonding any panels into place.

Once the bond breaking tool has been placed between the flange and panel, slowly tap it around the piece being removed. Make sure you keep the tool centered in the bonding adhesive. Do not dig into the fiberglass-mounting flange because they are tough to restore back to original strength if broken.

BODYWORK

Green masking tape is used to check the front end's bodyline in relation to the body. You want to make sure the front end is not running downward or upward. This is the last chance before gluing the panel in place to make sure the front end is positioned correctly.

For the '63, I need to check the fit before bonding: I had a really good looking 1966 convertible come into the shop in baskets, boxes, dollies, you name it. The bodywork was completed and the paint looked very nice. All I had to do was put it together. After being on the receiving end of so many of these "all you have to do is put it together" projects, you become highly skeptical of these jobs because they are never that simple.

The first tool I pulled out of the box was a tape measure. With the customer standing alongside me, I did a diagonal measurement of the frame. Sure enough, it was tweaked. The first order of business was having the frame straightened. But that was just the first of one problem after another.

Once the frame had been assembled, it was time for the body installation. At that time, I found some serious problems. Remember, I said the body had really nice paint. But when I began assembling the exterior, things went horribly wrong: None of the taillights fit properly in the rear surround. They weren't off just a little; the rear surround needed extensive reconstructive surgery to get the lights to fit.

What I am trying to stress here is that you make sure everything fits before any primer is sprayed and absolutely before any top coats are applied. That project cost plenty extra to fix everything so that the car looked presentable.

The doors should be fit prior to hanging the front end on the cowl. The front end can be held in place with screws as each area is fitted. Once you feel that the front has been fitted properly, go back and check the door gaps. The old adage "measure twice, cut once" applies here. Fit everything carefully, then check everything again for fit. Once you glue the panel in place, you risk damaging it if you have to remove it for placement changes.

You should have everything ready and waiting for the adhesive installation process. The fasteners holding the front end in place should be removed, and the front end set aside. Have all the fasteners in an easy-to-access location with the proper installation tools. Now, the bonding adhesive is mixed for application on the flanges.

Be sure to read and understand the bonding adhesive manufacturer's recommendations, especially on setup time. You have to apply the adhesive, then put the front end in place with the fasteners within a set time, dependent upon ambient temperature. Once the front end is set in place, your fasteners should be installed to align the assembly correctly.

Wipe off any excess bonding adhesive. General Motors did not do that, of course; they assembled plenty of cars daily, so the assembly line workers wasted very little time cleaning up. NCRS cars should not have the excess bonding adhesive wiped clean for authenticity. At this stage, it is a matter of waiting until the adhesive sets up, which often means letting things sit overnight.

Once all the major fiberglass issues have been taken care of, minor repairs should be handled. The details make a big impact on how well the finished project looks. During an earlier inspection, I noticed a few additional holes in the firewall from accessories that were added over the years. Screw holes in the fiberglass strip out easily and require repair to avoid having to use incorrect hardware. Look back at your notes from the disassembly phase and make the repairs before the paint is in place.

Final fit check is in order now. This is your last chance to make any adjustments or changes to component fit. Check the fit of each emblem in its respective position. Do they sit flat against the panel? Make sure the grille, rear taillights, etc., all fit properly. Check door gaps and hood fit. One final once-over can save you plenty of aggravation when it comes time to assemble.

Now, you're at an exciting point in the restoration when it's time to install all the exterior trim items, and you are able to see just how great the finished product looks. Or it can be a game changer with a "for sale" sign and multiple boxes of your pride and joy on the floor.

CHAPTER 4

Panel Removal

Prep Bonding Area

1 Use 36-grit grinding discs to remove any residual bonding adhesive. The aggressive grinding discs roughen up the flange to create a good surface for bonding adhesive bite. All the flanges should be cleaned of old bonding adhesive before fitting the front end. Clean any panel that is to be replaced before fitting.

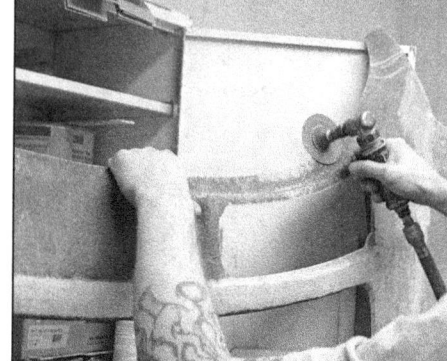

2 Use a 36-grit grinding disc to rough up the edges of the front end or panel to be glued. This is very important for proper adhesion of the panel. Once the grinding has been completed, blow off any remaining dust and debris.

Apply Bonding Adhesive

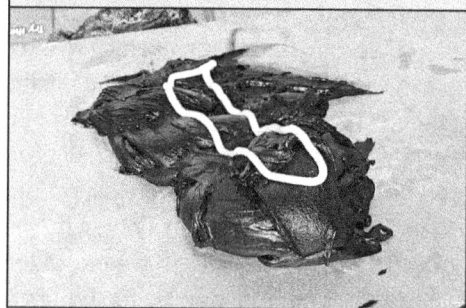

3 The bonding adhesive is ready for mixing. Be ready to quickly apply it because you have 20 minutes to spread the adhesive and have the panel or front end in place. Once the adhesive begins to set-up, you cannot get the panel to stick.

Position Fenders

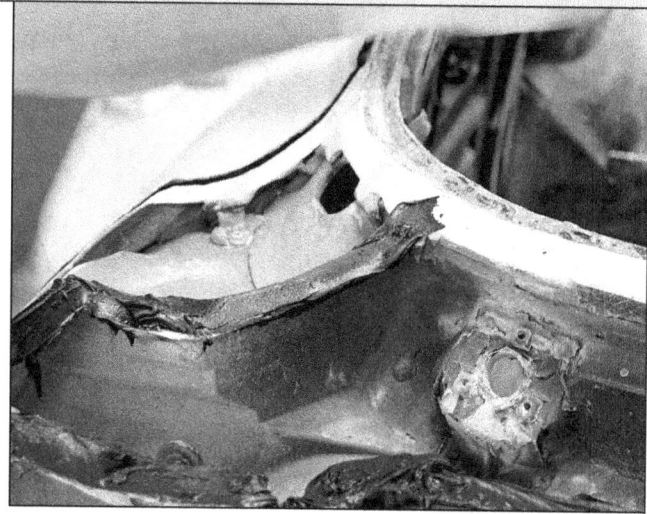

4 Apply panel adhesive to the flanges using about a 1/2-inch-thick bead, and now the process must continue. Apply adhesive to all of the upper flanges leaving the vertical portions for the next application because there is not enough time to apply adhesive to all the joints at one time. Don't try to do too much at once. Better to be safe or you may have to take the entire front end off and try again.

5 Now the front end with the inner fenders installed can be set in place. The side fenders need to be pulled outward to go around the cowl at the doors. You need to plan out the procedures before the adhesive is mixed. The front end must be placed back in the same position it was fitted in as soon as possible.

BODYWORK

Set Clamps and Tighten

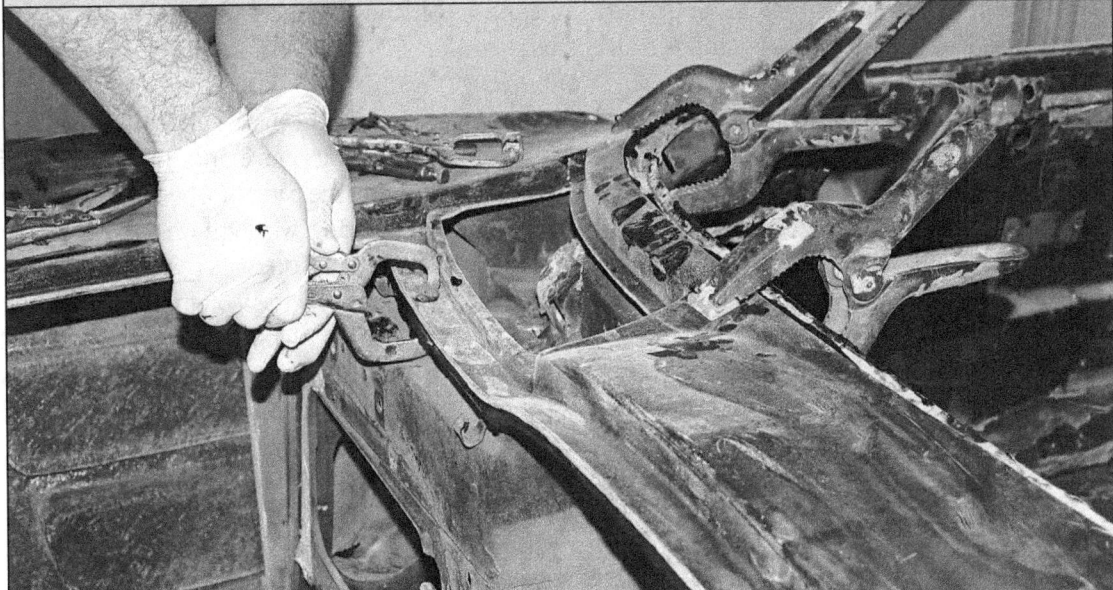

6 Place clamps every foot or so to make sure the adhesive is pushed level at all of the attachment points. Be careful with the clamps and do not apply too much pressure. It needs to firmly hold the panel in place, but you don't want to crush the panel. Therefore, do not overtighten the clamps. If you hear cracking, loosen the clamp immediately.

Set Proper Spacing Between Front End and Cowl Flange

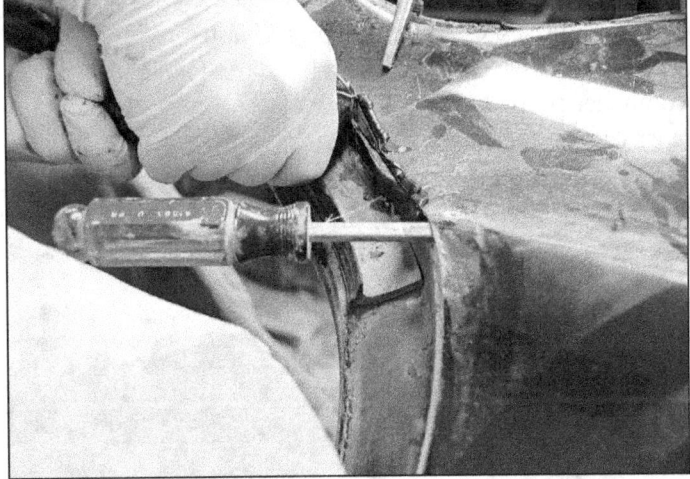

7 Force a screwdriver between the front end and the cowl flange. This allows for enough of an opening for the bonding adhesive to be squeezed in.

Install Screws in Fenders

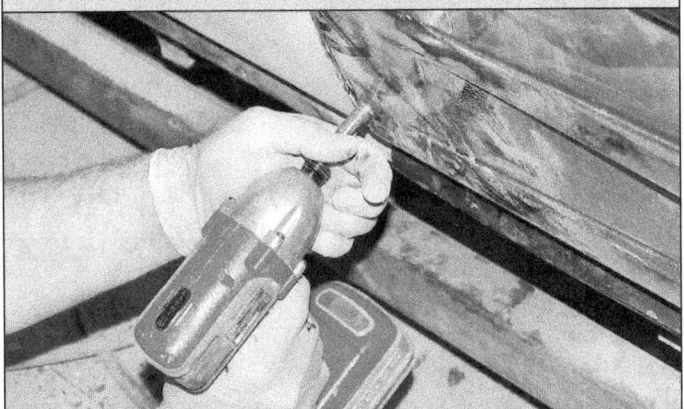

8 Now the screws used for alignment are put back into place in the side fenders until the bonding adhesive dries. Within an hour, the bonding adhesive should be cured if it was mixed correctly. If not, the panels pop off easily with a slight tug. Then you have to start back from the beginning grinding the flanges for a fresh start.

Frame Repair

I dabbled a bit in metal work on the body and more is needed. The chassis requires some work, either simple scrubbing and light sanding, or major reconstruction. My project had a junk frame, as I explained earlier. I had a couple of options: I could get a fresh frame from a known good source, or hit the swap meets. I chose a professionally-built original frame from Impact Restorations to be sure I had a solid, straight frame. The swap meet option could work, but can be risky. Since this is the foundation of the entire project, why take a chance?

Many pieces are available to repair an original frame. Replacing a frame rail at home is not for everyone. Care must be taken in aligning and making sure the frame is square. First, you need to find a perfectly level spot to repair your frame. Next, a fixture should be constructed to ensure correct installation while welding.

HOW TO RESTORE YOUR CORVETTE: 1963–1967

By then, quite a bit of money and time will have been spent with possibly questionable results. The cure for a corroded or tweaked frame is replacement or professional repairs. Let the experts take care of this very important piece of the puzzle. Once the frame's integrity is guaranteed, you can take over and do the prepping and painting.

Prepping to Paint

If your frame is indeed square, with minimal or no corrosion, or you are starting with a replacement, the next step is prepping it for paint. A thorough clean-up is in order, to avoid blowing debris from all the bodywork onto the fresh paint. Preferably, a complete wash down is the best way to eliminate the dust and dirt. Use a water-based solution from a body shop or paint supplier for the wash down.

Your paint supplier has a specific product that does the job without leaving any harmful residue.

By now, most original frames have been painted numerous times. This is actually a good thing though because bare frames corrode quickly. General Motors coated the frames with a mineral-spirits-based product that easily washed off. Engine oil, coolant, transmission fluid, and just about anything that dripped on the frame would remove the coating. This means that many frames are covered with rust if they have not been painted before. If by some chance the original factory coating is still on the chassis or the engine had massive oil leaks, rust or corrosion damage is minimal.

Before you select a method of metal preparation, you need to decide how your refinished components should look when completed. Bloomington Gold or NCRS chassis components must be carefully cleaned to avoid changing the base metals' raw surfaces. The options for removing the old dirt, paint, and corrosion are varied. Professional blasters are the easiest to use. Using a mix of professional blasting with manual removal of the crusty covering on the parts may save a few dollars.

Grease and Oil Removal

The first step is chemically stripping off the years of grease and oil. The grease you find under any car is a mixture of dirt and oil, and therefore sandblasting the oily grease away does not work. Grease contaminates the blast media making a mess of the equipment and media.

Forcing the grease into the metal with the blaster is not a good thing either. A thorough washing with an aqueous degreaser is best. Mineral spirits works well, but must be disposed of properly.

Make sure you consider where you can dispose of any hazardous waste before you generate it. Gasoline should never be used for cleaning any component or part. One spark from a scraper or wire brush can ignite and possibly destroy your project and you along with it.

Sandblasting

Once the pieces are degreased and dry, you can move onto the next step of restoring the part's finish. If you decide on sandblasting, what grit works best? Professional sandblasters are typically in a hurry to finish, so they often use aggressive, large grit in high-powered blasting equipment. The large sandblasting grit leaves pits and removes subtle machining marks.

If you decide to go the pro blaster route, make sure they understand what you expect. Ask them to use lower air pressure and finer sandblasting grit. If the blaster agrees to customize his work, be prepared to pay extra labor costs. Sandblasting is tough, hot, sweaty work, especially on a summer day. It cost me $650 the last time I had a chassis and all the attaching pieces blasted. While this may seem like a lot to pay for cleaning pieces, I would have spent 40 to 50 hours or more cleaning, so it was definitely worth

This is the correct way to check the frame using a tape measure. If the measurements are equal, you have a square frame. What you cannot check for is a raised rail or slightly bowed rail. Chances are that a square frame is safe to use.

BODYWORK

it. Also keep in mind that the cost of wire brushes, sandpaper, and blasting grit can be expensive.

Bead Blasting

Using a bead blast cabinet is an alternative pressurized cleaning method. Bead blasting grit is much finer and prevents surface damage, but it does take longer. Of course, a number of pieces don't fit in the standard bead blast cabinet.

Large, efficient bead blast cabinets save plenty of time, but are expensive. Plus, large cabinets take up a lot of valuable shop space. Smaller, less expensive bead blast cabinets are typically suction-fed blasters, which are not very efficient. The suction fed blasters can be painfully slow as they remove grime and corrosion. Small chassis pieces are more realistically blasted in small hobby-type bead blast cabinets.

Wire Brushing

Motorized wire brushing is an alternative that works fairly well. Wire brushes on bench grinders can remove years of crud quickly and easily. Bench grinder wire brushing does have drawbacks though, as it's often difficult to get into tight cracks and crevices.

Wire cup brushes spun in an electric drill are more versatile, making it easier to clean in tight spots. But these require care when operating because you can get hurt. Spinning brushes lose their metal bristles at high speed and they are flung at you. Slipping while using any high-speed tool can take off a large patch of flesh immediately.

Another serious concern is losing an object in the wire brush. The object could be thrown back at you, causing bodily harm. Be sure to wear eye protection and leather gloves when using any high-speed cleaning equipment.

A mix of wire brushing and bead blasting can save you time and quite a bit of money. Use the wire brush cleaning process as much as possible before blasting. Once you have the majority of the build-up removed with the wire brushing, blasting gets into the tight spots.

Avoiding Corrosion

After the raw oil-free pieces are finished with the cleaning process, a time sensitive situation begins. Washing the pieces with soapy water is required to flush out the loose particles and blasting media. Blow drying the pieces with dry, oil-free compressed air as soon as possible after washing limits inevitable corrosion. Touching the pieces with sweaty hands also starts the corrosion process. It is important to keep oily, sweaty hands and arms off the clean pieces. The use of nitrile or latex gloves while handling the pieces is recommended. The reason for all the cleaning and preparation is to promote good paint adhesion. The labor-intensive preparation process is necessary to ensure long paint life. Before primer is applied, I go one step further and apply a preparation solution to the raw iron metal surfaces.

Ospho metal conditioner is a rust-inhibiting coating that preps the raw metal for painting and can take a few hours to dry completely on hot, dry days, or 24 hours on cool, humid days. Light applications work best to avoid rough spots where the inhibitor has pooled.

New metal or raw blasted metal turns gray as the Ospho transforms the metal surface. If you prefer to skip the complete removal of the rust, Ospho treats the

What do you do with this frame? Unfortunately, a quick coat of cheap black paint was applied over rust years ago. Many hours of hands-on mechanical paint and rust removal was involved. The tough part is removing the paint, rust, and junk from all the tight spots. Media blasting makes the most sense fiscally and physically.

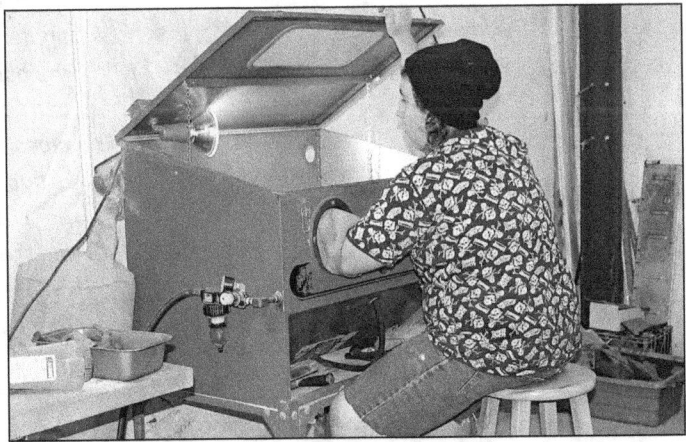

Bead blasting is a great fall or spring job. My grandson Phillip comes in after school to bead blast all of the small pieces. Have a seat and be patient because the process can take a while. For more efficient blasting, use an air-pressure regulator to drop air pressure to 90 psi. A floodlight bulb works much better than an incandescent.

pieces for primer. The scaly rust particles become black as the treatment turns them into iron oxide. Do not use this product on any aluminum or pot-metal pieces.

Dent Removal

By now, you may be wondering if all of the cleaning will ever end. Typically, the chassis requires the most labor and time to clean because it is assaulted not only by engine oils, transmission fluid, and differential grease, but also by whatever the road throws at it, whether it is water, salt, or cavernous potholes. Don't forget the time that it spent on automotive repair lifts or worse yet: floor jacks.

Many, if not all, the frames under Midyears have caved-in front crossmembers. A repair tool is available if the crossmember is not too banged up. The tool fits inside the crossmember and a fixture is placed on the outside to pull the dents out. One front spring must be removed to insert the tool inside the frame. The best time to repair the crossmember is while the frame is in pieces.

The 1963 project walk-through should put the bodywork and chassis prep requirements into perspective. This is not the worst-case body reconstruction. Many times windshield frames are severely rotted and require major panel removal to make repairs. I have even seen windshield and door pillar rot that required complete front-end removal. In some cases, the roof fiberglass required removal to access the bad pieces. The better the body is, the less you need to know about structure or worry about completely rebuilding your Corvette's body.

Apply Metal Surface Prep

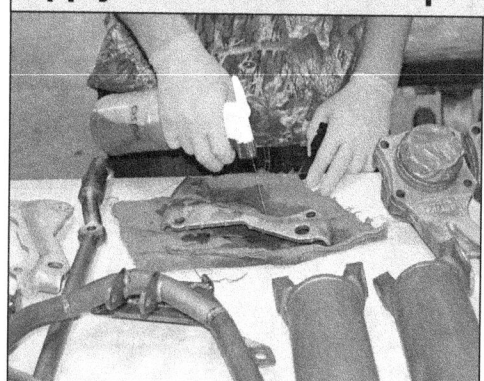

1 Apply Ospho metal surface prep with a sprayer then wipe it off. Try to avoid pooling of the material because it causes crusty formations on the pieces. Unfortunately, leaving the crusty particles makes them very noticeable after painting. Ospho contains phosphoric acid so make sure you use gloves and eye protection and avoid getting it on your body or clothes.

Remove Dents

2 This nifty tool kit from Corvette Central straightens the front crossmember. The upper fixture tightens down to push out the bumps and waves. Heat can be applied to the crossmember as the fixture is tightened. The crossmember should be cleaned internally of any grease or oil before applying heat. For the most part the front crossmember dent removal tool worked well. I applied a skim coat of all-metal body filler to slick it out completely. This is the perfect use for the extra tough all-metal filler. I used all-metal filler in a number of places on the chassis to smooth it before priming.

Clean Up Frame

3 One of my pet peeves is all the slag and debris left behind from the factory welding process. I use a cold chisel to knock off the welding beads on the entire frame. No, it is not NCRS correct, but it sure looks better. Another plus is less of a chance for bodily harm if your hands accidently brush against the frame while working on or near it.

CHAPTER 5

PAINT

The transformation is about to begin. All of your days spent repairing fiberglass and smoothing are over. The final paint prep work starts now, in anticipation of the overall paint application.

Paint materials are of considerable importance. Midyear owners and restorers expect a certain level of paint quality, which can only be achieved with base/clear coat paint systems. Single-stage acrylic enamel paint has been used in the past as an alternative, and when properly applied, holds up well, but the difference can be seen. Base/clear coat paint systems have it all: great looks and excellent UV protection.

Small exterior pieces are hung in preparation for the final overall paint using the same materials as the bodies exterior will receive. As tempting as it is to apply the top coat as soon as possible, look over the entire body one more time. Better yet, have a friend take a look; sometimes another set of eyes will see things that may have been missed. Every minor imperfection will be sure to show up when the shiny paint is on.

Safety Concerns

Automotive paint and painting procedures have evolved considerably over the many years since GM's use of acrylic lacquer on the Midyear Corvette. With some early Corvettes still sporting the factory paint, the durable acrylic coating speaks for itself. Of course, examples like this are rare and require that the car spend many days protected from UV ray exposure. Today, paint products are highly durable and as environmentally safe as possible.

Many governmental agencies regulate paint products because the proper use and handling of paint are critical to protecting public health and the environment. As a result of these regulations and protections, it's difficult for the do-it-yourselfer to purchase these products.

Regulations are one issue; another is the skyrocketing cost of paint, due to governmental regulations. For example, as of January 1, 2011, anyone purchasing paint products from an automotive paint supplier must provide personal information, unless he or she has a commercial business license to perform paint work. The law also states that an individual is limited to purchasing enough supplies to paint two vehicles annually. This is an effort to limit paint and solvent emissions and keep unlicensed shops from operating.

Because paint costs have increased dramatically, you need to know the correct paint mix ratios to prevent paint loss. Many professional paint suppliers keep the mix ratios privy to wholesale buyers. Altering the mix ratios or specific mix directions can result in adhesion problems. Ask your supplier for all the pertinent information to properly mix and handle the paints; in particular, ask for the Material Safety Data Sheets (MSDS). Many major paint suppliers post the paint mix ratios and MSDS sheets on their websites. Some paints, especially primers, have "cook times," or in other words, the paint manufacturer specifies certain ingredients to stand for a prescribed number of minutes before application. Make sure you adhere to the paint manufacturer's recommendations here, as well.

Waste paint is another issue you must deal with. Many local municipalities accept minimal amounts of waste paint without any associated fees. If in doubt, ask your paint supplier to recommend an organization for safe disposal of the waste materials. Water quality and safety is up to us to protect, so please dispose of any paint materials properly.

Paint safety was not a major concern for many early painters. Early photos show painters in enclosed areas full of vapors, breathing in either lacquer or enamel mist. Urethane paints are deadly, and you should never paint in a confined area without a respirator. A paint suit with positive air pressure is preferred to keep these deadly chemicals from finding their way onto your skin. Wearing gloves to prevent solvents and chemicals from leaching into your skin is equally important. Long-term exposure to synthetic paint and solvents can be deadly.

Choose a Shop

There are several levels of paint application. No matter how much money you have to spend on paint, it is hard to justify spending a lot on exterior bodywork and paint because eventually it gets damaged. Even works of art that live primarily in a garage get scratched, no matter how careful you are.

If you plan on hitting the car show circuit, paint damage will undoubtedly occur unless you plan on the added expense of an enclosed car trailer. If your idea is to have fun and enjoy your Midyear, keep in mind that things do happen. Why not hit some local car shows, so you can enjoy all the hard work? Once that first scratch occurs, others are a little less painful and then you learn the touch-up tricks. Not to make light of it, but you can call the road rash "badges of honor" from your road trips.

The best policy is to get at least three estimates, even if you plan on doing the work for yourself. You will then have a baseline against which to compare your options. Ask for written estimates outlining the complete procedure from start to finish. Explain to the shop doing the estimate how you intend to use your Midyear.

Your choice of paint shops can run a broad spectrum. Taking the time to have three estimates gives you a good idea of how each shop handles the required paint work. Look around each shop noting how they handle the vehicle and its components during the process. This should be an eye opener and give you a taste for what is to come, whether you tackle the job or farm it out.

Production Shops

Let's start with production paint and body shops (production being the key word). They typically do not like paint restoration projects because they want projects to come and go quickly without any delays. The theory is to limit the number of pieces they have to remove to save time. Minimal paint prep work is done in an effort to speed up the process.

Finding a production shop that paints any restoration project is unlikely because a restoration paint job goes far beyond a typical production-type paint job. And that's okay because it's probably in the best interest of both parties.

Independent Shops

Independent paint shops can surprise even the most particular customer with very nice paint work at a reasonable price. They usually have a broad area of work to cover, from crashes to overall paint jobs. These shops also prefer that customer cars get painted and leave in a timely manner.

I personally have had very good luck with independent paint shops, after carefully looking over their operations. Removing all the possible pieces from the body is one thing that I have found to help the bottom line and the finished product. The more parts that are removed from the body, means there is less masking of parts on the car. Less masking means less cost to the shop, and sometimes a better attitude toward a major project.

Removing and installing pieces takes time, and you can accomplish this if you are familiar with the vehicle in question. Unfamiliarity can be costly for the owner and the paint shop, such as when pieces are damaged during removal. Doing a lot of preparation on your own, can save you quite a bit of money if a deal can be struck with the shop.

Restoration Shops

Restoration shops are on the opposite end of the spectrum of the other choices, providing meticulous attention to detail on each step of the prep and painting process to produce show-quality paint work. Their word-of-mouth reputation typically keeps them very concerned about the finished product. A restoration shop is prepared to remove all the body's attaching pieces to allow for the ultimate paint job. They usually have shelves, dollies, and fixtures to properly store parts, while the painting process is underway. Knowing what it takes to prep raw surfaces for show quality paint is daily routine for them.

Typically, you're not going to be successful negotiating a lower price or striking a bargain deal on a paint job from a restoration shop. The shop has certain procedures that they follow every time, and cutting corners is not something they like to do or are willing to do to cut costs. Where do you or they draw the line and say "that is good enough?" That has been the age-old question for any show-quality paint work.

Make sure you and the shop owner understand what is expected before any work begins. Usually your project is a long-term job for most restoration shops. Periodic payments are expected, as each phase is completed.

What to Look For

When searching for a qualified paint shop, there are several aspects to consider. Look around the shop; if there is trash and debris everywhere, this is potential trouble because high-quality paint work is produced in a clean environment. If the shop is dirty, it's more difficult to produce a clean job. In addition, lost and damaged parts can be expected when things are strewn about.

Find out where they store parts that have been removed during the process. Ask to look at the paint booth. It should be clean and feature good lighting. Definitely inquire about what paint products they use. If you haven't heard of a particular paint manufacturer before, do some research on them.

It's difficult to collect on warranty claims from a paint manufacturer, because poor preparation is the most common culprit of paint problems. To prove the manufacturer's paint was defective is very difficult, and the manufacturers obviously know that. Ask what the shop's warranty is because they are ultimately responsible.

Remember, estimates for daily-driver paint jobs versus ultimate show car work are quite different. Time is money, and show-quality works takes more time. You may find that it makes more sense to have a professional paint shop paint your car. Or it might inspire you to work extra hard when doing the work for yourself.

Should You Do It Yourself?

Painting is an art and an acquired skill. A Midyear Corvette may not be the best candidate for your first paint job because these cars are quite valuable, and a professional, mistake-free paint job is difficult to achieve. Some of us have trouble painting with the best equipment, while others can produce really nice paintwork working in a breezy barn. The key ingredient to a show-quality paint job is patience and methodical planning.

Contamination Factors

Dirt, water, oil, and grease are the enemies that you must contend with. Paint contamination from improper handling and cleaning produces poor results. Contamination comes into play whether you are painting in your home garage or in a high-dollar paint booth. The worst possible scenario is contamination under your primer coating, such as when the first coat of primer or gel coat is applied to bare fiberglass. As each coat is applied, the contamination is being buried deeper and deeper until it pops up one day. Eventually, small bumps appear like heat rash on the top surface of the paint, and this means contamination has disturbed the paint's bond.

Contamination can occur many different ways. It may have been as simple as a mist of oily water in the air landing on the sanded surfaces. For example, contamination could have occurred from working near the mechanical side of the project. This illustrates just how sensitive the painting process is, and a simple oversight or mistake can have tragic consequences for a paint job. Unfortunately, contamination is all around you. Always be aware of it, and clean any suspect surface immediately.

Remember that your air lines themselves may be contributing to the problem. Water, debris, or compressor lubricating oil may reside in your compressed airlines. No matter how careful you are, water does end up in the piping system. I always use a water trap and filter for any painting project, even if it is an obscure part that may not be seen. Wiping down the surfaces immediately before painting with wax-and-grease remover is critical to prevent contamination.

Other contamination situations can occur. For example, imagine that you and your buddies are working around the car

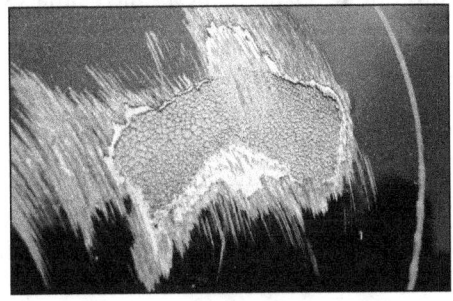

I found this crazed, light green acrylic lacquer paint under a very large paint bubble. It is hard to know for sure what attacked the underlying top coat. In some areas the reaction was not so severe and the paint held. This is why stripping is recommended on all early Corvettes. Why chance this happening?

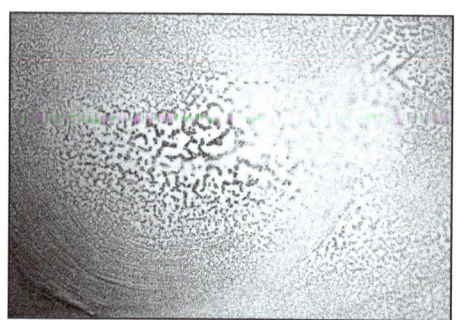

This is worst case with so many fisheyes they blend into one another. Silicone, oils or grease create this phenomena even incompatible paint materials can cause the problem. The best policy is to use wax and grease remover before applying any coating sometimes wiping off the surface with paint reducers will have the same paint adhesion problem. The paint is not sticking to the surfaces and the paint surrounds the contamination, worst part is no matter how many times you apply the coating it will not fill in the spots.

This air dryer is the key to an excellent finish. Anytime you spray off a piece during the bodywork or painting phase, use the line with the dryer. Drain the dryer frequently and definitely before spraying any top coats. Most good-quality driers have sight glasses to inform you of the desiccant's condition. Change the desiccant when recommended.

when someone accidentally spills something on the primer. If you don't deal with the spill immediately, it can have serious ramifications for your paint job. If it is anything other than a wax-and-grease remover, it should be removed immediately.

Another no-no would be wiping a drop of sweat from the primed surfaces with your hand. The touch of your hand and the subsequent introduction of skin oils can cause you to have to repaint an area. This is why I harp on the use of a water trap with filtered air for the paint spray gun air source and the blow gun. Using an unfiltered air supply to blow off a panel following body work can also get you into trouble. Remember to make a habit of wiping the panel or areas to be sprayed with a wax-and-grease remover, using clean cloths.

Sourcing Paint

A good place to research paint is on the Web, and you will find all kinds of deals on paint. You will see unbelievably-low to astronomically-high prices. Low-budget paint is most often from a no-name or obscure supplier, and these paints often require more paint, which negates any savings.

The additional paint material requirements may be obvious because the mixed volume is less. Or the coverage could be poor and require more paint. Then you could have to wait for the next batch of paint to arrive. The situation becomes far worse if you require more paint after the last coat has dried: then, you need enough paint to completely spray the entire body again. This alone probably makes a local paint supplier look like the better place to purchase materials.

Searching the Web can also give you an idea of pricing, even if you decide to buy at your local paint supplier.

Visit your local paint supplier to talk about your project, and let them know that you are planning a major restoration project, from top to bottom. They may help you on the cost, if you use them as your primary supplier for all the required materials. Exterior paint thinners, hardeners, and primers might be used on the other components that are going to be painted. Planning ahead can save you a significant amount of money, if crossover products can be safely used.

Wherever you buy, get what you need with a little surplus. There is no need to stockpile materials except with the exterior finish coat. I usually like to keep a quart of exterior color and a pint of chassis color on hand.

Paint Types

Enamels, acrylic enamels, acrylic lacquers, urethanes, and base coat/clear coat are the types of paints that you typically hear about. The factory applied acrylic lacquer on all Midyears. As with any exterior coating, there are short- and long-lifespan automotive paints. Cheap automotive paint doesn't last long. For the most part, the prep work is the same, no matter what paint you choose.

Trying to save money on the primer and top coat is not a wise move because you end up squandering your investment. Within a few years, you're left with poor appearing paint and may have to do it all over again to reach professional standards.

Enamels continue to be an economical top coat, and have a reasonable life. Keeping an enamel paint job looking good over the long term can be difficult, though. UV rays deteriorate the enamel and draw out the solvents, which oxidizes the paint surface. Enamel paint colors your polishing cloth as it is ever so slightly removed during the polishing process.

Synthetic or alkyd enamels are available, but should be avoided because they can be removed with solvents, even after curing. The slow dry time makes it very difficult to use without a heated paint booth. Weekend painters are hard pressed to keep dirt and debris from sticking on the surfaces before it dries. Poor coverage is another concern.

Acrylic enamels are much more durable than synthetic enamels. Dry times are shorter and finishes are much more resilient to solvents. Coverage is good, making this a viable, affordable choice for chassis and component painting. Durability can be enhanced with a clear coat to help ward off UV rays.

Water-based acrylic urethane enamels are found on the majority of today's vehicles. Activators are added to start the drying process. This base coat has a clear coat applied to provide the ultimate protection from UV rays and chemical attacks. This system is very toxic during the application and drying stages, so you must follow all the safety precautions when applying water-based acrylic urethane enamel paint or your life may be put in jeopardy.

Polyurethane was the first base/clear coat paint system. This highly durable paint requires a hardener and catalyst to begin the drying process. Most auto manufacturers used this in the early 1980s, and it's widely used in the aftermarket auto paint industry today because of its depth and color availability.

Corvette guys spot the low-luster finish of an enamel paint job immediately. Your Midyear project should have acrylic enamel with hardener and clear applied, as the median paint choice. Polyurethane-based coat/clear coat is preferred for long paint life with minimal upkeep. There are some downsides to everything, paint included.

Single-stage acrylic enamel paints (without clear) are easier to repair than polyurethane-based base coat/clear coat paints. After acrylic enamel paint damage is repaired, it can be blended in with a buffer.

When polyurethane base coat/clear coat requires spot paint work, the base paint material is applied to the spot and then clear has to be applied to the entire panel. Although the coats can be blended, they produce mixed results, and the base/clear repaired blend area is always noticeable.

The goal is to extend the blend area beyond the damaged area. When you look at the repaired area, chances are you do not see the blend line. If you look beyond the repaired area you do. This is why most base/clear repairs involve an entire panel, to avoid the blend line.

You may be wondering why I omitted an explanation of acrylic lacquer paint in the previous paragraphs. Today, lacquer is all but phased out because of environmental regulations. It can be purchased, but very few painters spray it, though. Painters prefer the ease of painting polyurethanes and acrylic enamels over the labor-intensive acrylic lacquer.

Lacquer is easy to work with considering its almost immediate dry time, which keeps airborne contaminants from sticking. With lacquer, you keep adding coats until the correct depth is achieved and then wet-sand to smooth it. After hours of buffing, you then have a lacquer paint job that is deep and shiny. Lacquer is always drying and shrinking. The shrinkage draws the paint into any imperfection it finds, and wet-sanding is necessary to make it look good again. Its durability is better than synthetic enamel, although UV rays affect either finish.

NCRS or Bloomington Gold Paint Refinishing

As stated earlier, General Motors applied acrylic lacquer on all the 1963–1967 Corvettes. Originally, NCRS wanted to see acrylic lacquer on any restored Midyear, and officials would subtly ask if the paint was other than acrylic lacquer. Today, they look for what appears to be "factory-applied material."

For example, NCRS judges look for tell-tale signs of orange peel in certain areas. The orange peel occurred in these areas because the factory painters were avoiding paint run or sag. To replicate a factory-type paint job, the painter has to have the right mind-set and leave the orange peel areas alone when wet sanding and buffing to achieve the correct look. Show-quality paint finishes are typically much better than what the factory turned out.

Bloomington Gold does not care what you paint your car with, but it wants a judged Corvette to appear the same as it left the St. Louis Corvette assembly plant. Provided there are no apparent differences in texture, gloss shade, or coating thickness, you are okay. A paint job that appears as though it were factory applied is given full credit, regardless of what brand or type of paint was applied. Detectable abnormalities and/or variations are penalized even if the original acrylic lacquer is used.

If your car is headed to Bloomington Gold or NCRS, you need to research this carefully before starting your paint job.

Practice Applying Paint

If you are painting exterior body surfaces, paint the suspension and frame-attaching pieces first, so you familiarize yourself with the spray gun operation and how to get good paint coverage in tight areas. It's not a big deal if you apply too much paint on a suspension part and get a run. You can wipe it down and start over again. If you quickly remove flawed paint, wait at least 15 minutes before repainting it. A quick wipe with solvent usually results in major fisheye formations. For the best results, wipe it down again with a wax-and-grease remover.

In my shop, I use spray guns to apply paint to all components that are to be painted. All chassis components have been cleaned and metal prepped.

Painting prep begins by applying wax-and-grease remover to a polyester cloth, then wiping down each piece while wearing gloves. Cotton rags are not recommended because they leave lint behind. I also apply wax-and-grease remover wet so that it evaporates off the pieces. If you have doubts about any oil or grease that has been left behind, soak the piece again with the wax-and-grease remover. Keep your bare hands off the pieces; they need to be painted as soon as possible.

I apply etch primer on raw pieces to improve adhesion. Etch primer is similar to a spray adhesive and enhances the bond between metal surfaces and subsequent coats of primer. Etch primer is a must for aluminum and pot-metal pieces. Primer does not stick to aluminum and pot-metal pieces unless a suitable etch primer is used. After the Ospho application, I apply etch primer to all pieces. Etch-primed pieces can be top coated without further priming if they don't require any further surface prep. Pitted or weathered pieces need sanding or minor filling before a coat of urethane primer is applied. Pieces that require major smoothing receive a light coating of all-metal filler, to fill in deep imperfections.

Once the etch primer or urethane primer has dried, the top coat is applied. Read the product application guidelines carefully. Many primers have a time period that allows the application of the top coat without sanding. If primed pieces sit for a long period, tedious sanding is required to promote the best top coat adhesion.

From start to finish, this process can take up to two days of non-stop work. It takes time to apply paint to each piece without missing some of the many obscure areas. Drying time depends on the paint chosen: Enamels can take 12 to 24 hours to dry, while urethanes can be dry to the touch in 4 to 5 hours. Urethane paints with hardeners can be dry to the touch within an hour on hot days. It is better to hang the pieces until they are completely dry.

Once you have 100 or so small pieces and the frame painting figured out, the body paint is a cinch. Even coverage is the key, following the paint manufacturer's recommended build-up of paint film. The final "wet coat" is the tough one to accomplish; the idea is to have that shiny, wet look without sags or runs in the paint. Applying too much clear coat is a bad thing because yellowing and cracking can occur. Make sure you understand how many coats of the products should be applied per the manufacturer's recommendation.

You need to put the final wet sanding into the clear coat equation. Most painters apply three coats of clear to have some to work with during the wet-sand and buff process.

Paint Facilities

Unless you use a climate-controlled paint booth, weather is a major factor in how well the paint sprays. Sunny and low humidity is best. With cloudy humid days, it could take months to finish the paint work. If you spray your car in your garage, you will find paint all over. I do not recommend nor advocate painting in a homeowner's garage, but the reality is that many people do. Your garage has many sources of combustion, whether from gas dryers or water heaters. Plus, chances are paint will end up in the house. Paint fumes will certainly end up in the house.

A temporary paint booth can be improvised utilizing a 10x20 tent. The enclosure is excellent for component painting, and in a pinch, the exterior could be painted inside the tent. These enclosures are inexpensive and can be used for storage when not used as a paint room.

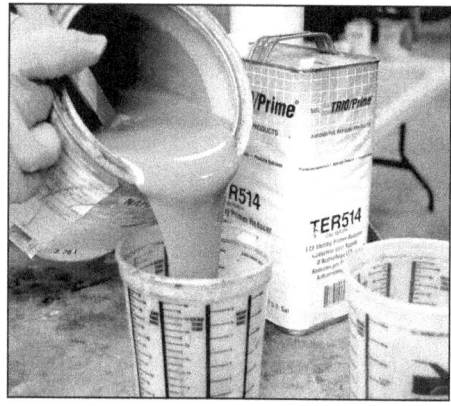

This syrupy etch coat being poured into a mixing cup reminds me of liquid adhesive. The tenacious liquid bonds well to all raw metal surfaces, especially aluminum and pot metals making it mandatory to aid good adhesion.

This enclosure works well for painting small pieces. When the sun is out, the light-colored material helps keep the pieces visible. Painting the intricate angles and blind holes makes this a great precursor to overall body painting. Note the paint mist in the air. That's why I'm wearing the respirator, glasses, hat, and gloves.

PAINT

The beauty of a tent is that the sun really heats the contents, providing an alternative to a factory-baked finish. The downside is that the enclosure may heat up the contents too well, meaning that you had better have your paint work done before 11:00 a.m. or be prepared to wait until the next day. Painting an exterior takes 3 to 4 hours for a professional. If everything goes well, be ready to start as soon as the sun is up.

Body Prep

Now that the body is roughed in, meticulous work begins to ensure that all the minor imperfections are worked out. As I have mentioned before, patience is the most important tool in the tool box now; take your time now or you could be disappointed with the results for years to come.

Gel-Coat or Urethane Primer

At this point, the body should be smooth enough for a coat of gel-coat or urethane primer. These seal the fiberglass and prevent loose fiberglass strands from showing up later. Urethane primer is much easier to spray than the thick gel-coat. General Motors did not use gel-coat and it is not mandatory for a good quality paint job. The general consensus is mixed on the importance of using the urethane or gel-coat.

Using gel-coat does add a thick coating that fills voids better than urethane primer. Gel-coat is harder to sand and smooth. Gel-coating is also best done on cool days or it dries before it lays on the fiberglass. You either have to borrow or buy a dedicated gel-coat spray gun.

For the first-time painter, the urethane primer makes the most sense for many reasons: Urethane is easier to prep, spray, and clean up. Using the urethane primer does not compromise the body work, if it has been done properly.

High-Build Primer

The next step is to spray high-build K2 primer-filler onto the previously-primed surface, to fill minor imperfections. Urethane primer is thick. K2 has even higher viscosity, so the spray gun needs a high-flow nozzle. For this reason, all painters have dedicated finish and primer paint guns.

In essence, the high-build primer is a coat of liquid body filler. The easy-to-sand K2 primer fills minor imperfections, for slick, blemish-free panels, and it's sanded off with 320-grit wet/dry sandpaper on a long block to start straightening the panels.

Follow the longest portion of the panel with the sanding block, using minimal pressure. Be extra careful on ridges, edges, and any body line, to avoid misshaped panels. Corners and edges can be quickly altered during the sanding process, and it takes a lot of work to correct them once they have been damaged. This time-consuming work requires plenty of patience to ensure good results.

A guide coat of high-build primer may be required to find low spots. A guide coat is a mist of dark primer that can be easily sanded to reveal any low spots. Next, you should sand the panel with 400-grit wet/dry sandpaper until the guide coat is removed without going into the urethane primer, gel-coat, or raw fiberglass.

Body filler should be applied if you find depressions more than an 1/8-inch deep during the blocking process. Spot putty is available for tiny imperfections, but do not use it for deep pin holes or gouges. Spot putty shrinks quite a bit, so applying large amounts usually causes it to crack as it dries. I avoid using spot putty because of its potential to shrink.

Block Sanding

Use a block (not your fingers) to sand large areas because they put ripples in the panel. In certain cases, a block is not used

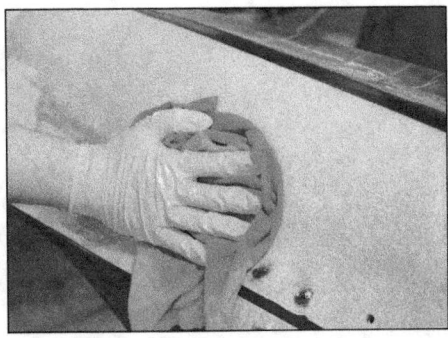

One final wipe down with wax-and-grease remover using a polyester rayon cloth. Cotton cloths leave lint behind and minute particles under the primer. The cloth is soaked so that the surface is flooded with the remover to flush out any contaminants.

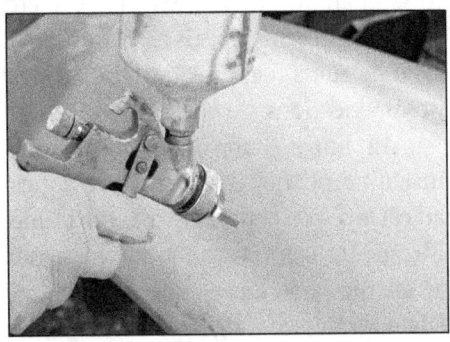

The body panels should have 2K urethane primer applied as soon as possible. Priming the area that was just sanded is the best way to end your restoration day. Apply one light coat, wait 5 to 10 minutes, then apply at least two or three good wet coats. You should dedicate an old spray gun just for the primer and make sure you clean it as soon as you finish.

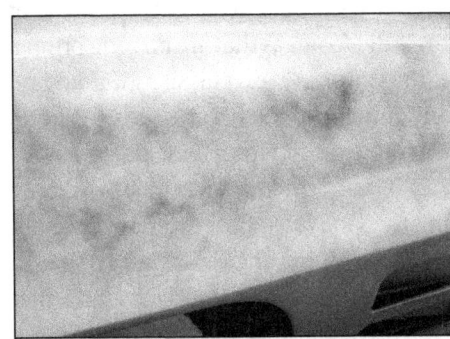

Spray a mist coat over the 2K primer to apply a guide coat. This should be done on each panel. As you block sand the panels, the low spots are revealed.

When sanding inside curves, I like to use this tube insulation as back-up for 400-grit wet/dry sandpaper. Various diameter tube insulators are available for about any inside curve you can imagine. When sanding large panels, follow the longest portion of the panel from front to back.

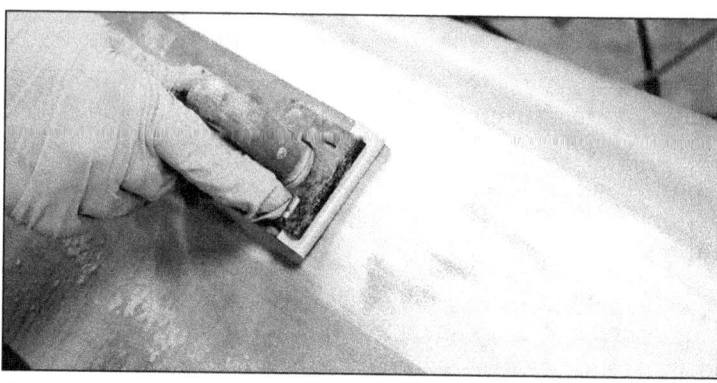

A block sander removes the guide coat and some of the 2K primer-filler. The dark areas in front of the sander are low spots that require more primer in order to smooth the panel properly. The idea here is for all of the guide coat to be gone with no tiny imperfections visible.

to sand around tight areas, crevices, etc. The 600-grit sandpaper is used as the final sanding guide coat pass until the smallest of imperfections are filled.

All imperfections, no matter how insignificant they may seem, are noticeable. Once you determine that the primer is ready for paint, take another hard look at all the large areas, especially around edges for missed rough spots.

Painting Procedure

If you paint the exterior yourself, careful preparation is very important after block sanding has been completed. Daytime is the best time to paint. Prep the body during the afternoon or night before, and then begin painting early in the morning. Immediately before painting, take the time to look the body over carefully for areas that are missing primer. If in doubt, reassess the situation and fix any imperfections because this separates a good paint job from a mediocre one.

If you rented a spray booth, changing the scheduled time often incurs additional costs, but this is the last chance to make corrections before you apply that expensive paint. It may cost more in the long run to stop and repair a suspect area, but it shows later.

Professional painters have a procedure that they go through to produce the same results each time: When the body or complete car is rolled into the booth, a metal chain is placed over the axle or body cart to prevent static electricity and the attraction of contaminants.

Next, the entire body is wiped down with wax-and-grease remover one more time. Seth, at Lucky's Customs, goes one step further by applying Lizard Skin to the inner areas that are not going to receive the body color. Seth explains that this seals all the inner panels and traps any possible dust and debris from blowing out onto the paint. Finally, a tack cloth is used to wipe down the entire body. Tack cloths are used to remove any lint, dust, remaining debris, or small pieces of trash. Many painters wet the paint booth's floor to keep from kicking up dust.

Outside contaminants are also considered, so you should avoid painting when grinding or sanding is being done nearby. Many painters go as far as avoiding painting when Diesel trucks are running nearby because the soot affects paint adhesion. Paint booths use filters to prevent contaminated air from entering, but opening the door can get you into trouble.

A dedicated area is needed for mixing paint. You fill your spray gun a few times during the process, so timing is essential. Have all the mixing supplies handy. Strainers, sticks, and cloths for clean-up and all of your paint supplies should be in one area.

Wear a respirator and gloves while handling any paint products. During the final paint application, timing is crucial to avoid dry spots. This is why it is imperative you have all your supplies ready to go. Place a fire extinguisher nearby just in case, too.

Please use the required safety equipment; it can save your life. Now, you are ready to apply the top coats.

Painting is an art; how much paint and when to apply it are the keys. For single-stage acrylic coatings, a tack coat is applied to obscure areas, such as tight spots around fender openings, to ensure that they are covered well. The paint can easily run, as two different depths are being sprayed.

Spray guns have adjustable spray patterns, from pinpoint round to fan. Using the pinpoint in tight areas works best for the tack coat. The spray gun pattern can be directed more carefully to prevent paint runs. The bottom of the doors, fenders, and body panels are often forgotten during the painting process. It's a good idea to apply a tack coat to these areas first. Once the tack coat is complete, a thorough overall wet coat is next.

Check your paint manufacturer's recommendations for between-coat times.

Begin Painting

Degrease Engine Compartment

1 Prepping the engine compartment can be time consuming. If rattle-can paint has been used for years of touch up, this semi-flat black paint usually adorns the entire compartment area. Oil and dirt is trapped between the multiple coatings and creates paint adhesion issues. Wash down the firewall and inner fenders a couple of times with degreaser before attempting to remove the paint; this prevents sandpaper clogging. Additionally, you won't be pushing the grease and oil into the raw fiberglass as it becomes exposed. Remove all the paint possibe using thinner and then sand. Another wipe down is necessary with wax and grease remover before any primer is applied.

Paint Engine Compartment

2 The painter used a single-stage acrylic enamel exterior car color to paint the engine compartment. The paint was applied before the exterior paint to ease the masking chores. If you scratch the engine compartment or inner fenders you can easily touch up the single-stage paint. You may have noticed that this photo was taken after the exterior was painted.

Apply Base Coat

3 The painter applied the silver base coat starting at the roof, and it has a typical dull finish. The doors and hood were painted separately to ensure complete coverage. Applying a good coat of paint to the edges of the doors and hood is difficult when they are still on the car. Take a few moments to spray the material on a piece of scrap material to adjust the material flow.

Apply Coat at Edges

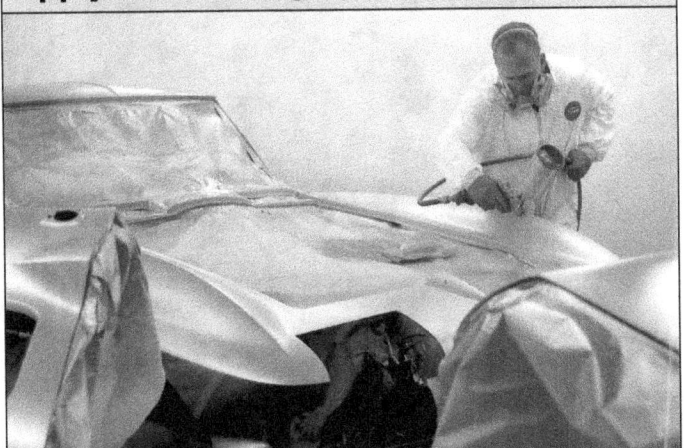

4 Applying an even coat at corners and edges is very critical. The spray gun can be adjusted to limit material flow and fan pattern to avoid puddles of base coat. Pay careful attention at enclosed areas because the paint sprays back at you. Usually the spray-back also ends up with sags.

Paint All Areas

5 Low points are often missed or just barely coated. Extra attention needs to be paid during the base and clear coat application. Note that the windshield and engine compartment are masked even though the body is bare. This is an effort to keep overspray off areas that may be painted later. No one wants to do extra sanding to blend the overspray into the original paint.

Fix Flaws

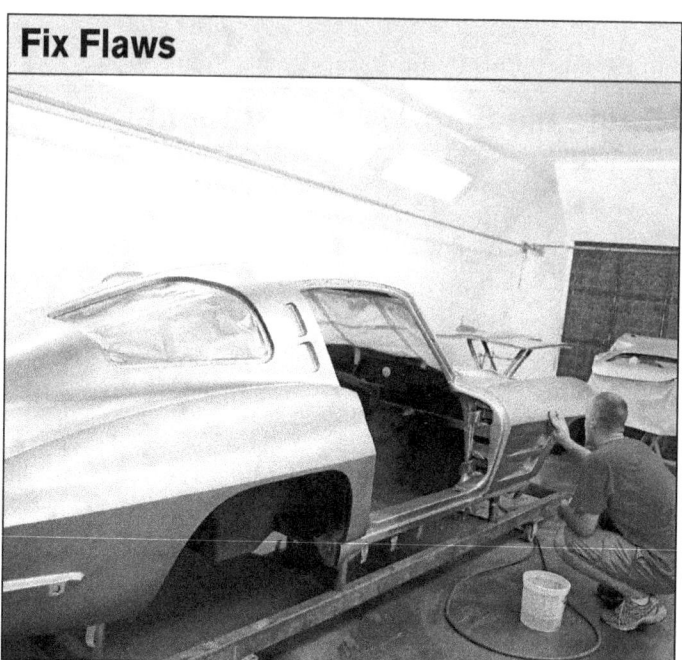

6 A couple of minor flaws were spotted after the second coat of base was applied. The painter lightly wet-sanded the area with 600-grit wet/dry sandpaper. If you end up at the primer, remember to apply a couple extra passes in the area. Even color is important. If you see "tiger stripes," they are further enhanced with clear applied. Look over the entire body for imperfections and missed base coat.

Touch Up Paint

7 Like the body, a few minor areas may need attention. This is your last chance to take care of any suspect areas. Remember to look over the edges and any areas with depressions for missed base coat. Give the entire body a once-over, especially the lower areas. Any area that is wet sanded should be wiped with a wet, clean cloth. Once the area is dry, a tack cloth should be wiped on the area also.

Apply Clear Coat

8 Begin spraying the blind holes and crevices while maintaining consistent material application. Make sure that all the tight areas are coated well before the overall clear coat is applied. You must remember how many times you have applied the clear coat in an area. Too many passes in one spot and the clear sags. As with the base coat, take some time to adjust the clear coat flow on a scrap piece of material.

Apply Clear Coat (Continued)

9 The distance from the spray gun to the panel should be maintained at 8 to 12 inches. This means you must be constantly moving your body to keep the spray gun correctly aimed and at the same distance. Long panels require you to move your body following the panel as material is applied. A painter has a natural tendency to stay in one spot, creating an arc as material flows from the gun. So the center of the panel receives the majority of material while the outer edges are lightly coated with material. The panels must stay wet until the entire car body is painted or dry spots result.

10 Applying paint to flat surfaces is easier than applying it to vertical surfaces. Too much clear can make the base coat color appear irregular. For best results, maintain the same distance and application rate as with the body. You naturally want to let go of the trigger when you get to the end of the painted surface, but the material must keep flowing past the end of the panel. Each pass of the spray gun should overlap 3 to 4 inches of the previous pass to keep the material wet to prevent tiger stripes. You must be committed to finishing the paint application without interruption or plan on sanding the entire car before applying the next coat.

Allow Paint to Dry

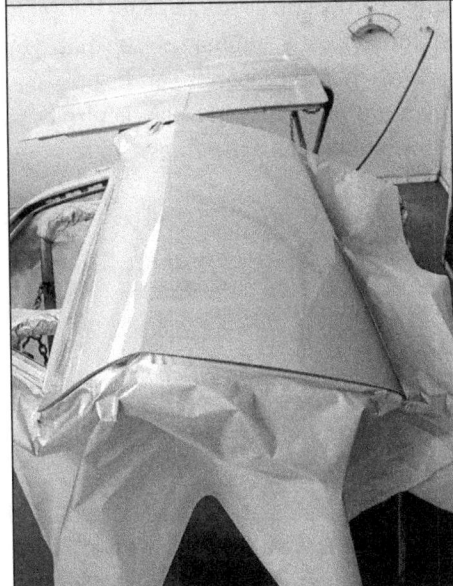

Mask and Paint Hinge Area

11 After carefully inspecting the doors and hood, they are finished. The heated, humidity-controlled paint booth has the pieces dry to the touch within an hour. The body and pieces should be left to dry for at least a day before handling them though.

12 The clear is glistening in the light on the metallic silver base coat. This is another area that can get you into trouble very easily. The recessed cove areas are sprayed first and then a top coat is sprayed across the whole area.

13 The hinges and doors were fitted before they were removed for painting. This way you only have to set the door up on the marked hinges. Trying to adjust the hinges in the pillars also messes up the paint. The hinges were masked to keep paint out of the bolt threads.

Tech Tip: Painting Tips

- Have all your materials ready.
- Take time to look everything over carefully before spraying.
- Read and understand the paint manufacturer's recommendations.
- Practice using the spray gun on vertical and horizontal surfaces before spraying top coats. A pinpoint spray pattern increases paint volume application dramatically compared to the fan pattern. Adjust the spray gun accordingly and test before spraying again.
- Order enough paint supplies: add 10 to 15 percent to what the paint supplier suggests.
- Record the paint formula codes and spray techniques in a safe place.
- Clean the spray equipment as soon as possible after finishing, before the paint dries in the nozzles and cups, making it easier to clean up. ∎

Required skill level increases to do this; wet coating with acrylics involves a delicate touch to get a good, deep coat of paint without runs. If the paint is too wet, it runs, but if it's too dry, it has rough, dull areas. While it is very difficult to level a run with acrylic paint, rough dry areas are almost impossible to smooth out. This means correct paint application is paramount to an excellent final product.

Base/clear coat paint systems are more labor intensive to apply and finish than acrylics. The base coat requires an even application, as the urethane did.

Metallic finishes require the correct metallic dispersion; changing the paint gun air pressure affects the metallic color from light to dark. If you see overlapping strokes in a metallic base coat, they will be more noticeable once the clear coat is applied.

This gives you an idea why it is so difficult to repair damaged base/clear coat finishes. The base coat has a low sheen when dry. Clear makes the base come alive as it brings the depth and shine to the surface. After a couple of base coats have been applied, the clear coats must be applied quickly enough to avoid dry areas.

The problems start when you have to go away to mix another cup of paint. Make sure you have at least three cups of clear mixed and ready for application. The upside to the clear-coat application is that most everyone ends up wet-sanding and buffing to get the maximum amount of shine. But you need to avoid significant dry areas, as I mentioned earlier.

Plan on applying three coats of clear and waiting for the paint manufacturer's prescribed amount of time between each coat. Those interested in show quality may add another coat of clear, so that they can slick all the panels when they are wet-sanding.

Wet Sanding

Finishing the paint work is critical. You need to wait the required time for the paint to harden before beginning the wet-sanding process. Acrylics with hardeners and base-coat/clear-coat finishes are typically wet-sanded within 24 hours after painting. Always consult the paint manufacturer's guidelines so that you know when the process can begin. Temperature and humidity play key roles in how quickly the paint dries.

These 3M products are used to level and bring out the shine. The color-sanding wet/dry sandpaper is used first, then the rubbing compound. Wrap up the buffing with the foam polishing pad glaze. The glaze removes swirl marks that the buffing pad leaves behind. Do not wax any of the surfaces for at least two months so the paint can cure without locking any of the solvents.

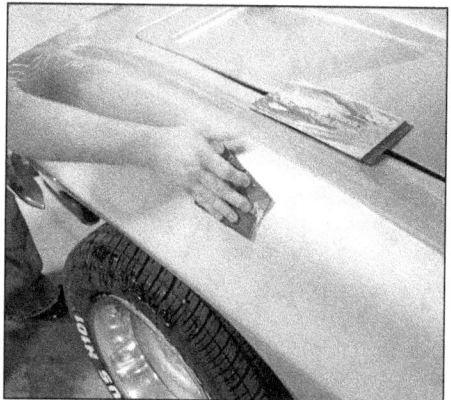

Begin the wet-sanding process following the fender's longest portion of the panel. In this test area, you find out how much sanding is required. Once you get an idea how much time you have to spend on an area, you can gauge when to stop and check your progress.

Within about three minutes, the wet sanded area is dull and smooth without any imperfections. The area should be flushed with clean water to prevent deep clear coat scratches. You do have to be careful as you approach edges where all paints have a tendency to be thinner. Never run the sandpaper on the top of the edge; go up to it, not over it.

PAINT

The reason for wet sanding is to level the clear coat while removing any minute particles of debris. It is very hard to prevent absolutely all contaminants from finding their way to the paint surface during the painting process. Today, high-tech paint booths have filtered, cross-ventilation systems to keep the environment free of dust and debris, but even so, you can still usually find a bit of debris here and there. Do-it-yourselfers invariably have some errant debris in the paint, but with careful sanding, these can be removed. Edges often have less clear or topcoats. Never sand over the top of the edge itself; you need to come up to it as you sand.

Before you start sanding, assess how much work you need to perform. How does the overall paint surface look? For the most part, is it clean and smooth, with light orange peel? Is there quite a bit of orange peel with debris? Wet-dry finishing sandpaper comes in 1000, 1200, 1500 and 2000 grits. If your paint is rough, you may have to start with the 1000 grit and move up to 1500 grit. To avoid many hours at the buffer, the final overall sand should ideally be with 1500- or 2000-grit sandpaper.

Really great paintwork takes a lot of elbow grease to make it slick. The better you apply the paint, the less extra sanding you have to do.

Start wet-sanding using a wet cloth to wipe down a 10-square-inch area to remove any grit. Put your wet/dry paper on your sanding block. Wet the paper and slowly sand the area, following the largest portion of the panel. In other words, sand the fenders front to back, not up and down. Follow this same procedure on all panels. Work from front to back or vice-versa.

After you have sanded for a couple of minutes, stop to see how things are going. Wipe off the area with a clean sponge soaked in clear, clean water. Let the area dry and see what you have. In the early phase of sanding, you should see evidence of tiny divots similar to the surface of a golf ball. As you sand further, the divots should disappear and the entire area should have a dull sheen, without any imperfections. Exercise caution: you want take away the imperfections without taking away any more material than necessary.

Once you get the feel for the time it takes to sand an area, you are ready to repeat the process on the rest of the car. Finish wet-sanding one area at a time, before moving on to the next. After wet-sanding an area, flood it with clear, clean water, then wipe it down. Sponges work well to flood the area, and cotton baby diapers work best to dry it off. If you happen to drop your sandpaper, sponge, or drying towel in a dirty area, throw it away or make sure it is clean before using it again.

Buffing

Buffing an edge can also remove the clear from the surface within seconds. Buffers and orbital waxers are options. Buffers use a straight-drive, high-speed pad to scrub the paint. Orbital waxers gently apply and remove wax on painted surfaces. Their circular, orbital action helps avoid swirl marks that the buffer's straight-line rotation would not. You need to utilize a high-speed buffer to bring the deep shine back.

You need to carefully buff the painted surface. If you use the wrong technique, buffing pads, or speed, you can damage the paint. Use a corded electric buffer with a maximum speed of 2,500 rpm. Stay away from air-powered buffers that have high-RPM capabilities. Hold the electric buffer at approximately 1,200 rpm (half speed) as the wool pad applies light pressure on the fender. The buffing pad should never rotate into or over an edge. As the pad's wool fibers hit the edge, material is quickly removed.

The mirror-like reflection shows that the hood is just about ready for the foam pad and swirl remover. Use masking tape to prevent clear coat damage at vulnerable edges with height differences. Place a cloth to raise the hood at the rear, so the buffing pad can rotate off the edges of the hood during the buffing process. Care has to be taken so that the buffing pad doesn't rub the fender edge as the hood's edges are buffed.

As you progress through the buffing process, you use finer-grit materials to remove the scratch marks from the surface. 3M Super Duty rubbing compound should be used first to remove the ultra-fine sanding scratches. 3M's Perfect-It rubbing compound removes swirl marks.

Foam pads are easier on the paint than wool pads. Wool pads remove material quickly and can get down to the primer. If the surfaces have been wet-sanded properly, the foam pad should remove sanding scratches. You can carefully use an aggressive wool pad, but you have to then use a foam pad to remove the swirl marks. I use different pads for each material. Rubbing compound needs its own pad, and so does swirl remover.

It's best to do the wet-sanding and buffing of the overall paint surfaces before the emblems are in place, or you have to be extremely careful to avoid damaging the paint and emblems with the buffer.

Post-Paint Work

The factory did not sand the entire body. The emphasis was on the top portions and sides of the painted surfaces. The factory used heated paint rooms with a 45-minute, 250-degree-F heat cycle to accelerate the drying time of the acrylic lacquers. A temperature of 325 degrees F was used on metal bodies to get the acrylic lacquer flowing. The fiberglass bodies were not subjected to the high heat so they required wool pad buffing. Like the sanding during the paint process, the factory buffed the panels starting at the beltline and went upward.

Be extra careful during the wet-sanding process or you may have to fire up the spray gun again, to replicate the correct orange-peel finish. NCRS judging manuals specify where and how the paint was applied. They also cover how the factory did the final wet-sanding and buffing. There is no clause in the judging manual that says the paint cannot be too shiny. Remember, they are trying to preserve history one Corvette at a time. If you ask Bloomington Gold and NCRS judges, they will explain how the paint finish should look.

Body Reinstallation

If the body has been removed from the chassis, it should be prepped before it is reinstalled. I begin with the engine compartment splash shields because it is so much easier to install the rubber shields with simple tools while the body is off the chassis. General Motors used a heavy-duty stapler to install upper control arm splash shields onto the inner fenders, as well as the rubber shields on

Body Reinstallation

Attach Splash Shields

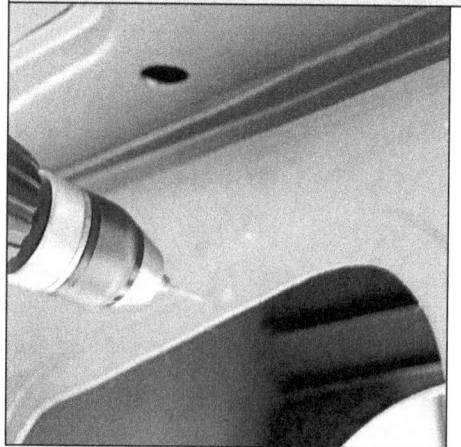

1 Drill the new inner fenders for the splash shields after checking the staple placement in the original inner fenders. Use a hole punch to prep the control arm splash shields for the stainless-steel staples. Be gentle with the 1/16-inch drill bit; it can be broken very easily.

2 Insert the staple through the splash shield from the inside then use a small ball-peen hammer to bend over the legs. This is the best way to complete this task. I would like to see the factory tool that performed this procedure of stapling through the fiberglass. The inner fenders get the black lizard skin coating before you install the shields.

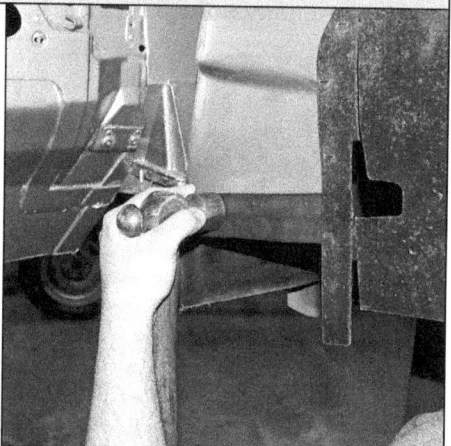

3 On the back side, hold the staple with a larger hammer during the clinching process. It takes some skill to hammer the legs over while holding the large hammer tightly against the rubber shields. You can also hammer too hard and rip into the rubber. Check the progress a few times until you get the hang of it.

Rivet Shields

4 This nifty tool from Corvette Central is used to clinch the aluminum rivets. It has an inverted dome so the rivet has that factory-finished look. The tough part of this job has a helper inside the passenger compartment holding a large hammer as an anvil during the clinching process.

Use Lift

5 This is where the lift comes in handy with the body being so close to the chassis rear mount support. Some clearance can be gained if the fuel tank is left off the chassis during the body installation. The chassis can be rolled forward during the body drop allowing more clearance. Take a look upfront at the radiator core support as the body is lowered. The area gets tight as the core support drops between the frame rails.

Shim Body

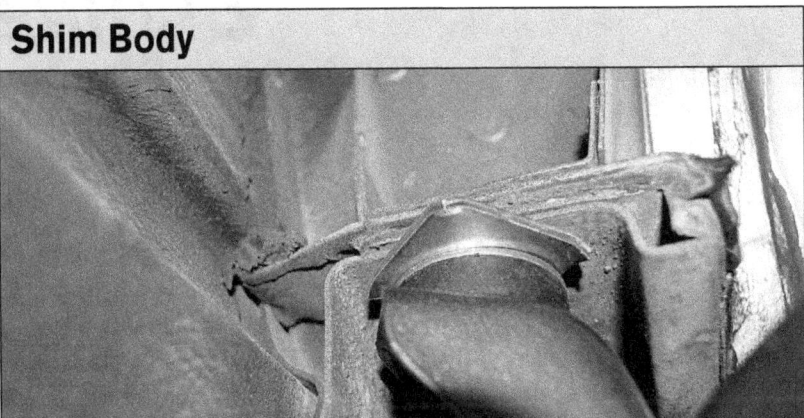

6 A couple of shims are required at the number-1 body mount, which should be installed in this manner. Since the frame was replaced I had to start with just enough shims to fill the clearance between the cushions and the body. Once the spaces are shimmed check door fit and if necessary add shims to align the door gap. If the door gap is too tight at top, add shims to the body mount behind the door for example. Once the door openings are set add the appropriate shims to the rear body mounts. The same goes for the front: you want the center body mounts shimmed then the radiator core support. The shimming process must be done on level ground with all the tires on the ground.

the lower edge of the inner fenders. The shields can be installed with the body on the chassis, but it is much more difficult.

The underside also has some items to inspect before the body drop. Reinforcements were used to strengthen the body mounts, which rust badly over the years. This is the only time to replace the body mounts.

Check the seat mounting and seat belt reinforcements, too. General Motors used rivets that require bucking to cinch them, making them difficult to install after the body is in place.

Check and clean all of the threaded holes from front to back. This is the last chance to make sure all the underside pieces are easy to install.

After the underside reinforcements have been installed or repaired, you should consider what, if anything, will be done to the underside fiberglass. General Motors left the underside fiberglass raw, which means it soaked up any oil or grease. A good scrub with mineral spirits removes much of the contaminants.

For originality, the fiberglass should be left raw. Many restorers apply a low-sheen clear finish to make the underside easier to clean. I use clear finish to keep the underside nice. I also use rubberized undercoating in the fender wells, to help prevent rocks from scarring the fiberglass.

Something to think about is that the front inner fenders are also the outside fenders on the top. The undercoating helps keep rocks from damaging the fenders where you might see the damage on the top side.

CHAPTER 6

ENGINES

Multiple options are available when it comes to second-generation Corvette engines. The original engine can be restored, rebuilt, or replaced.

Engine restoration consists of rebuilding the engine from top to bottom to factory specifications and finishes. Restoration also includes checking and replacing any incorrect numbered or date-coded components. Painting engine components requires special attention to detail during the restoration. The NCRS Reference Manual specifies all the correct finishes for the engine parts. A restoration makes sense if your car has many original, salvageable major engine components. It can also make sense if you have all the correct pieces except the original engine block. Or it may be best to restore the engine after finding a correct block and stamping it. NCRS allows re-stamped engine blocks with the correct date code and part number casting number. This makes it possible to recreate a Midyear with the correct pieces.

At some point, restoring an engine just does not make fiscal sense, such as when all ancillary items are gone, unless you're talking about a low-production-number, high-optioned car. I know that some would say it makes financial sense to restore any Midyear engine to original specs. In reality, the expense may be so high that the car is never driven, except in and out of the trailer.

Rebuilding, on the other hand, entails completely freshening the engine. It may be a later small- or big-block with performance engine components. This is a common find, as many owners added aftermarket cylinder heads, headers, intakes, and carburetors. The performance parts can possibly be rebuilt to save you a few dollars and gain some power.

Another option is to buy another engine, such as a performance rebuild or new crate engine, to which you could add personal touches such as an upgraded carburetor or intake manifold. You can also apply personal artistic touches to the engine, such as matching its color to the car's exterior paint. That is why I personally like the crate or rebuilt engine route over the matching-numbers, everything's-correct engines.

A few other thoughts: Does it make sense to use the original, numbers-matching engine if you plan to drive the car? Or does it make more sense to store the original engine away and use another engine altogether? If you are

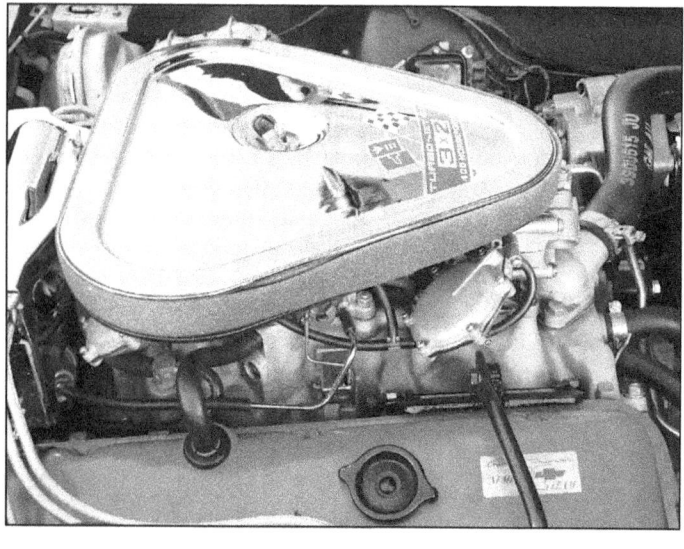

427 cubic inch tri-power engines are the most sought after Midyear power-plants at 435 HP with three Holley two-barrel carburetors they command big money. This fine example has all the correct colors, stickers, and finishes to compete in a Bloomington Gold or NCRS event.

lucky enough to have the correct original engine, you know it will not be hurt if it is prepared for storage, set aside, and periodically maintained. Swapping the original engine back in place would not be an issue, if that was what a new prospective owner wanted. Remember to keep all the fasteners related to the engine, if you do decide to store it.

Disassembling the engine for rebuilding takes some effort and does make a bit of an oily mess. Automotive machine shops generally help you decide the best route to take. They do all the critical measuring of the engine block's cylinders, crankshaft, pistons, and connecting rods. All of the machining (cylinder block, crank, and cylinder heads) is done by the machine shop, leaving you to handle the final assembly. That is, if you decide to disassemble and assemble the engine yourself. Most machine shops only warrant the machine work. You are responsible if there is an engine failure. Because of this, I always double-check the clearances of all rotating components during assembly to be safe.

Machine shops also offer complete engine rebuilding services. Drop off a greasy, oily engine assembly, and within two weeks, you can pick up a fresh, shiny, ready-to-install engine. You should get a warranty on the assembled engine, if you choose this option. The machine shop supplies instructions on start-up and break-in. Be sure to follow warranty instructions.

Use the best oil for your restored, original engine. Zinc was eliminated from many engine oils to prolong catalytic converter life, but zinc is vital for flat-tappet camshafts. And it's been part of engine oils for the past 70 years. Engine rebuilders had to deal with sudden cam and lifter wear. Thankfully, it was rectified before too many engines were destroyed. The oil has no zinc unless it specifies ZDDP for off-road or Diesel use.

Diesel oil provides the zinc protection, but the viscosity is not great for stock-built engines. Brad Penn oil has multiple viscosities available for all applications.

The solution is to add ZDDPlus to your favorite oil. ZDDPlus has the correct amount of zinc for the typical 5-quart engine requirements. To preserve your flat-tappet engine, make sure you always use the correct ZDDP level in your engine oil.

Other Factors to Consider

At this point, you've decided whether to restore or replace. You also need to consider how the car will be used. Engine compression is a very important consideration, no matter what path you take. High-compression engines require premium fuel and possibly an octane booster to avoid spark knock or detonation (also known as pre-ignition). Early, factory-correct, high-compression engines can benefit from changing to lower-compression pistons. No one will know (even during NCRS judging) that the compression has been dropped enough to run on today's fuels. I keep the compression at a maximum of 10:1 for street-driven engines with cast-iron cylinder heads. Aluminum cylinder heads allow for slightly higher compression ratios in the 10:0 to 10:8 range, thanks to their improved cooling capabilities.

All engines built before 1974 should have hardened cylinder head valve seats installed, or use a lead supplement in the fuel. This means all Midyear cylinder heads should have hardened valve seats, to avoid valve seat erosion. It's unclear how long lead supplements will be available, so it makes sense to upgrade all cylinder heads to avoid dependence on substitutes.

Camshaft selection is as important as the compression ratio you choose. Reproduction stock-grind camshaft profiles are available to bring your engine back to factory specs. Reproduction camshafts give you the sound and feel of an early Corvette. For example, the 300-hp Midyear 327-ci engine idles well and has great low-end torque with its factory cam, which is readily available and inexpensive.

With early camshaft technology, however, the reality is that as the engine's horsepower increased, drivability decreased. If you plan on changing the camshaft, make sure you factor in compression, intake manifold, and carburetor.

Engine Disassembly

The first steps in the rebuild process are to get the engine apart and inspect all of its components.

The engine should be completely disassembled down to a bare block. If you do not have an engine stand, now is the time to get one. Engine stands are not expensive, so buy a stable and safe one.

I stand by my rule that you should separate questionable pieces by placing them in a specific area. This prevents missing pieces that should have been ordered, when it comes time for assembly.

Use Special Tool

1 *This inexpensive harmonic balancer tool removes the balancer without damaging it. Harmonic balancer removal tools are available at all major parts retailers for rent or sale. You also need a harmonic balancer installation tool so you avoid beating the balancer back onto the crankshaft.*

Remove Valvetrain Parts

2 Remove the valve covers, rocker arms, and pushrods and place them in their respective spots in a valvetrain tray or on a bench. Place the rockers and pushrods in their respective places. You need to put the valvetrain pieces back in the same location they came from, so the wear patterns are kept the same. Pull the lifers to place them in the valvetrain tray. Most likely, the lifters are not going to come out easily. Years of hydrocarbon buildup make them stick in the engine block bore. You may need to pull the lifters out with pliers. Spray carburetor cleaner around the lifter to help free them, and then use a pair of pliers to work them up and down until they come out. In some cases, the lifters cannot be pulled out. You may have to wait until the camshaft is pulled and see if they can be helped out with a brass drift and hammer.

Remove Cylinder Heads

3 The cylinder heads have seventeen 5/8-inch bolts on each side. The outer and cylinder head bolts can be difficult to get a socket onto fully. These special, small Snap-On sockets help get into the tight spots. You can use a short, 5/8-inch socket and extension in lieu of the special socket. The cylinder heads have dowels to hold them in place until you are ready to remove them.

Number Connecting Rods

Remove Connecting Rods

5 Back off the connecting rod nut until the nut is even with the rod bolt, and then tap on both sides of the rod to loosen the cap. The rod cap protects the crankshaft during the tapping process.

4 Now that the oil pump and driveshaft have been removed, you can number the connecting rods. The factory did not number the upper and lower part of the connecting rods or crankshaft main bearing caps. Numbering the rods and main bearing caps is an absolute must because the crankshaft does not turn if you mismatch the rods or main bearing caps. When connecting rods are manufactured, the upper and lower halves are assembled then line-bored and honed. If you try to change the lower half from one connecting rod to the other, the centering of the bearing surfaces is off. This in turn makes the connecting rod seize on the crankshaft. Number stamp sets are available at most hardware stores.

Remove Pistons from Block

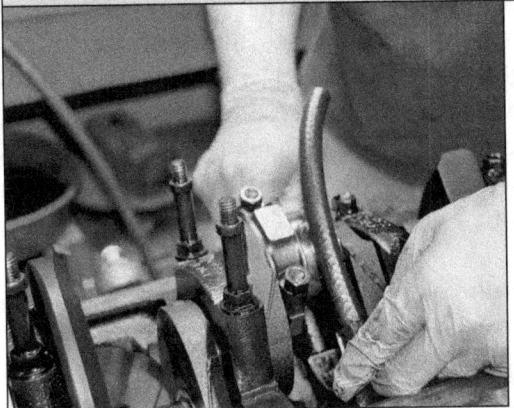

6 A couple of pieces of 3/8-inch fuel hose work well to protect the crankshaft as the pistons are tapped out. If you let the connecting rod bolts crash into the crankshaft as you push them out, crankshaft journal damage results. The crankshaft journals are precision ground and polished. Imperfections in the crankshaft journal tear into the connecting rod bearings and eat up the softer material. As the bearing material is consumed, an oil pressure loss occurs.

Remove Crankshaft from Block

7 Remove the crankshaft once all the pistons and the crankshaft main bearing caps have been removed. Use a ball-peen hammer to lightly tap on the side of the main cap, which jars the cap loose. Keep away from the crankshaft bearing surfaces with any tool that can nick or gouge it.

Remove Crankshaft from Block (Continued)

8 Make sure you have a good grip on the oily crankshaft and lift straight upward. Hold on tight because the crankshaft is heavy, and it gets stuck if lifted off to one side. Once the crankshaft is out, lay it on a secure surface. Watch your fingers as you set it down because there are plenty of pinch-points. Some people believe that laying a crankshaft down causes it to bend over a long period of time. They like to set the crankshaft straight up on the flywheel side, which is fine unless it gets knocked over.

10 Tap out the oil dipstick lower tube from the block. The lower tube keeps the dipstick away from the crankshaft and guides it into the pan. Many of these tubes are lost, making it difficult to get the dipstick in and out easily. This 5/16-inch threaded bolt works great to knock out the dipstick tube. Do not leave anything that protrudes on the block such as bolts, tubes, etc. During the machining process they tend to get lost or broken.

Remove Freeze Plugs from Block

9 Freeze plugs should all be replaced. Use a hammer and a punch to tap on the outer edge of the freeze plug to get them popped out of the block. These pop inward and require you to dig them out of the block. I usually use a big screwdriver to get behind them and pry them out. The prying action reduces their size enough that they can be easily removed.

Remove Dipstick from Block

CHAPTER 6

Machine Shop Service

Once the rotating components have been removed from the engine block, you are ready for a trip to the machine shop. I leave the cam bearings in the block because they will be removed at the machine shop. All automotive machine shops have specialized tools to properly remove and replace cam bearings. I can understand that you may want to fully disassemble and assemble the engine, but having the machine shop replace the cam bearings and clean the engine block just makes good sense. You negate any potential savings if you have to purchase a few sets of cam bearings while you practice learning to install them correctly. Camshaft bearing installers are relatively expensive, considering the limited use they get. When the machine shop cleans the engine block, it gets a submersion bath that internally cleans all the interior surface areas.

The engine block cylinder wall condition should be sonically tested to see if it has the minimum wall thickness for rebuilding. All Midyear engine blocks (General Motors calls them "cases") have lower nickel content than later engine blocks, which means that the cylinders wear more quickly in early engine blocks.

Even low-mileage cylinder blocks can have egg-shaped cylinder walls with a noticeable ridge at the top of the cylinder. The ridge occurs as cylinder wall material wears away from the extreme combustion pressure placed on the upper piston ring forcing it outward. Chances are the engine block requires boring and the pistons then need to be replaced.

Before boring, discuss with the shop the pistons you want and the desired bore size.

Early engine blocks (1968 and older) can be bored beyond the customary .030 inch, but with the lightweight engine blocks of today, I would stop at .030. Boring to .030 is the norm, and pistons in that over-size are readily available.

Cylinder liners or sleeves are available in cases where the bore is badly damaged or worn. When installed properly, there is no reason to junk a block that requires a sleeve. The replacement pistons must be available, so they can be fitted to the cylinders properly. The machinist measures the crankshaft bearing journals for proper dimensions, then polish it or grind it under-size if necessary.

There is a misconception that worn oil pumps cause low oil pressure. Excessive bearing clearances cause low oil pressure. When the bearing clearances exceed .003 inch, oil pressure drops exponentially.

Unless you're an experienced engine builder, rebuilding an engine for a Midyear may not be a wise decision. A reputable machine shop produces a professional rebuild. They need the engine block, piston/connecting rod assemblies, crankshaft, and cylinder heads.

I also take the tin pieces for cleaning, such as the oil pan, timing cover, valve covers, etc. Engine shops typically clean aluminum pieces, too, but beware: their process may not be NCRS friendly.

Engine Machining

Cylinder head service is required, so expect that to be extensive and costly on early cylinder heads. As explained earlier, installing hardened valve seats is common. I commonly have the valveguides and all valve seats replaced in Midyear cylinder heads. The parts and labor cost for cylinder head service can easily approach the cost of a new, assembled cylinder head.

Bore Engine Block

1 *The cylinder block is bored to straighten and square the bores. The cutter head moves down the cylinder bore, set on auto feed. This is where you have to depend on the machinist's accuracy. The block deck is placed squarely on the bottom side of the machined surface to ensure accuracy. The machinist must leave enough material to allow for final honing and correct piston fit.*

ENGINES

Hone Engine Block

2 This hone is also a precision machine that straightens bore imperfections. The machinist checks piston diameter then hones the cylinder bore until .002-inch clearance is achieved between the bore and piston. The .002 clearance figure is for cast pistons. Forged pistons require .004 for the additional thermal expansion that occurs during operation. The honing process requires careful timing as the hone moves in and out to create a crosshatch pattern, which retains oil to prevent piston and ring damage during the break-in period.

True Crank Journals

3 This crankshaft is ready for the under-size grinding process. The bearing journals require .010 inch of material to be removed. As with the cylinder boring process, enough material must be left for polishing the crankshaft after the machining. This crankshaft grinder is an expensive piece of machinery that requires a highly skilled individual to operate it. One slip and the crankshaft could be junk.

Repair Crankshaft

4 It was a surprise to find a precision crankshaft welder in my little sleepy town of Scottsboro, Alabama. John at Market Street Performance can save just about any severely worn crankshaft. As long as the crankshaft is in one piece, he can weld the bearing journals back to standard dimensions. If necessary, he can repair crankshaft thrust surfaces also. This high-tech welder auto feeds the welding materials and rotates the crankshaft at the speed required for perfect welding. This can save your early 327-ci small-journal crankshafts, which are hard to find.

Deck the Block

5 The engine block is mounted in the surface grinder for deck machining. There is a noticeable difference in cleanliness in comparison to the previous photos. Although the shop was always dirty and there was junk everywhere, they turned out excellent work. Word of mouth works best when it comes to finding a competent machine shop. Do not be deceived by ultra-clean, modern equipment. Knowing how to operate the machinery is the most important factor.

CHAPTER 6

Valve Seat Machining

When the machine shop completes its work, the engine is ready for assembly. Keep your assembly area clean. Clean all the parts (new and old) and set them on a workbench or shelf off the floor.

Every engine I build follows the same routine, time and time again. The first step is to remove the lifters from their packaging and clean them. The lifters may look clean, but the manufacturing processes can leave some metallic residue behind. Wash them thoroughly in a mineral-spirits bath, scrub them with a brush, and then blow them off with compressed air. Once they are dry, set them in a container of 10W30 engine oil so they can soak for quite a while, until they are needed. Cover the container that holds the lifters to keep any airborn debris out.

Press In Valveguide

1 John is using a Berco cylinder head servicing station to machine the original cast-in valveguide for the new press-in cast guide. Do not be surprised if the machine shop says that all the guides need to be replaced. Loose valvestem guides cause all kinds of problems, from poor valve sealing to noisy valvetrain. John recommends cast-iron replacement valveguides for street use. Bronze valveguides are available at higher cost for use in race or high-performance applications.

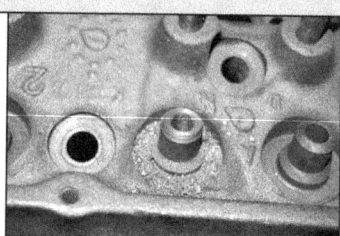

2 This is the installed valveguide ready for cleaning. Various cutters are used to machine the top of the guide back to the stock appearance. This rifling in the new cast-iron guide stops within 1/4 inch of the bottom of the guide. This prevents oil from reaching the combustion chamber while still lubricating the valve stem. Knurling is an alternative to replacing the valveguides. A cutting tool goes into the existing guide, cutting and forcing material outward to tighten the valvestem in the guide. This is a stop-gap approach, however, that does not last for the life of the engine.

Remove Valve Seats

3 Like valveguides, valve seats are part of the casting and require machining for removal. This takes experience to machine the seat out without cutting too deep and striking coolant. One thing to remember is that these cylinder heads are 40 years old, plus cracks can occur from the pounding that they have received over the years.

Install Valve Seats

4 The new hardened valve seat is installed with this specific driver. The seats must be installed squarely to avoid cylinder head damage. On a positive note, the valve seats can be replaced easily in the future.

Machine Valve Seats

5 Once the valveguides and seats have been replaced, valve seat angle machining is performed. Valve seats are machined in two ways: grinding with a stone or cutting with a machine tool. This Berco cylinder head service bench uses machine tools for precise valve-angle cutting. Once completed, early cylinder heads can withstand today's fuels.

Short Block Assembly

Engine assembly starts with the short block and some very important rotating components. You don't need any special tricks or techniques to build big- or small-block Chevy engines, just careful methodical procedures that will produce reliable long-life engines. Lay out the engine parts on the workbench in the order that they should be assembled. It is imperative that you torque all the fasteners. Those who say, "I don't need a torque wrench, I can feel how tight the fasteners are" end up with engines that perform poorly. Along those lines, make sure all the fasteners are torqued before taking a break; you would be surprised how many engines are damaged because one or two fasteners were left loose when the assembler decided to take a break. Lubricate all rotating components with engine assembly lube. Lastly, ensure that you keep your work area clean for the best results.

Inspect and Clean Block

1 This is what you can expect to find after receiving your engine block back from the machine shop. The boring and honing process leaves metallic particles behind. Use a stiff brush and soapy water to scrub the cylinder and block thoroughly so metallic particles are removed. Keep a compressed-air nozzle and oil nearby. Immediately after the cleaning job is complete, blow the water out of the cylinders and then apply oil. The cylinders rust almost immediately if you do not get the water out quickly. Use a clean cloth with oil to wipe the cylinders and see if any metallic dark streaks are left on the cloth. Any evidence of gray metallic streaks on the cloth indicates metal left behind so you need to go through the cleaning process again to prevent unintended wear.

Set Piston Ring End Gap

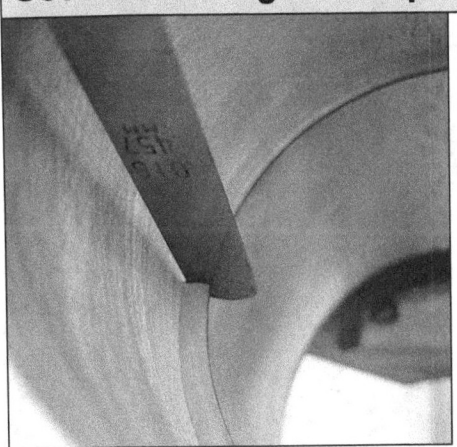

2 Piston rings have minimum ring end gap requirements to prevent them from binding. As heat builds, metals expand, and therefore, piston ring manufacturers have a minimum end gap for good sealing while minimizing friction. Insert the compression rings into the cylinder where they eventually end up during the build. Use a feeler gauge to check the minimum end gap of each compression ring. If necessary, use a ring file to remove the required material and place the rings in a secure area to ensure the rings go back in the same cylinder. I have been told that this fitting is not necessary because if one ring fits they all do. That is true to some extent, but we are talking thousandths of an inch. If just one ring was made incorrectly, that piston could be too tight or create excessive blow-by.

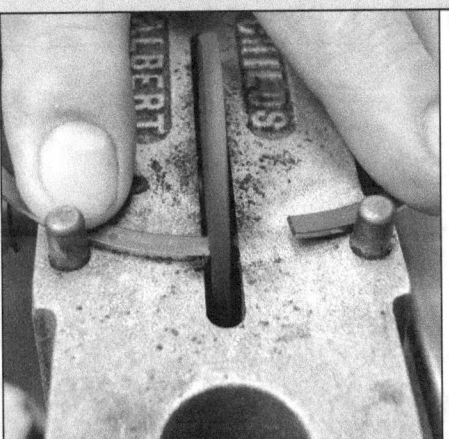

3 Piston rings come in many forms: chrome, cast iron, and many alloys. Cast-iron piston rings work best for all-around engine performance. The majority of stock cast-iron replacement rings do not require any machining to fit them to the bore. They usually have the prescribed .004 per inch of cylinder bore clearance figured in. These performance rings are "file fit" for exact ring end gap clearance. This is a tedious job using a ring end filer to carefully remove material and check for proper fit. You have to hand-crank the Childs and Albert ring filer, but it is much easier than using a hand file. The ring filer makes it easier to keep the ring end square during the machining process. Once the ring end gap is correct, use a hand file to barely touch the outer edges to remove any build-up.

Install Pistons and Rods

4 Pistons usually have a notch or mark that identifies the front of the piston. Your machine shop should have orientated the piston notch correctly on the connecting rod but mistakes do happen. Connecting rods are not symmetrical, and the rod bearing surface is offset to keep the connecting rod in the center of the piston. There should be two sets of four piston-and-rod assemblies with the bearing lock on the outside of each set. (This is with the piston lying down on the bench, front notch facing upward.) The piston shown has been installed on the odd bank of cylinders (1, 3, 5, and 7). The caps bearing the lock on the left (yellow tab) are on the left as shown. The early small-journal connecting rod has a channel cut through it on the right side of the cap. This channel was for oil spray on the camshaft and was deleted when the large journal crankshaft was introduced in 1969.

Install Piston Rings

5 It's time to install the rings that were fitted to each cylinder. The rings usually have a "pip" mark, which is a round depression that is usually installed in the up position. Make sure you read the piston ring manufacturer's instructions before installing any rings. Pay careful attention to the three-piece oil ring, and do not overlap the center expander ring. You can use an inexpensive set of piston ring expanders that prevent scratching the piston during ring installation. Set aside the piston and rod assemblies for installation after the crankshaft.

Measure Main Bearing Clearance

6 Set the crankshaft in place with new bearings and a strip of green Plastigage placed on the bearing surfaces. The main caps have been installed. Torque the inner bolts to 70 ft-lbs and the outer bolts to 65 ft-lbs. Do a few dry runs to check bearing clearance before moving forward. Do not rotate the crankshaft. Install a few connecting rods in the same manner to check connecting rod clearances.

7 The Plastigage plastic strip crushes when the bearing cap is assembled and torqued. Remove the bearing cap to see how far the plastic was crushed and then compare it to a gauge printed on the Plastigage package. If you have .0015 to .0025 inch, you are in the ballpark and the clearances are correct. The machine shop is not responsible for incorrect clearances. Their reply will be, "You should always double-check clearances because all the variables can alter clearances."

ENGINES

Apply Sealer to Rear Main Seal Lip

8 In my shop, I am very particular about sealer use. I apply a coat of Permatex Aviation sealer to the rear main seal lip. Permatex Aviation sealer is impervious to gas and oil while staying somewhat flexible. It bonds well to the rear seal material, which is the most important fact. This block is for use with a late-model, one-piece rear main seal. The crankshaft is an early two-piece style that requires this adapter for rear seal installation. The procedure for rear seal or rear main cap is the same; this is just in two separate pieces.

9 This rear main seal may look out of place jutting above the side of the adapter, but it is not. It is the latest technology, placing the parting seam away from the seal adapter parting seam. This ensures that the seal-adjoining seams are not going to be slightly off if the adapter or rear main bearing cap seal surface halves do not meet up perfectly. Place a dab of aviation sealer on the seal ends and across the main cap or adapter to prevent oil from leaking past the machined surfaces. It is very important that the rear seal lip faces inward to keep the oil in the engine.

Lube All Main Bearing Surfaces

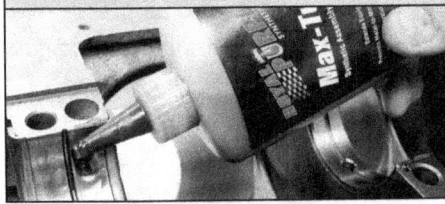

10 Apply a liberal coating of assembly lube to all the main bearing surfaces. The rear main seal should also have a bit of the assembly lube wiped on the surfaces away from the sealer to prevent seal burn-up until the engine has run for a while. The crankshaft can be installed now. The rear main bearing cap should be hand-tightened, and all the other main cap bolts can be torqued for the final time.

Center Rear Main Cap

11 The reason behind hand-tightening the rear main cap is to set the rear main thrust surfaces. Use a dead-blow hammer to hit the front and rear of the crankshaft. This centers the rear main bearing cap providing a 360-degree thrust bearing wear surface for the crank to ride against. This procedure is particularly important for manual-transmission cars where you may find poor bearing fit between the upper and lower bearing halves, causing premature bearing failure. Do not forget to torque the bearing when you are finished.

Check Main Bearing Clearance

12 The dial indicator proved there was .005 inch of rear main bearing thrust clearance, which is under the acceptable .008. I used a large, flat-bladed screwdriver to move the crankshaft back and forth to check the clearance. This type of checking is what is required to ensure that the engine enjoys a long life. It takes a bit more time, but preventative measures are important to avoid the necessity of going back into the engine.

Position Piston Rings

13 It is important to minimize blow-by and oil usage. These piston ring end gaps are approximately 12 degrees apart. The oil ring end gap is on the opposite side. Make a habit of placing all the ring end gaps in this same position on all pistons. This routine prevents mistakes from happening. Do not get me wrong; mistakes happen. We just employ routines to minimize them.

Install Pistons in Block

14 First place crankshaft protector boots on the connecting rod bolts, then install the pistons. Dip the pistons into 10W30 engine oil to coat the rings. Liberally apply assembly lube to the connecting rod bearing surfaces before inserting the piston into the ring compression sleeve. Use piston ring compression sleeves to compress the rings and ease assembly. The cost of the sleeve is reasonable but is limited to the particular bore size you are working with. As each connecting rod is installed, put the correct rod cap on and hand-tighten the 9/16-inch hex nuts.

Recheck Fasteners and Clearances

15 Once all the pistons have been installed, turn the engine over in the stand with the oil pan surface facing upward and torque the rod nuts. Use a feeler gauge to take out any slack between the connecting rods for the torqueing procedure. The connecting rods twist during torqueing and apply side pressure to the bearings, which you want to avoid. A good assurance procedure is to recheck the torque on all the connecting rod nuts and main cap bolts. Anything can happen; you can get sidetracked and leave one nut loose and ruin all your hard work.

Install Cam

16 Liberally coat the camshaft bearing surfaces with assembly lube before carefully installing the cam into the new bearings. A medium-size Phillips-head screwdriver shaft goes into one of the camshaft bolt holes. This provides a handle for careful cam installation. The idea is to keep the cam lobes from digging into the cam bearing material.

Prepare Timing Gears

17 Applying heat to the crankshaft timing gear eases installation. When you see smoke just starting to come off the gear, it is ready for installation. If it's properly prepared, the gear slides right onto crankshaft and seats. Handle the hot gear with a pair of leather gloves during the installation. I do not recommend using an acetylene torch to heat the gear. It is too easy to overheat and damage the gear with the high-heat torch.

Install Chain Assembly and Gears

18 After soaking the timing chain in oil, install the double-row timing chain assembly and gears. The white dots on the gears must be aligned for correct camshaft timing. This timing chain and gear set is adjustable for camshaft advance or retard. I chose zero on this application, but consult your cam manufacturer for a recommendation.

ENGINES

Install Pick-up Tube in Oil Pump

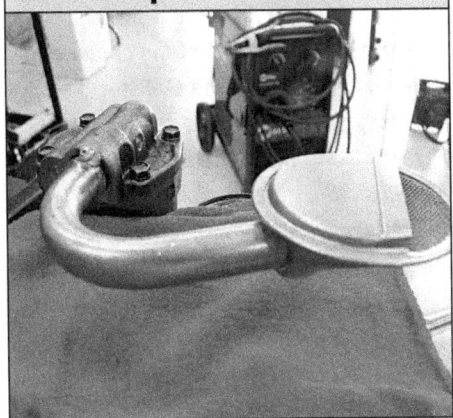

19 GM pick-up strainer tubes are a press-fit in the oil pump. They require quite a bit of force to install when new. If the strainer goes into the oil pump without effort, it should be replaced. A 5/8- or 3/4-inch open-end wrench works well to tap the strainer in place. To be safe, always spot weld the oil pump strainer to the oil pump body.

Apply Sealer to Timing Cover

20 Apply Permatex Aviation sealer for the front seal in the timing cover. Many times an oil leak appears to be coming from the seal when it is actually coming from between the seal and housing. Once the seal has been tapped in place, smear some of that assembly lube on the seal's inner surfaces.

Install Oil Pan

21 Correct oil pan installation is important to prevent oil leaks. Applying silicone sealer on both ends of the rear main bearing cap and timing cover keeps the oil in. This is one of the few places to use silicone sealer because it bonds with the one-piece gasket. These retro one-piece gaskets really work well. They have spacers at each bolt to prevent over-tightening. Those using the cork pan gaskets need to avoid crushing the material because it causes immediate oil leaks. The one-piece gaskets are not NCRS friendly, but they sure minimize oil leaks.

Top End Assembly

With the short-block buttoned up, turn the engine upright and prepare for cylinder head installation. Clean, straight threads are essential to ensuring proper fastener torque is reached and to prevent component damage. Cracks can occur as the bolt tries to make room for debris left in the threads. Every threaded hole in the cylinder head should have a thread tap run through it. A 3/8-16-inch thread tap is run through the cylinder head, intake, and exhaust threaded holes.

You must take the time to properly torque fasteners. Torqueing fasteners is very important to ensure long engine life and for that matter any component's life. Engine torque specifications are used to minimize the distortion of cast-iron and aluminum components. Using an "it feels tight enough" attitude can get you into trouble. The torque values were studied and specifications were put in place that made each component happy throughout its thermal cycling. Torque wrenches are not that costly and can be used for many uses on every vehicle you own. I have foot-pound and inch-pound torque wrenches available at all times during an assembly process.

Wash the remaining debris out of the threaded holes with brake cleaner, then blow them out. Be careful not to break off a tap in the block or cylinder head. Use oil during the tapping process and back the tap off frequently to clear the metal shavings from the thread tap.

Cylinder head bolts should be replaced with new ones because the originals have been stretched and

Cleaning the engine block cylinder head surface is something that should be done carefully. You can use brake cleaner or alcohol to remove any residual oil left over from the piston installation. T-shirt cloth material works well for the solvent application because it leaves behind few cloth fibers. Once the head gasket has been set in place, carefully set the head on the dowel pins and try to prevent moving the head, which could tear the gasket material.

Install all the head bolts and then hand-tighten them with a small ratchet or speed handle. Using the correct bolt tightening sequence, first tighten the bolts to 35 ft-lbs with the torque wrench. The bolt tightening sequence starts at the center and works out. This information is available in the GM service manual and should be strictly adhered to. The second pass torques the bolts to 50 ft-lbs using the same sequence. On the final pass, torque to 65 ft-lbs. This procedure is not found in the GM service manual, but it works very well for long head-gasket life. As the head gasket gets compressed between the deck and cylinder head, the material spreads outward and the three passes allows it to spread evenly.

stressed. The 34 head bolts require wire brushing to remove all the debris from the threads. If the threads are suspect, a 7/16-20 thread die should be run over them.

The original bolts are "correct looking" since some of the outer short bolts are visible. New bolts usually feature a reduced-size hex head, to make it easier to get the socket on the head during the tightening process. Either direction is fine, as long as the bolt threads and the cylinder head threaded holes are clean.

Adjust the valves before the engine goes in the chassis, whether solid or hydraulic lifters. Hydraulic lifters use oil pressure and valvespring tension to keep them loaded onto the valvestem with just enough clearance to allow lubricating oil between them. When the valves are adjusted, the specifications usually call for three complete turns of the adjuster nut after zero lash. When the lifter is preloaded with the three turns, oil pressure takes over and keeps the inner piston in the lifter floating.

I have found that the three turns can be extreme when you are revving the engine to redline frequently. I set my lifters at 1½ turns to alleviate the possibility of valve float at higher RPM. Leaving the adjustment less than 1½ turns can beat up the top of the valvestem and eventually cause lifter noise and unintended wear.

Valve Adjustment

Adjusting the valves starts with positioning the number-1 cylinder at top dead center (TDC) using the timing mark on the cover and balancer. The number-1 intake and exhaust valves are adjusted by turning the adjuster nut down until you can feel a slight load on the pushrod as you rotate it. This is the zero lash point.

Then you turn the nut down an additional 1½ turns. If you are careful and watch how you turn the crankshaft, each cylinder can be adjusted in two full revolutions of the crankshaft.

The next set to adjust would be the number-8 valves. Rotating the crankshaft exactly 90 degrees puts the number-8 cylinder at TDC.

Watch the number-8 intake valve as you turn the crankshaft. As you begin to move the crankshaft, the number-8 intake valve should just finish closing.

Use a small screwdriver to make sure the piston is at TDC before the adjustment. It is critical that you only move the crankshaft 90 degrees in either direction or it negatively affects each cylinder you adjust.

After cylinder number-8, you keep moving the crankshaft the 90 degrees doing the next cylinder in the firing order. Firing order for all Chevrolet small- and big-blocks (except the LS engines) is 1-8-4-3-6-5-7-2.

Alternative Engine Options

New, remanufactured, or used engines are great options depending on your comfort level. Remanufactured or new engines make sense if you feel that engine assembly is not your forte. Rebuilding used engines can be a money pit; you must be careful that the engine you decide to build is not a pile of junk. Inspecting a used engine thoroughly is as important as the build itself.

The L-98

This 1963 split-window coupe project will receive a 1987 Corvette engine transplant. You may be thinking: why go for mediocre performance when there are plenty of high-output crate engines available? Cost and aesthetics is why I chose this powerplant. The engine is a complete take-out, with all the necessary wiring and accessory drive system.

This is where saving dollars makes sense. I can use the complete accessory drive system from the 1987 engine, for instance. I also wanted to keep that old-school look you expect to find under the hood of a Midyear.

Intake Manifold

I will rebuild the 1987 Corvette engine and add some accessories. General Motors put together a fuel injected small-block with a Ramjet intake manifold reminiscent of the early fuelie engines. The styling cues came from the earlier fuel injection units with one drawback concerning putting it under the hood of the Midyear. The original fuelie unit had a side-draft throttle body with the air filter mounted on the driver-side inner fender. GM's latest rendition has the throttle body mounted at the front, which creates hood and accessory drive system clearance issues.

Arizona Speed and Marine recognized the potential of this latest Ramjet manifold and re-engineered it to develop the Superjet Dropped Top intake manifold. Aesthetically, they machine fins into the top of the intake to look similar to the original Ramjet intake, circa 1962. The front-mounted throttle body is moved to the driver's side like the early unit. The Superjet Dropped Top unit allows for extra clearance at the front for placement under any Midyear hood. The Superjet system provides the look of the early fuelie unit with all the conveniences of late-model fuel injection.

I had the shop machine into the top of the unit, similar fins to those that the 1963 Fuelie sported. Although the top of the intake is not as wide as the correct 1963 fuelie intake, the look is cool. I won't fool anyone into thinking this is a GM-assembled Midyear, but I will be able to enjoy it.

Although this does not meet NCRS standards, I will have the best-driving,

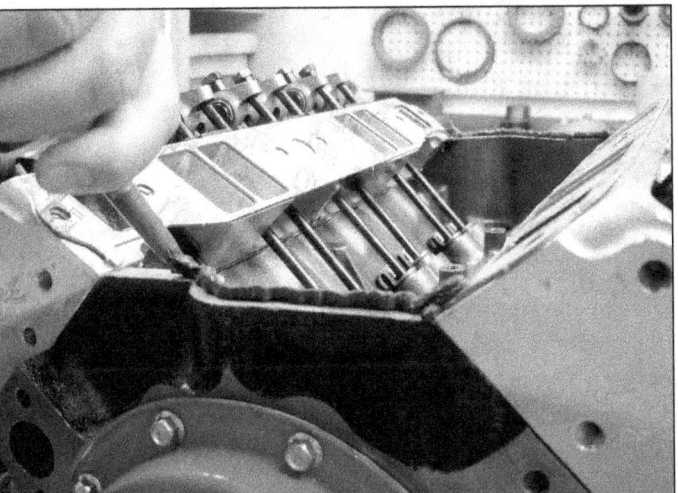

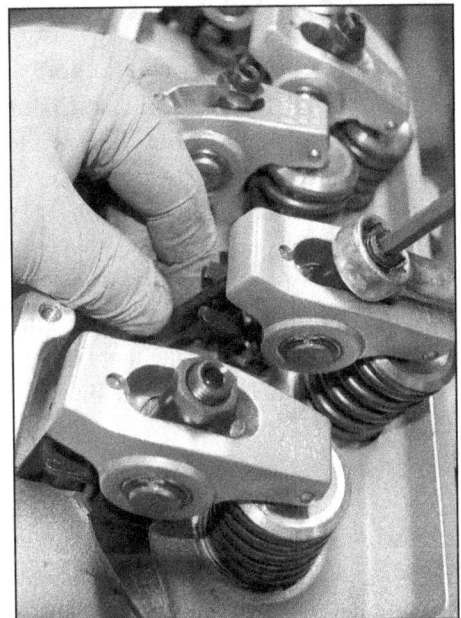

I prefer to adjust hydraulic lifters with the intake manifold off the engine. This allows you to "feel" the adjustment better. You need to find the point when zero lash occurs, and then continue to tighten for 1½ turns. New lifters may not be pumped up fully, allowing you to possibly tighten the rockers too much and push the inner piston downward. Once the engine starts, oil pressure pumps up the lifter preventing the valves from closing fully. Finding an engine miss from tight valves can be a real pain. Usually the engine idles very poorly when the valves are too tight.

Make sure the cylinder and engine block surfaces are clean. Use brake cleaner to remove any oil residue from the surfaces. Use just enough 3M Weatherstrip Adhesive to hold the gaskets in place. Use hot, oil-resistant silicone sealer for the front and rear intake manifold sealing. This is a time-sensitive sealer application, and if the silicone skins over, it does not adhere to the surfaces. Hot summer afternoons give you about 5 minutes from the time the sealer is applied to when the intake should be set in place.

Carefully set the intake in place as close to its installed position as possible. The silicone may allow it to slide around, which is not a good thing. Install two bolts, one in each far corner to keep the intake in the desired installation position. Coat the bolt threads with Permatex Aviation Sealer and install them. Snug the bolts from the center out with a small ratchet or wrench. The final torque for these bolts is 35 ft-lbs.

CHAPTER 6

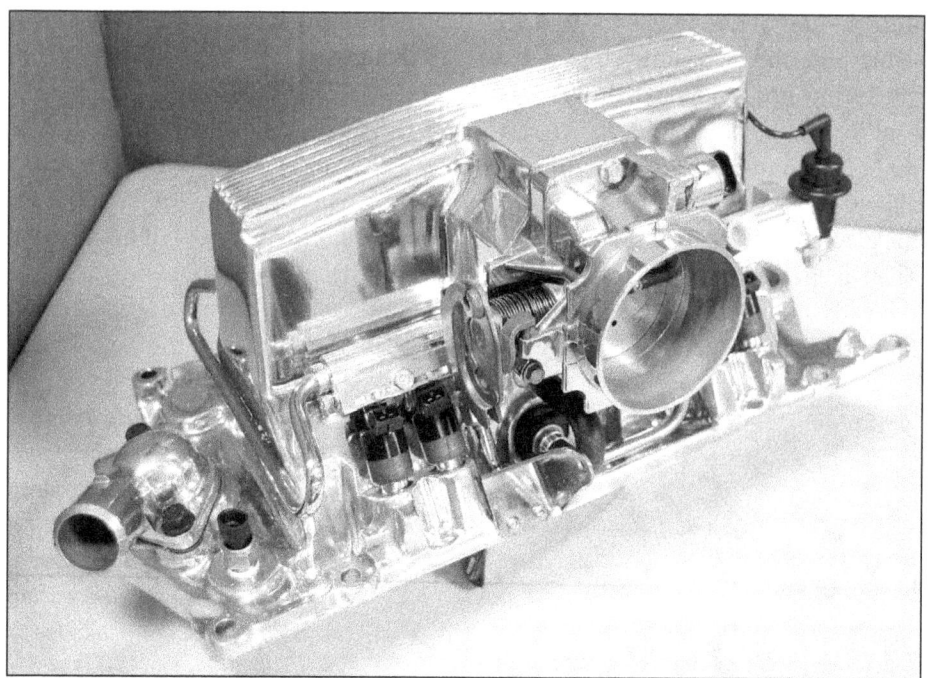

Wow, does this Arizona Speed and Marine "Superjet" Dropped Top intake manifold look cool! The transformation from the original GM Ramjet intake manifold is spectacular. It certainly has the look I wanted for my 1963 coupe project with the side-draft throttle body. There will be plenty of double-takes when the hood is raised because people initially think it has an early fuelie unit. The late-model electronics gives the fuel mileage an early fuelie owner would envy. Quick cold and hot starts can be expected as well with the precision fuel control.

early-appearing Midyear possible with decent fuel mileage. Quick starting in cold or hot weather with all-around top performance can be expected with the electronic fuel injection. The standalone electronic fuel injection does not require major electrical system modifications. If I wanted to put an original engine back in place, it would not be difficult.

General Motors designed the modern small-block Ramjet intake to work only with Vortec cylinder heads. The intake bolt configuration is completely different with eight bolts instead of the traditional 12 bolts of classic small-block heads. As a result, I need Vortec cylinder heads to to use the Ramjet intake. While this is an additional cost, there is a major benefit to the cylinder head change.

Production cylinder heads are typically not known for optimizing airflow. Installing the correct set of cylinder heads can provide a huge horsepower gain. Of all the performance pieces, installing aftermarket cylinder heads is the most beneficial to improving performance. I chose Racing Head Service cylinder heads to couple with the Superjet intake. In spite of the additional cost required to install the Superjet, it makes sense for this complete package to be used. There is plenty of low-end torque with the large intake plenum. These RHS cylinder heads are able to use the fuelie intake's air efficiently and create lots of horsepower on the top end.

Camshaft

As explained earlier, compression is a concern and you need to choose your camshaft wisely. Proper camshaft selection is the key to good power with a manageable idle. I want my Midyear coupe to sound period-correct with a lope at idle. Too often, an overly aggressive camshaft selection delivers poor street performance. This is where restraint is important. Too much camshaft duration and/or overlap causes rough idling. Idle quality is especially important for cars with an automatic transmission. Long-duration camshafts require higher idle speeds and high-stall-speed torque converters to avoid slamming into gear from "Park."

You can either go online or contact an aftermarket camshaft supplier to help select a cam. Camshaft manufacturers ask many questions before selecting a camshaft for you. This is when you want to make sure that you give accurate information to the cam tech who will be making this important decision for you. Listen to his recommendations; they know what works and want you to be happy. My discussion with the cam tech ended with the selection of a Comp Cams camshafts (grind number 268XFIHR13) for plenty of torque with a noticeable idle. I do not want my Midyear to sound and idle like a Cadillac, after all.

Lifters

While this may seem insignificant, the 1987 L-98 engine that I chose has some major advancements over early small-blocks. Roller hydraulic lifters are the number-one advancement; they reduce friction and allow the use of newer oil formulas. Roller hydraulic camshaft conversion kits are costly, so going with an L-98 allows you to save a few bucks but still have roller lifters. Oil leakage is a thing of the past, too, thanks to the one-piece rear main seal and redesigned cylinder head and valve cover.

The cylinder head valve cover mounting rail is higher than on the early cylinder heads, so oil does not soak into the valve cover gaskets while the engine is running. Those early valve cover gaskets are going to leak no matter what quality they are or who installs them.

The Corvette L-98 has a shallow oil pan for better ground clearance, mimicking the Midyear oil pan. From the bottom side, the L-98's pan looks very similar to the original Midyear oil pan. This means that the basic L-98 short block can be used without any changes. If I put an early set of cylinder heads and period-correct intake on this short block, it would perform wonderfully and it would be hard to detect the change. Of course, the numbers guys will know it, but I will enjoy all the benefits of the later engine.

Electronic Control Unit

The Superjet Dropped Top manifold comes with the Delphi MEFI 4B electronic control unit. While this system works fine, you need to buy specific software to tune it with a laptop. I used a Comp Cams F.A.S.T. fuel-injection controller for tuning with my laptop.

Although not necessary, I installed an electric radiator cooling fan, which is also supported by the F.A.S.T. controller. I am able to tune on-the-fly, and if I make changes down the road, I can make the required tuning changes with a few keystrokes. The MEFI controller can be modified if sent away, but I would prefer to be able to do the programming myself and avoid downtime.

I decided not to use the factory harness with the factory computer. General Motors used batch-fired fuel injectors in the early years, which inject fuel whether the intake valve is open or not. This is not very efficient fuel control at low engine speeds. I need to keep the batch-fired fuel injectors in mind when selecting the camshaft. My decision to use an

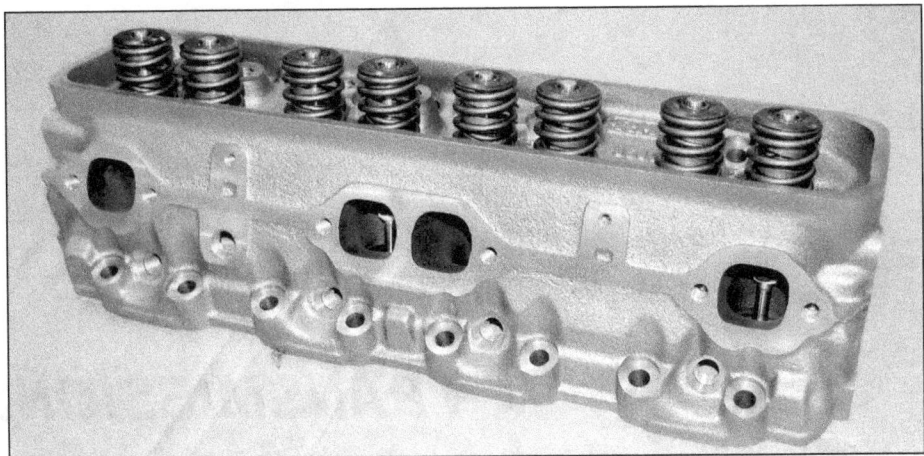

These Racing Head Service Vortec cylinder heads replace the L-98 cylinder heads. For all-around performance the 64-cc combustion chambers with 170-cc intake runners improve airflow, especially at higher RPM. These are early perimeter "Corvette" scripted valve covers that require adapters for the Vortec center bolt heads. The taller outer rail keeps even those early valve covers leak-free.

aftermarket fuel control system allows for a more radical duration camshaft. As you can see, many systems are intertwined, affecting each other.

Crate Engine

Buying a crate engine is a good alternative to rebuilding your original engine—one that can save you time and money. GM Performance Parts has crate engines that range from mundane to real fire breathers. Remanufacturers also have plenty of crate engine options.

Bloomington Gold/NCRS Requirements

Judges look for correct gaskets sticking out from between engine components. If the original gaskets were cork, they had better be cork and the correct color cork, too. For instance, later big-block engines had silver-colored cork valve cover gaskets that had tabs showing. Judges also want to see cork gaskets at the front and rear of the intake.

Judges also look for incorrect bolt heads and their markings during inspection. You should have all the clips and hardware installed per the assembly manual. Exhaust manifold bolts also require the correct markings on their heads. General Motors did not use any gaskets on the exhaust manifolds; instead, it relied on perfectly flat exhaust manifold and cylinder head surfaces to provide an acceptable seal.

Judges do not want to see any gaskets protruding from the exhaust manifolds. Your machine shop can check the exhaust manifold and exhaust manifold cylinder head surfaces and machine them if necessary.

Something as simple as painting the engine requires careful attention. Overspray from painting the engine commonly made its way into intake and exhaust manifolds during the factory build. The bellhousing was installed before the engine was painted, which ended up creating a band of orange due to overspray from the painting process.

CHAPTER 7

Transmissions

Saginaw 3-speed manual transmissions were used in the base model for all the Midyears. The cast-iron case and two shift linkages identify this 3-speed when it is removed from a car. Reportedly, late in the 1963 build year, BorgWarner-built 4-speed transmissions were installed rather than the GM corporate-built Muncie M20 manual 4-speeds. Warner-built 4-speeds have a nine-bolt side cover while all Muncies have a seven-bolt side cover. All of the BorgWarner cases have a distinct rib running parallel to the case mounting pad.

For the next two years, there was one 4-speed option available, the Muncie-built wide-ratio M20 unit. In 1966–1967, two more Muncie 4-speeds were available: the M21 close-ratio and M22 close-ratio, heavy-duty units. The M22 was a heavy-duty version of the M21 with gear sets that were cut on a different helix (gear) angle to lessen the thrust load on the main and input shaft.

The M20 and 21 have an approximate 30-degree angle, while the M22 uses an angle of just over 20 degrees. The straighter-cut, higher-grade nickel alloy teeth produced a whine that was hard to cover up. The M22 was dubbed "Rock Crusher" because of the inherent noise from the 20-degree gear set.

The 1963–1965 M20 4-speeds are wide-ratio gear boxes with 2.56:1 first gear ratios for better launch. The 1966–1967 M20s had a slightly lower numerically ratio of 2.52:1. The wider spread between the remaining gear selections in the M20 worked well with lower-torque engines.

Austin is ready to wrestle this M20 into one of our 1964 Midyear projects. The transmission tailshaft is inserted above the transmission crossmember then pushed back as far as possible. With the correct rotation of the transmission case the input shaft will then barely pass by the bellhousing for installation into the clutch assembly. The upside is that the Muncie gearbox is not extremely heavy.

This late 1963 Muncie case (casting number 3831704) was used for the first batch of M20s. I say late, meaning this was the casting number used after the T10 Warner gearboxes were phased out.

TRANSMISSIONS

Finding any early GM spec T-10 is just about impossible. They were last used in early 1963, then Muncie-built 4-speeds took their place. This beauty was found in a pile of cores at a local transmission shop. The quickest way to distinguish a T10 is the tab near the front of the case at the bottom. The nine-bolt side cover also tells you it is a T10. Additionally, all the cases I have seen have a drain plug.

The M21 and M22 close-ratio boxes had 2.20:1 first gear ratios, making them suitable for big-block engines with plenty of torque. Less spread between the gear changes also suited the big-block's lower-RPM redline and keeps it in (or close to) its powerband from one gear to the next.

Identification

Finding the right numbers-matching transmission components is a game to some. Just remember to remove the transmission's side cover for gear inspection. Keep in mind that the early Muncies have most likely have been disassembled and assembled numerous times with who knows what installed to make them keep going. Expect mismatched pieces internally and externally.

Casting Numbers

The 1963 Muncie cases should have casting number 3831704, while the 1964–1965 cases should have casting number 3851325. Not all 1965 cases have casting 3851325. Some may have casting number 3885010, which was used until 1967. The 1963–1965 cases (3831704 and 3851325) have 7/8-inch-diameter countershaft shafts. All 1966–1967 cases (3885010) should have 1-inch-diameter countershaft shafts. But some things are fuzzy.

The 1963–1965 M20s and M22s should have no identification grooves around the input shaft splines. Supposedly the 1966–1967 M20 has two grooves cut into the input shaft. The 1966–1967 M21s should have one groove cut into the input shaft splines. Early on, the grooves were used to identify the unit during the build sequence, but later on, the practice was stopped.

Over the years many input shafts have been changed, so there is no absolute way to use the rings for identification. All Muncies of the era have 27-spline output shafts. M22s built after 1970 have 26-spline input shafts with 32-spline output shafts.

Unfortunately, the only way to know for sure is to remove the transmission's side cover, and count the teeth on the main drive gear located at the front of the transmission. As you look at the car, the main drive gear is the first gear to your left and is part of the input shaft.

This Muncie case is out of a 1965 coupe. There were two 3851325 castings. One had a round upper bolt boss for 1964. Then in 1965 the case was modified and the upper boss was square. The date code stamped vertically at the rear of the case (to the left of the casting number) is P01 15– "P" for Muncie Plant, "01" for January, "15" for the build day. (Photo Courtesy Ed Hartnett)

The 1963–1965 M20 units should have 24-teeth main drive gears. The 1966–1967 M20s have 21-teeth main drive gears. The M21 and M22 have 26-teeth main drive gears, and straighter-cut teeth distinguish the M22 gears. All other Muncies have the same gear angle, so the best policy is to familiarize yourself with the angle difference by taking a look at a few boxes first. The angle difference is obvious after you have seen some.

Transmissions

In the 1960s, the Powerglide was GM's primary automatic transmission. The popular 2-speed transmission was offered as a Regular Production Option M35 in the Corvette. The Powerglide's 1.76:1 first gear ratio and its torque converter's torque multiplication provided decent off-the-line performance. The unit was very simple to maintain and repair, if necessary.

Not a lot of Midyear Corvette buyers checked option M35 during the ordering process. If you are compelled to rebuild your own Powerglide, there are plenty of publications available to guide you. Due to their popularity on the dragstrip, however, finding a complete and correct Powerglide for a reasonable price can be difficult today.

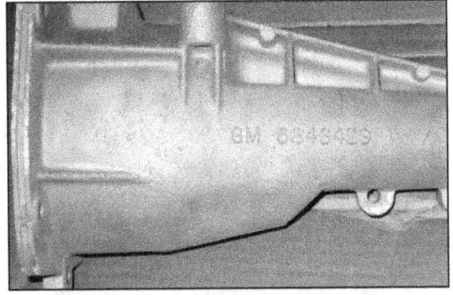

This 3846429 extension housing casting number is correct for a 1964 coupe. Over the years many parts have been replaced due to wear and abuse. Check all major exterior components for correct casting numbers because chances are many are incorrect. (Photo Courtesy Ed Hartnett)

Muncie 4-Speed Setup

Early Muncie transmissions had internal issues that require some extra attention. In the past, I would carefully rebuild an M20, M21, or M22, and then find out I had gear clash on a road test. Bronze blocker rings are used to slow down the rotating gears before the shift occurs, to prevent clashing or grinding. The interior of the blocker rings has a conical shape that fits onto the conical section of the drive gear. Grooves and slots are placed into the inner coned area of the blocker ring to force gear oil from between the gear and blocker ring. If the blocker ring does not grab the gear properly, grinding or clashing occurs.

Poor-fitting replacement synchronizer bronze blocker rings are a common problem, and it's important to recognize it. Poorly constructed off-shore synchronizer blocker rings are suspected. When I used NOS GM rings, I solved my gear clash problem. I also found that if I carefully checked the fit of the blocker ring on the gear, some of the off-shore pieces would work. The casting tolerances of the off-shore rings that I've encountered are much looser than the original Muncie pieces, so choose your pieces carefully. While good quality off-shore pieces are out there, they are tough to find.

Research is the key to finding good-quality parts suppliers, so ask other Corvette owners. NOS pieces are priced at the seller's discretion and are often expensive. It might be worth spending some time fitting and using the offshore synchronizers. You may have to buy two or three sets to find four good-fitting synchro rings.

The early units of 1963–1965 should have later internal gears and synchronizers installed. Many experienced restorers use all the original aesthetic pieces, and then replace all the internal gear assemblies. This is especially sound advice for actively driven 1963–1965 Midyears.

Another Muncie malady is worn main gear cases, particularly in the countershaft shaft support area. The countershaft gear assembly is located in the bottom of the case, and it rides on 112 pin-type roller bearings. The transmission case supports these rollers that ride on a hardened shaft. To keep the gear assemblies in alignment, the countershaft support shaft has an interference fit in the case.

As mentioned earlier, transmission gears have a tapered helical-cut design; as the rotational load is applied to the opposing gears, it forces them apart and outward. This puts an enormous load on the supporting bearings and shafts. Eventually, this load wears the aluminum case, loosening the countershaft support shaft's interference fit in the case.

When the support shaft interference fit becomes sloppy, you end up with a small, tell-tale drip at the countershaft support shaft. The drip shows up at the front of the transmission, between the case and bellhousing. Gear oil passes between the countershaft support shaft and main case. Many temporary fixes have been used over the years such as applying sealer around the shaft. However, the bellhousing doesn't fully cover the shaft seal job, so fluid leakage may be slowed, but it's not resolved.

Wear is going to happen, so replacing the case is the only long-term solution. The loose shaft fit in the case is not good for gear alignment or long-term transmission life. The rear bearing support plate partially covers the countershaft gear support shaft to prevent rotation. As the case wears, the possibility of the shaft rotating increases and in turn damages the rear support plate. Irregular gear wear occurs, causing shifting issues and terrible internal noises. The noise does not mimic the M22 "Rockcrusher" gear whine. The leak is the result of the loose shaft-to-case fit and needs to be addressed.

This loose countershaft support shaft is a difficult problem to solve, especially if you plan on using a numbers-matching early case with one-inch-diameter countershaft gear shaft. The original support hole can be bored and bushed, but you need a skilled machinist to do it and keep the countershaft gear assembly in proper alignment. Riverside Gear offers an aluminum bushing with a new thrust-bushing surface to fix just about any case for reuse. This is a great long-term solution to save your numbers-matching case.

The 1963–1965 7/8-inch countershaft gear assembly can be bored to the later one-inch-diameter support shaft. Machining the case is easy enough at just about any machine shop. The correct one-inch-diameter countershaft and installation pieces are easy to find and to match your original gear set. Be sure to count the teeth on your countershaft gear assembly and replace it with the like amount.

I have applied sealer on the shaft before I seat the shaft in place but I only attempt this with shafts that still require effort to install. Sealing in this manner is very challenging, due to the assembly grease used to keep the countershaft support bearings in place during shaft installation. The area at the front of the case must have every bit of the assembly grease removed and be squeaky clean or the sealer does not work. For added protection, I make sure to clean the bore area about 1/4 inch before the shaft is fully installed.

Then silicone sealer is applied inside the bore area and the shaft is seated. I carefully wipe the silicone around the shaft and bore area to ensure that there is no sealer left behind to prevent the transmission from seating flat on the bellhousing. This is not my preferred method of repair, but it is an inexpensive alternative for good numbers-matching cases.

The ultimate fix to this age-old problem is a new Supercase kit from Autogear. Autogear has designed a plug to positively seal the countershaft support shaft. The case itself is reinforced at the known weak points to permanently prevent flex and leaks. The exterior of the case looks like an original Muncie, aside from the casting and date codes. If you are not hung up on originality, this is the case for you.

In the past, Autogear had an overdrive gear set available for Muncies, to make them a 3-speed with overdrive. The .82 overdrive gear set was in limited supply, however, at the time this was written. I am hesitant to say whether the gear sets will be available in the near future or ever again. If they do become available, you could have an original, matching-numbers Muncie case with overdrive. The .82 does not make a substantial drop in engine RPM, though. If you choose the 2.52:1 first gear and have a 3.36:1 differential gear ratio, you would still have good acceleration. You could be cruising at 70 mph with the engine at 2,000 rpm.

Silicone sealer came be found on many Muncies at the countershaft bore area. You can be pretty well assured this case was leaking due to a loose-fitting countershaft. This is a temporary fix and the leak will reappear unless the loose shaft fit is resolved.

The Autogear Supercase is the ultimate fix for the original weak Muncie case. High-strength aluminum alloy with increased case thickness allows better bearing support. Best of all the countershaft leak dilemma has been solved with a specific case plug. (Photo Courtesy Autogear)

Manual and automatic transmissions have the same requirements for NCRS and Bloomington Gold certifications. Do not be surprised if a judge crawls under the middle of your Midyear to see if the numbers are correct. At some national NCRS events, they even put Corvettes on a lift to verify as much as possible.

Given the Corvette's performance use, the majority of Muncie transmissions have been rebuilt numerous times. If your plan is to use the original gearbox, check its numbers carefully.

Unless it was an NCRS restoration, it's unlikely a Saginaw 3-speed would be put back into a Midyear Corvette, though the restoration of one is similar to that of Muncie 4-speeds. BorgWarner transmissions have a few differences that are easy to understand, compared to the Muncie, during a restoration.

Manual transmissions require very few special tools. The Muncie's unique, thin front bearing retainer nut requires a special wrench. Corvette Central has the extra-thin steel wrench available (PN 532117) that can remove a very tight nut. A pair of good snap-ring pliers, typical sockets and wrenches are used to disassemble and assemble the unit. The tough part is removal and installation of the manual transmissions' bearings. Your

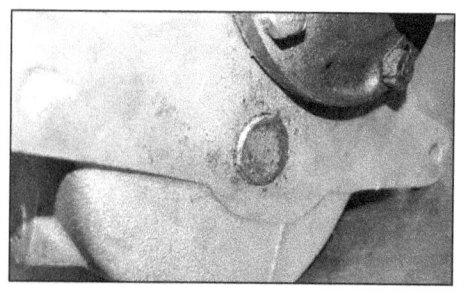

local machine shop has made an investment in expensive service equipment and are well-versed in the use of hydraulic presses and bearing removal equipment. By the end of the project, you will be on a first-name basis with your local

I hadn't seen this before. The countershaft support shaft did not allow the case to sit flat on the bellhousing. As the transmission retaining bolts were tightened, the bellhousing must have been under enormous pressure. Who knows what angle the input shaft was at in relationship to the engine crankshaft? Vibration, anyone?

machine shop.

Intimate knowledge of the common issues plaguing vintage 4-speed manual transmissions can take plenty of years to acquire. Test drive your Corvette to determine the problems and to establish a base-line before disassembling any component. If you have any concerns during the test drive, record them.

Disassembly

Removing the transmission is simple enough, once you sneak it by the bellhousing. When I pulled this 1964 transmission out, I noticed that it appeared to be spring loaded when the transmission-to-bellhousing bolts were removed. Strange for sure; the countershaft gear assembly support shaft was protruding out past the case surface.

Remove Side Cover

1 *I found only one correct "TR" marked bolt head holding the side cover in place. Be careful with these original pieces. Use a sharp-bladed scraper to break the gasket bond for side cover removal. Many of the covers are gouged and beat-up from the many times someone has repaired the assembly. If the cover gasket does not break loose, use the scraper to gently pry at least three other areas.*

Remove Extension Housing

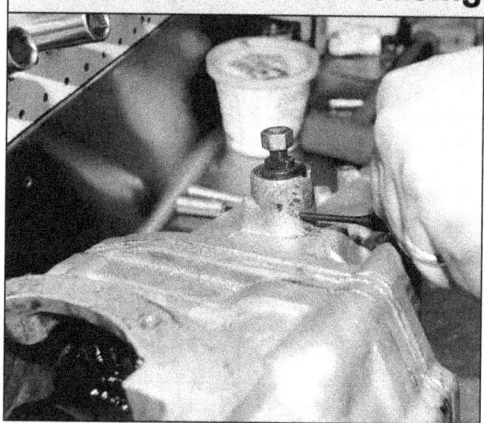

2 *The reverse gear shift shaft retaining pin must be removed to free up the linkage and remove the extension housing. The solid, tapered pin must be driven up from the bottom of the transmission extension housing or bad things can happen. Once the pin has been removed, the shift shaft pulls upward, releasing the shift lever from the reverse gear.*

Remove Reverse Shift Linkage

3 *The extension housing takes some finesse to remove the reverse shift linkage from the reverse gear. I usually roll the transmission onto the side cover side to let the linkage pull away from the reverse gear. From the looks of things the yoke must have been out and water was nearby, causing rust to form on the output shaft.*

Remove Reverse Idler Shaft and Gear Assembly

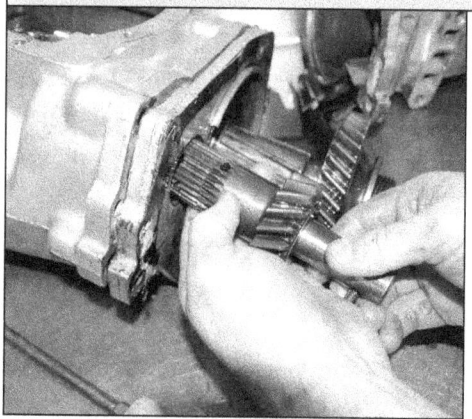

4 *Now take the reverse idler shaft and gear assembly from the case; it is a slip-fit into the main case. The idler shaft goes in and rides on the countershaft for reverse operation.*

Remove Input Bearing Retainer

5 Bend back the French lock tabs to allow removal of the bearing retainer bolts. New French locks are available; replace them every time. I found a mangled bearing retainer nut when I removed the input shaft retainer housing. The nut was also flipped over and installed incorrectly. You cannot remove the input shaft from this side with the cover off; however, it allows enough movement to remove the mainshaft.

Remove Mainshaft from Case

6 The mainshaft came out of the case as an assembly with a little wiggling. Moving the one-two synchronizer ring toward the front of the case gives some room to move the assembly straight back out of the input shaft. The main drive gear set goes like this, starting from the left. Third gear sits next to second gear, then the synchronizer sleeve, with first gear at the mid-plate.

Remove Countershaft Gear Assembly Support Shaft

7 Tap on the countershaft gear assembly support shaft with a hammer to loosen it. Surprisingly, the shaft fit tighter in the case than expected. Some transmission guys remove the countershaft support shaft before attempting to remove the mainshaft. The countershaft gear assembly drops down to give additional clearance. I do not use that procedure, because when you assemble the transmission, there are a lot of things to juggle. Placing the shaft into the countershaft gear assembly often takes some time and patience to get it to fit.

Remove Speedometer Gear Drive

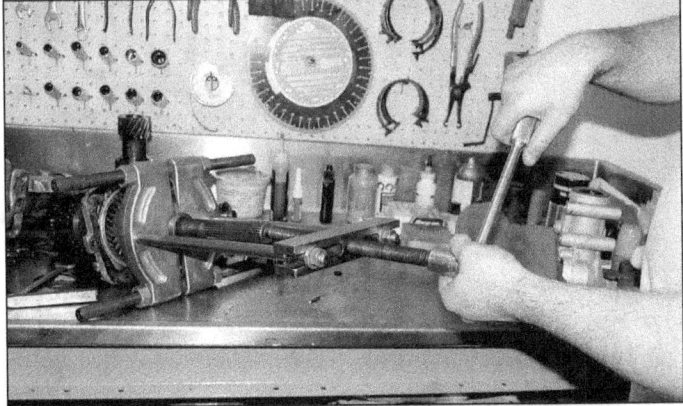

8 This is the correct way to remove this bruised and battered speedometer drive gear. I have a hefty investment in these two Mac tools for one measly gear removal. On a positive note this same puller assembly can be used to remove the front bearing from the input shaft. The puller has three sets of bolts to allow for differing depths making it very versatile for any bearing you may need to remove without the expense of a hydraulic press. I am not too proud to say in the old days we used a hammer to remove the speedo gear when gears were plentiful and cheap. The problem was those gears stuck sometimes, and there were few other alternatives.

CHAPTER 7

Remove Mid-plate

9 Use a good pair of compound snap-ring pliers to squeeze the snap ring to the fully opened position. Capture the rear bearing in the mid-plate with the snap ring. Once the snap ring is expanded, tap off the plate. This is one of those "if I had three hands this would be much easier" situations. Once the plate is tapped back far enough, you can let go of the snap ring. I use a Snap-On plastic hammer for the tapping process to avoid damage to the soft aluminum. Do not kid yourself; the plastic hammer can still do some damage. Tap the plate evenly to avoid cocking it and getting it really stuck.

Remove Rear Bearing

10 What a mess! The compound snap-ring pliers make easy work of the rear bearing removal. Snap ring pliers wear at the tips making them very aggravating to use at times. Snap rings can also hurt you when the energy is released unexpectedly; for example, if the ring slips off the tips and comes at you.

Remove Rear Bearing (Continued)

11 With a plastic hammer, note how tight the rear bearing is on the shaft. Like the front bearing, the well-worn rear bearing should come off easily with just a few taps. If necessary you can use a hydraulic press.

Remove Third Gear and Synchronizer

12 One more snap ring to remove. Now this one can get you if it gets loose from the pliers. Sometimes the snap ring is tight in the grooves requiring a slight tap on the tips either way to free it. Put light tension on the snap-ring pliers while tapping to avoid an unexpected snap ring flying in the air. One modification for your workbench is to cut a 2½ inch hole in the top to allow shafts to protrude. This makes work much easier during assembly or disassembly.

Keep it Clean and Organized

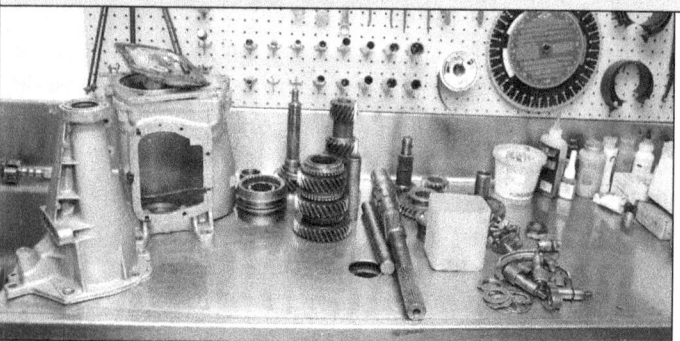

13 During disassembly, it is difficult to keep things clean and organized. Now is when organization is important to prevent missed or extra pieces during assembly. All parts were cleaned in a mineral-spirits wash tank and scrubbed with stainless-steel brushes. Compressed air was used to make sure no debris was left behind. Wiping internal pieces with shop rags or any rag for that matter is not a good practice. Fibers from the rags are left behind and stick to the rough surfaces. This is hypercritical when dealing with automatic transmissions.

Inspection

This is the most important part of the entire transmission restoration process, so don't rush through it. You have one chance to find, repair, or replace the necessary pieces correctly. Sometimes, a worn or failed piece can damage other newly-installed pieces and this is the time to find it. Inspect all parts and threaded holes carefully because these become corroded and torn up in the soft aluminum housings.

I usually install Heli-coils, which are stainless-steel windings that are inserted into the stripped or damaged holes, renewing the threads. Now that all the pieces are ready, I can assemble the transmission. The typical wear items are replaced: ball bearings, countershaft support shaft needle bearings, and thrust washers. These wear items are included in any rebuilder's "small parts kit." The big parts can sometimes hurt financially, especially the replacement of the countershaft gear assembly. Using a good original gear assembly can cost as much as the reproduction pieces. Try to buy the majority of pieces at one supplier as they are more apt to work with you on price.

Bad omen perhaps? None of the fasteners are correct including the washers and only one of the original 5/18-18 bolts were in place. The shift shaft seals had been leaking and most likely they were the originals. Many rebuilders do not go the extra few steps and replace all the seals, even though they come in each rebuild kit. When you find incorrect fasteners and an overall shoddy paint job it makes you wonder what lies ahead.

All too often this input shaft bearing retainer nut is installed incorrectly as shown here. The input shaft bearing retainer nut has a collar on the outside to keep gear oil from leaking out onto the clutch assembly. The correct installation of this crucial retainer is shown on page 102. What this does tell me is that the previous rebuilder was not well versed in how a Muncie four speed was assembled and I had better be on guard.

The speedometer gear and fitting was also painted as an assembly from the previous build. It appears that all of the main case pieces were painted with little regard for the dirt and grease under the shiny aluminum paint. This "aerosol overhaul" approach to any major component is a red flag; most likely short cuts were taken. I look extra careful at all the components when so many obvious suspect rebuild techniques are present. Bloomington Gold nor NCRS would accept components that look like these shown as originals or correct overhauls.

Check Countergear Shaft Fit

1 If you want to use your original case, check the shaft fit after disassembly. You may think that the shaft has plenty of interference fit with the bearings and countershaft gear assembly in place. Once the shaft has been removed and the gear assembly is out of the way, check the fit. The shaft should just start into the front end of the case and require considerable force to push it in further. Use a ball-peen hammer to tap it into place.

Examine Countergear First Gear

2 Metal "gremlins" have eaten away at the countershaft first gear drive area of the teeth. It is very important to look at first gear on the main shaft for similar damage. This causes a growling noise when in first gear (but not like an M-22, unfortunately). The reverse idler gear rides on the same area as the first gear teeth. Reverse is on the left side of the area; you can see the distinct line between the gears showing.

Examine Synchro Blocker Ring

3 To prevent the possibility of gear clash, check the fit of every synchronizer blocker ring before assembly. Synchronizer ring top land fit is extremely important and many times brand-new rings are too loose or tight right out of the box. This means that the lubricant cannot be forced out from between the blocker ring and gear quickly enough and gear clash occurs. Cone mismatch synchronizer rings are another problem. The taper from the synchronizer ring to the gear does not match properly, and the fit may be tight at the top or bottom. You should have at least 90-percent contact on the taper. Use a set of feeler gauges to check the outer fit of the bronze blocker ring to the drive gear. There should be at least .025-inch clearance between them.

4 You can see scuff marks where the blocker ring scrubbed on the drive gear. The cone fit was loose enough so grinding occurred whenever there was any quick shifting. As unbelievable as this may seem, the metal tapered section of the drive gears do wear. Make sure you check the fit of the new blocker ring on the old gear; do not assume everything is alright.

Inspect Synchro Ring

5 This is a synchronizer ring from a transmission that was jumping out of gear every time the throttle was released or applied quickly. Synchronizer rings engage a gear on either side of the gear depending on what gear is selected. The tapered synchronizer ring engagement teeth force the drive gear teeth out, causing the jumping. On the other side of the synchronizer ring, you can see the engagement teeth are straight and this is what you need for positive shifting action. Pay attention to the engagement teeth and check them for flat spotting. This photograph of the rust/corrosion in the gear teeth shows you what happens when the gear oil is not changed for many years.

Replace Side Cover

6 This correct-casting side cover (PN 3831707) replaced a well-worn incorrect casting. It was used from 1963 through 1965 and has a non-shouldered pivot pin for the detent system. Later 1966-1967 covers (casting number 3884685) had shouldered pivot pins to keep them tight in the casting.

Here is a tell-tale sign of not clocking the countershaft support shaft position properly during installation. The countershaft support shaft produced this crescent-shaped wear spot on the mounting flange below the casting and date codes. The countershaft support shaft has a similar raised section on the end, and that should have been rotated during installation. The crescent-shaped raised area sits inside the recess and prevents shaft rotation. This is why the support shaft was sticking out too far at the front of the case, which was found during disassembly. For some reason the mid-plate was not damaged as it forced the support shaft beyond where it should go. The gaskets were leaking, and that is why there was not enough pressure on the gasket.

Replace Bearings

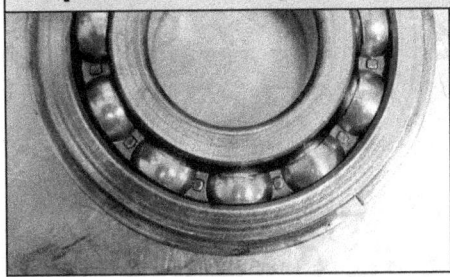

7 This front bearing assembly is so worn out that the ball bearing retainer has been wearing on the inner race as it rolls. Ball bearings should not be tight like a tapered bearing; there should be some radial movement. When the bearing race is this loose, everything that comprises the bearing wears and requires replacement. The front bearing depends on the pilot bearing or bushing in the crankshaft to keep the correct alignment. This is why replacing and maintaining a good pilot bearing/bushing is important. You can imagine the amount of centrifugal forces applied from the spinning clutch disc as the clutch is disengaged trying to push the input shaft off-center.

Inspect Reverse Gear

8 These reverse-drive and driven-gear teeth look rough, but surprisingly enough this is typical wear and there is no reason to be concerned. The unsynchronized reverse gear set takes a lot of abuse as it tries to stop the spinning input shaft. Once you drive early Corvettes, you realize it is always a good idea to put the transmission in first gear before going into reverse. This stops the input shaft from spinning so the reverse gears can engage smoothly with minimal grinding. If you still have problems shifting into reverse there are a couple of possible reasons. A sticky pilot bearing/bushing can exacerbate the grind going into reverse. Oil- or grease-contaminated clutch discs do not let go after disengaging the clutch. Warped pressure plates or broken springs also keep the input shaft spinning during the shift.

Assembly

If you decide to use an original transmission and shifter, remember to restore the complete assembly, including the shifter. All too often, I find freshly restored transmissions with gummed-up, worn-out shifters that result in complaints from the owner. Missed gear shifts in which you get stuck between two gears are telling you the shifter is worn. The shifter is exposed to all the elements: water, sand, oil, and grease. Grit-filled oil and grease wear away at the shifter, loosening components.

On a positive note, today you can find all the pieces to restore the original shifter. Zip Products has a kit (PN ST-378) to bring the shifter back to new condition. All the common wear items are included, along with a new shifter ball and reverse T-handle. The rebuild process is not difficult and is well worth the effort. Of course, you have the option of using an aftermarket shifter, which is more durable and smoother to use.

If you do not feel comfortable tearing into your 4-speed gear box, you can crate it up and send it to a rebuild shop for service. Ed Hartnett has spent many years researching and rebuilding these early transmissions. If necessary, Hartnett can supply you with a ready-to-bolt-in unit. Ed was good enough to help with many of the photos for this section and kept me straight on what casting number meant what. This is the person you want building your transmission for a daily driver or a Bloomington Gold-certified Midyear.

All late-model transmissions use different gear oil formulas. None of the late-model transmissions used today call for 90W gear oil; light-viscosity oils are the norm. Look for 90W gear oil with the designation GL5 MT1. There are plenty of gear oils without the MT1, but it is very important for any early manual transmission, as MT1 denotes its compatibility with bronze synchronizer rings.

None of the major transmission restorers or suppliers recommend synthetic lubricants for the Muncie or Warner gear box. Synthetic lubes are too slippery, causing gear clash. If you use a late-model transmission, use the recommended fluid for that transmission.

Assemble Countershaft Gear Assembly

1 This is the countershaft gear assembly roller bearing layout. The long inner spacer loads the rollers from the inside. Then one row of needle bearings are placed in a circle inside the countershaft gear followed by a thin spacer washer. The next row of bearings is installed then another spacer finishes the load at one end. Yes, that is the bad countershaft gear assembly; the replacement hasn't arrived yet.

Assemble Countershaft Gear Assembly
(Continued)

2 Once you load a few of these countershaft gear assemblies it becomes easy to finish the assembly. Use automatic transmission assembly lube (similar to petroleum jelly) to hold the rollers in place during the process. The coloring helps distinguish whether the rebuilt component is leaking or there is just residual lubricant. Special assembly shafts have slightly smaller diameters than the countershaft support shaft to load the bearings easier. I have heard people using a correct-diameter broom stick, for example, to load the bearings. With care they can be loaded in this manner.

Assemble Synchronizer Assembly

3 These synchronizer hubs show you the right way to install the blocker ring key springs. Springs are used to put pressure on the keys that fit in the machined recesses. The keys extend into the blocker rings to prevent them from spinning. The keys have a raised area in their center to engage in the center of the synchronizer ring. This keeps the synchronizer ring centered away from the blocker rings while the gear set is in neutral. If the spring is installed (left), there is one key with no tension. Worse yet is if the spring were like those on the other side of the hub. There would be pressure only on one side of the key. The loose key could cause binding during shifting. Smooth shifting is difficult if the springs are incorrect.

Install Case Thrust Washers

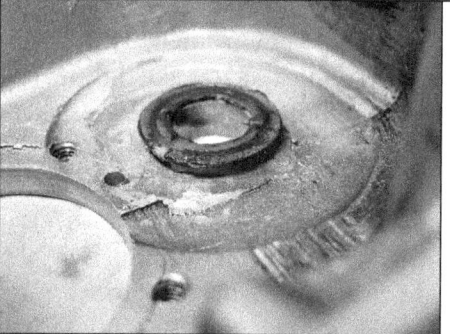

4 Use transmission assembly lube to stick the thrust washer onto the case pad area for the countershaft gear assembly. There is another thrust washer for the other side supplied in the small parts kit that gets the same treatment. Both of the thrust washers have tabs that keep them from spinning in the housing. Make sure the thrust washer tabs are orientated correctly and the washer is sitting flat on the case.

Install Countershaft Gear Assembly

5 Place the countershaft gear assembly into the case in preparation of shaft installation. Take care to avoid pushing the thrust washers out of place that you just installed. In the event that the washer gets pushed off-center, make sure it easily goes back into position. If there is any force required the thrust washer's tab is out of the slot and must be rotated until it slips back into place.

Install Countershaft Support Shaft

6 Use extreme care when installing the countershaft support shaft. It must be pushed through all the needle bearings and spacers without knocking any of them out of place. The thrust washers must be in position before the shaft is tapped into place. Always check to see if any rollers are left on the bench before setting the shaft in the case. If you find any loose needles, you have to figure out where they came from and put them back in place. Note the raised crescent area on top of the shaft's position. This area has a straight line that should be running horizontally. The shaft's horizontal line is when the transmission is installed in the car.

Assemble Mainshaft

7 The mainshaft is assembled next, starting with second gear and synchronizer assembly. To save some aggravation, look carefully at how the hubs are orientated to the outer synchronizer rings. This synchronizer assembly has the flat part of the hub pointed upward. The outer ring has the tapered portion facing upward. This is the assembly that goes between first and second gear.

Install First Gear Bearing Collar

8 This first gear bearing collar fits snugly but you should be able to push it on. The collar should bottom out against the synchronizer hub and mainshaft. Once in a while, you need to use a heat gun to heat these collars, and then they drop in place with no trouble. Do not use a torch because the excessive heat damages the bearing surface.

Install Rear Bearing and Blocker Ring

9 Slip the bearing on after first gear, and then install the blocker ring. You can apply heat to the bearing to prevent the use of the hammer, but you may have to give the bearing a little help with a small hammer and punch to get it in place.

Seat Snap Ring

10 This simple procedure can save you plenty of grief. Make sure the snap ring is fully seated in the groove. Use a small pin-point chisel to give the ring a little nudge.

Install Third/Fourth Gear Synchro

11 With the mainshaft pointed upward, set the third/fourth synchronizer assembly in place. Note that the synchronizer inner hub has the raised area pointing upward with the synchronizer outer ring taper also pointing upward. When you are installing the synchronizer assemblies, pay attention to where the blocker ring slots are for the synchronizer keys. The slots must correspond with the keys or the hubs do not seat properly. Install the snap ring and check it to make sure it is fully seated in the groove.

Install Input Shaft Roller Bearings

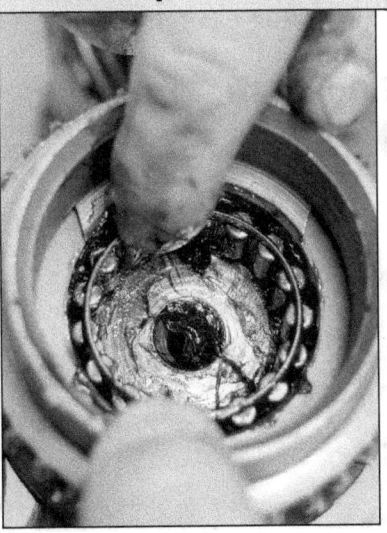

12 It's a bit of a trick to install the input shaft roller bearings into the race using assembly lube. The race is then installed in the input shaft with plenty of assembly lube to keep it from falling out. The assembly lube works much better on a cool day, as hot days tend to melt it.

Prepare Mainshaft for Installation

13 The mainshaft assembly is ready for installation after carefully placing the input shaft on the mainshaft. Note the brass blocker ring is installed in the synchronizer assembly sitting flush with the outer synchronizer ring. This is how all the synchronizers should sit if the keys are aligned. Rotate all the driven gears to make sure there are no binding issues.

Install Mainshaft into Case

15 This method of inserting the mainshaft assembly into the case works easily. The mainshaft assembly is in the bench-top cutout hole for stability. Lower the case onto the shaft assembly. As you did during disassembly, place the synchronizer rings in the fourth and second gear position to help get the center line of the gear set close to the countershaft gear assembly.

Install Reverse Shift Shaft

Install Reverse Drive Gear

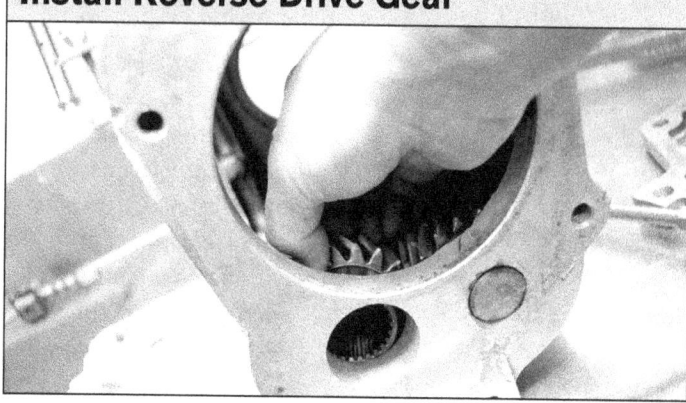

14 Before proceeding, the reverse drive gear must be installed. The gear has a flat side that goes toward the front of the case. Use assembly lube to install the reverse drive gear thrust washer in the same manner as the countershaft gear assembly washers.

Install Bearing on Front Input Shaft

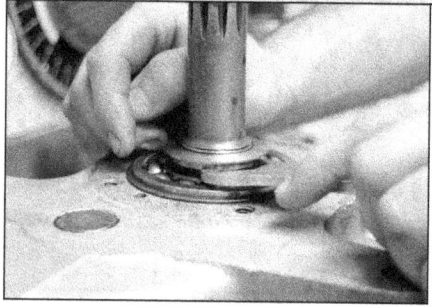

16 Once the mainshaft is in place and the midplate is sitting flat on the case, install the front bearing onto the input shaft. All Muncie transmissions lack a front input shaft seal, and therefore the gear oil is held back with a specially designed nut that fits closely to the front bearing retainer. Installing the nut for the first time can fool even an experienced mechanic. The nut flats used for tightening it are on the inside requiring a special wrench for proper tightening. Another important aspect of this particular information is that overfilling the transmission can be disastrous. Gear oil is forced onto the clutch disc and pressure plate. When that happens, you almost always need to remove the transmission and clutch to clean up the mess. Warner transmissions has a snap ring with a seal in the input shaft housing.

17 This reverse shift shaft can be tricky to install. The detent ball protruding out of the housing rides on the shifter shaft. When the shaft is installed the ball must be pushed down while the shaft is pushed past the ball. Once the shaft is installed with the detent ball in place the shaft is bottomed out against the case for reverse shift dog installation. Once the extension housing is in place push the reverse shifter shaft inward engaging the reverse gear.

TRANSMISSIONS

Repair Shifter Assembly

18 These early shifters are easy to disassemble and repair. The C-clip on the right pops off, the pin comes out, and the levers are loose. The housing that keeps the shift levers together spreads from rough shifting. The extra play lets the stick go between the levers causing "stuck between two gears" syndrome. Place the housing in the vise and flatten it out to reduce the play between the levers. Make it as tight as possible without binding the shift levers.

Install Shifter and Linkage Rods

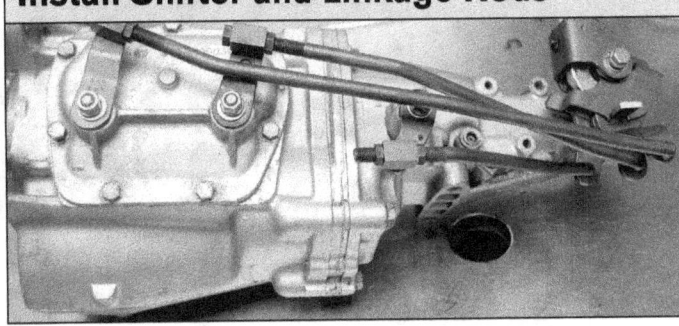

19 Install the shifter and linkage rods while the transmission is on the bench, to save you a big hassle later. The shifter requires a flat-adjustment gauge, available at Zip Products (PN ST-406) for a couple bucks. Place the gauge in the shifter gate and adjust the linkages accordingly. At this stage, worn pieces typically give you a tough time. Every time you shift the transmission the neutral gate feel changes because of the sloppy linkage and shifters. This shift linkage is in decent condition so I am going to replace the shift levers at the transmission to tighten things up. Only one shift lever is correct and it is worn out. I will remove the shifter for transmission installation.

Repair Case with Heli-coils

Installing Helicoils should be part of your repertoire when restoring any Midyear Corvette. These handy little wire coils bring back life to many components that otherwise would be sent to the scrap heap. Helicoils can be used in any cast iron, steel, aluminum, or pot metal component.

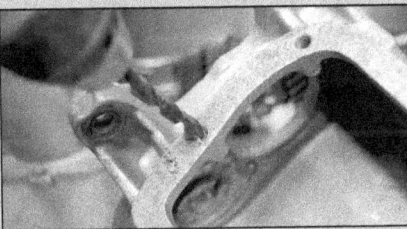

Aluminum case plus age equals the insertion of many Heli-coils. Heli-coil installation starts with drilling the proper oversize hole. Be sure to use the recommended drill bit, not just one that looks like it works. Use cutting lubricant during the drilling process. Most hardware stores have specific cutting lubes for aluminum. The waxy cutting lubricant prevents aluminum from smearing and overheating during the drilling.

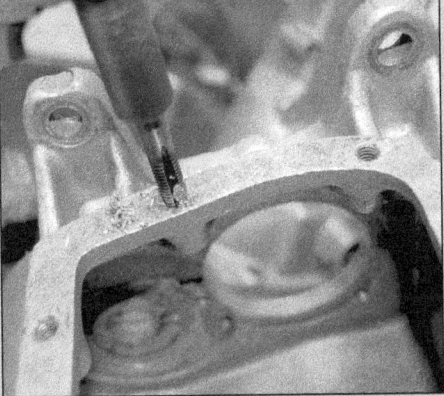

Tap the hole with the proper Heli-coil tap for the 5/16-18 thread insert. As with the drilling process, apply lubricant to the tap. Back the tap off every couple of revolutions to clear the chips. Wash the threaded hole and blow out any chips with compressed air.

Install the 5/16-18 Heli-coil thread insert with the supplied installer. Heli-coil kits are inexpensive and available at most hardware stores. Install Heli-coils in all of the case's threaded holes. This way you know that the case is leak-proof and there are no surprises of stripped threads.

CHAPTER 7

Transmission Options

If you're on a tight budget, an overdrive transmission and matching differential gear set makes sense. If you need to, scale back your engine plans to save a few bucks for a late-model overdrive transmission. Putting the money in the correct transmission and differential gear set choice makes driving your vintage Corvette more enjoyable.

Driving a Corvette with the original transmission on long road trips is not very comfortable. As you approach highway speeds in a 1963–1967 Corvette, the tachometer needle is between 3,200 to 4,000 rpm, depending on the differential gear ratio, and you wonder where the overdrive gear is on the knob. Try to carry on a conversation in a '60s-era vehicle as you rumble down the highway and you find out just how frustrating it is.

There are other benefits to the lower engine RPM: Engine wear is minimized, as is heat produced by the engine, which keeps the under-hood area cooler. Rubber components live longer with the lower engine compartment temperatures, which is a benefit for both the driver and vehicle.

It is very important to consider all the factors before choosing any drivetrain component. Engine, transmission, differential gearing, and tire diameter choices need to be included in your equation, before the first component is purchased.

Keisler, for example, has a really neat speed analyzer that allows you to compare what you have against the overdrive offerings. The beauty of the Keisler RS gear box is that it is available in one complete, engineered package. All hardware is included; fluid is the only additional purchase you need to make. If, by chance, a Powerglide transmission is in place, Keisler has a kit to install the RS. The correct pedals, clutch pressure plate, and disc with clutch linkage are included.

Tremec TKO 500 and 600 transmissions have become popular retrofits for Midyear Corvettes to add an overdrive gear to slow down cruising RPM. These units work well, but you can expect rubbing or very close clearances at the upper portions of the transmission tunnel. 1963 Midyears have the tightest fit with the body sitting directly on the chassis which creates rub points when using the Tremec TKO units.

Keisler Automotive has many available gear ratios in their RS transmission line-up. RS600 has a 2.80:1 first gear with .67:1 overdrive ratio. The 2.80:1 first gear ratio works perfectly behind higher torque or large-cubic-inch engines. The RS500 and RS400 has a 3.37:1 first gear ratio to get low-torque-output engines moving. All of the RS transmissions have the .67:1 overdrive ratio. FYI: the 400, 500, and 600 denote maximum torque loads that the respective transmission should handle.

Another choice is a Richmond 5-speed transmission, utilizing a 1:1 final drive. Its low 3.28:1 first gear provides excellent acceleration even with just a 3.08:1 differential gear set, which drops your cruising RPM approximately 1,000 rpm compared to a 4.11:1 differential. The Richmond 5-speed box has close gear ratios for quick shifting: Second gear is 2.13:1, third is 1.57:1, fourth is 1.24:1 and fifth is 1:1. The Richmond gearbox uses an external shifter, like the original Muncie or Warner shifter.

The Richmond gearbox, however, requires some engineering on your part. Richmond supplies the transmission, shifter, yoke, and speedometer gears at an additional cost. You have to come up with the crossmember and all hardware, and your driveshaft requires shortening and balancing. You may also want to consider the torque load requirements: the Richmond is rated to 450 ft-lbs.

There are also alternatives if you would rather not shift through the gears. The GM 700R4 automatic overdrive can be installed in place of the 4-speed or Powerglide 2-speed. General Motors welded all 1963–1967 transmission crossmembers in place. The 700R4 automatic overdrive can be shoehorned in place without cutting out the transmission crossmember;

Gearing Choices

While I have been extolling the virtues of having an overdrive transmission, there are gearing choices to consider. To put this into perspective here are a few examples of the cruising engine RPM you can expect:

RS400/500
- 3.37:1 first gear ratio
- 3.36:1 differential ratio
- 2,000 cruising RPM at 70 mph
- first gear accelerates like a 4.49:1 differential gear

RS600
- 2.80:1 first gear ratio
- 3.36 differential ratio
- 2,000 cruising RPM at 70 mph
- first gear accelerates like a 3.73:1 differential gear

The Muncie/Warner gearbox would have you cruising at 50 mph with nowhere near the same acceleration as either RS gear box. Here are some Tremec TKO options and how they work:

TKO 500 5-speed (wide ratio)
- First gear ratio 3.27:1, Second 1.98:1, Third 1.34:1, Fourth 1:1, Fifth 0.68:1
- 3.36:1 differential gear ratio
- First gear performs like a 4.36:1 differential gear
- 2,000 cruising RPM at 68 mph

The 3:27:1 first gear helps get small-cubic-inch Corvettes rolling quickly, and then a major drop to second gear occurs. Wide torque band engine performance is required to avoid flat spots in acceleration.

TKO 600
- First gear ratio 2.87:1, Second 1.89:1, Third 1.28:1, Fourth 1:1, Fifth 0.64:1
- 3.36:1 differential gear ratio
- First gear performance feels like a 3.82:1 differential gear
- 2,000 cruising RPM at 72 mph.

TKO 600s work well with larger-cubic-inch engines producing high-torque output. First gear is usable in parking lot maneuvering and low-speed city driving.

There is another TKO 600 available with a .82 overdrive ratio. The lower overdrive ratio benefits engines that have long-duration camshafts that require higher RPM highway cruising speeds. All other ratios are identical to the .64:1 TKO 600. At 2,000 rpm you cruise at 56 mph using the 3.36:1 differential gear set. At 2,500 rpm you cruise at 70 mph using the same 3.36:1 differential gear set.

---

the trick is getting the transmission in place without removing the engine.

This is where planning pays off. While the frame is being prepped for assembly, a removable crossmember can be fabricated. In my shop, I have duplicated the factory automatic transmission removable crossmember mounts. This allows a factory removable crossmember from a later automatic transmission Corvette to be installed.

Besides the obvious benefits of not shifting an automatic transmission, you have another acceleration tool to work with. Automatic transmission torque converters have multiple stall speeds available to enhance performance. Stall speed refers to the point at which the torque converter has minimal slip. Raising the stall speed helps off-the-line acceleration.

If you decide to use a 700R4 with a high-stall converter that retains the lock-up clutch, you have the best of both worlds: great acceleration with no torque converter slippage while cruising. The torque converter clutch is a hydraulically actuated clutch piston that couples the input and output sides of the converter, eliminating slippage. Now, the decision is yours—automatic or manual?

My 1963 Corvette coupe project car will receive a Keisler-prepped T45RS overdrive transmission with the correct differential gear set to match. Over the last few years, the trend has been to enjoy your ride. That is my angle; I want to sport the body of a 54-year-old with new running gears. I figured my engine would be spinning at 2,000 rpm with a T45RS overdrive transmission spinning the 3.36:1 differential gear ratio at 70 mph. Using this formula allows me to get the best fuel mileage possible while enjoying around-town driving.

There are modifications required to make the transmission swap, but the upside is they are reversible, if need be. Now is the time to make a major change. I can fit every component for a dry run, so to speak, before the final installation and painting.

CHAPTER 8

DRIVELINE

Engines, transmissions, and driveline components are subjected to considerable wear and abuse. Inexperienced drivers cause driveline abuse, especially in manual transmission cars. Aggressive driving also takes a toll on all the components. Restoration after 50 years of use is the only way to bring back like-new performance.

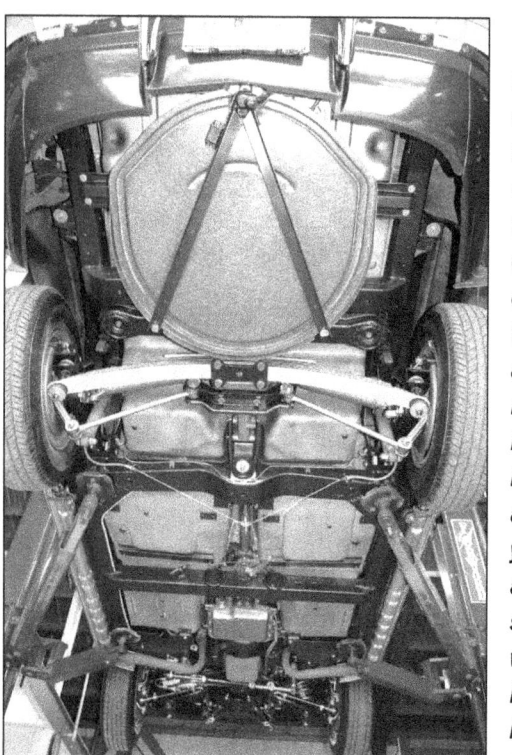

Restoring the Midyear driveline is one of my favorite phases of a restoration. Although the job is usually messy upfront the tasks are rewarding. The tough part is cleaning all the different pieces and removing the years of corrosion and road grime. Multiple refinishing coatings are applied and figuring out what coating to use makes the job interesting. NCRS and Bloomington Gold documents are very helpful in identifying what coating to apply where. If natural steel is what you want to look at, clear coat can be applied in various sheens to keep raw steel pieces from corroding. No matter what your restoration plans are, applying a coating to each and every piece is essential to keep corrosion from forming.

Clutch Linkage

Clutch operation can only be as good as the pieces connecting it to your left foot. After 40 plus years, you can expect some wear on any metal-to-metal contact joints. Clutch linkage wear occurs slowly, over a long period of time. The subtle changes are generally not noticed until you find the clutch pedal binding or sticking. Clicking and popping noises when operating the clutch pedal warn that failure is imminent. Poor lubrication exacerbates the clutch linkage wear, until failure occurs. Linkage restoration is simple, inexpensive, and recommended. Taking the time to disassemble, inspect, and restore the clutch linkage allows for smooth clutch release and engagement, making the drive more enjoyable.

Free-play

Very few drivers realize the importance of proper clutch linkage adjustment. The advent of hydraulic clutches on newer vehicles has eliminated the need for clutch adjustment, but all Midyear Corvettes should have 1½ to 2 inches of free-play when stepping on the clutch pedal. This means that when the pedal is at rest, you should be able to lightly touch the pedal and feel free-play before noticeable resistance is felt. A few factors can make you think there is no free-play or an incorrect amount of free-play. A hefty clutch pedal return spring is used to keep the pedal against the upper clutch pedal limit stop; if the return spring is broken or weak, it can prevent the pedal from returning to the upper stop, tricking you into thinking that there is no free-play. Worn, poorly lubricated linkages can bind, which also prevents the pedal from returning fully.

You might be thinking, "Why worry so much about free-play? It just cannot be that important." As the clutch disc wears, the clutch pressure plate apply fingers move towards the transmission assembly and free-play is eliminated. Clutch linkage free-play is adjusted at the equalizer push rod, using two 9/16-inch wrenches to loosen the jam nuts holding the equalizer clevis. The position of the pushrod clevis is a good indicator of clutch disc wear. If the equalizer clevis is at the inner portion of the threaded push rod you can be certain the clutch disc is worn to its lowest limit. It can be quite interesting how much information that clutch adjustment position can tell us. For instance, someone that was abusing the clutch would require frequent free-play adjustments. Frequent free-play adjustments would also be necessary with an incorrectly-chosen differential gear ratio. For example, a tall (numerically low) differential gear set or first gear would require a long, slow engagement (slipping) of the clutch to get the vehicle moving, causing premature wear.

Another casualty from poorly-adjusted clutch linkage can be the clutch release bearing or "throw-out bearing," as it is sometimes called. Constant clutch pressure plate load on the bearing wears the bearing assembly prematurely. On the flip side, too much free-play can cause transmission damage. The additional free-play causes gear clashing or worse: the transmission may not go into gear. Every time you force the transmission into gear, metal is grinding off the engagement teeth. Once your restoration is complete, keep an eye on the free-play adjustment; it could save your clutch and transmission.

Under the hood the clutch free-play adjustment is next to the steering column, below the brake master cylinder. From the position of the clevis pin, this clutch has worn about 50 percent.

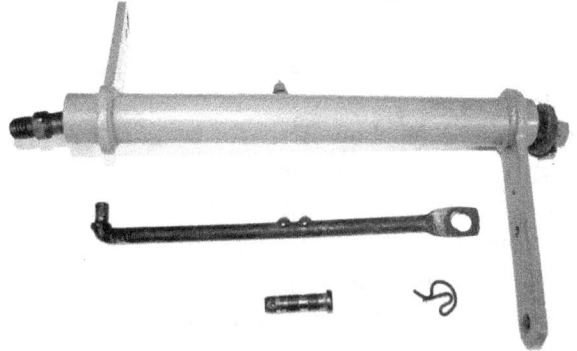

These are the majority of the clutch linkage pieces. The equalizer or cross shaft usually withstands the test of time. Below the equalizer is a well-worn linkage rod at the clevis pin connection. Original-equipment Clevis pins are hardened and wear very little while they wear away at the linkage rod.

These anti-rattle springs that connect to the equalizer, clutch fork, and clutch linkage rod may seem insignificant but they are not. There are two springs (one on the clutch fork and the other on the equalizer) that connect to the linkage rod. They keep any slack in the linkage tight, preventing rattles.

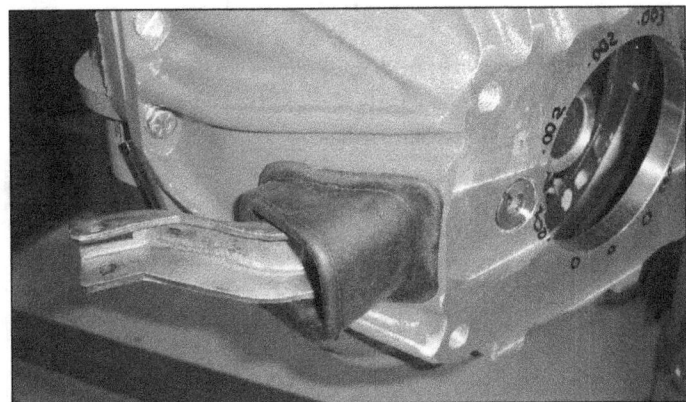

Notice the clutch fork deep offset, along with the rib removed from the upper edge. The 1963-1967 Corvettes use this deep-offset clutch fork to clear the firewall. Incorrect Chevrolet clutch forks damage the firewall and require structural repair.

CHAPTER 8

Flywheel

Your flywheel has multiple functions: it provides inertia for vehicle movement; the starter engages with it to start the engine; and it provides a suitable surface for clutch engagement. We rarely worry about the flywheel until the starter does not engage. Many times, the flywheel is neglected during clutch service, causing clutch chatter or slippage after the job is completed. The flywheel clutch disc engagement surface takes a beating each time the transition from standing still to full clutch engagement occurs. Heat is generated as the disc slips on both the flywheel and clutch pressure plate surfaces. Hot spots or checking cause hard spots to form on the flywheel and pressure plate surfaces. Distortion of the surfaces is commonplace and causes uneven clutch disc application.

New clutch components have flat, even wear surfaces. So should the flywheel, to aid in full clutch engagement. Flywheels can be resurfaced to machine off the uneven surfaces and some hard spots, to reuse an original piece. Like brake drums or rotors, there is a limit to how much material should be removed. Unlike brake drums, there is no good place to measure the thickness and no set discard dimension. If you know for sure that the flywheel has been resurfaced in the past, it really should be replaced. I limit resurfacing to .02 inch. If that does not clean up the surface, I suggest replacement. In most cases, the hard spots (caused by the excessive heat I mentioned earlier) do not go away during the machining process: the resurfacing tool bit bounces over the spots and causes irregular high and low spots. When you are dealing with a vintage vehicle, the best policy is to replace the flywheel.

If you decide to replace the flywheel, there are a few things to consider. First is size; is your replacement flywheel the same diameter? General Motors used either of two flywheels, depending on the engine's power output. Low-horsepower engines used the 153-tooth ring gear with an external diameter of 10½ inches, while high performance engines used a 168-tooth, 11-inch-diameter flywheel. If a different diameter flywheel is used, the starter must coincide with the change. General Motors also used two different bellhousings. As you can imagine, the large diameter flywheel does not fit into the small bellhousing.

The flywheel needs the correct balance weights. When General Motors redesigned the crankshaft rear seal area in 1987, the new design required a flywheel with the proper balance weight. General Motors also thoughtfully changed the bolt pattern to prevent incorrect flywheel installation. You need to make sure you have the correct bolt pattern for your engine. There is one exception: Stroker engines, which have specific weights that may be configured differently. For a stroker engine, always use the flywheel recommended by the engine builder.

Flywheel materials have certainly evolved from the early cast-iron pieces. Today, we can find aluminum, cast iron, and high-strength steel-billet flywheels in just about any configuration. Aluminum flywheels have their place in lightweight vehicles or behind mega-torque, large cubic-inch engines. The old, reliable, cast-iron flywheel works fine when used within its limitations. Engine RPM is the main limitation to the iron flywheel; below 6,000 rpm, it is fine. Steel billet flywheels have higher RPM limits and tougher clutch application surfaces for performance applications. Heavy vehicles, such as our 1963 Corvette with moderate torque, benefit from a heavier cast-iron flywheel and don't need the high-rpm capability, so this is an area where we can save a few dollars. Why pay for something we really do not need?

Inspect Ring Gear Teeth

1 *Clean the starter ring gear area to look at the ring gear teeth. All of these teeth look just like they should, with square corners and smooth tapers.*

Install Roller Pilot Bearing

2 *I prefer to install a needle roller pilot bearing in place of the original bronze bushing. A 7/8-inch socket fits around the outer circumference of the bearing to avoid damaging the bearing's integral seal during installation.*

Torque Flywheel

3 This is a later, one-piece rear main seal, small-block engine. Torquing the flywheel bolts on the one-piece rear main seal crankshaft is mandatory to prevent crankshaft hub distortion. Over-tightening the flywheel bolts create a rear main seal leak. Torque the 7/16-20 thread bolts to the maximum 65 ft-lbs.

Clean Flywheel and Clutch Disc

4 Both the flywheel and clutch disc have a protective coating of petroleum products. Wash the surfaces with a clean cloth and brake cleaner to prevent clutch chatter. Keep washing until the cloth does not show discoloration when you wipe the surface with a clean spot on the cloth. Unfortunately, this step is rarely done in the haste to assemble the clutch quickly.

Align Clutch Disc

5 Use the supplied alignment tool to put the Spec Stage 3+ clutch disc in place. This particular clutch disc includes a carbon semi-metallic material capable of handling 750 pounds of torque. As simple as this may sound, make sure you heed the instruction, "Place this side towards flywheel."

Torque Clutch Bolts

6 Begin by tightening the bolts incrementally until they are all seated, to avoid pressure plate distortion. Torque the 3/8-inch thread bolts to 45 ft-lbs using the star pattern procedure.

Clutch Assembly

You need to carefully select a clutch assembly that works well for your application. Your clutch assembly must effectively clamp the clutch disc between the pressure plate and flywheel with the least pedal effort. As RPM, horsepower, and torque rise, so do the requirements for the clutch assembly. For safety's sake, it makes sense to order a clutch assembly that handles at least 10 percent additional horsepower. After all, you may decide that you want to boost the horsepower down the road. However, if you go overkill with the safety factor, the increased pedal effort makes you regret your decision.

You need to factor your differential and transmission first gear ratios into your clutch selection process. The equation works like this: high differential gear ratios (which are lower, numerically, like 3.08:1) require higher clamping force clutches to avoid constantly burning up the clutch disc. Low gear ratios (like 4.11:1) are much easier on the clutch assembly. As far out as this sounds, transmission or differential gear ratio choices may require reconsideration if the clutch choices do not work. It is all about balance. You want a clutch that is going to grip well without giving you leg cramps in city traffic. Do not forget about parades to show your beauty off; idling and constantly working the clutch pedal is tiresome.

CHAPTER 8

Bellhousing

Bellhousings seem simple enough: they cover up the clutch and flywheel, while connecting the transmission to the engine. This un-sung hero has to do all of the above with tremendous torque loading applied. To verify the bellhousing's integrity, check for concentricity and parallelism, which are of utmost importance to prevent transmission vibration and damage. The bellhousing must keep the centerline of the transmission input shaft concentric and parallel to the engine crankshaft. This is quite a feat, considering the mass production of all three items: engine block, bellhousing, and transmission. "If it ain't broke don't fix it," applies here, if all the original components are used and everything is put back just the way it came apart.

Bellhousings are indexed (or positioned) using dowel pins on the back of the engine block. The transmission input shaft retainer or collar indexes the transmission to the bellhousing. If the bellhousing-to-engine bolts become loose over time, the bellhousing's softer aluminum material wears. The ensuing wear allows movement around the indexing dowels, which changes the transmission input shaft to crankshaft concentricity. If the bellhousing does not fit the indexing dowels tightly, concentricity is likely to be out of spec. To be safe, any time a major component is replaced (whether it's an engine block, bellhousing, or transmission), you need to check for concentricity run-out. Offset dowel pins are available to correct for concentricity run-out misalignment. The original dowel pins are removed, and with some careful placement, the concentricity can be set below the maximum .004 inch.

Parallelism is not achieved when the engine-mounting surface of the bellhousing is not parallel with the transmission mounting surface. Most machine shops can correct bellhousings that are no longer parallel. Careful measurement of where the high and low spots are must be relayed to the machinist. I check every bellhousing for both concentricity and parallelism, whether they are new or used, to ensure long transmission life.

Verify Bellhousing Concentricity

1 This is the set up for checking bellhousing concentricity. Position the dial indicator's magnetic base on the flywheel hub area. It does not have to be centered perfectly for the test. Divide the total run-out in half. For example if the run-out is .008, you need to be below .004.

Check Parallelism

2 Here, the parallelism check is taking place. As was done with the concentricity check, affix the dial indicator's magnetic base to the crankshaft. Rotate the crankshaft while watching the dial indictor. This example was below the allowable .003 parallelism run-out.

Select Dowel Pins

3 Offset dowel pins come in .007, .014, and .021 increments. The one on the right shows the original out of the engine block.

DRIVELINE

Lessons Learned

Improper component installation is often the culprit of failure of parallelism. For example, I had a customer bring in a 1965 Corvette with a transmission vibration issue. The owner explained that he had someone install an overdrive transmission kit recently. The problem was getting worse and more noticeable as engine RPM increased. Once I had the Corvette in the air, it was easy to spot the most likely cause of the problem: the transmission was not sitting tight up against the bellhousing. There was a very noticeable gap between the bottom of the transmission mounting surface and the bellhousing. I could fit 1/8-inch worth of feeler gauges in the gap. Upon disassembly, I found that the clutch fork pivot ball had not been fully screwed into the new bellhousing. The clutch fork pivot ball prevented the transmission case from seating fully on the bellhousing.

In this case, the bellhousing itself was not the parallelism problem. The really bad thing was that the transmission retaining bolts had been cranked down hard, forcing the transmission mounting ears against the bellhousing. As hard as it may be to believe, the transmission case itself was bent at the lower mounting ears. Unfortunately, the fix was costly: a replacement transmission case. Luckily, no other pieces were hurt, thanks to the short time that transpired from the vibration complaint until the repair.

We are all susceptible to making mistakes, but being careful to make sure each piece fits flat without forcing the assembly together goes a long way.

Differential

Does it make sense to buy the special tools needed for differential restoration? What about skill level requirements? Purchasing differential bearing service tools costs quite a bit. You may buy these with buddies or you can rent them. Or you can take everything to a gear specialist who has the equipment and skill to do the job quickly and precisely.

When you consider the tools and skill level required for a complete differential overhaul in most cases, it makes sense to leave it to the pros; however, I am going to cover the steps required for a complete transmission and differential overhaul so that you can make your own decision.

From 1963 until 1979, General Motors used Eaton Corporation differentials. Like

Hydraulic Clutches

Options or upgrades are available for the tried and true mechanical clutch linkage. Today, 99 percent of manual transmission-equipped cars have hydraulic clutch actuation systems. Hydraulic clutches have advantages, such as reduced pedal effort, flexibility during installation, and self-adjustment. The downside is that hydraulic clutch failure requires that the transmission be removed to perform a repair. Today, when you repair a hydraulic clutch system, you replace everything: master, slave, and hose assemblies. Many of them come pre-bled and full of fluid. Just install them and you are ready to go. On a positive note, the clutch never requires adjustment, lubrication or service.

If you convert from an automatic transmission to a manual transmission, hydraulic clutch assemblies can save time and money. One reason you may consider installing the hydraulic clutch actuation system is to avoid having to weld in a very difficult area. The mechanical clutch linkage equalizer uses a support bracket on the frame; if you plan to use mechanical linkage, the support bracket must be welded onto the frame. Probably the most significant beneficial of a hydraulic system is that it allows for just about any exhaust or header system. My inclination on the 1963 Corvette project is to use the hydraulic pieces to ease pedal effort and eliminate any adjustment concerns.

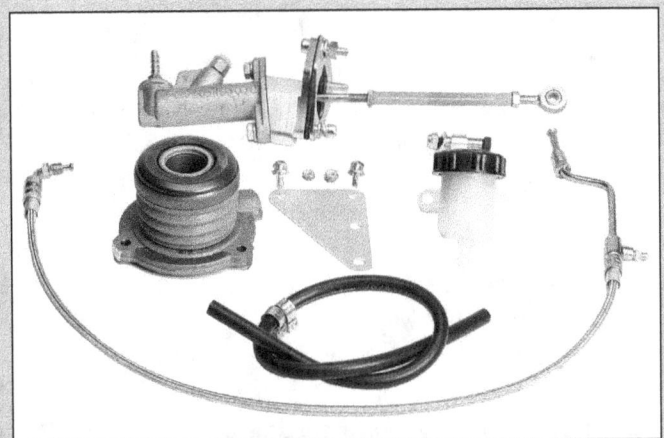

This Keisler automotive hydraulic clutch kit has all the pieces you need in one convenient package. The engineered kit was designed for easy installation with simple hand tools and fits easily into the confines of the engine bay. This latest version has a bleeder screw integrated into the pressure hose to speed up the bleeding process.

all differentials, they are stout enough for almost any overhaul procedures. On the other hand, a misplaced adjustment shim can leave yours howling at any speed.

Setting up a differential for the first time takes patience. General Motors used a shim under the inner pinion bearing to determine pinion depth. You can cross your fingers and hope the pinion depth shim you selected is correct, but the better option is to use a set-up tool. I have a removal tool that allows me to remove the pinion bearing without damaging it, but it is not something in which most people would want to invest.

Ring gear to pinion gear backlash must also be checked, and that requires a dial indicator for the measurement. I learned a very hard lesson in the shop a long time ago: always check this backlash before disassembly. New bearings can move the ring gear or pinion enough to change the backlash, which can bring about a wicked howl from the freshly-overhauled differential.

When I rebuilt one differential a while ago, all the bearings were replaced, but the odd thing was that the backlash had changed slightly. I made the appropriate shim changes to bring it back to where the backlash was before the disassembly. On the road test the differential had a slight howl on acceleration above 35 mph.

After spending way too long trying to figure out what happened, I found a slight difference in inner pinion bearing thickness. My pinion depth had changed just enough to cause the noise. This explained why I had to make a minor change in shims to correct the backlash.

Gear Ratios

Gear ratios affect every aspect of your Corvette's performance, so it's helpful to "know the lingo" so to speak concerning gear ratios before you start working on them or making changes because it can be a little confusing.

When people say they have a low gear ratio like 4.11:1, they are referring to the mechanical advantage not the numerical factor.

Conversely, a 2:73.1 differential gear ratio is considered a high gear ratio requiring more torque to get things rolling, even though the numbers themselves (2.73:1) are lower than a "low gear" 4.11:1.

Traditionally, gear ratios numerically below 3:54.1 are typically considered highway cruiser gear sets–3.36;1, 3.23:1, 3.08:1, 2.73:1, etc. Lower gears, such as 3.73:1, 3.90:1, 4.11:1, and so-on, have been the traditional performance gears. Remember, modern overdrive transmissions can provide the same mechanical advantage as performance gears with much more economical highway gears.

In this book, I refer to "low" and "high" gear ratios for their mechanical advantage not their numerical value. I use this valuable information to help you choose the correct differential gear ratio for your Corvette.

So, what differential gear set complements my 1987 Tuned Port Corvette engine? I created a formula to find the combined transmission first gear ratio and differential final gear ratio to help make this important decision. Here is an example:

I decided to start with the Keisler T45RS 5-speed manual transmission with its 3.37:1 first gear and .67:1 overdrive gearing and a goal of keeping the combined first gear ratio in the 10.0:1 range, to get my project Corvette rolling easily.

I found that multiplying the T45RS' 3.37:1 first-gear ratio by the 3.08:1 differential-gear ratio yields a 10.37:1 combined ratio. At 1,800 rpm I cruise at 70 mph in the T45RS .67:1 overdrive fifth gear with the 3:08.1 differential gear ratio.

My early Tuned Port Injection engine is "in the zone," utilizing its excellent torque for off-the-line performance and highway cruising. Balance is what I am after for my long-range cruiser. I can also save a few dollars because I won't need an exotic clutch with this combined gear ratio. Stop-and-go traffic is easy to contend with; no extra stiff clutch pedal to constantly strain my left leg.

Another major benefit is that my conservative RPM cruising range keeps my fuel costs reasonable. Remember to check how the tire size affects your final drive ratio for the exact figures for your car.

If you are on a tight budget, it makes even more sense to spend your money on proper gearing for your Corvette. Leverage is the opportune word. Selecting the correct differential gear ratio aids acceleration. Selecting an overdrive transmission gives you the best of both worlds. Now is the time to make this decision. Down the road, you can pump up your engine's horsepower, if necessary. Build a modest engine up-front, and use the money you save to buy the optimal transmission and differential gearing.

DRIVELINE

Check backlash before disassembly if you plan on using the original differential gear set. Set the dial indicator probe as close to the centerline of the ring gear as possible for the most accurate reading. Here, I am checking the typical .008- to .010-inch clearance between the ring gear and pinion gear teeth. This tight clearance can be difficult to feel. If necessary the pinion flange can be held stationary with a large pair of pliers. This helps you feel the backlash clearance between the gears. Check the backlash at three or four places on the ring gear then average them. Record the backlash reading and put it in a safe place for reference later. Original gear sets should maintain the same backlash found before disassembly.

Beware! Just because the bearings look the same, does not mean they have the same stacked height. This is why it is important to check backlash and the gear pattern before disassembly.

If it was not for the Corvette's Positraction clutch plates that eventually chatter, most differentials would probably never receive a fluid change. Positraction metallic clutch plates rub against each other every time you make a turn, which sloughs off metal into the gear oil. The clutch plates become gummed up with the worn-out gear oil and metallic particle slurry causing them to chatter. Popping during cornering is the next indicator that the fluid was ready for service a long time ago.

Crush Sleeve

Restoring or rebuilding a differential is not for everyone. Now you need to decide whether you are going to rebuild the ancillary items off the differential assembly, or have a shop do it. When considering this, ask yourself: was the differential noisy or leaking badly from the pinion yoke area? If the differential was quiet and not leaking badly, chances are, your results will be good if you decide to tackle it.

You may want to rethink your game plan if the differential is noisy and leaking. Noisy, leaking differentials require more specialized tools and knowledge. General Motors used a crush sleeve to capture the inner and outer pinion bearings. The crush sleeve needs to collapse inward until the bearing pre-load is set. The crush sleeve takes a set, and as a result, positions the bearings correctly for the life of the bearings. A leaking pinion seal usually means the bearings are worn or damaged, causing the pinion yoke to go off center, damaging the seal. This often explains why numerous seals may have been installed yet the leak keeps returning.

The fix is to replace the pinion bearings and crush sleeve. When you have both a leak and noise, the pinion has been off-center for quite a while, damaging the ring and pinion and a complete overhaul with ring and pinion gear replacement is necessary.

Differential Carrier

A few problems are inherent in the C2/C3 Corvette differential. If you find

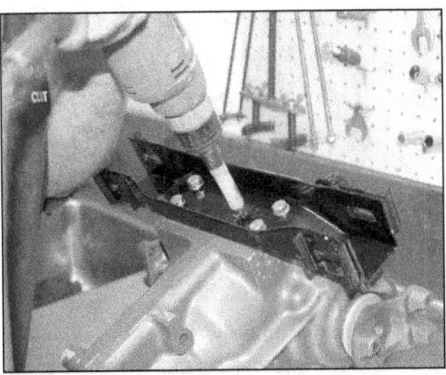

You may want to modify your differential case to allow for future servicing. The Petris Enterprises differential drain plug installation kit hole saw cuts the strut rod bracket first. Then a 5/16-inch drill bit opens the hole up for the national pipe tap.

With a 1/8-inch NPT tap in hand, tap threads for your new differential drain. Thread-tapping fluid or oil should be used to keep the threads sharp during the tapping process.

Install the 1/8-NPT drain plug with Teflon tape. Draining and filling the differential annually keeps it going for many trouble-free years.

popping and chattering during your pre-teardown road test, you should inspect the differential carrier. The ring gear is bolted to the differential carrier, and the pinion gears or spider gears are housed inside the carrier. Pinion gears allow the left and right tires to turn at different speeds without chirping.

There are four pinion gears in total: two idler gears and two side gears, which drive the side yokes. A limited-slip clutch assembly rides against the axle pinion side gears inside the confines of the carrier. The idlers ride on a cross pin or shaft and pin wear occurs as a result of on and off the throttle loading. Quite often the cross pin wear is minimal, as the carrier itself wears from the load. When the carrier is worn at the pin area, popping can occur during cornering or when taking off from a stop. The only fix for the worn carrier is a replacement assembly. If you decide to go into the differential, you need to go all the way. Chances are it has been a long time since it was completely disassembled and inspected. We have found broken Positraction clutch plates hidden in the middle of the stack.

Watch for sticking steel shims when you remove the pinion side gears. The steel shims stick inside the carrier at each end sometimes. Set the shims aside, so that they can be reinstalled on the same side from which they came. When replacing bearings, be careful to check for proper bearing and bearing race installation. Each bearing must be seated completely flat against the housing or component. A differential that was quiet before may not be again if the bearings are not seated properly, because the difference can change pinion depth.

Backlash

Check the backlash before disassembling any portion of the differential. Check the ring gear and pinion pattern with some grease paint. Interpreting the gear pattern does take some practice. The idea is to set up the gears in the same location to avoid a whiny differential.

If replacement differential gear sets have been installed, they require .008 to .012 inch of backlash. I try to get as close as possible to .008 inch to prevent clunking when loading the drivetrain.

Rotate the ring gear 90 degrees, check backlash, and do this again in at least three other locations. Debris trapped between the ring gear and carrier can cause run-out issues. The ring gear should be removed and both surfaces checked for burrs, high spots, etc., if there are tight and loose spots.

Differential Installation

Seat Pinion Bearing

1 The inner bearing race can be easily cocked during installation, and that prevents it from seating properly. Heat cycling may allow the bearing race to seat fully but this changes the pinion depth and creates bearing clearance. The resulting pinion depth change may cause your differential gear set to howl. Worse yet, the resulting loose bearings allow the pinion to float around, ruining the new differential gear set.

2 Also fully seat the outer pinion bearing race to avoid pinion bearing pre-load changes. It takes some getting used to, but you can hear the change in the tone of the hammer hitting the installer when the bearing is seated. The tone changes to a dull thud when the bearing race is seated. Tight pinion bearing tolerances are required to keep the pinion centerline from changing. You can check the bearing-race-to-case fit from the backside of each bearing. You can see whether the bearing race is seated in the housing from the backside of the inner pinion bearing when the outer pinion bearing is installed, and vice-versa.

Install Differential into Carrier

3 Install the loaded differential side gear into the carrier. Install the differential Positraction drive and reaction clutch plates by hand onto the side gear beginning and ending with a reaction plate. Lube each plate with 90W gear oil during assembly. Do not forget to place the steel shims on the last reaction plate.

Install Pinion Gears

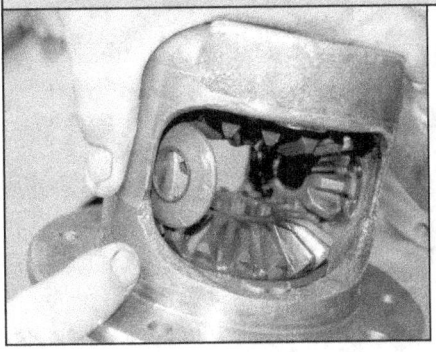

4 Rotate pinion gears into position and install them. Install the gear's coned wear prevention washers next. These washers can be difficult to fit behind the pinion gears, which is why the gear is out a bit, to aid installation.

Install Pressure Plates into Carrier

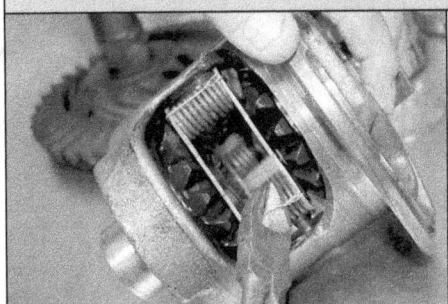

5 This trick works well to keep the Positraction clutch pressure plates and springs together for installation. Place the spring and pressure plate assembly into a vise and then tie the plates together with safety wire. The spring and pressure plate assembly should slip into the differential carrier with little effort; that is, if the springs were coil bound when the wire was installed. Sometimes you need to lightly tap the assembly into place. Once installed you simply cut the wire and make sure to remove it.

Install Pinion Gear Rotation Pin

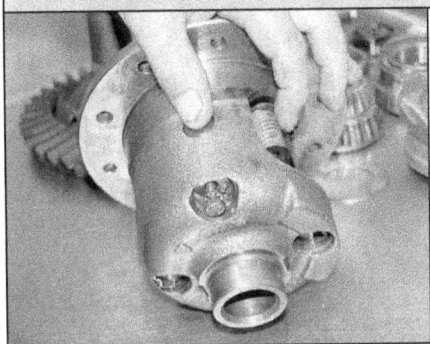

6 Install the pinion gear rotation pin and make sure the retaining screw installs easily. This can save you a lot of aggravation from misplaced pinion gear wear washers. Once the posi pressure plates have been installed, the pinion gears become loose and allow the wear washers to fall out. Keep the pinion pin in place until you are ready to install the yokes, which is one of the final steps.

Torque Ring Gear Bolts

7 Use new Grade 8 ring gear bolts and washers to retain the new ring gear to the carrier. Torque the bolts to the recommended 55 ft-lbs.

Install Differential Side Bearings

8 Use a large socket and hammer to install the differential side bearings onto the carrier. Using a flat installation tool prevents the bearings from seating completely. The carrier bearing hub protrudes above the bearing when the bearing is seated fully. The large socket (installer) must have a large enough inner diameter to clear the raised carrier hub.

Install Shim

9 Place the correct or same-thickness shim as the one removed from the original pinion gear under the inner pinion bearing to set the correct pinion depth. If you do not have pinion depth set-up tools start with a .028-inch-thick shim. I prefer to press the inner bearing onto the pinion. Heat can be applied to the inner bearing race to ease installation.

Install Pinion

10 Install the outer pinion bearing without the crush sleeve and pinion seal. Place the outer bearing onto the pinion with plenty of lube. Pinion bearings have a snug fit on the pinion and require some light tapping with a small ball-peen hammer for installation.

Prep for Pinion Pattern Checking

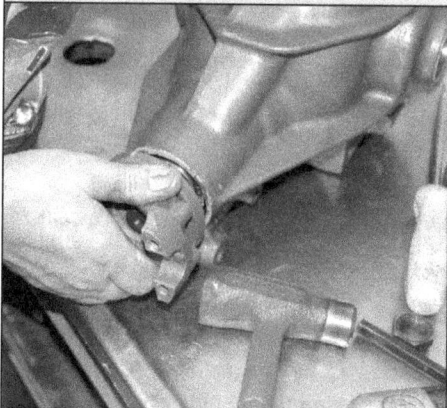

11 Install the pinion yoke by lightly tapping it in place with a plastic hammer for pattern checking. The trick is to tighten the pinion nut enough so that there is movement with bearing drag for ring gear pattern checking. Do not over-tighten the nut and prevent rotation, which causes bearing damage.

Set Backlash and Carrier Bearing Preload

12 Put the assembled carrier into place. Use the shims supplied with the differential gear installation kit replicating the same amount of shims you had before on each side. The aftermarket shims allow you to tap them into position. Factory cast-iron shims can shatter when you tap on them, even with light taps.

Set Backlash

13 Make sure there is some backlash (clearance between the ring and pinion gears) before you torque the main cap bolts to 65 ft-lbs. Check again for backlash as you approach the required bolt torque limit. Do not force the ring gear into the pinion without any backlash because the gears can crack (shatter) due to their extremely hard surfaces. If necessary the carrier side bearing shims can be changed to achieve .008 to .012 inch of backlash before proceeding. Add shim to the right-side carrier bearing and remove from the left to add clearance or remove shim from the right side add to the left side.

Set Pinion Depth

14 The coast side of the grease-painted ring gear teeth tells a story. Unfortunately, it is not the one you like to see. The close proximity to the crown requires a pinion depth shim change. Remove the carrier and pinion gear so you can remove .004 from the pinion depth shim under the pinion gear. Conversely, if the pattern is to the outside of the ring gear teeth you add shims under the pinion gear.

15 The drive-side ring gear teeth contact pattern is close to center, and that tells you that you are close to achieving the correct pinion depth. The removal of .004 pinion shim should make the difference you need. Once the pinion depth has been achieved, you get to take it all back apart.

Install Crush Sleeve on Pinion

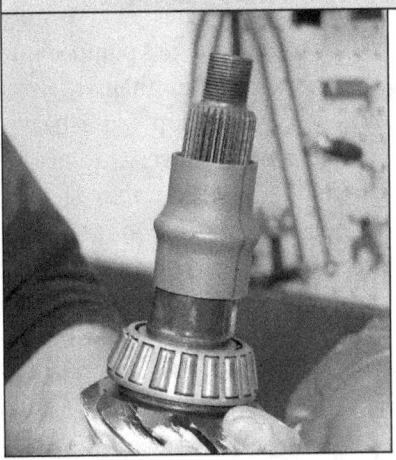

16 Disassemble the differential completely to install the crush sleeve on the pinion. Pinion bearing pre-load is retained with this bell-shaped crush sleeve. The idea is to collapse the crush sleeve until the bearing pre-load is set. The tough part is to hold onto the pinion flange while you tighten the large pinion nut. Aftermarket supplied crush sleeves collapse much easier than GM sleeves. The aftermarket crush sleeve is recommended and works fine.

Apply Hot Oil Sealant

17 First, install the pinion seal. Then, before installing the pinion nut, apply a bead of hot oil resistant silicone sealer to the pinion yoke washer. Next, tighten the pinion nut, collapsing the crush sleeve until you have pre-load drag on the bearings. Rotate the pinion as you are tightening the pinion nut, feeling for bearing play. At the point when the bearing free-play is eliminated you are close to achieving the correct pre-load and it can sneak up on you quickly. If the pinion nut is over-tightened, creating too much bearing pre-load, a new crush sleeve should be installed. Bearing pre-load requires 20 inch-pounds of force measured with an old-school beam torque wrench to rotate the pinion yoke when the correct pre-load is achieved.

Install Yoke Side Bearings and Seals

18 You can now install the yoke side bearings and seals. Washing the gear oil off the seal installation surface with a cloth and brake cleaner. The seal installation bores can become nicked and gouged during servicing and require a sealer for a leak-proof seal.

Apply Sealer to Bore Surface

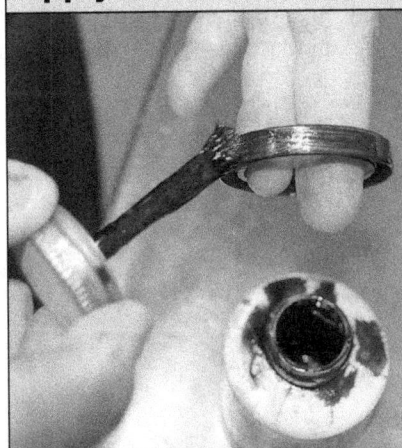

19 Nasty stuff, but it works well if the seal surfaces are clean and free from oil and grease. An application of Permatex aviation sealer on the seal bore surface ensures no leaks or weeping results from any metal clad seal like these used for the side yokes.

Install Side Yokes

20 First lube the previously installed side yoke bearings and seals, and then install the side yokes. Check the side yoke seal and bearing surfaces for nicks, gouges, and corrosion. They can be polished with steel wool before installation if necessary.

Install Snap Rings

21 Insert snap rings to keep the side yokes secured. These can be a pain to get into place properly, but make sure they seat into the groove all the way. Once they have been installed, use a screwdriver to push them around and make sure they are fully seated. If the snap ring is out of position it does not rotate in its groove.

Install Differential

22 Mission accomplished. Now it's time to button it up! Install new 7/16-14 thread bolts and lock washers to secure the rear differential cover. Watch the length of the bolts because the housing can be damaged if the upper and lower bolts are too long. Torque the twelve 1¼-inch-long bolts to 65 ft-lbs to finish the install.

Driveshaft/Axleshaft

The 1963 to 1967 Corvettes have six universal joints: two in the driveshaft and four in the axleshafts. You can use standard-duty or heavy-duty universal joints. High-performance universal joints have solid trunions with special heat-treated coatings. Standard-duty universal joints are rifle drilled with lubrication passages. The lubrication passages that weaken the universal joint's structure, but, conversely, they usually help the joint last longer by ensuring it's properly lubed. However, drilled universal joints require service.

Many shops ignore universal joints; if they do perform a lube service, the grease fittings typically are not cleaned properly, so when the grease gun is stuck on the dirty fitting, grit gets pumped into the joint, which causes them to wear prematurely. In my shop I use heavy-duty, non-greasable, universal joints for strength and long life, unless the car owner requests greasable U-joints.

After 40-plus years, your driveshaft and axleshafts could likely benefit from a trip to the driveline/driveshaft specialty shop. Driveshaft specialty shops check the shaft for straightness and replace the universal joints at very reasonable costs. If the shafts spin true, they balance them for smooth operation.

Why wait until the first road test to find out that there is a vibration? With three shafts and six universal joints, finding vibrations can be a daunting task.

Driveshaft/Axleshaft Installation

Replace Universal Joints

1 Here's a handy way to replace the U-joints. The chrome socket is large enough to allow the U-joint cup to receive it. Use a smaller-diameter U-joint cup than the one you are removing, so you can apply force and press the U-joint out. If the parts have not been corroded, this often works well. If the cup is old and corroded, it is often frozen in place and this won't work; you may need to use a vise.

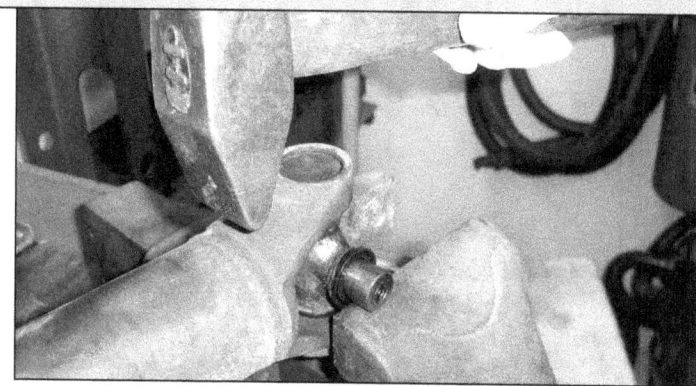

2 This method also works well, but you must be careful to hit between the weld and yoke flange. The sharp impact of a hammer and tool loosens corroded, stubborn, universal joints. This large hammer works well to get them moving when the vise attempt fails. Be sure to hit squarely at the weld area.

3 You can apply localized heat with a Map Gas torch to the yoke to help break the corrosion loose. In some cases, a big hammer is also required to get badly corroded U-joints loose. Remember that as the joint heats, the resulting grease expansion can cause a loud bang. Be prepared for the bang if the U-joints do not have grease fittings to remove.

Replace Universal Joints (Continued)

4 This is the preferred method of universal joint replacement. This massive OTC tools C-clamp has multiple uses, and here it pushes the U-joints out effortlessly. The C-clamp also makes easy work of installing the new U-joint cups.

Check Axle Flange Trueness

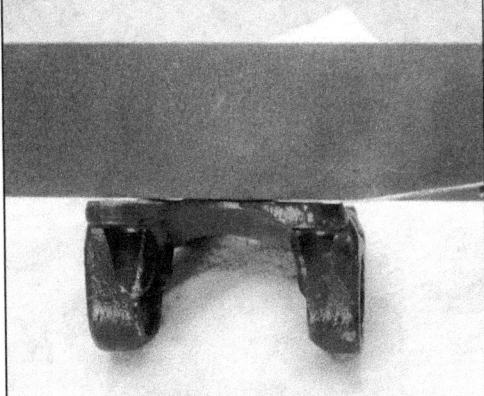

5 After removing stubborn universal joints, you typically find axleshaft flanges have been distorted. Use a straightedge to check for distortion. In this case, I found one that is bent. Oh well, it is to be expected when extra force is necessary to remove stubborn U-joints.

Straighten Axle Flange

6 Careful work at the hydraulic press can straighten the flanges for reuse. The trick is to go beyond straight slightly, then when the flange springs back it is straight. If you leave them distorted it is almost impossible to seat the universal joint retaining clips.

Remove Corrosion from Shafts

7 Once the driveshaft or axleshaft has been disassembled and cleaned, use a 3/4-inch-diameter flap wheel to remove any remaining corrosion. Tread lightly here because it is easy to remove too much material and have loose-fitting universal joint cups.

Install U-Joint Cups

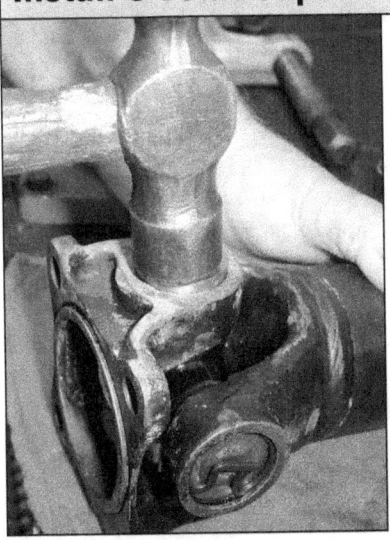

8 Carefully and precisely use a light-duty hammer to install the U-joint cups. Lift the U-joint up and out of the previously installed cup just enough, so that the one you are installing has the rollers on the U-joint trunions. This is somewhat tricky so avoid letting the U-joint trunions drop. If it does drop, it can knock a roller loose.

Seat U-Joint Retaining Clips

9 Make sure that the U-joint retaining clips are fully seated in the groove. If the retaining clip comes out of the flange, the U-joint cup follows. It does not matter how tight the cup fits in the flange.

CHAPTER 9

BRAKES

Midyear Corvettes went through many brake system changes. Production began with drum brakes, which were similar to those on first-generation, solid-axle Corvettes. Brake fade or loss was typical when drum brake systems became wet or excessively hot. Nothing was more unnerving than stepping down hard on the brake pedal, only to find that it did very little to halt vehicle motion.

Earlier, I touched on GM's very special optional drum brake system, RPO J65, which was available with the big tank, road race 1963 and 1964 Corvettes. RPO J65 used segmented, sintered-metallic brake shoes with finned, aluminum, 11-inch brake drums. The finned, aluminum drums helped dissipate heat much more quickly than cast-iron drums. Ventilated brake backing plates further helped alleviate heat build-up. Unfortunately, the J65 optional brake system came with compromises that drivers had to contend with. Temperature was still a concern, as cold brake shoes caused uneven braking until heat built up. Chances are good that very few folks work with the rare J65 option.

I cover the most common Midyear systems and possible upgrades, in order to eliminate safety concerns.

Early Midyear brake hydraulic systems were very simple: A single master cylinder actuated all four brake assemblies. Wheel cylinder piston diameter and brake shoe width determined the drum brake system balance. Wider brake shoes and wheel cylinders with a larger diameter were used up front for greater braking power, due to weight distribution. General Motors used the Corvette platform for many first-run mechanical advances, and brake systems were no exception, such as the introduction of disc brakes and dual-circuit hydraulic brake systems. For the first time, Midyear Corvettes had a power brake option. Many positive changes occurred with the braking system in the five years of Midyear production.

The 1965 Corvettes have front disc brakes as standard equipment. Disc brakes

This 1965 has had a rough life. There is a very good possibility that it had knock-off wheels at one point. At about five o'clock on the rotor's position as it sits you can see a flat spot from the rotor rubbing on asphalt for a pretty good distance. The ACDelco caliper is also an original which means this Midyear will require a complete brake overhaul to ensure proper brake operation.

on the Midyear Corvette are not perfect. Like any new product, problems surfaced. In spite of a few issues, General Motors used the same style caliper in place on all Corvettes until 1982. The Delco-designed Midyear disc brake caliper had four pistons in a fixed housing. The "fixed" calipers use four caliper pistons to apply pressure to both sides of the rotor surface. The design applied equal pressure to the rotating disc and provided excellent braking.

Brake pedal travel is relative to fluid displacement, which presents a challenge when you have 16 caliper pistons to actuate. To limit caliper piston travel, light-duty compression springs were placed behind the pistons, to keep the disc pads close to the rotor. This minimized caliper piston movement during rotor rotation and limited brake pedal free travel. The number-one concern or problem with any fixed caliper is ensuring that the rotor centerline is parallel to the caliper centerline. Centerline variations past .004 inch at the outer edge of the rotor cause a low brake pedal. Excessive brake pedal travel also occurs as caliper piston movement introduces air into the hydraulic system. The calipers become much like a little engine with the pistons pumping air into the hydraulic system.

Caliper piston seal wear was another issue, due to excessive rotor run-out. One more malady that plagued the early design calipers was corrosion of the caliper piston seal surface. When calipers leaked (and they all did) expensive housing replacement was required. In 1969, when floating calipers were introduced for all other car lines, the caliper piston seal design was changed: The caliper pistons became the seal surface, and the pistons were made of stainless steel. This meant that, in the worst case, floating caliper corrosion only required piston replacement.

As you can imagine, a lot of 1965–1982 Corvette calipers were in the field. Additionally, in limited numbers, GM and other U.S. vehicle manufacturers used fixed calipers on their high-performance vehicles until 1968. This brought about an industry focused on repairing and enhancing the original, fixed, four-piston calipers. Early on, stainless-steel sleeves were pressed into machined original housings to restore corroded calipers. Aluminum pistons were replaced with new, improved lip seals, making them better than new. Many of these remanufactured calipers are used today with excellent results.

Brake caliper design has evolved with some crossover of fixed and floating caliper ideas. Floating calipers have square-cut caliper piston seals. The significance of the square cut O-ring seal is its adaptation to the fixed caliper pistons. As mentioned earlier, fixed calipers use lip-style piston seals for the loose-fitting pistons, which were more susceptible to excessive rotor run-out. The square cut O-rings held the pistons better than the original lip seals. Consequently, the rotor run-out concerns were not nearly as troublesome.

The caliper piston square-cut O-ring seal design has been improved to increase fuel mileage. By modifying the square-cut O-ring with a tapered edge, caliper pistons pull back very slightly when the brake pedal is released. The slight pull-back of the caliper piston relieves disc brake pad drag, thus increasing fuel mileage. Vette Brakes and Products utilized this square-cut O-ring technology for their remanufactured calipers. You can purchase either style O-ring or lip-seal-type caliper assemblies from Vette Brakes and Products.

The beauty of the stainless-steel-sleeved calipers is that you can have your original set of calipers restored. Without disassembly, no one can detect that stainless-steel sleeves or O-ring-style pistons have been installed. There are other remanufacturers, such as Stainless Steel Brakes Corporation, that do fine work making original calipers look new and ready for the NCRS judges. If you are inclined to restore your project back to Bloomington Gold or NCRS standards, make sure you have original GM caliper housings. Date codes were stamped onto the caliper housings, which are important for a correct restoration. Over the long history of the Corvette fixed caliper, many companies have made new, look-alike replacement calipers. You certainly do not want to have the calipers restored, only to find out that the calipers are not GM originals.

I do not attempt to restore or rebuild calipers. These days, there are very few original, non-sleeved calipers available. The vast majority of calipers have been sleeved multiple times with new

The disassembled caliper has stainless-steel sleeves underneath all the corrosion. Brake fluid weeps past the lip-type sealing rings causing the rust stains and build-up of debris. I do not rebuild the calipers because the remanufactured caliper costs only a few dollars more by the time you buy seals and pistons.

components installed. When you find stainless-steel-sleeved calipers leaking, there are a few causal factors to look for. The number-one most common factor is rotor run-out, which causes wear to the sleeves. Contaminated brake fluid contributes to caliper leaks, too, especially with lip-type piston seals. I have disassembled many leaking, stainless-steel calipers to inspect them, hoping that I would be able to replace the seals. No such luck. I found damaged stainless-steel sleeves every time. The fact is that the stainless-steel-sleeved, O-ring-sealed calipers should last a lifetime if rotor run-out is maintained. Periodic brake fluid flushing is also necessary to keep the calipers in good condition.

The 1965–1982 Corvette calipers are available in kit form from specialty suppliers. The most common kit consists of four calipers, disc pads, hoses, and rear lines. Beware when it comes time to buy replacement calipers. Many of the major discount automotive supplier chains cannot come close to the pricing from the specialty suppliers. Every time I compare prices at discount stores against specialty stores, the specialty stores win. Another concern is the discount chains may not have stainless-sleeved calipers. I have found them without stainless sleeves in new aftermarket and remanufactured calipers from the discount chain suppliers. Instead, these sources are using the cast-iron bore as in the old days. At the very least, you want the stainless-steel-sleeved calipers, whether they are new or remanufactured. I always use the stainless-steel-sleeved, O-ring version for all of my restorations.

Don't forget about rotor wear. Rotors wear as a result of aggressive disc brake pads and dirt. Rotors should be checked for minimum thickness before and after machining. General Motors stamped a minimum wear limit inside the rotor; please heed the allowed limit. You might think that machining the rotor removes excessive run-out. This statement would be true if the rotor is still riveted to the hub, as General Motors originally manufactured them. When front rotors are replaced, rivets are drilled out and the assembly becomes two pieces. Companies, such as Corvette Central, have replacement rivets if you desire to make the assembly one piece again.

Rear brake rotors are another story. The rotors must be removed to access the parking brake assembly. The alternative method to access the parking brake is to press out the spindle and rotor as an assembly. When rear rotors are replaced or machined, the rivets must be drilled out. One rotor machining option is to machine the rotors on the car. On-the-car rotor machining is more commonplace today, due to the majority of front-wheel-drive cars on the road. By now, however, the majority of Midyear rear brake rotors have had the rivets drilled out. Riveting a new rear rotor onto the spindle requires major work disassembling the spindle. It really makes no sense to worry about riveting rear rotors to the spindles, unless you are planning an NCRS or Bloomington Gold restoration.

Once the rotors have been removed, check for minimum thickness, and if they are within limits, they can be machined. After machining, the rotors should be washed thoroughly with soap and water. Many shops blow off the metallic dust and slap on the spindle, ready for service. Like engine cylinder walls, the machining process leaves the rotors and drums coated with a fine metallic dust that should be removed. The dust accelerates wear, causes squeaking, and shortens rotor or drum life. I use Purple Stuff, Simple Green, or a similar type of acidic cleaner to remove dust and grease. Scrub the rotor and then wash it down well with water.

Now, the trying part begins. Each rotor should be checked for excess run-out with a dial indicator. I always knock off any high spots on the rotor and hub before installing the rotor onto the hub. Place five lug nuts on the hub and rotor assembly and tighten them with a wrench. The following photos show you how I address high and low spots that cause rotor run-out.

This is my in-house-built multipurpose wheel stud installer and rivet crimping tool for NCRS rotors and drums. The rotor and hub are placed in the fixture with the rivet in place as shown. A hydraulic press is used to peen the rivet on the inside of the hub. The upper peening tool is machined out to mushroom the rivet head.

Bloomington Gold or NCRS calipers need this Delco Moraine stamping with the logo above it. Judges also look for the casting number and date code centered below it. This is a 1973-1982 front caliper casting number. Casting numbers for 1965–1966 are 5465954, 5465952, 5465902, and 5465905. Those for 1967 are 5452270, 5452273, 5452281, and 5452284.

Brake Rotor Replacement

Measure Brake Rotor Thickness

1 Using this dial caliper is not the ideal way to check rotor thickness but it gives you an idea whether to machine the rotor or not. This rotor is an original, riveted to the rear spindle with plenty of meat for machining. I measured the flat, smooth rotor at 1.256 inch thick, well above the 1.215 discard limit.

Replace Brake Rotor

2 Rotor replacement starts by drilling out the factory-installed rivets. Use a 3/8-inch drill bit to remove just the head of the rivet. Use a center punch first to dimple the rivet as close to center as possible. The rivets are soft steel and using a drill press makes it much easier to cut them out.

Punch Rivets Out of Brake Hub

3 Once the drilling has been finished, use a flat punch to drive out the remaining rivet shank. After the rivets have been punched out of the rotor, the remaining portion of the rivet needs to be driven out of the hub. Pushing the rivet piece out of the hub can start trouble that shows up during rotor run-out checking. Keep the punch centered; do not let it get stuck in the hub's rivet hole. The rivet hole becomes raised if the punch gets stuck and causes one or more high spots.

Clean Brake Rotors

4 Use a degreaser or brake cleaner on new, used, or machined rotors. Machined rotors have metallic dust embedded in the surface. A good cleaning with a scrub brush helps keep the disc pads healthy and squeak-free. Once the surfaces are clean keep your hands off the disc pad wear areas.

Clean Brake Hub

5 Machined rotors require more rotor hub area preparation. Use a high-speed grinder with a 3M Scotch-Brite disc to knock off the corrosion and any high spots from the axle flange area. Run the grinder around the entire axle flange area in the rotor hub area until it shines. The better you prepare now the more it helps the run-out testing.

Measure Brake Rotor Run-out

6 Use a magnetic or Vise-Grips base dial indicator to check rotor run-out. Set up the indicator at the outer edge to find maximum rotor run-out. Note the low spot to the closest wheel stud. Tighten all five of the lug-nuts with the flat side against the rotor to 50 ft-lbs to ensure the rotor is tight and flat against the hub.

7 This run-out was 0.012 at the high end. I placed a 0.005 piece of brass shim stock on the stud opposite the low spot. This can be tricky. Sometimes you have to place the shim to the right or left of the perceived low spot. Install the rotor and try the run-out check again until the run-out is 0.004 or less. Do this same procedure on new components as well as dated, hard-driven Midyear examples.

Prepare to Install Caliper

8 In preparation for the caliper installation, run a 7/16-20 thread tap through the mounting plate's bolt threaded holes. This is for a rear caliper that bolts to the mounting plate. Be extra careful cleaning these threaded holes with the rotor in place. The tap can easily bottom out against the rotor and chew it up.

Install Piston Retainers

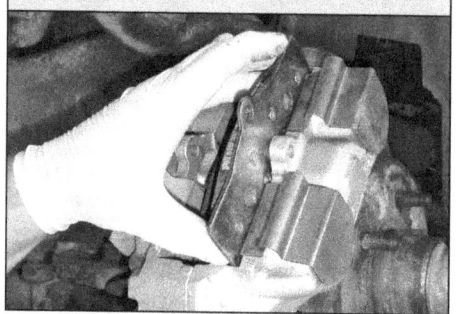

9 Use caliper piston retainers to keep the pistons in the bores until the pads are installed. Push the caliper pistons back into their bore then install the retainers. It is much easier to install the retainers when the calipers are off the car. Or the retainers can be put in place before the pads are removed. The retainers work well when it comes to replacing the disc pads to keep the caliper pistons out of the way. Apply a light coating of silicone grease to the disc pad's back plate before slipping it into place. This caliper kit has new pins that hold the floating disc pads in place.

Torque Caliper Mounting Bolts

10 Use a click-type torque wrench to torque the mounting bolts to 65 ft-lbs after the Stainless Steel Brake Corporation caliper is bolted into place. Leave the brake fluid supply hard line loose and the hose off until you torque the caliper.

1963–1965 Drum Brakes

The tried-and-true duo-servo drum brake system was used on all the Midyears. The front brake shoe is the primary shoe, with a rear, secondary shoe. The duo-servo design increases braking effort as the primary shoe drags the secondary shoe into the drum. Another first for the Midyear were self-adjusting front brakes on the '63 to '64, and rear brakes were self-adjusting from 1963 to 1965. When applying the brakes in reverse, a lever pivots off the secondary brake shoe and turns the adjuster wheel one position. The system worked well for those who came to a full stop. If you had a tendency to let the transmission make the transition from rearward motion to forward, brake adjustment did not occur.

Drum brake service is simple enough and requires very few special tools to address the most common problems: wheel cylinder leakage and brake shoe and drum wear. For the most part, drum brake replacement parts are inexpensive. In the past, I usually rebuilt the wheel cylinders, which have aluminum pistons with a cup-type rubber seal to actuate the brake shoe pin. The aluminum cups corrode and stick in the wheel cylinder bore. Water-saturated brake fluid ends up finding its way between wheel cylinder cup seals, contributing to corrosion. Corrosion eats away at the wheel cylinder surface, leaving irregular low spots. Wheel cylinder hones are used to smooth and refinish the seal surface. In the majority of cases, honing the cylinders to remove the irregular low spots is impossible. The cylinder bore ends up oversized and allows fluid to leak past the wheel cylinder seals. For these reasons, replacement is the better option.

If you are doing an NCRS restoration, original wheel cylinders can be restored for judging. There are companies that machine and install brass or stainless sleeves in your wheel cylinders. Apple Hydraulics machines and sleeves all brands of wheel and master cylinders. Like the calipers, make sure you have the correct Delco wheel cylinders before sending them out for service. The cost is higher, but the wheel cylinders should last the life of the car with periodic brake fluid servicing.

Unless there is a record of recent replacement, you should replace the return spring hardware. Over time, the spring loses its rate due to heat, which weakens the brake shoe hold-down and return springs. Zip Products has all the return springs, clips, and pins available in one kit, making it a simple job. The price is low enough that it is not worth cleaning the tired pieces and hoping that they do the job correctly. After 48-plus years, the self-adjuster hardware most likely is worn and in need of replacement, too.

Midyear brake drums were also Delco products, and chances are they have been changed multiple times by now. You can buy Delco replacements, but they are not Bloomington Gold or NCRS correct. Checking the drum diameter is very important for maximum brake performance and safety. The drum has a maximum safe oversize limit stamped on the outer surface. If the drum has enough material for machining, make sure the shop checks the finished diameter. Drums or rotors worn beyond limits are not safe because they can crack under hard braking. Automotive machine shops and brake specialty shops can service drums and rotors, if necessary.

When drum brakes were popular, brake shoe arc grinders were used for maximum brake shoe-to-drum contact. The arc grinder was set for the exact drum diameter, then the brake shoes were ground accordingly, to fit the drum very closely. The beauty of the brake shoe arc grinder was that the brakes felt good immediately; however, over time, shoes that have not been arc ground wear into the oversize drums, making better contact. Maximum brake shoe contact and correct adjustment is critical for minimal brake pedal travel.

Drum Brake Rebuild

Remove Drum Brake Spring

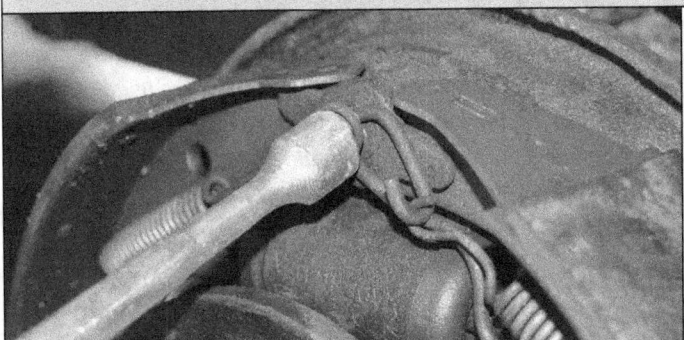

1 *Ah, drum brakes. Had to get out some tools that were lonely in the brake service drawer. This is one valuable brake spring removal and installation tool. Hook it on the spring, give it a simple twist, and the spring is off. Remember, these springs have plenty of stored energy and can hurt you if you are not careful.*

CHAPTER 9

Replace Drum Brake Wheel Cylinder

2 This is what you typically find when peeling back the wheel cylinder boot: a blob of rust and corrosion formed around the aluminum cup. Today it makes sense to replace the cylinders, considering the cost of materials and labor time. Two 1/2-inch hex bolts hold the wheel cylinder to the brake backing plate from the backside. Break the hose or brake line loose before removing the 1/2-inch retaining bolts.

Install Brake Shoes

3 Set the brake shoes in place as an assembly with the star wheel adjuster and return spring installed in the shoes. Make sure to install the parking brake actuator lever and E-clip in the rear shoe before proceeding.

Install Brake Shoe Spring

4 Use the special installation tool to install brake shoe hold-down springs and retainers. This can be tricky since you have to place the self-adjuster lever in the shoe while installing the hold-down spring. The hold-down spring retainer fits into the special tool to aid in pushing down the retainer until the pin is far enough out to allow the retainer to be twisted. Twist the retainer a quarter turn until it sits into the retainer depressions.

5 Install the new primary and secondary brake shoe return springs. The spring (here) is on the primary side. The spring ends have a tendency to open up after installation, so use a pair of pliers to squeeze the spring closed.

Confirm Adjuster Lever Operation

6 This short red spring is part of the self-adjuster assembly. The adjuster lever rocks downward and tightens the brakes each time the brakes are used in reverse. Make sure the adjuster lever is engaging the adjuster's star wheel. You should be able to move the lever downward by hand to tighten the brakes.

Drum Brake Options

Consider changing your front drums to discs if you have a '63 or '64 Midyear. This suggestion is especially worth considering for any Midyear you want to drive on a regular basis. Changing from drums to discs on the front is simple with readily available kits. The rear drum brakes are fine and take quite a bit more work to upgrade. Rear disc conversions are usually done when rear wheel bearings and trailing arm bushings are replaced. All of the available kits are complete with conversion brackets, calipers, disc pads, and hardware. By far, front disc conversions are the best brake upgrade for the dollar.

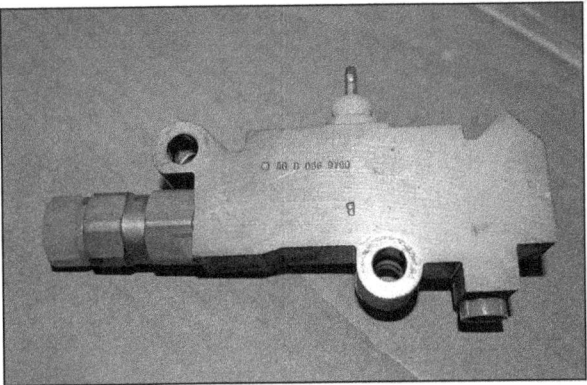

Combination valves, as the name implies, do multiple tasks. The switch at the top warns of pressure loss on one side of a dual system. Internal valving shuts down the side with the fluid pressure loss. Finally, the large brass fitting with double hexes proportions the fluid pressure for optimum brake balance.

Hydraulic System

Single-circuit hydraulic systems worked for years with one common pressure source: the master cylinder. If you have not driven an early car and experienced a brake system failure, it's quite exciting. When a single-circuit hydraulic system springs a leak, complete brake failure occurs. Today's dual-circuit braking systems have two, separate hydraulic systems in one unit. The front brakes are independent of the rear brakes. If the front or rear brakes experience a hydraulic leak, valving shuts down the offending side of the split system. The remaining front or rear brake system provides some stopping power. Of course, if you lose the front brakes, stopping distances are much greater. Due to weight distribution, the front brakes normally do more work.

Disc Brake Options

There are other caliper options for the original Delco heavy iron calipers. Stainless Steel Brakes Corporation (SSBC) has a new-design, replacement caliper available. SSBC's fresh design of the fixed calipers are direct replacements on the original Corvette spindles and utilize cast-aluminum housings to lighten the load significantly. The calipers are also available in red, black, and natural aluminum. The powder-coated calipers add some beauty if you decide on aftermarket specialty wheels. This is an area that you might consider upgrading, especially if you plan on driving your Midyear.

The 1963 split-window coupe project has these really great looking SSBC lightweight aluminum calipers at all four corners. It also has the SSBC "Big Bite" cross-drilled, slotted rotors for maximum stopping power under extreme conditions. These calipers are available in red, black, silver, and natural finishes.

Another option is Wilwood direct-fit aluminum housing calipers. Corvette Central supplied the gold-cadmium-plated, cross-drilled rotors. Calipers come in red, black, and natural. The aluminum calipers offer a 28-pound weight savings overall. They certainly look good with wide-open custom wheels.

The good thing is, you can still stop if there is enough distance between you and the next car.

Most brake valves are multi-purpose, diverting brake fluid flow when hydraulic system failure occurs and warning of system failure. Some valves serve a third purpose, proportioning the brake fluid pressure for the best possible brake balance.

GM brake technology was cutting edge for 1965, using a dual-circuit master cylinder on cars equipped with power brake. This early dual-circuit system had a control valve with a warning light switch. By 1966, all Midyears had a dual-circuit hydraulic system with or without power brakes. This is one very smart upgrade for any single-circuit hydraulic system. Brake lines require reconfiguring for the dual-circuit system, which is easily done during restoration.

Master Cylinders

Like many of the normal wear items, most master cylinders have been replaced multiple times, by now. The correct, date-coded cylinder requires a brass or stainless sleeve for sure. In that case, pack up the master cylinder with your calipers and send the whole batch away for restoration. As I mentioned earlier in this chapter, it makes sense to upgrade to a dual master cylinder. The task is easy enough with most major Corvette suppliers carrying all the pieces needed for quick installation.

Master cylinders leak at the rear, where the pushrod from the brake pedal forces the piston inward. Cars with manual brakes may have brake fluid stains or possibly liquid on the backside of the carpet under the dash. Power-brake-equipped Midyears with master cylinder leaks do not readily show the fluid loss. As the fluid seeps out of the rear of the master cylinder, it can end up in the booster, where the fluid causes internal damage. Master cylinder failure is gradual in most cases. Many times, the problem is noticed when waiting at a stop light, the brake pedal creeping toward the floor. If you have to wait for an extra-long light, the pedal may actually end up on the floorboard because brake fluid is bypassing the compression seals, causing the brake pedal to drop slowly. Eventually, the seals do not hold pressure at all and the pedal has a slight drag when depressed. After the slight drag, the brake pedal hits the floor. You can pump the brake pedal, and it has resistance, but the pedal just heads to the floorboard a moment later.

Brake Lines, Fittings, Hardware

Finding corroded brake lines and fittings is commonplace. If the brake lines are more than 10 years old, chances are all the brake lines are in poor condition. Brake lines corrode externally and internally. With all your hard work, it would be a shame to crash over the cost of new brake lines. If you are planning a body-on restoration, brake line replacement is very tough. I don't want to say it is impossible; it can be done. Of course the lines can be modified to fit without body removal. The problem there is that it is very obvious to a potential buyer. If you decide to just lift the body enough for body mount replacement, go a little further and replace the brake lines.

Removing old brake lines is usually difficult. Either the line wants to twist off or the fitting nut is rounded off. If you want to save the lines, here are some tricks. Heat the fitting nut when replacing a front brake hose with a seized fitting. To avoid a small explosion, cut the flexible brake hose, close to the hose fitting. (I got a surprise the first time I heated up the fitting to loosen a line: The ensuing pop blew the rubber hose out of the hose end. No danger or damage, just a very noticeable surprise.) If you find a slightly rounded fitting nut, Vise-Grips

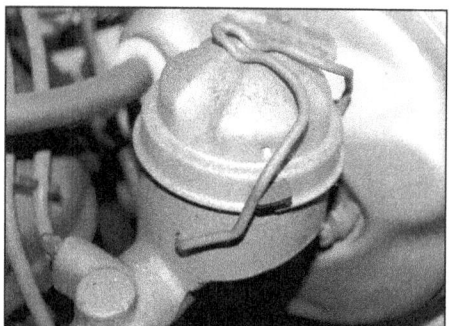

This is a single master cylinder with power brake booster from 1964. It has the correct-looking cap, but the cylinder itself has been replaced. If you decide on an NCRS early Midyear this is what you have to deal with. A brake system leak = no brakes at all.

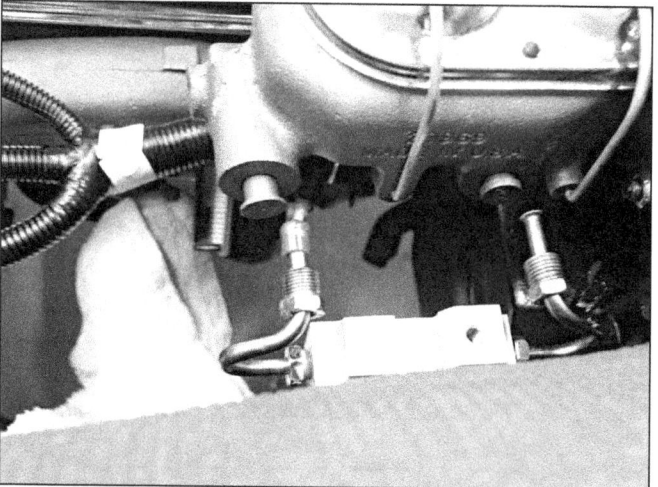

This 1964 Coupe is about to receive a much better option, the late-model, dual-reservoir system master cylinder. All-new late-model brake lines are used from a 1970 Corvette to avoid the hassle of making custom lines. Yes, the body has to be lifted to access and change the new brake lines.

pliers applied to the line wrench helps loosen it. Clamp the Vise-Grips onto the open end of the line wrench to prevent slippage of the wrench.

All Midyear brake lines are carbon steel with double inverted flare ends and steel flare nuts. If you plan on repairing steel brake lines, they should be double flared. Stainless-steel lines should be single flared. Under no circumstances should compression fittings be substituted for flare fittings. If you do splice a brake line, use inverted flare coupler fittings to make the connection. Brake system pressure is 50 to 100 psi and any leak is a problem. Besides the obvious loss of fluid, system pressure is reduced from even a small leak.

Power or Manual Brakes?

Disc brakes require additional pedal pressure to move the multitude of caliper pistons. Vacuum-diaphragm, power-assisted boosters were introduced to ease the extra pressure requirements. Power brakes also make drum brakes feel better if the drums and shoes overheat.

New 1964–1967 date-coded brake boosters with correct cadmium plating are available from all the major suppliers. Long Island Corvette Supply has a rebuilding service for your original unit, if you desire. Keep in mind that the rebuilding service takes approximately a month. With proper planning, the booster is ready for installation when you need it.

Let's face it: We are getting soft with all the latest automotive options available. Driving an early car with manual disc or drum brakes is hard to accept after cruising around in your daily driver. Converting to power brakes is routinely done with readily available parts. Brake boosters are available remanufactured and new with correct master cylinders. If you do convert to power brakes, make sure you also purchase the appropriate master cylinder.

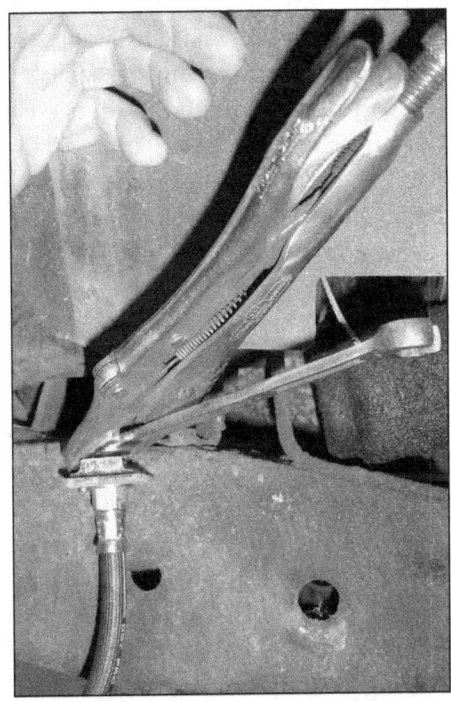

Here is another trick to save a brake line fitting nut. Someone had just installed a new hose on a leaking caliper and I wanted to try to save the hose. The Vise-Grips provide extra tension on the fitting nut. The Vise-Grips are placed over the line wrench applying pressure on the open end wrench. The Vise-Grips cuts into your line wrench but sometimes it is worth disfiguring a wrench.

Whether loosening or tightening the line, always use wrenches to hold both the hose end and brake line fitting nut. The nut must come loose to release the brake line. If the hose end is not held properly, the brake line can twist while you attempt to loosen it and you can possibly break the line.

This 1964–1967 NCRS-correct booster came off a '64 coupe converted to disc brakes. While restoring the pedal assembly I decided to remove the booster and master cylinder. I found a trail of brake fluid on the booster from a faulty master cylinder. Luckily I found it before the brake fluid did damage to the brake booster's rubber diaphragm.

I found this after raising the body on a '64 coupe, making me wonder if someone lifted the body for a repair. Someone did a lot of work to put a compression fitting in a very difficult location. Why not replace the entire line? When replacing the brake lines, you need to note how the driver-side brake block is installed. It is easy to flip the block over and have the clip on the opposite side of the tab. The lines screw in but requires extra force due to the improper thread match and leaks occur.

Brake Fluid

Brake fluid is the culprit of almost all problems in the brake system. DOT 3 and DOT 4 glycol brake fluid is hygroscopic and draws water from the atmosphere. Master cylinder caps have rubber diaphragms to prevent air intrusion into the system. The diaphragm expands and contracts as brake fluid level changes. It is imperative that the rubber diaphragm seals tightly to the master cylinder reservoir. Water ends up in the hydraulic system no matter how careful you are. The worst thing to do is use a previously opened can of brake fluid that has been sitting around for many months. When you check the brake fluid, put the cap back on the reservoir as quickly as possible.

DOT 5 or silicone brake fluid is an alternative to the glycol fluid. Silicone fluid is non-hygroscopic, although moisture in the system is still possible. The use of silicone fluid is somewhat controversial because of spongy brake pedal concerns. Another concern is silicone fluid's inability to mix with any moisture that may be present. Water in the system is in specific areas and not disbursed throughout the hydraulic system.

I use silicone brake fluid in all Midyear project cars to prevent damage to painted surfaces. My personal cars all have silicone fluid with no ill effects especially concerning the spongy brake pedal claim. The chance that water intrusion is an issue with proper maintenance intervals is greatly reduced. If you plan on road racing or high-speed auto crossing use the glycol fluids and change it often to limit moisture intrusion.

Silicone-based fluid is particularly dangerous in areas with freezing temperatures because the water freezes within the system, potentially preventing brake operation or causing component failures.

Brake System Service Tips

- Anti-squeal products that are applied to the disc pads should not be used. When the disc pads stick to the caliper pistons, caliper housing damage occurs. The disc pads and pistons follow any deviation in the rotors.
- "Spongy" brake pedals after long drives indicate excessive rotor run-out. The best policy is to check rotor run-out every time the rotors are removed for any reason.
- Wheel bearings must be checked for excessive play to keep the rotors in check.
- Flush the brake system every two years regardless of miles driven.

DOT 5.1 glycol-based fluid is a good solution for cold temperatures.

Parking Brakes

Like the vehicle brakes, parking brakes went through numerous changes during the 1960s. The 1967 parking brake system was refined and a similar design was used until 1982.

The 1963 parking brake cable system had some trouble spots. The parking brake front cable was secured to the fiberglass floorboard. After years of use, the parking brake weakens the fiberglass floorboard, eventually tearing out the cable support. The front cable pulls on a frame-mounted lever that connects to the rear parking brake cables. The frame-mounted lever is easily damaged from road debris or improper jacking during repairs.

The 1964 model year brought a much-needed change: the front parking brake cable was mounted to the transmission crossmember. There were a couple of different rear parking brake cable configurations for the drum and disc brake cars. A much easier to use, center-mounted parking brake lever was brought into production in 1967. The center-mounted parking brake lever was easier to use, thanks to greater leverage. Throughout all the changes, two mechanical parking brake assemblies were used. The 1963–1965 drum brake-equipped Midyears mechanically applied the rear brakes, while 1965–1967 Midyears with disc brakes had a unique, miniature drum brake system incorporated into the disc brake system.

The mini parking brake assembly worked poorly, at best. The mini drum brake shoes and cables had to be adjusted frequently for any parking brake reliability. To top it off, the brake shoes were hidden behind the rear spindle. Many parking brake shoes and hardware have been removed because of the difficulty in servicing them. Specialty tools are available to service the brake shoes, but even so, the task is quite difficult.

The best policy is to replace the parking brake shoes and hardware when servicing the rear spindle bearings. I use stainless-steel hardware with steel parking brake shoes.

No matter what Midyear you own, operate the parking brake frequently. All parking brake cables have a tendency to freeze from non-use. Always adjust the parking brake shoes before adjusting the cable. In most cases, I back off the parking brake cable, leaving it loose while I adjust the brake shoes. Make sure the wheels rotate freely after adjusting the parking brake. Excessive brake shoe drag causes high heat, which possibly damages the wheel seals and bearings. Of course, brake shoe wear and damage does occur and requires the dreaded parking brake shoe replacement.

BRAKES

Bleeding the 1963–1967 Corvette brake system is a major pain and at the very least an annoyance. The multitude of air pockets within the calipers makes it very difficult to get all the air out. Having a friend pump the brakes is an option. Expect an all day affair in the quest to get a really good, hard pedal. Today, pressure bleeding systems work well and can be purchased at a very reasonable cost. If you use a pressure bleeding system, you do not need anyone to pump the pedal; just pressurize the system and bleed. You can also use the pressurized bleeder to check the system for leaks. Leave the system pressurized for half an hour after bleeding the system. Any leaks can then be spotted before heading out on your maiden voyage.

Motive Products has a very reasonably-priced brake bleeder unit that works like a garden sprayer. Be sure to buy the appropriate adapter for your Midyear's master cylinder. After installing the adapter, the cylinder is pumped up and the bleeding begins. Another nice feature is that with the multitude of adapters available you could flush any of your other vehicles' brake systems easily.

Brake Setup

Remove Brake Adjuster Nut

1 First soak the parking brake cable with PB Blaster to help break the adjuster nut loose. Sometimes heat must be used to get frozen nuts loose and a propane torch does the job well; however, always remember you are working around a fiberglass floorboard that burns quickly.

Connect Brake Cable to Lever

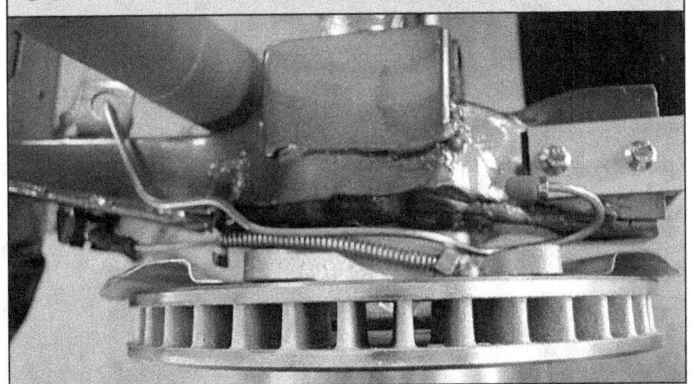

2 This gives you an idea how the parking brake cable connects to the lever. The caliper has to be removed to access the parking brake cable. The rear caliper brake line should be set in place before the caliper is installed. I often find this brake line incorrectly placed on top of the trailing arm. The line sits under the caliper conforming to fit alongside the trailing arm.

Replace Parking Brake Springs

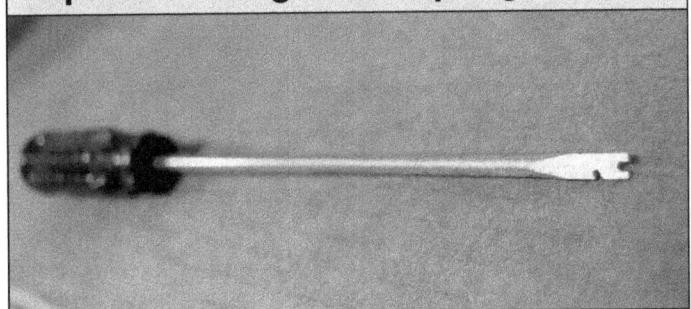

3 Use this special tool to remove and replace the springs for parking brake service with the spindle in place. The notches grab the spring for the contorted installation of the springs. Although feasible, this tool is no miracle device, it allows you to service the parking brake shoes. Mid America Corvette has this tool available along with all the necessary parking brake pieces.

Restore Parking Brake Assembly

4 This is the condition of many parking brake assemblies found hidden under the rear spindle. Broken return springs cause a constant clicking noise as the wheels rotate. Grease on the brake shoes from incorrectly installed spindle seals is commonplace. This is why I always recommend disassembling the spindle and restoring the entire assembly.

Remove Rivet Stud from Spindle

5 Someone has drilled the rivet heads off leaving the remaining rivet stud in the spindle. It seems harmless enough until the rivet stud backs out into the parking brake assembly. I always remove the entire rivet to prevent floating shrapnel from tearing up the parking brake's internal components.

Install Brake Shoes

6 This is what I like to see: New steel cadmium plated brake shoes with stainless steel hardware installed. Use Never-Seeze to lube the adjuster threads during assembly. As you can imagine, working through a couple of 1/2-inch holes to install the pieces is very difficult. If you can master installing the shoes with the spindle in place, shipbuilding in a tiny bottle is right up your alley.

Set Brake Adjusters

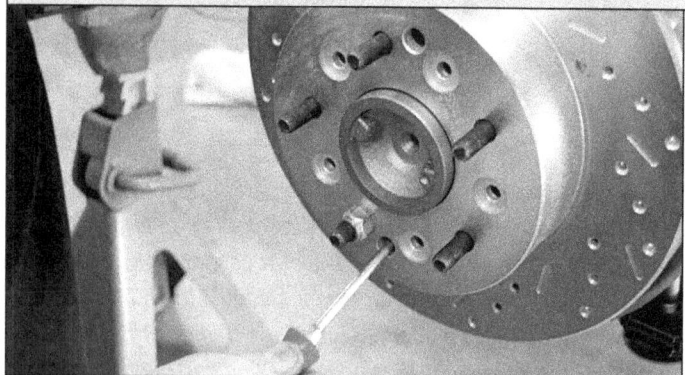

7 Old-time brake adjusters that are not right- or left-specific need to be adjusted now. One side goes up to lengthen the star wheel adjuster while the other side goes down. Tighten the parking brake adjuster until the rotor does not turn, then back it off five to six clicks. The rotor should turn with minimal brake shoe drag. I usually tighten until the rotor does not turn and back off the adjuster procedure twice to set the shoes in the drum.

Bleed Brakes

8 Using a pressure-pot assembly is the preferred method to bleed brakes on all Midyears. The cover plate fits tightly on the master cylinder and 15 to 20 psi of pressure is applied from the pressure tank filled with fresh brake fluid. This is absolutely the quickest and easiest way to bleed brakes.

9 As you bleed the brakes, clear, fresh DOT 5 silicone fluid flows from the remanufactured O-ring calipers. The hose is used to prevent spilling brake fluid. To check operation, also look between the disc pad and caliper and check to make sure the caliper pistons have come out and are pushing against the disc pads. Once in a great while, a piston sticks slightly and prevents it from seating on the disc pad.

CHAPTER 10

SUSPENSION

Zora Arkus Duntov wanted a suspension that would provide a competitive edge for the 1963 Corvette. The 1953–1962 Corvettes carried GM's early kingpin-style front suspension, and although it had proven to be reliable, the early suspension had limited adjustability hindering high-speed handling. If General Motors wanted to be able to show the new Corvette Sting Ray's merits, an entirely new suspension was required.

Design Innovations

The new front suspension design incorporated unequal-length control arms with ball joints. Rear suspension changes were radical with independent control of each rear wheel.

The use of unequal-length front suspension control arms kept the tire/wheel geometry stable. Balancing suspension travel and geometry had been an ongoing battle with the kingpin setup. The newly designed suspension balance was much better, proving to be a major improvement in handling on inconsistent road surfaces. Ball joints were used for steering knuckle/spindle connection to the control arms in place of the antiquated kingpins. Anti-roll bars were added to further improve handling on the all-new front suspension. The new front suspension was so effective that the same basic design is still in use today, albeit with some tweaks on the latest Corvettes.

Designing a cost-effective rear independent suspension assembly was a challenge. The use of a transverse-mounted rear spring for vehicle lift had the added benefit of acting somewhat like an anti-roll bar, since it was connected to both trailing arms. The newly designed rear suspension proved to be road race worthy while minimizing unsprung weight. The rear trailing arm housed the rear spindle assembly and maintained rear-wheel toe alignment. Strut rods were used to control and adjust rear suspension camber. The real engineering brilliance was in maintaining tolerable alignment during suspension travel, without upper control arms to help locate the trailing arms.

Think about your intended plans for your Midyear and select the preferred spring rates and shock absorbers for comfortable road cruising. Suspension work requires careful thought. This spring's potential force can be applied when released suddenly.

HOW TO RESTORE YOUR CORVETTE: 1963–1967 133

CHAPTER 10

The cost savings centered around the axleshafts and the deletion of rear, upper control arms. Other fixed, rear independent suspension used constant-velocity-style axleshafts, requiring axleshafts that allowed overall length changes while utilizing two universal joints. Constant-velocity axleshafts were expensive to design and produce, back in the day. Conversely, the plunging axleshaft would not maintain correct wheel alignment, but the idea worked; it saved money while allowing a true independent rear suspension, but only because of a carefully designed-in balance: Simple geometry shows that a fixed-length straight line becomes too short as the line goes off center; the challenge was to control the rear wheel camber without using telescoping axleshafts. The Corvette's fixed differential mounting allowed pivoting the axleshaft off it. The idea of using driveshaft-style components for axleshafts saved money. Universal joints with flanges were used to attach the axleshaft to the spindles and differential.

Another engineering fact was that the fixed axleshaft length did not allow the use of the upper control arms. Binding would have occured as the fixed length axleshaft attempted to travel through the up and down motion.

There are a couple of downsides with this differential/suspension design. For one, the weight of the Corvette is transferred onto the differential axleshaft yokes and internal differential pinion gear cross shaft. Over time, vehicle weight wears on the differential yokes and pinion gear cross-shaft pin, negatively affecting rear suspension alignment. For another, major changes in suspension movement meant radical changes in camber(explained earlier). At full suspension droop, when the rear wheels are hanging free with no load upon them, axleshaft universal joint binding can occur. While the shock absorbers limit travel, binding can still occur within the shock absorber travel.

Exacerbating the binding issue was GM's use of axleshaft universal joint caps to retain the axleshafts on the differential side. High-torque engine applications used the caps in place of flat straps. Low-torque applications received straps to retain the universal joint caps. Some of the strap-retained axleshafts do not bind at full downward travel. The best policy is to avoid raising the rear wheels and running the drivetrain, no matter what axleshaft shaft retainers are used.

The same style of rear independent suspension is found underneath three generations of Corvettes, 33 years later. The concept was sound and the design provided exceptional performance. And over three decades, it was refined and improved. A few minor changes were incorporated in the suspension, front to rear, during the Midyear's existence. The beauty of the long suspension run is interchangeability between the 1963–1982 model years. The only major change in 19 years was the 1980–1982 Corvette rear differential manufacturer and material. As you can imagine, there were tweaks to all the front and rear suspension components especially in the early years.

The 1963–1966 early, upper front suspension control arms are the same and feature rectangular control arm shafts. The 1966 late-production through 1982 control arms are the same and feature round control arm shafts. Early-1963 front suspension lower control arms are unique, minus a reinforcement pad. General Motors welded a sway bar support pad to the underside of the late 1963–1982 lower control arms.

The 1963-1966 control arm (top) is an early upper control arm with rectangular control arm shaft. The late 1966 through 1982 production upper control arm (bottom) has a round control arm shaft. This is one of many things you need to know for an NCRS or Bloomington Gold restoration.

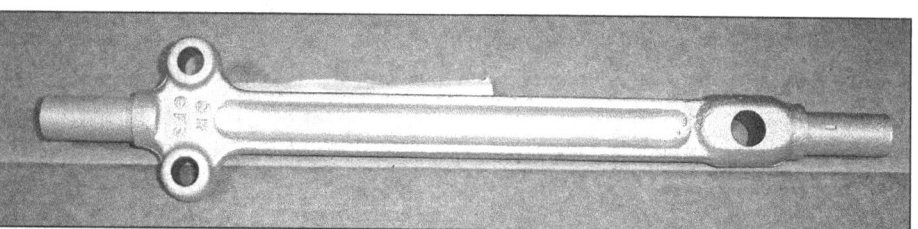

This early lower control arm shaft was used reportedly until 1964. Lower control arms manufactured before December 4, 1962, were part numbers 3817549 and 3817540. Later lower control arms were part numbers 3840603 and 3840604 with additional support bracket for the sway bar. This is where verification of correct pieces can become difficult, with the lower control arm shaft being used in both the early and late lower control arm.

SUSPENSION

Alignment Terms

Caster describes the angle of the vertical centerline of the spindle (how far forward or rearward the top of the spindle is tipped) and largely determines spindle load placement affecting high-speed handling or lead. Incorrect caster causes a load bias on the steering wheel right or left while you are driving down a straight road. When the steering wheel is released, the vehicle immediately heads in that direction. Caster can be difficult to understand, since you cannot see differing wheel/tire relationships or tire wear problems.

Laying the top of the spindle back farther from vertical creates positive caster. Positive caster promotes better handling with more vehicle load to the rear of the spindle, which aids the steering wheel's return to center, after cornering. Early on, 1 degree of positive caster was the norm. With the advent of radial tires and improved power steering, positive caster was increased to 7 degrees on performance vehicles.

As you might surmise, non-power-steering Midyears with increased positive caster exhibit high-effort steering. Non-power steering cars upgraded to power steering benefit from less effort while allowing increased positive caster.

Cross caster helps keep your vehicle rolling down the highway without having to hold onto the steering wheel. The typical alignment has 6½-degrees positive caster at the left wheel, but the right side caster is set at 7-degrees positive caster to keep your vehicle from running off of crowned roadways.

Camber is the angle at which the wheel is tilted inward or outward, vertically. If the top of the wheel is angled inward (toward the engine) relative to the bottom of the wheel, the suspension has negative camber. Hence, if the top of the wheel is angled outward, the suspension has positive camber.

Incorrect camber alignment is easily seen when out of adjustment. You commonly see the top of the rear tires leaning slightly inward on 1963-and-up Corvettes. The typical alignment setting for street-driven Corvettes is 1/4 degree of negative camber. So that oh-so-slight inward lean at the top of the rear tire is normal. Remember, the rear suspension has some limitations due to design. The ¼ degree of negative camber setting helps with these limitations while keeping the rear tires in maximum contact with the pavement through typical suspension travel.

Corvettes set up for road racing handle better with increased negative camber settings even though additional negative caster causes wear at the inner edge of the tire tread. A compromise can be reached with street-driven, occasionally-raced Midyears: Set the rear camber to 1/2-degree negative to promote better handling with minimal tire wear. For the record, any positive camber causes poor handling and the tire tread shows smooth wear, depending on how positive the camber setting is.

Toe measures the angle of the wheel, front to rear. Zero toe means the wheels are running precisely parallel to each another, and pointing straight ahead. Toe-in describes a situation in which the front of the wheels are closer together than the rear of the wheels. Toe-out is the opposite of toe-in.

Toe-in or toe-out affects handling, tire wear, and fuel mileage. Excessive toe eats up the tires very quickly on the inner or outer edges. Unlike camber, the tire tread wear is feathered and looks like the

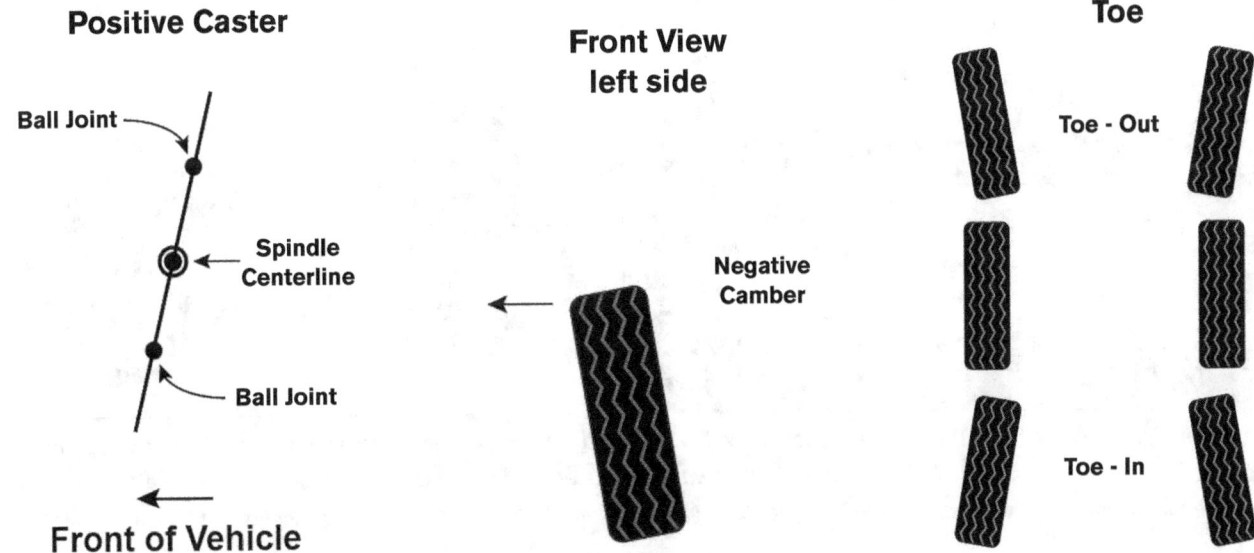

Mike Urquhart of Petris Enterprises Inc. put together this diagram explaining alignment terms.

tire has been chewed up. Fuel efficiency decreases because the tires are scrubbing all the time on the road surface. Handling is adversely affected, and as a result, the car does not roll easily. Rear toe alignment adjustment has to be performed on 1963–1967 Corvettes to keep the back end rolling freely.

Thrust line is another alignment term that comes into play. The idea is to make sure the rear wheels are tracking in the same line as the front suspension. A complete four-wheel alignment includes checking the thrust line, caster, camber, and toe. Finding a shop that knows how to properly align your 1963–1967 Corvette may be difficult. Originally, General Motors required trailing arm pivot bolt removal when changing the shims for toe adjustment. Later-design trailing arm toe shims are slotted, requiring only that the bolts be loosened to change them. This is why many alignment shops are not too happy to see an early Corvette come in.

I learned the hard way why General Motors drilled the frame and installed a cotter pin to keep the new-design, slotted trailing arm shims in place. If the cotter pins are not used, the later-style slotted shims can fall out, and you have a wicked rear steer issue. I always drill the frame, so the cotter pins can be used with the later trailing arm shims.

Vehicle weight also makes major differences in ride height and alignment. I suggest filling the fuel tank about half full for a realistic ride height and checking

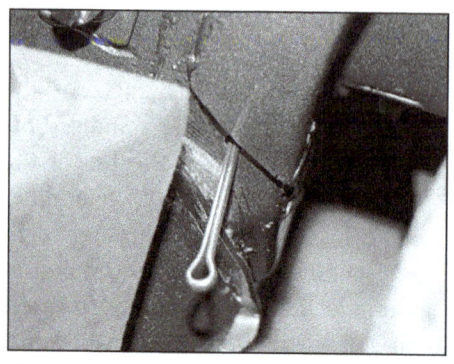

The later model frame converted for this '63 project has the 7/32-inch holes drilled for the trailing arm shim cotter pin. The cotter pin is inserted through the inner and outer shims (meaning the inside of the frame), so it also has to be drilled. Drilling the frame is really tough with the body on, but it must be done when using slotted trailing arm shims.

Rear Steer Concerns

The 1963-and-later Corvettes can suffer from a phenomena called rear steer. The feeling can be scary and possibly dangerous when all the wrong elements add up. The rear trailing arms pivot on rubber bushings, and these same bushings are shimmed to adjust rear toe alignment. Failed rubber bushings allow the trailing arms to shift around under load, which changes the toe adjustment. The worn trailing arm bushing rear steer problem is exacerbated when you accelerate or decelerate. Handling feels fine in a steady cruise state, but when you accelerate or decelerate, the handling feels somewhat unpredictable because you and your prized possession can head into traffic or off the road.

Use a 5/8-inch drill bit to cut off the securing washers with a drill press. Sometimes you have to hold the outer washer with adjustable pliers when rubber bushings are worn badly.

Bad news here. These severely worn trailing arm bushings caused very noticeable rear steer concerns. The rubber bushing material was oozing out of the trailing arm bushing outer sleeve.

the tire pressure before having the alignment done. The best policy is to check the pressures yourself and set it to the tire manufacturer's recommendations before a trip to the alignment shop.

Suspension Restoration

Inspect and evaluate the chassis and suspension components before disassembly. As unbelievable as this may seem, a trip to the alignment shop before any disassembly takes place should be considered. Early Corvette frames have been subjected to years of abuse and possibly even collisions. It would be bad news to have all your suspension restoration completed and discover that your Corvette's frame is tweaked. Discretion comes into play here. If you know the history of your project Midyear, the frame's integrity may not be a concern.

A "basket case" Midyear project is another challenge altogether. All the suspension pieces, including the frame, may look fine, but they may be hiding tweaked components. To be safe, the suspension should be assembled and the drivetrain in place, then the alignment and frame condition can be checked if necessary. The drivetrain must be in place to have the Corvette at ride height before the alignment check. If the alignment shop calls to say they cannot align your Corvette properly, now is the time to know.

After considering the possibility of frame damage affecting your Midyear's suspension alignment, you need to verify the frame's integrity. Severe corrosion may require removal of the body to properly repair the frame. This may be the turning point for your project, and may determine the direction of your restoration. Severe frame damage may necessitate removal of the body. If you have to deal with frame damage that requires straightening, the shop may recommend loosening the body mounts before any frame work begins, which is a very smart thing to do because twisting and pulling on the frame can break or distort fiberglass panels very easily.

If frame straightening has been performed, it's wise to bring the Midyear back to the alignment shop. Similar to body problems, it would be really disheartening to find out that there was an alignment issue after frame work. Bent chassis components may have compensated for earlier collision damage that could have otherwise caused alignment problems. Distorted suspension control arms and control arm shafts are a very real possibility. Before work begins, you need to verify that the frame is straight, and that the alignment is good. The frame is the basis for the entire project, including the body structure. Trying to save a few dollars here, may cost you big bucks down the road.

Once the frame has been checked, the suspension disassembly can begin. You might want to leave the engine in place until the front suspension has been taken apart. The front springs are under an extreme load, making them difficult to remove with a light front end. All of the front suspension bushings should be replaced. Front suspension lower ball joints wear quickly, and they take the majority of the vehicle's road load. Upper ball joints do more stabilization than load carrying and as such tend to experience minimal wear.

All wheel bearings should be checked and, in most cases, replaced. Rear wheel bearings should always be serviced and replaced, unless you have absolute proof of recent servicing. Disregarding the rear wheel bearing's condition could potentially cost you. One unlucky Midyear owner was riding in his newly purchased prize when the right rear wheel bearing failed. Adding insult to injury, the bearing spindle was damaged and let the wheel go, damaging the rear fender. This is an extreme situation, but there are warning signs.

Failing wheel bearings rumble or growl early on, and get louder as speed increases. Two bearings retain the wheel spindle. Bearing loads increase during cornering and exacerbate the growl on the loaded bearing. As the failing bearing's load increases, so does the growling intensity. Decreased bearing loads lessen the growl.

I use this road test procedure to determine a potentially failed bearing: it involves driving on a long sweeping turn, right or left. If I find the growling noise increases during the wide sweeping turn, the next step is to turn around and go in the opposite direction. If the noise decreases, I know that a wheel bearing is failing. Now, how do I know what side is failing? The direction I am traveling in that caused the most noise indicates which side has the problem. So, if I found the noise greater on a long, sweeping left-hand turn, the left rear bearing is failing.

This information is very good to remember, now that you are a Corvette owner. You can prevent yourself from being stuck on the road because of this preventable, major problem.

Corvette rear wheel bearing replacement is not for the first timer. Specialty tools are required for wheel bearing disassembly, replacement, and assembly. Corvettes used the same rear wheel bearing configuration from 1963 to 1982. After that, new technology came into play, eliminating the need for a myriad of special service tools. Understandably, many shops do not want to invest in the correct early rear wheel bearing service tools. The possibility of performing just a few early Corvette bearing service jobs does not make good fiscal sense.

The 1968–1982 Corvette rear wheel bearings require specific adjustment to keep the wheel in check without causing excessive heat. General Motors used shims between the rear wheel bearings to adjust and maintain bearing end play. In some cases, the original shims can be used with the new wheel bearings. If the bearing end play is not correct, you must have the correct shim. This compounds the difficulty during rear wheel bearing service.

Also, the inner and outer wheel bearings have an interference fit onto the rear spindle. The interference fit is tight enough to require a hydraulic bearing press and/or bearing removal tool. Every time a wheel bearing shim is changed the wheel bearings have to be pressed on and off. You could conceivably end up buying many extra wheel bearings before the correct shim is found. Although the chances may be slim that you will service your own rear wheel bearings, I have outlined the process below. Knowing the correct procedures can save you from major issues if you are looking for a reputable rebuilder or repair facility.

Rear Wheel Bearing Service

As with the unique Corvette disc brake calipers, a cottage industry sprang up to service rear wheel bearings. People like Artie, at Van Steel, specialize in rebuilding 1963–1982 Corvette trailing arms. They have all the right tools and equipment to properly service rear wheel bearings. Long-standing Corvette specialty shops possibly have the early bearing service tools because they had to deal with them. Most GM dealers had the tools but by now they have most likely disappeared. Ask whether they have the correct tools or are going to improvise. Request a top-quality synthetic wheel bearing grease and the best bearings available. Most major oil suppliers have a synthetic wheel bearing grease available.

Remanufactured trailing arms come in a few different configurations. You can purchase an entire trailing arm assembly ready to bolt on. The rear spindle housing can be bought with fresh bearings and seals for installation into your trailing arm. Due to brake backing plate design, the plate has to be installed during assembly of the bearing and spindle. This is a good reason to consider purchasing the complete trailing arm assembly. GM rear disc brake rotors are for regular braking and emergency brake operation, with the miniature brake shoes under the rear spindle assembly. Installing or replacing the mini brake shoes is challenging, even for experienced Corvette service technicians. You definitely want to check into how difficult it is to replace the brake shoes before going the spindle and housing route.

The rear wheel bearings are a major concern, one that must be completely understood. In addition, front wheel bearings are also important. General Motors used the same front tapered roller wheel bearings from 1963 until 1968, while 1969–1982 Corvettes had larger front wheel bearing assemblies with stouter spindles. When restoring Midyears that will be driven spiritedly, I recommend using the later spindles. The larger front wheel bearings and stouter spindles are more reliable. Also, servicing or replacing the front wheel bearings is easy. You do need to precisely adjust the front wheel bearings though, as loose wheel bearings can affect the brake calipers, causing a low brake pedal from air intrusion into the hydraulic system.

Wheel studs are often forgotten until a lug nut is tough to remove. My policy is to replace all 20 wheel studs while servicing the rear spindles and front hubs. After all, the studs are more than 40 years old and chances are they have stress fractures. You should also consider your wheel choice if you decide to change the wheel studs. I install longer studs if wheels or wheel spacers require them.

Wheel Housing Rebuild

Install New Wheel Bearing

1 *This hefty rear spindle bearing press is a must have for rear wheel bearing service. The bolt placed in the spindle support prevents the bearing press hold-down bolt from coming out of position at high speed. After putting some torque on the forcing screw, use a large hammer to shock the bearings loose. If necessary apply more torque then hit it another couple of times. If not, caliper mounting plate distortion occurs.*

SUSPENSION

Spindle Bearing Tools

2 This tool was designed to remove the outer bearing with the rotor still in place. It works well if you don't have a hydraulic press and collar to remove the bearing. If you fully tighten the clamping bolts that capture the inner bearing race, the bearing can be removed without damage. Apply pressure with the Allen head forcing screws then tighten the clamping screws a little bit more before trying to remove the bearing. This comes in handy if the wrong bearing shim is installed.

Remove Inner Wheel Bearing Race

3 This is more evidence of grease leakage from the outer seal with the build-up of dirt around the bearing housing area. With the spindle out, knock out the inner wheel bearing and race with a round, flat punch. If you wipe the grease away from the bearing race you find there are two areas cast into the bearing housing, to allow better purchase on the bearing race during the removal process. Work the punch back and forth tapping the bearing race out evenly preventing housing distortion. Accessing the parking brake shoes is quite a pain with the spindle in place.

Mount Spindle Housings In Correct Position

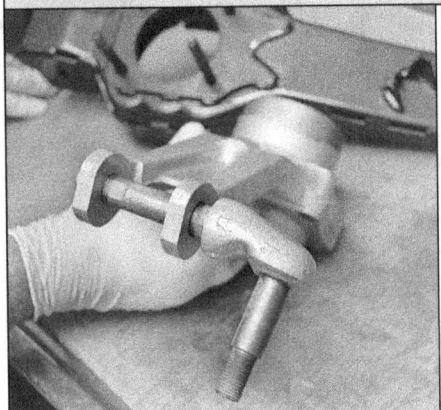

4 Be sure that left and right spindle housings are re-installed in the correct position. The factory machined a flat on the shock mount to prevent rotation. The shock mount doubles as the strut rod retaining bolt. During complete trailing arm restoration, it is very easy to swap the right for the left spindle housing or vice-versa. Check carefully for proper placement. If the housings are swapped the shock mount does not go into the housing. That means you have to re-do all of your hard work installing new bearings.

Use Proper Specialty Tools

5 I prefer to use these bearing installation tools. They come in multiple sizes to fit many bearing races. Bearing installers ensure square bearing race installation without bearing damage. Although bearing races are very tough, damage can occur when using punches to force them in place.

Install Spindle Bearing

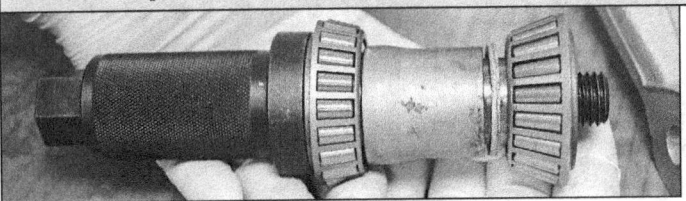

6 This rear spindle bearing setup tool has the same dimensions as a rear spindle. Insert the setup tool into the spindle housing with inner bearing, outer bearing, sleeve, and shim. Check bearing end play before final assembly. Check end play before packing the bearings with grease.

Check Spindle Bearing End Play

7 Here are the bearings, sleeve, and shim setup with the end play setup tool. Rear wheel spindle tapered bearings should have 0.00 to 0.004 endplay per the GM service manual. Check the endplay with lightly oiled bearing for the best possible feel; wheel bearing grease masks any minute play when using the set-up tool. The best policy is to have zero endplay, which means you can feel no perceptible sideway movement in the set-up tool. If the bearing end play shim is too thin you have a difficult time rotating the set-up tool. A dial indicator can be used to check end play; if you want to go to the high end play limit, it is difficult to tell the difference between .004 and .008. Shims come in nine sizes from .097 to .145 thick making it feasible to keep the end play at the low limit.

Pack Wheel Bearings

8 This inexpensive wheel bearing packer is very easy to use. Place the bearings as shown then connect your grease gun to the grease fitting. Pump your grease gun, filled with synthetic chassis grease, until grease forces out of the bearings. Place approximately two tablespoons of grease in the spindle housing in case of excess bearing heat.

Lube Spindle Housing

9 Place two tablespoons of grease in the housing cavity before you place the sleeve and shim in the spindle housing. Make sure the large tapered end of the sleeve is installed toward the outer bearing. Place the shim on the small end or toward the inner bearing.

Install Spindle Housing on Trailing Arm

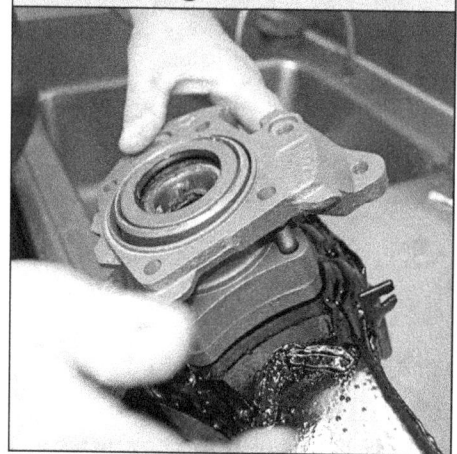

10 Place the spindle housing into the trailing arm then install the caliper mount onto the four trailing arm studs. Place the large parking brake anchor threaded hole at 12 o'clock when installing the mount on the trailing arm. Always check and chase the threads for the caliper mount and parking brake anchor bolt threads before installing the mount. The caliper mount threads are 7/16-20 tap while the parking brake anchor threads are 1/2-20.

Apply Grease to Rubber Seals

11 Once the bearings and seals have been installed, make sure you apply grease to the rubber seal. This prevents seal burn-up for the first few miles of operation.

As you are rubbing your finger around the seal, feel for installation damage. Bent seals cause leaks. Replacing an outer seal means major work and bearing replacement is likely.

SUSPENSION

Install Backing Plate

12 Install the backing plate with parking brake shoes with four 3/8-24 thread nuts and lock washers. Torque the nuts to 45 ft-lbs before installing the spindle assembly. If necessary, replace the wheel studs before installing the spindle.

Install Axleshaft Flange

13 With the trailing arm turned over, install the axleshaft flange. Use the special assembly tool to finish the bearing installation. The special tool pulls the spindle into the bearings as the 1¼ nut is tightened with a large pull bar. The spindle should be rotated while pulling the bearings together. Seals pinch as the spindle assembly comes together taking a chunk out of the seal.

Install Bearing Races and Wheel Studs

14 Front hubs get the same treatment as the rear spindle bearings did. Replace bearing races and wheel studs after a thorough cleaning. I use an in-house-built wheel stud installer to ensure straight stud installation on the hydraulic press. This tool doubles as a rotor rivet clinching tool for NCRS-type rotor replacement.

Make a Plan of Attack

Having a procedure plan can make things immensely easier when disassembling the suspension and steering. By now, you should know whether the frame will be rolled out from under the body. If the idea of a total body-off restoration was not in your plans, tackle one end of the Midyear at a time. There is no use in having pieces lying around all over the shop. The task seems less daunting when you are doing the project in stages. For that matter, maybe you want to drive the Midyear as the suspension restoration takes place. Actually this is not necessarily a bad idea, once an area is completed; you know that you can proceed with confidence. Starting at the rear suspension makes the most sense with a piecemeal situation. Know the condition of the rear wheel bearings before any road miles were put on the project. As the rear trailing arms are removed, put them aside for shipping, if you plan on using remanufactured assemblies. You may have decided to use ready-to-go trailing arms. If so, the removed trailing arms need to be returned to the parts supplier for re-manufacturing. They can be shipped back for a deposit refund as soon as the cores are checked. You should check the existing trailing arms carefully for any parts that may not come with the replacement trailing arms.

When you consider the weight of the trailing arms as an assembly, it makes sense to attend a Corvette show. Why? Because you can bring the trailing arms with you and swap them, saving the core charge and shipping. There are a few restorers who frequent the shows and bring ready-to-go items with them. Vtech Corvette for instance has trailing arms in complete or partial form. It is good sometimes to compare notes with your parts supplier face-to-face also. They usually are happy to give you hints on how to properly install the products you purchase.

As the disassembly progresses, please understand the suspension has plenty of stored energy. Front springs can do tremendous damage to fingers or hands that get in the way. Rear springs can also give you an unintended whack, if you are not careful.

Chassis Disassembly

Earlier, I recommended spring removal while the engine was in place, which makes the task safer and easier. My plan is to completely disassemble the chassis, front to back, or vice-versa. Remember to put into one specific area all the worn pieces to be replaced. This gives you an opportunity to check the new parts against the originals. While you are at it, record the damaged fasteners to be replaced.

Remove Rear Springs

1 Unloading the rear spring can be dangerous, so you need to be very careful and use proper precautions. Use the C-clamp to keep the jack from slipping. When the rear spring bolt nut is removed the body can jump upward. Important: You must make sure the spring is unloaded fully before taking the nut off.

2 Removing the rear spring can be difficult. Let the exhaust hold the spring up until you are ready to remove it from the chassis. Move to the outside of the heavy awkward spring holding onto the outer end of the spring as you work it out over the exhaust.

Remove Axleshaft

3 Begin the axleshaft removal at the outer flange by removing the 5/8-inch hex head bolts. Originally, French locks were used to prevent the outer flange bolts from loosening. Substituting lock washers for the French locks is difficult. The split lock washers have a tendency to split open as they come out from under the bolt, preventing correct torquing.

Remove Shock

4 This shock mount knocker will test your mettle. Shock mounts have a serrated end to lock them into place. The Zip Products shock mount knocker must be tightened with a wrench to prevent thread damage before use. Depending on the condition of the strut rod bushing sleeve, a few whacks and the shock mount is loose.

SUSPENSION

Remove Trailing Arm Bolt

5 Removing the trailing arm pivot bolt is the next test. In a perfect world the bolt pushes out easily, but half of the time, this does not happen. Use an air impact hammer to rattle the pivot bolt to shake it loose. The impact vibrations break up the rust holding the bolt.

6 As the rusty bolt begins to move, use a long rod to push it out completely. The rust you see on the bolt's shank comes from interaction with the trailing arm bushing sleeve. I was lucky with this bolt. The sleeve corrosion was not too bad and the bolt let go easily.

Remove Trailing Arm Bolt (Continued)

Remove Front Springs

8 This is a potentially dangerous procedure and extreme caution must be exercised. Front spring removal is much more dangerous than rear spring removal. To safely complete this procedure, the floor jack must roll with the control arm as it moves downward or it slips off the jack's lifting cup. The jack must not slip. If it does, the spring could come flying off the vehicle and cause serious injury. Leave the spindle in place until the spring is out of the control arm. Hopefully, it slows the spring if it comes loose unexpectedly.

7 All too often you end up cutting out the trailing arm pivot bolt with a reciprocating saw. Remove the trailing arm shims first to gain access to the bolt. The trick is cutting the bolt without the saw blade hitting the frame pocket. Cutting the bolt with a torch can be disastrous, damaging the frame pocket or causing a fire.

Remove Control Arm Bolt

9 Trouble ensues when the upper control arm bolt is spinning in the frame. The upper control arm bolts are serrated, and that prevents them from rotating during alignment. Flip over the upper control arm, so you can hold onto the spinning bolt. When it comes time to align the front end, accessing the bolt to hold it is very difficult. Spot weld the bolt in place to prevent any chance of spinning bolts.

CHAPTER 10

Subassembly Disassembly

Once I have all the chassis pieces removed, I move to the work bench to disassemble subassemblies, like the steering box, steering linkage, and upper and lower control arms from the front end. (By the way, restoring the steering box is not too difficult and does not require any expensive, special tools.) As each assembly is disassembled, designate an area or storage bin to keep all the pieces in one place.

Remove Trailing Arm Bushing

1 Use a reciprocating saw to cut the outer washer and sleeve off. This is often the best way to remove the trailing arm bushing. After the washer is cut off, use your hand to push out the other washer and sleeve.

Remove Strut Rods

2 Sometimes you have to cut the shock mount to release the strut rod; it just depends on how long you want to play with it. This shock mount had damaged threads anyway so I did not really lose much.

3 Now that you have the strut rod loose from the spindle housing, push the strut rod bushing sleeve out of the rubber bushing. Some people burn the rubber out of the bushing. It's an alternative if you don't have a press.

Remove Ball Joint from Spindle

4 You can use a pickle fork mounted in an air hammer to force the ball joint stud off the spindle. Watch the positioning of the pickle fork as pressure is applied; damage can occur to the control arm if the tool digs into the arm. The downside is the ball joint boot is typically damaged when removed this way. Damage occurs to the spindle and lower control arm if you are not careful while hammering the joint apart.

Remove Control Arm Bushing

5 This in-house-made control arm tools prevent control arm damage during bushing removal. I cut a longitudinal piece out of a 2-inch-diameter piece of pipe to place between the control arm bushings. This keeps from distorting the arm when I press the shaft and bushing out. As I apply pressure the control arm shaft pushes the lower bushing out then I turn the arm over and push the other bushing out.

SUSPENSION

Remove Outer Sleeve From Control Arm

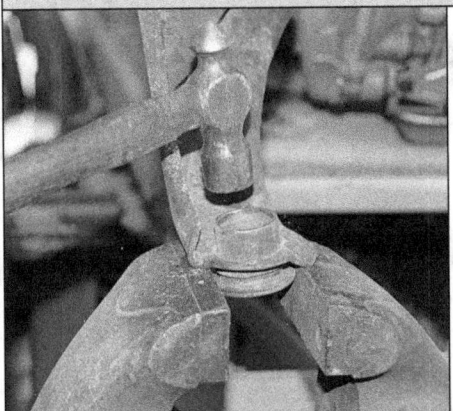

6 Sometimes the outer sleeve stays in the control arm. A few taps with the hammer and it comes out. I often find the control arms distorted and chewed up from the various methods used to remove the bushings. Check the control arms carefully for cracks around the bushing areas.

Remove Pitman Arm

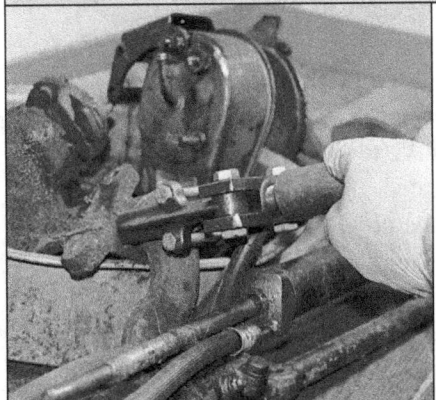

7 My favorite puller is at work again pulling off the Pitman arm from the well-worn steering box. This puller was sold as a Pitman arm puller, which means it has a striking surface on the forcing screw. The forcing screw is tightened and then hit with a hammer if necessary to break the taper loose.

Rear Trailing Arm Installation

The rear trailing arms may require installation of new pivot bushings, if you are restoring your trailing arms yourself. Urethane bushings come with a swaging tool to properly secure the two bushing halves in place. Rubber bushings require a special tool to swage the heavy-wall original equipment steel sleeves. This may be another good reason to buy the complete, remanufactured trailing arms. Purchasing the special swaging tool is expensive for one-time use. The best policy may be to have the rubber bushings professionally installed and install the urethane bushings yourself.

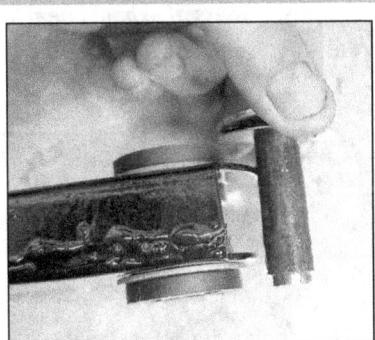

Install Vette Brakes and Products' urethane bushings in the trailing arm with shims to make sure they are tight once crimped into place. Some new replacement bushings have smaller-diameter outer sleeves causing them to be loose in the trailing arm. For this reason hold onto the original outer sleeves until you know if you have tight sleeves or not. If necessary you can reuse the original outer sleeves.

Rubber trailing arm bushings are comprised of four pieces requiring a special tool to crimp the assembly together. Tap the bushings into the trailing arm then place one washer onto the sleeve. Then install the sleeve into the bushings with the other washer placed on the opposite side. Use this special tool to crimp the washer onto the inner sleeve. Tighten the fixture to compress the bushings slightly. Hit the center punch with a hammer or squeezed in a hydraulic press to crimp the sleeve. Check the progress of the crimp frequently, during the process. Ultimately the sleeve should be even with the bushings tapered washer. If too much pressure is applied the pivot bolt does not go through the bushings.

Steering System Installation

With the trailing and control arms ready for installation, it's time to focus on the steering system. General Motors used the same steering gear box for Midyears with manual or power steering. Power steering cars had a hydraulic cylinder connected to the drag link to provide steering assist. "Assist" is the key word here because General Motors wanted the Corvette to have road feel at speed.

Cadillac had power steering that required only a pinky finger to turn the steering wheel in a tight parking lot. To accomplish this, the steering-assist cylinder applied pressure when the control valve mounted on the drag link was loaded right or left. The control valve used fluid pressure supplied by the engine-mounted pump assembly.

The assist cylinders leak and the control valves fail. I replace assist cylinders and control valves with Vette Brakes and Products' remanufactured assemblies. The steering box, on the other hand, is overhauled in-house.

You really do not want to leave the old gunk-filled steering box in place after all the other work that has been done. The steering box lubricant is located close to the exhaust manifold, and therefore it's subjected to heat and contaminants. General Motors used a chassis-lube-based lubricant that uses wax to suspend the lubricating oils. The excessive heat boils off the lubricant, leaving dirty wax as the only lubrication.

Years of exhaust heat leave this nasty sludge in steering boxes. Long ago the lubricant left the wax base. The only fix for steering boxes like this is complete disassembly, cleaning, and overhaul.

Ball Joint Installation

While at the workbench, you can install the lower and upper ball joints to finish off the control arm subassembly for installation. The original ball joints were riveted into place, but replacement ball joints are bolted in place, allowing for easy installation.

Do not install the lower rubber bump stop on the front lower control arm, since it gets in the way during spring installation.

Set aside the control arms until you have all the other subassemblies prepared.

Corvette Central has the correct rivets and tools to properly cinch the rivets into the control arm, so the ball joint installation adheres to NCRS or Bloomington Gold standards. The rivet cinching tools are much easier to use on the work bench. The rivet tools are not too expensive and you can use them on your Corvette buddies' cars.

Install the lower ball joint rivet clinching fixture from Corvette Central in an NCRS-built control arm. Tighten the 3/4-inch nut holding the center of the ball joint in the control arm hand-tight until you clinch the rivets.

This air hammer rivet setting tool is available from Mac and Snap-On tools. With the clinching tool holding the backside of the rivet hammer, tighten the 3/4-inch center ball joint nut to 50 ft-lbs.

SUSPENSION

Suspension Fastener Torque Specifications

Front Suspension

Lower control arm shaft to frame rear bolt	135 ft-lbs
Lower control arm shaft to frame front bolts	70 ft-lbs
Lower Ball joint to spindle	80 ft-lbs*
Upper control arm shaft nuts	60 ft-lbs
Upper ball joint to spindle	50 ft-lbs*
Steering link to spindle bolts/nuts	75 ft-lbs
Idler arm to frame bolts	45 ft-lbs
Idler arm to center link	50 ft-lbs*
Steering gear to frame bolts	45 ft-lbs
Tie rod ends to center link and steering arm	40 ft-lbs*

* then continue tightening until the castle nut aligns with the cotter pin bore

Rear Suspension

Differential crossmember to frame	60 ft-lbs
Differential front mount to frame	50 ft-lbs
Trailing arm to frame	50 ft-lbs
Axle shafts to axle flange	75 ft-lbs
Axle shafts to differential yoke strap type	15 ft-lbs
Axle shafts to differential yoke cap style	35 ft-lbs
Strut rod bracket to differential	35 ft-lbs
Strut rod to differential bracket	60 ft-lbs
Strut rod to rear spindle assembly	75 ft-lbs
Rear spring to differential housing	70 ft-lbs†

† using O.E. 9/16-18 thread bolts

In the end, steering box overhaul costs are minimal in the grand scheme of things, so send your steering box out while the other pieces are in progress. This way, you have a tight, safe steering box for the long term.

Next, check the tie rod ends and idler arm. Tie rod ends are similar to ball joints, housing a ball stud in a socket. Idler arms are rigid during their rotation. There is no up-and-down movement, only side-to-side movement. Tie rod ends have a heavy spring pushing the ball stud tightly into the socket assembly. Using pliers to apply pressure to the tie rod can move the ball stud into the socket, revealing what appears to be wear. Many shops believe that this is a reason to replace tie rod ends.

Instead, I look for movement when the steering wheel applies load to the steering linkage. If the tie rod ends move then, I know they are worn.

Steering components typically wear faster from poor maintenance than from expected steering movement. Poor maintenance includes pushing a dirty grease gun nozzle onto a sand-encrusted grease fitting, forcing grit into the tie rod with the fresh grease. Over time, the grit wears the components, loosening the ball within the socket.

A restoration is all about giving your Corvette a fresh start, so why not replace all the tie rod ends anyway? I make it standard practice, to ensure tight steering. Plus, how much time will you spend cleaning and prepping your tie rod ends for painting? New replacements eliminate nearly all of that effort.

The idler arm takes a lot of punishment, since both tie rod assemblies are pushing and pulling on it. This wears on the rotation joint and eventually the idler arm moves up and down. The unintended up-and-down movement of the idler arm negatively affects the steering geometry. Excessive free-play is felt in the steering wheel. As with the tie rod ends, I recommend replacing the idler arm. I also opt for the heavy-duty idler arm assembly, to keep the steering tight for many miles.

Before frame and component assembly begins, it's good practice to check bolt threads and threaded holes. No matter how careful you are during cleaning and prep processes, thread damage can occur. Paint and primer can end up in and on threads, preventing proper fastener torque. Make a habit of properly tightening and torqueing each and every fastener.

Subassembly Installation

After all the prep, you are finally ready to install your subassemblies onto your bare frame. The safety concerns are installing the front springs and connecting the rear spring bolts to the trailing arms. I start by installing the front upper and lower control arms, then I either need to set the engine in place or use a spring compressor to install the front springs. If I am going to install the original front springs or a set of springs that are similar, I need both the compressor and the engine in place. The original Midyear small-block coil springs are long, with many coils, making them difficult to install. Replacement springs are shorter with fewer coils requiring less effort to install.

CHAPTER 10

Install Spring

1 The spring compressor set up must be correctly placed to avoid the lower control arm and spring pocket. You may end up removing and replacing the spring compressor a few times until you get all the restrictive areas figured out. Safety Tip: coil spring compressors are dangerous! With just one slip severe bodily injury can occur. Do not use air-impact wrenches to draw the spring compressor into place. The impact wrench can cause the compressor to slip off. Replacement springs do not require a spring compressor.

2 Once the compressed spring is in the proper location install the spindle assembly onto the upper and lower ball joints studs. If that was not enough hassle, the upper portion of the spring has to be in the spring pocket depression, while the lower part of the spring is oriented into the lower control arm correctly. This tie down strap does help during installation with replacement springs and just the weight of the frame.

Check Coil Spring Orientation

3 The front end is taking shape with the spindle in place with the steering arm and caliper mount ready to be torqued. Check to make sure the coil spring orientation is correct in the spring pocket. Always paint the components to prevent rust from showing up.

Install Gaskets

4 This simple foam gasket slips over the spindle keeping dirt and dust out of the wheel hub area. Some spindles require two gaskets per side to seal the backing plate to the spindle correctly. These small pieces are sometimes left out and really do serve a purpose keeping the grease seals from getting chewed up from dirt.

Install Dust Caps

5 Another small way to show you care is to cut a piece of exhaust tubing that fits tightly onto the dust cap. Now you can install dust caps without the typical dents you see in them.

Trailing Arms Installed

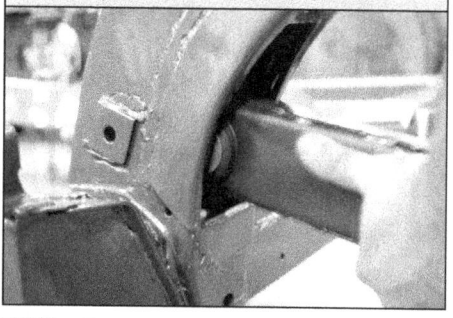

6 What a difference installing fresh trailing arms in an ultra-clean frame can make. Use stainless-steel trailing arm pivot bolts to ensure easy removal in the future. The pivot bolts must be installed from the inside of the frame. This is obvious when the body is on the frame.

HOW TO RESTORE YOUR CORVETTE: 1963–1967

SUSPENSION

Install Washers on Strut Rods

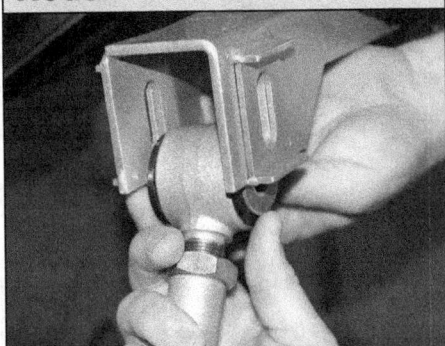

7 Strut rods should have specific washers installed on the bushings to aid in holding the alignment position. The same washers allow the strut rods to move during alignment preventing the bushing sleeves from digging into the bracket. The correct washers have a raised lip that slips into the bushing sleeve.

Prepare for Shock Mount Installation

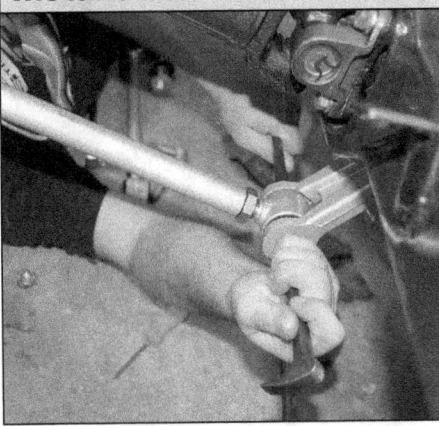

8 At the outer end of the strut rod use a line-up bar to prepare for the installation of the shock mount. Never use your fingers to line up any component. If the assembly moves for any reason bad things could happen.

Install Rear Spring

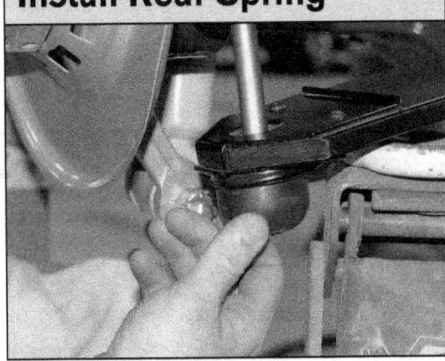

9 Hook up the rear spring to the trailing arm using a floor jack. The fiberglass spring has a metal reinforcement plate top and bottom where you place the jack pad. The lip prevents the jack from slipping off as the jack is raised. Fiberglass springs are very tough but one gouge can cause a failure so keep the jack off it.

Component Installation

Now you have some real progress to show for all the hard work you have done thus far. You're also ready to move on to engine and transmission installation, if you haven't already set the assemblies in place, to add some weight during front spring installation.

After you do a few of these restorations, you learn how to streamline the process while avoiding unnecessary additional labor operations. I leave the assembled chassis on jack stands so that I can install as many pieces as possible. It is so much easier to work on the wide-open chassis without the confines of the body in place. The complete exhaust system, ignition shielding, and engine accessories can be installed now, if you desire.

After the completed engine has been installed, add the bellhousing in preparation of transmission installation. This Corvette Central project has taken a different route as a custom-built Midyear. The silver engine mimics the exterior color with the dark gray as the contrasting color.

Take a couple of minutes to run a 7/16-14-inch thread tap into the body-mount caged nuts. Dab a bit of anti-seize into the caged nuts to ease assembly. Now you are ready to install the body onto the prepared chassis.

HOW TO RESTORE YOUR CORVETTE: 1963–1967

Rubber Versus Urethane Suspension Bushings

Bushing choice is important. Rubber bushings are bonded to inner and outer sleeves that encase them. The bonding results in the rubber twisting, as the suspension component moves. Eventually, this shearing or twisting motion breaks down the rubber. Rubber bushing longevity is tough to determine. Heat and contaminants shorten the rubber bushing's life, and they become soft and deteriorate as oil coats them. Power steering fluid leaking onto the Midyear driver-side, lower control arm bushing has the same effect.

Stability-wise, rubber bushings allow suspension components to move around more than stiffer urethane. This can be a good thing for rough roads and cars that are driven frequently because the ride is softer and more forgiving. The downside is that the forgiving rubber bushings are not good for extreme handling in race conditions.

Urethane bushings squeak. There, I said it. Urethane bushing manufacturers like to tip-toe around the subject, but squeaks happen. The dense urethane bushings are bearing-like in their operation; the inner and outer sleeves are not bonded to the urethane and allow rotation of the sleeves in and around the bushing, which allows full movement of the suspension component with minimal resistance. Movement of the sleeve in the urethane causes some noise, depending upon the weather conditions. Cool, wet days seem to increase the noise level and hot, dry days lessen the squeaks. Silicone lubricants are supplied with most bushing kits, to alleviate the inherent noises. Over time, the lubricants dry up and the squeaking begins. Some owners have drilled the outer sleeve and bushing to install grease fittings, which can help quiet some of the noises. I really think the trade off is worth the minor noise issues.

Urethane bushings also keep the suspension pieces in alignment much longer without deflection. The bushings themselves are not harmed by heat and fluids. Age is not a factor, either, as urethane bushings do not crack or develop dry rot. They do wear, though, since they are more bearing-like in operation. In spite of the possibility of wear, you most likely will never need to worry about future bushing replacement. Another plus is bushing installation is easier, due to the three-piece design. I prefer a blend of urethane and rubber bushings, to enhance suspension and steering without sacrificing ride quality.

My blend of bushings for street-driven Midyears calls for:

Urethane
- Upper and lower control arms
- Anti-roll bars
- Trailing arms
- Rear strut rods

Rubber
- Body mount bushings
- Engine mounts
- Transmission mount

You want to have maximum suspension and steering control, while isolating engine and transmission vibrations in the chassis. The use of rubber body mounts also minimizes the transmission of driveline vibrations to the passenger compartment. I have logged many miles with this very combination with great results. Tight suspension and steering feel, with a quiet, vibration-free interior is my goal. Total urethane bushing use is for hard-core street and race use.

Safety Warning

Incorrect bushing retaining bolt torque can lead to catastrophic suspension failure. A control arm's normal up-and-down motion loosens the bushing retaining bolt/washer assembly. Once the retaining bolt comes out completely, the urethane bushing easily pops out of the sleeves. True disaster strikes when the control arm comes off the shaft, leaving the control arm dangling in mid air. At that point, the upper control arm is no longer holding the wheel in alignment, allowing it to point in whatever direction it wants. A complete loss of steering is next. Please make sure that the control arm shaft bolts are properly torqued. Check them twice.

CHAPTER 11

ELECTRICAL AND WIRING

Electrical systems intimidate many owners and simple problems can seem daunting, but the reality is that the most heavily optioned Midyear is fairly simple to diagnose and repair, especially compared to any late-model vehicle.

Wiring resistance is a major factor in correct electrical component operation. Dash gauges, for instance, use resistor-style sending units relying on minimal resistance wiring feeding current to resistance coils in the gauges. High resistance means that the gauges provide incorrect readings, making you believe all is well.

The stranded electrical wiring used in harnesses is subjected to underhood engine heat. Internal heat increases as the wiring ages and corrosion builds up. Electrons flow on the outer surface of the wire strand and any contamination slows the process. Anything that impedes the electron flow adds heat to the wiring. When you strip the wiring insulation and find a black coating, corrosion has begun. The best policy is to replace any corroded wiring, even if the wiring you are using is supposed to be new. Wire insulation does dry up and become brittle and causes exposed wire strands.

Of course, underhood temperatures take a toll on the wire insulation, too. High-amperage load circuits usually have stiff, broken insulation. GXL cross-linked polyethylene has replaced the original GPT PVC insulation found on Midyear wiring. GXL wire insulation is much more resistant to heat and it stays flexible for many additional years, which is another justification to use new wire harnesses.

General Motors used specific terminals for its components, with wire strain relief to prevent insulation damage. The idea is that the wire terminal captures the stranded wire and wire insulation. Vibration, over long periods of time, damages the wire insulation, especially at the terminal connection. Once the wire insulation breaks at the terminal, wire strands also break. It's common to see broken wire strands limiting current flow

The dash gauge cluster requires low resistance wiring to provide accurate engine information. The best gauge cluster restoration won't work properly with high resistance wiring caused by years of corrosion build-up. Many hours of aggravation can be avoided by using fresh main and engine harnesses.

to components. Terminals themselves corrode, adding to the electrical system resistance. The first year General Motors used a firewall bulkhead connector to connect the main harness to the underhood harnesses was 1963, and it used this for many years to come.

Main harnesses connect to the forward lamp, engine harness, and rear lamp harness. A/C harnesses are considered auxiliary, interfacing with the main and underhood harnesses. More importantly, the main harness has the fuse panel to protect the wiring and components. I find many fuse panels with corroded fuse connection terminals and wiring connections. Corroded fuse terminals also cause extra resistance, and many times cause open circuits. Although the cost of the main harness is significant, it usually makes sense to replace it. There are cases where the main harness is in very good condition. Low mileage and humidity make for long wire life.

Electrical System Inspection

You need to do a thorough inspection of all the wiring components, including the harnesses. Check the fuse panel carefully for corroded fuse holders and the main harness for stiff, brittle wiring. Also check the backside of the fuse panel, which is the bulkhead connector. Poor-fitting bulkhead terminals are hard to overcome. Inspect the ignition wiring that passes through the firewall, connecting to the ballast resistor and wiper motor. If the bulkhead and fuse panel look good, you can replace any damaged underhood wiring.

While you are under the hood, headlamps are another area to check. Remember, poor connections cause electrical problems. The headlight motors are powered through the bulkhead connector, from the headlight rotation switch. Check the headlamp rotation motors' plastic connectors and wire terminals for corrosion. If the headlamp motor wires are stiff, heat has taken a toll on the wiring and insulation.

Inspect the alternator output lead wire and the terminal at the alternator. Poor connections here cause extreme heat and many problems. Hard starting to poor performance can be contributed to this important wire lead. If the harnesses are not replaced or any single wires are replaced, this one absolutely should be.

I would be remiss in not covering component grounding despite these cars having a fiberglass body. Grounds are always problematic, whether you have a steel or fiberglass body. Corvettes rely on many ground wires placed throughout the vehicle. Ground wires are required at all metal surfaces ensuring that the ground path ends up back at the battery. Electrical components must also have an adequate ground path that ends up back at the negative battery cable.

Ground wires must be kept clean and tight. Loose ground wires create really strange electrical phenomena. Components that seek a ground use the path of least resistance. In many situations, the component seeking the ground likely uses another component for a ground circuit. When that happens, lights come on when the wipers are turned on, for example. During your inspection, look closely at the ground wires and replace them if they are in bad shape.

Midyear negative battery cables are bolted to the engine to provide an adequate ground to the engine during starting. The concern is the engine-to-frame grounding. Make sure the engine mount-to-frame ground cables are solidly attached.

If you are set on repairing the harnesses, heed the following recommendations: GM-specific T-56 terminals and connectors are used throughout the early harnesses, which are available from many suppliers. Using the correct T-56 components allows correct factory reliable repairs. For many years, I have removed the plastic connectors from the harnesses I have replaced. Because of this, I have stockpiled plenty of factory connectors available for minor repairs. If you have

This bulkhead connection for the main harness can be the root of many electrical issues on the Midyear. High-amperage current comes in and goes out here. The best policy is to avoid removing this connector if possible. Each time the terminals are wiggled around they become looser and potentially create a poor connection.

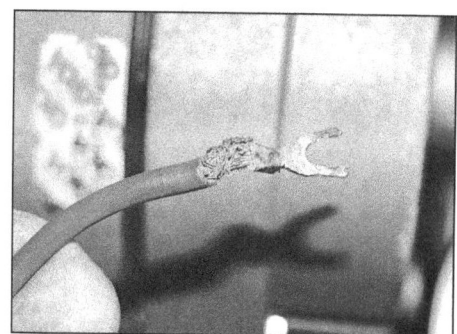

This 14-gauge alternator output wire has an exposed terminal with no wire strain protection. Wire strands are broken with a poor crimp. Don't blame the alternator or battery when hard, hot starting occurs. This connection overheats and limits amperage sent to the battery.

ELECTRICAL AND WIRING

This engine-to-frame braided ground strap is difficult to access, but very important. Midyear negative battery cables connect directly to the engine. This vital link provides ground for many components directly from the battery.

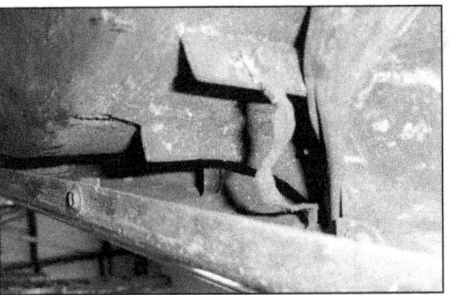

This is another very important ground strap used for interior compartment component grounds. The strap clips onto the driver-side body mount support. Gauges and dash components require this ground circuit for proper operation. Many times this ground wire is left off after the body has been lifted.

Fiberglass car bodies need a ground plane (plate) below the antenna for good signal input. This flat ground strap connects to the plate below the body at the antenna and the frame. Poor radio reception occurs when this ground is loose or disconnected.

trouble finding connectors, try Corvette-specific service centers, as they may have stockpiled some of the difficult-to-find connectors.

Aftermarket terminals and connectors are not recommended. Universal connectors and terminals typically do not provide proper strain relief nor secure connections. Plus, you can spot the aftermarket terminals easily, when showing your Midyear.

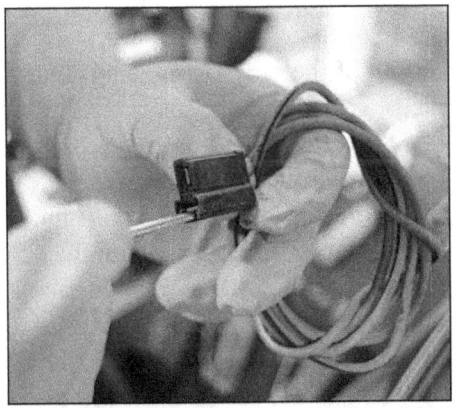

Midyear terminals are simple to remove from the connector. You can flatten the terminal's lock blade with a small, flat-blade screwdriver. If the connector has been melted, a poor terminal connection caused the extreme heat. Replacing the connector does not fix the problem, but the terminal itself requires replacement.

One of my pet peeves is the incorrect use of aftermarket terminals and the wrong wiring gauge. Plastic sleeves denote the wire gauge to be used in a specific terminal. The problem is that many times the largest terminals (yellow sleeve) are used for the lightest-gauge wire.

Wiring Advances

Stock Midyears have low amperage requirements, compared to late-model vehicles.

A pair of Wurth W-crimp crimping pliers produces the factory crimp. NAPA has a more versatile tool with additional W-crimping capabilities. For some reason, these male T-56 terminals are much tougher to crimp. If in doubt, solder the terminal connection after crimping. Removing this terminal from the connector requires pushing the tab inward to close the gap.

Air Conditioning

Air conditioning consumed the largest amount of energy when the blower was on high and the compressor was engaged. General Motors used an in-line, plastic fuse to supply current for the high blower position. This proved to be somewhat unreliable, as the poorly-connected high-amp fuse melted the in-line fuse holder.

Alternator

The alternator power lead that charged the battery is another area of concern. The same forward lamp harness with 14-gauge alternator lead wiring was used for A/C or non-A/C Midyears. Using the same 14-gauge wire to keep up with the higher amperage requirements of the A/C-equipped Midyear guarantees that the alternator lead wire will overheat.

Late-model vehicles have 8- and 6-gauge alternator lead wires supplying current to the battery. The late-model alternator lead wire also follows the shortest route to the battery or battery positive cable. Many of the Midyears I restore end up with aftermarket A/C installed. Because of this, I replace the 12-gauge alternator lead wire with a minimum 8-gauge wire. In addition, the

CHAPTER 11

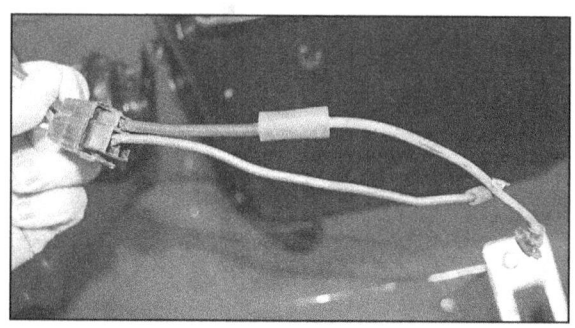

For example, this short replaceable section of fuse-link wire burns if you inadvertently touch the headlamp rotation motor circuit breaker with it.

An aftermarket wire harness supplier installed this factory-style fuse link. The black rubber connector with the smaller gauge wire is the section of fuse-link wire. I add these to all my projects that are not NCRS-correct to prevent accidental fires and major wire damage.

To do the best possible repair or restorations, apply DE-OX Oxide Inhibitor. This product prevents corrosion to the terminal and therefore helps prevent shorts and ensures a good, long-term connection. Also apply this material to bulb bases before installing bulbs.

Midyear alternator lead wire is routed to the horn relay, then back to the positive battery cable. The already-overloaded alternator lead wire has to push current over an extra long wire. I route my new alternator lead directly from the alternator to the starter positive terminal.

My policy is to make the electrical system more reliable with added safety features. That is, of course, if the project in question is not an NCRS or Bloomington Gold restoration. Many of my projects have a late-model internal voltage regulator Delcotron alternator installed. I modify the new engine and forward lamp harnesses for the late-model GM alternator, before installation.

Early on, wire fusing was minimal, making underhood fires a real concern. Today, fuse links are used to protect high-amperage load circuits at the source. Fuse links burn a small section of wiring cutting current to the circuit. I add fuse links at the starter to the alternator lead and interior circuits. It makes sense to protect the circuits as much as possible. The changes are easy enough while promoting fire safety.

Battery Cables

Battery cables are often neglected, only being replaced when all other options have been exhausted. Then, inadequate battery cables are often used as replacements, making you wonder what the heck is going on. Although the battery cables are short, the Midyear engines have higher compression, requiring high amperage at start-up. When you go to major auto parts retailers for battery cables, expect four-gauge cables for four-cylinder engines. You need a minimum of two-gauge battery cables for a small-block and one-gauge cables for big-block engines.

Better yet, order the correct gauge and fit battery cables when you order your wire harnesses. Ground strap packages are also available, to bring the entire system up to new specifications. In many cases, your supplier may give a discount if you purchase all the required harnesses and cables in one package. Some electrical suppliers like to bundle their products, providing discounts when large purchases are made. Chances are good that there will be fewer warranty concerns for them, if all the wiring is replaced. You can expect to spend in excess of $1,000 for all the harnesses and correct battery cables. In the grand scheme of the project, the cost is minimal, considering the benefits.

Component Restoration

Delco-Remy supplied all the electrical components for all Midyears. Although all of the items are date coded, none are serial numbered and plenty are available. There are a few areas of concern though, for NCRS or Bloomington Gold restorers. By now, many of the original components may have been replaced and the cores turned in. Early on, few Corvette owners thought about rebuilding the original components. It was much easier to replace these items and turn in the core for rebuild. If by chance, a GM dealer was chosen for service, the original component was typically rebuilt. If you are concerned with matching numbers, check the components' casting and date codes carefully before restoring what you have.

All of the early Delco-Remy components were well built, able to withstand the test of time. No integrated circuit electronics come into play, so they can be restored to original specs easily. All Midyears have an external mechanical regulator with a Delcotron alternator. The tough part of their restoration may be finding reliable replacement parts.

General Motors dropped the use of the Delco external regulator alternators in 1968; starters were dropped in 1987. Automotive electrical shops rarely deal in the early Delco-Remy alternators or starters anymore, so they have few parts available. NAPA stores are the exception: they do have quality, early repair pieces available.

ELECTRICAL AND WIRING

If you feel uncomfortable restoring your pieces, I recommend contacting John Pirkle of Masters City Classic Car Parts to perform the work. He has dedicated many years to restoring early GM alternators, specifically for Corvettes. He has correct starters, alternators, regulators and relays for all Midyear applications. This is his primary business and you can be assured that the components you receive will work properly and pass any judging standards. If necessary, he can supply you with any date-coded electrical component you may be missing.

Corvette Central also has correct date-coded electrical components available, as well as all the correct component mounting hardware available.

The other alternative is to be on the hunt at Corvette swap meets. Have your NCRS numbers figured out and check out each component carefully. This is where research pays off; you may find what seems to be a good deal on a restorable correctly numbered part, but when you purchase all the pieces and the restorable core, you may find that you could have purchased the professionally-restored item for only a little bit more.

Alternators

Alternators are simple three-phase generators that use diodes to convert the alternating current to direct current voltage. Diodes are one-way electrical valves, allowing current to flow in one direction. DC generators were replaced by the alternator because alternators charge better at low RPM. There are three rectifier diode banks; among those there are three positive and three negative diodes. Slip-ring brushes supply electrical current to the rotor windings. Stators are the outer wire winding found in the case, which works with the rotor to create magnetism and ultimately electrical power.

Worn slip-ring brushes are the most common failure. The symptom of worn brushes is good power output at idle, but as soon as the RPM is raised, power output drops.

Failed diodes are another common failure. Early Delco alternators have the diodes pressed into the alternator case. The diodes have date coding and are visible for the judges.

Rarely, stators and rotors fail from bearing failure or overheating. NAPA part numbers are ECH AC2N negative diode (3 required), ECH AC2P positive diode (3 required) and ECH R429 alternator brush and holder set.

Performance Testing

Testing and repairing an alternator is easy enough. The tough part is refinishing the alternator's aluminum housing; Bead or sandblasting of the housing is not recommended for NCRS refinishing. I use a stainless-steel brush to manually remove the years of build-up.

This correct 1965 Corvette alternator is in remarkable condition with very little corrosion or brush wear. Tough is the word for these reliable units unless someone repeatedly causes voltage spikes removing the battery cable to check system charging. Use that old-school way of checking for alternator output by removing a battery cable to see if the engine dies. Voltage spikes in excess of 100 volts can occur when battery cables are removed and replaced, taking out alternator diodes. Use a voltmeter when checking for the required minimum 13.2 volts at idle during an alternator output test.

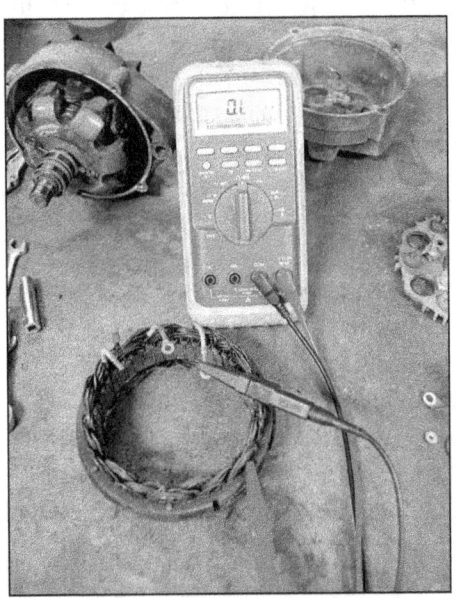

Alternator component testing requires a decent multi-meter. Checking the stator windings for a possible short to ground. Check each set of windings (terminals). The ohm reading should be infinite (open circuit).

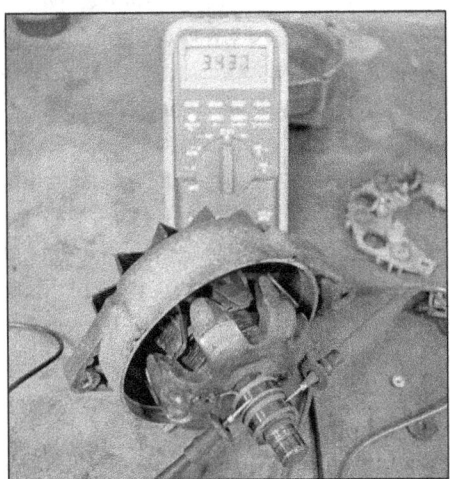

This rotor checks out to have 3,000-plus ohms of winding resistance. If it had zero ohms there would be a shorted winding. Shorted windings usually occur due to overheating from high-amperage requirements. A shorted battery or constant battery drain, causing the alternator to work at full output continuously, overheats the rotor.

HOW TO RESTORE YOUR CORVETTE: 1963–1967

CHAPTER 11

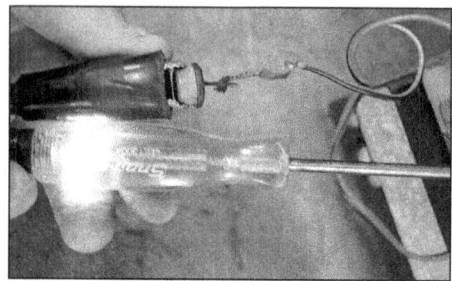

This is one of the six diodes required for alternating current conversion to direct current. The test light is connected in series with the diode. The test light probe is connected to the positive side of the battery. When the test light connections are reversed the test light should not light. There should be three diodes that flow current positive to negative and three diodes that flow negative to positive.

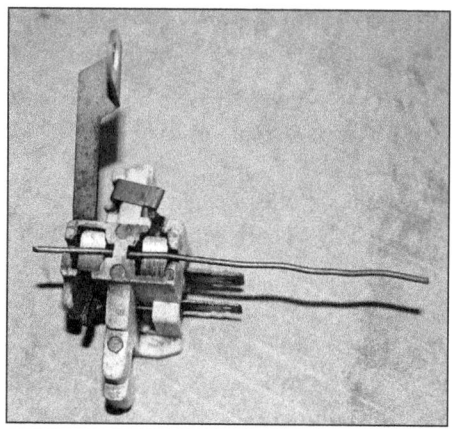

The alternator brushes require replacement if the overall length is less than their width. You can use a piece of .060 wire to hold back the sprung brushes. It's much easier to remove this assembly from the alternator to load the brushes.

This same 60,000 mile original 1965 Coupe has never had the regulator replaced. I removed the cover to check the condition of the points that regulate charge rate. A quick filing with a points file and the assembly is fine. Always make sure the ground wire on the lower case is tight and clean.

Using a Multi-Meter

Once you have your components restored and installed, a performance check should be done to ensure proper system operation. All Midyears have battery gauges monitoring voltage, which (when working) gives you a good idea of system performance. Alternators charge at lower voltage levels when they are putting out high amperage. A good example is when an engine is first started, the top charge is drawn off the battery, and the alternator shows a low charge level on the battery gauge, at first. As the battery reaches full charge, the battery gauge begins to show higher output. When the battery is at full charge, the gauge shows maximum output.

Let's face it, if you plan on doing a restoration, you should have a multi-meter in your tool repertoire. You can test many electrical components and systems with a multi-meter, such as battery condition and alternator and voltage regulator performance.

Automotive 12-volt batteries are comprised of six cells with 2.1 volts each. Fully-charged batteries in good condition should have 12.6 volts during testing. As 12-volt batteries degrade, so does the fully-charged voltage reading on the multi-meter. When you hear the term "dead cell," the battery has 11 volts or less.

Alternator output can be checked with the multi-meter. You are looking for alternator output voltage to be above 12.6 volts to surpass the battery's charge level. Voltage is a measurement of electrical pressure; you want at least 13.0 volts at idle with all accessories on, to keep the battery charged. When the electrical system is working properly, you should see 13.6 to 14.5 volts at high RPM with all accessories on. Failed diodes limit amperage output, which is seen when electrical system loads are maxed out.

All Midyears have mechanical voltage regulators that control alternator output. The voltage regulator has a set of points that open and close rapidly with a set of coils that become magnetized as electrical current runs through them. The rapid movement of the points switches the alternator field on and off, controlling voltage.

Checking the regulators internal switches (solenoids) requires a multi-meter. Contact points used to switch the alternator can be cleaned with a point file. In most cases a good cleaning and point filing takes care of regulator maintenance.

Voltage output is adjustable at the regulator coils, following an involved procedure covered in the GM service manual. You want to see a maximum of 14.5 volts at high RPM with a fully-charged battery.

Starter Motors

Starter motors are simple devices with an armature, field coils, and brushes. Solenoids are used to engage the starter's high torque armature. Initially, starters require high amperage to activate the solenoid and spin the armature. This info is very important because poor connections severely affect starter performance. Battery cable condition should always be considered when the starter drags initially at start-up. Heat, which drastically shortens starter life, builds up quickly when low amperage current is used to turn the starter. The same scenario occurs when the engine is hard to start and requires long crank times, such as when the engine is fuel-flooded. You should let the starter cool down any time it requires more than three to four seconds to get the engine started.

You can usually tell pretty quickly if the starter has been overheating: the familiar smell of burned wire insulation is apparent during disassembly, and field coils show shiny areas where the bushings allowed the armature to rub against it.

Like the alternator, starters have brushes for the armature's commutator. Brushes and support bushings wear, while armatures and field coils burn up due to overheating or short out when bushings wear. Starter drive-gear assemblies engage the flywheel, using a one-way clutch incorporated into the drive gear itself, to avoid spinning the starter armature at high RPM when the engine starts.

Starters are simple to restore and parts are available from several sources, including NAPA, which is one of the most convenient and most reliable. NAPA's starter rebuild kit (PN ECH SRK104) comes with all the internal items: starter brush set, thrust washers, bushings, brake washer, stop ring, and starter drive. I also use the ECH ST124 starter solenoid, if required.

You rarely see these original starter braces and heat shields on any Midyear. Usually the first time the starter is replaced someone thinks that he knows more than the engineers who designed the system. The pieces get tossed away, and the starter solenoid gets baked while the back end of the starter is unsupported.

These are not the least expensive pieces to buy, but they are the most reliable. Replacement armature or field coils are hard to find. Check with an auto electrical shop that has been around for a while. They may have some pieces left over from when these starters were popular.

Refinishing the starter field housing is easy, with its semi-gloss black coating. Depending on the application, the starter nose may be cast iron or aluminum. A

Some starters may require shims for proper contact between the flywheel ring gear and the starter drive gear. A .035-inch-thick wire gauge is in place to check for proper clearance. GM requires a .020 minimum clearance between the starter drive and flywheel ring gear teeth. Placing a .015 shim between the starter and engine block increases the clearance approximately .005. In some cases, more than one shim is required. In rare cases, the clearance may exceed .060; if so the starter can be shimmed only at the outboard bolt to tilt the starter inward.

stainless-steel wire brush is used on the aluminum nose, but cast-iron noses can be bead blasted before refinishing them with cast-iron coat for a natural, cast look. The starter's rear cover should be painted semi-gloss black.

Starter Motor Repair

Remove Starter Pivot Pin

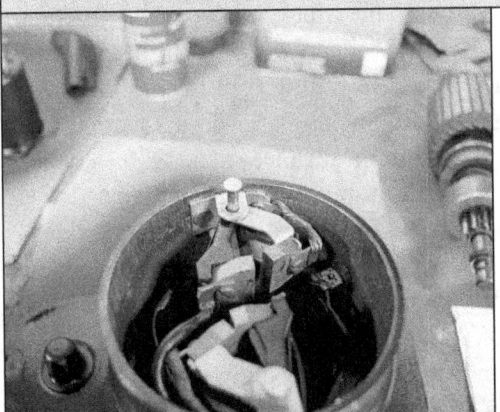

1 The brushes pivot on the raised pin while holding a tension spring in place. It is much easier to remove the pivot pin and then unscrew the brushes. Over the last 40-plus years, the brushes were the only major wear items on this original unit.

Check Armature Fit

2 NAPA Auto Parts stores have the starter armature bushings for the cover and nose assembly. Always check the armature fit before assembly. If the bushing is tight, pressure must be relieved, or the starter drags at high temperatures. Tap on the cover around the bushing to seat the bushing.

CHAPTER 11

Clean Starter Solenoid

3 Starter solenoid service is easy enough. The center plate is pushed upward as the solenoid is activated. The disc then completes the high-amperage circuit turning the starter motor. Clean the disc surface with a brass brush to polish it.

Adjust Solenoid Cap

4 The solenoid cap has the positive battery cable terminal in place. Loosen the nut holding the terminal and rotate it 180 degrees. This provides a new wear surface for the high-amperage terminal.

Seal Starter Motor

5 ACDelco placed a strip of caulking to seal the starter at the solenoid. You can use 3M black strip caulk to simulate the original material. These starters are very reliable until they are overheated. Low battery output causing slow starter speeds ruins the armature and field coil windings from overheating.

Replace Thrust Washer

6 Pull back the starter armature brushes with your fingers to let the field coil assembly drop down onto the starter nose. When you pull back on one set of brushes, they drop down onto the armature then the other side is pulled back for that set to drop down. We Replace this thrust washer to keep correct clearances.

Ignition Distributors

The ignition distributor is an often-overlooked but important part of the electrical/ignition system. Distributors may or may not get an external cleaning before being dropped into place without further thought during an engine overhaul. Distributors provide the primary electrical signal to fire the ignition coil and route spark, while driving the oil pump and tachometer cable. The load on the distributor from the oil pump is greater than you might think: supplying 80 psi of oil pressure at high RPM puts extreme torque loads on the distributor shaft and bushings.

Consider that 1963–1965 mechanical fuel injection distributors also drive the fuelie units' high-pressure fuel pump. Ignition distributors should undergo a complete restoration to ensure many more years of trouble-free operation.

Dirty, debris-filled engine oil wears on the distributor shaft bushings and, in most cases, the distributor shaft itself. Shaft wear occurs at the bushing area and tachometer drive gear. Wear also affects ignition timing advance, causing poor overall performance. Centrifugal and vacuum systems advance ignition timing for optimum engine performance. Centrifugal advance is handled with weights placed on the distributor shaft. As engine RPM increases, the weights force the distributor rotor plate ahead, advancing the timing. Vacuum advance actuator units move the ignition point plate to advance the timing. It's common for centrifugal advance plates to become stuck under the distributor rotor. Advance plates can become stuck at base timing, causing poor acceleration. Sticking also occurs at maximum ignition advance, making it very difficult to start hot engines.

Companies such as Mid America Motorworks have all the pieces to make your distributor like new again. This is an easy restoration project, with bushing replacement being the toughest job. All of the components need to be cleaned in preparation of the replacement of worn pieces.

Distributor Reconditioning

Inspect Distributor

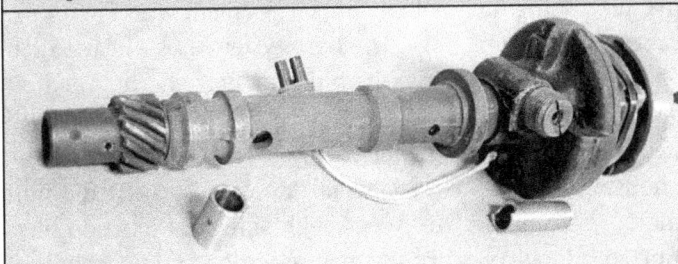

1 On a vintage RPO K66 transistor ignition distributor, the bushings laying beside the unit are typically worn. Remove the drive gear retaining pin by tapping it out. Note the dimple to the left of the retaining pin. The dimple should be in line with the rotor's brass tip for correct TDC phasing.

Set Bushing Height

2 Check and record the original bushing's installed height before removing the distributor upper bushing. Measure with a machinist's rule from the top of the bushing down to the raised ring of the distributor housing that surrounds the bushing. Bushing height is critical for correct breaker-plate retention. After the bushing has been installed, place the correct lubricant supplied from Corvette Central into the distributor housing. There is no engine oil in this area, but periodic maintenance is required to clean out the old grease and replenish with new grease.

Install Nylon Washer

3 Apply grease, then install the nylon washer and a felt ring. This replacement nylon ring works, but if possible use the original nylon washer because it sealed better. Sometimes the original washer can be saved with careful removal. The felt ring should be soaked in engine oil before setting in place.

Examine Advance Weights

4 Make sure the centrifugal advance weights are free and move easily. Look closely at the centrifugal advance mechanism for worn components. Aply a dab of white grease to the ignition-advance limiting pin. Slip a bronze sleeve over the pin to limit total ignition timing advance. Most sleeves are missing. Without the sleeve, total ignition advance can exceed 50 degrees, causing misfire at high RPM.

Examine Reluctor Ring Teeth

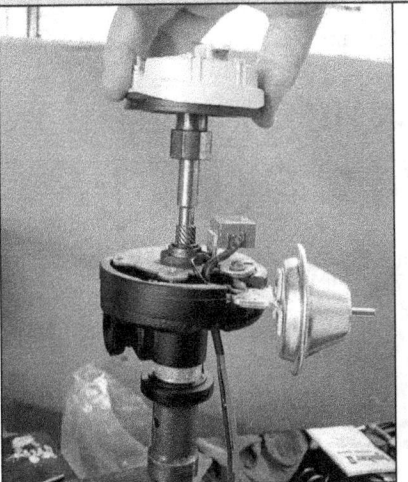

5 Secure the Pertronix magnetic reluctor ring to the bottom side of the rotor. Note the tach drive gear just about to go into the distributor bushing. Make sure the gear teeth are square and not chipped. The additional red wire coming out of the base of the distributor supplies ignition power to the electronic ignition module.

Electric Motors

Midyears were built when we repaired components like wipers, headlight rotation, power windows, and antenna motors. Delco protected each of these motors with overheat switches, preventing total motor failure. It takes a lot of work to totally destroy any of these early motors. Corrosion from water damage is about the only reason to replace any motor. All of the motors have commutator brushes, which wear. Unfortunately, the brushes are not readily available. But, fortunately, none of the motors are in continuous use, so brush wear is minimal.

I have had very good results disassembling and cleaning each of the various motors. Most of the time, refinishing the exterior of the motor casing is the tough part. The wiper motor has an upper aluminum housing with a steel motor housing. Careful stainless-steel wire brushing takes care of the upper housing.

Once the steel motor housing is rusted, it is difficult to make it look correct. Pitting and discoloration occurs from corrosion, which is almost impossible to remove. I use a stainless-steel coating that resembles the raw steel motor housing.

Relays are used on Midyears to control the horn and A/C high blower relay. All relays function the same, controlling a high amperage circuit with low amperage. The horn system uses a relay to activate the high-amperage horns. The horn button supplies the ground to activate the relay.

General Motors also used the horn relay as a high-amperage junction block for the main electrical system load. High blower relays work a bit differently; while they, too, supply high amperage current to the blower, the blower switch sends low amperage current to the relay.

Wiper Motor Rebuild

Disassemble Wiper Motor

1 Delco appliance wiper motors are also very reliable; fire is about the only thing that kills them. Take plenty of photos as you disassemble the unit. A thorough cleaning is typically all that is required. Wash the housing and all mechanical pieces with mineral spirits; try to avoid soaking the electrical components. Mineral spirits do not harm the wiring or electrical components unless they are soaked for a long period of time. The exterior can be cleaned with a stainless steel wire brush. Once the cleaning is completed, including wire brushing, wash the electrical components with electrical contact or brake cleaner. Years of debris build up in the lubricating grease, slowing the motor's operation and causing more heat build-up.

Inspect Wiper Motor

2 The outside of this '64's wiper motor looked horrible with layers of paint over dirt and grease. On the inside the brushes are barely worn with slight corrosion on the internals. The majority of motors are in this condition. The trick is getting the armature back in place while holding back the brushes. Use a couple of angled picks to hold them as the armature is installed.

Sync Pump Actuator Wheel

3 Midyears equipped with windshield washers have this pump actuator wheel that must be synched with the motor's drive-wheel pin. Place the plastic slot over the steel pin then align the cover to the motor assembly.

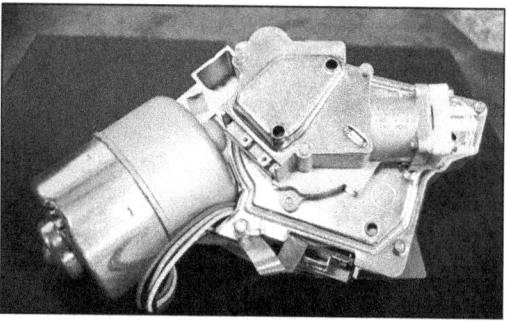

Corvette Central supplied this correct Midyear wiper motor. The steel motor housing and wiper cover have a silver cadmium plate finish that is difficult to reproduce at home. Sometimes it makes sense to pay the professionals for their expertise when you want a factory-correct look.

ELECTRICAL AND WIRING

Headlight Rotation Motor Service

Clean Headlight Rotation Motor

1 Headlight rotation motors are also reliable, but after years of use or misuse they require cleaning. This is what you find under the gear case cover. Most of the time the rotation motor gear internals simply require cleaning and greasing for correct operation.

2 This headlight motor looks similar to the wiper motor brush assembly. To the left of the brushes you can see a set of contact points. This is the thermal limiter, which saved the majority of the motors. The wiper motor has this same limiter.

Position Plastic Washer

3 Watch where you place the plastic washer's notch in the motor housing. The motor housing has a raised tab to keep the washer from spinning. Use grease to hold it during assembly. If the motor is hard to turn, check the washer; it may have slipped out of position.

Install Motor Cover

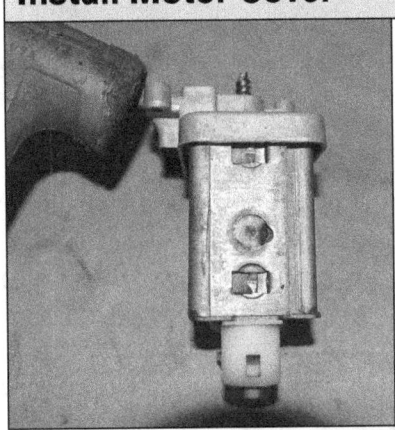

4 Use a plastic hammer to tap the motor cover around until the motor's shaft spins freely. Then finish tightening the screws and check the motor's shaft for binding. If it is bound, tap the housing again until the shaft rotates easily.

Check Shaft End Play

5 Shaft end play must be checked on both the wiper and headlamp rotation motor. In theory, the adjustment should be maintained if all the same components are used. I set end play at .020 to .035 if required to prevent wear on the geartrain.

Clean Relay Contacts

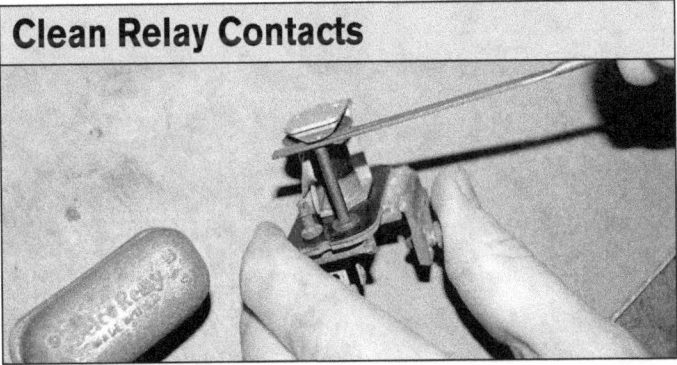

6 Horn relays have one set of contact points and a solenoid coil to pull the contacts together. Corrosion is about the only thing that hurts these assemblies. As with regulator points, a couple of strokes with a point file and the surfaces are clean. Disconnect the battery or remove the relay when you are working on it. High-amperage battery current is always present.

HOW TO RESTORE YOUR CORVETTE: 1963–1967

Gauge Clusters

Gauge restoration is big business, with a number of companies specializing in Corvette clusters. Restoration practices have gone through a few different stages. Take the main instrument cluster, for example: early on, original Delco replacement gauges could be found, but when that source dried up, original gauge faces were silk-screened. Today, complete gauge assemblies are available and cost less than the expense of the silk-screen process. This is where careful consideration comes into play to make the correct decision.

You may want to do the cluster restoration yourself, and it may make good sense. All of the small gauges are available new, with good-looking, original faces and needles. The problem comes in if the speedometer or tachometer requires any major replacement pieces. Many gauge specialists do not sell the very limited supply of pieces they have available, or they may have invested big dollars in having someone make a limited quantity of the valuable reproductions.

Contact Zip Products or Corvette Central after you evaluate the condition of your cluster. If the major Corvette suppliers do not have what you need, send the cluster to a specialist for restoration. Roger Scott at Corvette Instrument Service, does excellent work at very reasonable prices.

Maybe your gauges look good, but a few don't work quite correctly. The battery, coolant, and fuel gauges work off variable electrical resistance. Remember that all electrically operated gauges are affected by high-resistance wiring, though the coolant and fuel level gauges are affected the most. When the coolant gauge was calibrated at the factory, the sending unit was heated to a specific temperature, then the resistance in the sender dictated where the gauge needle should be.

The Midyear fuel gauge is in a class all by itself: voltage is sent to the fuel-sending unit in the tank, then the rheostat in the tank sends regulated voltage back to the gauge. The rheostat varies resistance (voltage) as the needle passes over the rheostat electrical windings. This means that you have two wires that could be a resistance problem for the fuel gauge.

The speedometer, tachometer, and oil pressure gauges are mechanical with no electrical intervention.

The only other electrical concerns with the gauge cluster are the dash illumination, brake warning, and turn signal lamps. The dash lighting current begins at the light switch, then travels to the fuse panel's cluster fuse. From the cluster fuse, current is sent to the gauge cluster and clock. Turn signal lamp current comes from the turn signal flasher to the turn signal switch. Current flows out of the turn signal switch to the front parking lamps and dash indicator lamps. Brake warning lamp current is constant ignition power, with a switch mounted on the parking brake assembly to provide a ground.

Ignition condensers are mounted on the back of the cluster. These are capacitors to quell electrical interference, which was a major problem with the original, old-school radios. Capacitors are used in numerous places on the gauge cluster and behind the dash. Switch pop was the reason most of the capacitors were in place. This means that you really should keep the capacitors in place. Missing capacitors can also affect new radios, in some situations.

The 1965 gauge cluster is disassembled and ready for assessment. Always take apart the assembly to check its condition whether you send it out for repair or make the repairs yourself. Photograph what you have for your records.

This gauge is from an earlier GM car but the theory is the same. The gauge face looked good but did not work from the corrosion on the terminal posts. In this case a careful wire brushing took care of the inoperative gauge.

ELECTRICAL AND WIRING

Midyear interior number-90 courtesy bulbs are unique, with ground and power terminals in the socket base. Installing a later number-631 single-terminal bulb can get you into trouble: the bulb shorts out across the ground and power terminals in the socket. I recently worked on a very nicely restored '65 coupe with some electrical issues: the courtesy fuse kept blowing. The customer decided to keep replacing the blown fuse with a 30-amp fuse. I found melted wiring in the main harness, which required major work to replace the damaged wiring. So, make sure the courtesy bulbs are correct, and do not use higher amperage fuses.

Watch the headlight rotation motor circuit breaker terminals when working under the dash. The unprotected circuit breaker terminals have battery voltage on them at all times. If that isn't enough to be concerned with, the circuit breakers battery supply wire has no fuse in-line. There will be some serious welding going on if you accidentally hit the terminals.

There is one very simple solution that is often disregarded: disconnect the battery's negative cable before working on any electrical circuits. Using a battery cable quick disconnect is a really great idea. When your pride and joy is sitting in the garage for any period of time, disconnect the battery.

When your Midyear is in storage, be good to the battery. Dormant batteries lose available cranking amperage as they lose their charge. Activity is the best medicine for any lead acid battery, whether it is absorbent glass mat or wet cell composition. Battery Tender chargers work really well at maintaining the battery charge without causing overheating. The 2-amp floating charge rate is monitored, turning the charger on and off to maintain peak battery charge level.

Check the battery posts and terminals often for corrosion, and clean if necessary. Battery mats placed below the battery keep any acid weepage from damaging the battery tray or the frame below the tray. Midyear batteries had factory-installed heat shields, due to close proximity of the exhaust manifold. Installing the shield and all battery hold-down hardware is very smart.

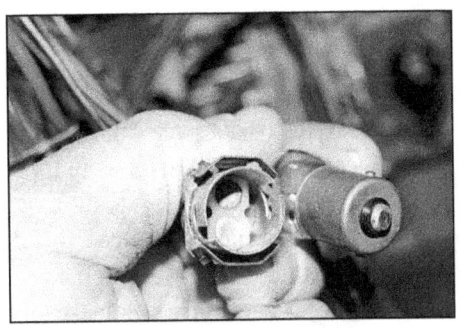

It is so simple to avoid, but installing the wrong bulb often happens. The early Corvette courtesy lamp bulb must be a two terminal design. As you can see, the single terminal shorts across the socket terminals.

Electrical welding anyone? This headlamp rotation motor circuit breaker is connected directly to the battery without any fusing. The circuit breaker is mounted to the cowl area right above the driver side cowl vent. Both of the always-hot terminals are exposed. Working under the dash could result in inadvertent contact creating a high-amperage short. One more of many good reasons to disconnect the negative battery cable during service work.

CHAPTER 12

INTERIOR

The Midyear interior was by far the most driver-friendly Corvette cabin until the C5 Corvette was introduced. The Midyear Corvette was also the last generation that you could rest your arm on the door comfortably for that big car interior feel. And the Midyear's classy metal housing instrument cluster with full gauges and trip odometer as standard equipment were easy on your eyes during long trips. After spending many hours on the highway in the cockpit of a Midyear, you really appreciate how comfortable they are. Maybe the interior is not the only reason you enjoy the ride. The whole package works, and making any trip in a Midyear is a great experience!

The original Midyear interior components are, indeed, durable. The original vinyl or leather seat covering materials held up well, if any maintenance at all was performed. UV rays took a toll on the original carpeting and caused it to fade quickly, but the rest of the interior color held up well. Making a decision on how far to restore a decent interior is tough. Doing a halfway restoration usually looks that way when finished. It really does not matter how much cleaning and preserver you apply to old pieces; new pieces stick out. Once the restoration begins, you need to follow through and do the entire job.

Interior restoration is much like working with the paint and body. All of your work is on display every time you get in the car. When you have paint damage, invariably it happens on the driver's side where you can see it every time you enter. Any problems during the interior restoration generally occur in an area you see constantly. That being said, careful installation of interior components is very important to avoid damage. Additionally, you want to be comfortable behind the wheel while on a long cruise. After all, this is going to be your home away from home on cruise nights and car show trips.

To the restorer's advantage, the majority of interior pieces have been reproduced. Both interior restoration facets (factory original or custom look) are

This is an award winning 1966 interior with one very nice late model style Flaming River tilt column installed. What I like most about these Midyear interiors is the use of metal throughout the dash because the screws are easy to find and access. The Midyear interior can be restored by the novice with excellent results if care is taken during disassembly and time is taken investigating how the factory assembled the components.

available. Suppliers like Al Knoch Interiors have excellent factory original reproductions. Their seat covers come in leather or vinyl with correct material grains. For that like-new feel, Al Knoch has reproduced seat foam with correct density and shape, and their factory original-look door panels have correct vinyl grain material.

Corvette America is another major interior supplier with plenty of original materials and colors for your Midyear project. They, too, have very nice seat covers and door panels for your project. One of their nicest products is a reproduction dash pad. Correct color and vinyl grain make the dash pads look factory-correct. In the past, reproduction dash pads have had issues with thickness inconsistencies. Corvette America has worked diligently to make theirs as accurate as possible, along with the rest of their complete interior packages.

Personalized interiors have become popular for Midyear show cars. I've seen many attractive, two-tone interior combinations. Seating upgrades are also popular, and many use later model Corvette seats. Mid America Designs has been at the forefront, producing some unique two-tone interior combinations for late-model Corvette seats. They work with you if you decide to upgrade the seats to later Corvette seat assemblies. They work with you to design custom interior packages at a reasonable price. Mid America manufactures its own carpeting and offers very nice fitting original and custom, plush, molded carpeting.

Corvette Central has the "nuts and bolts" of seats. They also have seat covers and foam available, along with all the pieces to make the seat frames correct. Hardware items, like seat release levers, catches, handles, and seat springs for a reliable seat, are all in their catalog. Seat track assemblies with the required return springs can also be found. They also have all the unique pieces to retain the seat track assemblies to the floorboard. Many items are manufactured in-house and inspected for quality, to ensure consistent product reliability.

As with many areas of your restoration, purchasing the majority of your interior supplies from one vendor can save you some money. There's also a greater likelihood of the color of all the interior materials matching when purchasing from one supplier. After your new pieces have arrived, immediately look them over carefully for shipping damage. Months can go by, even years, before you get to this part of your restoration and if you find damage after unpacking it, it will not be covered under any warranty. The best plan is to repack the items carefully to keep off dirt and debris. Watch that the repacked items are not bound up; it creates impressions in the material. And absolutely do not lay anything on top of the soft interior material because the impressions will be there to stay.

If you feel uncomfortable working with the soft goods (seat covers, convertible top, etc.), Al Knoch can replace your seat covers or convertible top at one of the many Corvette shows they attend. If that is your intention, make sure you contact the guys at Al Knoch months ahead of the show you plan to attend. They take reservations and stay busy at every show from dawn until dusk. If you plan on doing your own seat covers, stop by and watch the guys at work. Keep in mind, his crew has done hundreds—if not thousands—of seats and convertible tops, making it look very easy.

Seat Covers

Leather is what everyone wants and what prospective buyers want to see. The leather look is more refined and feels better. Vinyl is less costly and easier to install, since it is more stretchable. Water does not harm the vinyl, so it is easy to clean and maintain, too. If you plan on driving your Midyear quite a bit, vinyl may be your best bet.

No matter what material you choose for the covers, using new seat back and bottom foam is a very good idea because it creates the foundation and fit for the new seat covers. You can expect wrinkles and loose areas when old, shrunken foam is used.

Original seat cover hog rings are available in an installation kit that includes all the different-length retainers to secure the seat covers to the foam and seat frame correctly. In addition, they also contour the seat cover to the original factory shape. I see pieces of wire and about everything you can imagine used to install the seat covers. That's why you see Midyear seats with flat backs and bottoms with no shape.

Once the seat covers and foam have been stripped off, the seat frames are sand or bead blasted. On rare occasions, I just clean the seat frames and prime and paint them. Usually, the frames are really deteriorated and require complete blasting, priming, and painting.

Now is a good time to assess the seat track and hardware. Loose-fitting seat tracks are usually not the problem. Stiff, corroded tracks are common. The seat tracks should be cleaned with mineral spirits to remove dried grease. Soaking them in a pan with mineral spirits works well. After cleaning off the corrosion and old grease, you might find the seat tracks are loose fitting. Replacement may be the only option to restore a tight feel without the "rocking chair" effect.

After the tracks have been cleaned, brush on chassis grease to lubricate them. Run them back and forth to distribute the grease, then wipe off any excess.

You need seat covers, foam, and an installation kit for easier installation with the correct look when finished. Vinyl covers are easier to install when they are hot, from sitting in the sun. The vinyl stretches, but it does have limitations; watch the stitched seams during installation. If you see the seams are pulling away from each other, back off, and apply silicone spray lube. Leather is also easier to work with when warm, but the stretch is very limited without hurting the cover.

Silicone spray lube works to ease installation no matter what cover you are using. Be gentle with them and use plenty of silicone to let the covers slide, as opposed to relying solely on stretching. I have also seen wax paper used to let the material slide over the foam during installation. Silicone works best, in my experience.

The scary part is cutting holes in the new covers for the hinge or any trim that must be installed. I always have the seat cover material fully installed before punching any holes to keep from making any incorrect cuts. Once the covers are installed, place the seats out in the sun for them to heat up and remove some inevitable wrinkles. New seat side rails and hardware are usually required to make the seats look factory finished.

After you have done many interiors, a few things come to light and should be considered. I have some strict rules to avoid damaging new components during interior component installation and finishing. I use a razor knife for all the interior trimming. I also go through about five blades, to keep the blade sharp to prevent a loss of control. Dull blades require more pressure to do their job, making it easy to make a mistake. Using a battery-powered screwdriver with a tension clutch prevents overtightening of the interior screws.

Seat Cover Installation

Remove Seat Cover Retainers

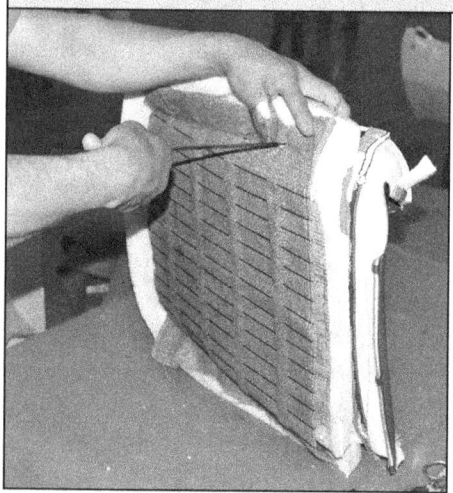

1 Pull the seat cover material retainers through the seat foam and burlap and hook it onto metal retainer strips. Multiple wire retainers follow the inner portion of the seat cover material to shape the seat back and bottom.

Apply Heat to Attach Seat Covers

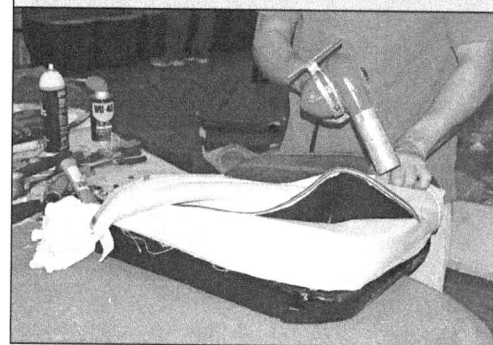

2 I use soft blankets to cover the worktable to prevent material scratches. All the typical supplies are on-hand, including that roll of first aid tape (duct tape). After the seat retainers have been secured, apply heat to ease the attachment of the covers at the bottom. Be aware of how hot the seat cover is getting; any discoloration or smoke means it is way too hot.

Apply Heat to Attach Seat Covers (Continued)

3 As soon as the heat is applied turn the seat over and install the unique clips that retain the seat cover to the frame rail. Install the clips on the seat cover material first then fold over the material to capture the clip on the rail. Clip the long, straight sections in place first, then the corners.

Install Hardware

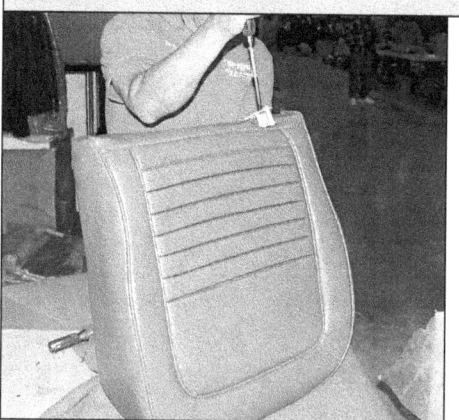

4 This Al Knoch Midyear seat cover has the correct contoured look on the seat bottom with no wrinkles. Install hardware after carefully punching holes for each item. Cut a round hole if possible. Slitting the material can promote tearing. Over time the tear generally keeps expanding until it becomes visible.

INTERIOR

Headliner and Insulation

I start by installing the headliner. Just about any project starts at the top and works down. I want to keep the headliner installation materials off of all the other components.

Firewall and cowl area insulation is next on the installation list. General Motors used a jute-backed, asphalt fiberboard to insulate the firewall. Jute is comprised of scraps of wool tightly pressed together to form 1/2-inch-thick sheets. The cowl area above the firewall was covered with jute padding material to keep some noise out and prevent sweating.

For ultimate sound and heat control, I apply Suppressor Acoustical and Heat Control Mat from Thermo-Tec under the original firewall insulators. The Thermo-Tec mat adheres to vertical surfaces and the underside of panels tenaciously, making installation of the original materials easier.

General Motors glued the pre-cut jute to the cowl with a high-tack adhesive. Mid America Motorworks sells pre-cut jute and firewall insulation, which avoids the time and aggravation of cutting pieces to fit.

You can really tell the difference when the additional soundproofing materials and original insulators are in place. It results in a quieter interior with less heat intrusion, allowing for a more comfortable ride in all climates.

Dash Insulation Installation

Install Soundproofing

1 The interior compartment insulation begins with Cool It Thermo-Tec acoustical and soundproofing material. The Cool It mat really sticks well and allows the jute insulation to be installed with confidence.

Measure the mat twice and cut once. Use contact cement to secure the jute insulation to the mat. Remember this contact cement works best if the adhesive is dry to the touch. You can wait up to a half hour on cool days for the best results.

Install Firewall Pad

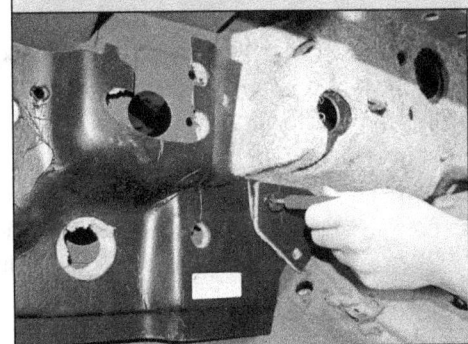

2 Install Thermo-Tec material and jute, and put the factory firewall pad from Corvette Central in place with the dreaded push-in retainers. Overlap these two pieces of factory insulation, and then position the right side insulation panel on top. Be cautious as you push the retainers in place. Rotate the tool as you push inward.

Cowl Vents

Air from the cowl vents placed at the kick panels ventilated the passenger compartment. Simple foam sealed the doors, but the foam breaks down over time. At some point, all Midyears need vent and seal restoration to prevent unwanted air intrusion. Cables beneath the dash cluster control airflow through the vents. The cable-retaining tab is broken off most plastic cowl vent covers. Corvette Central has high-quality reproductions of the covers and control cables available, for like-new operation.

Factory or aftermarket A/C-equipped Midyears must have the passenger-side vent door serviced before the A/C components are installed. Driver-side vents or non-A/C-equipped passenger-side vents can be accessed at any time. I like to make sure the vents are operable and that the cowl drains are open before I proceed with interior installation. Years of debris is usually found in the bottom of the cowl area and cleaning it minimizes the chance of puddles on the floor as rain or washwater backs up in the cowl.

Replace Foam Rubber

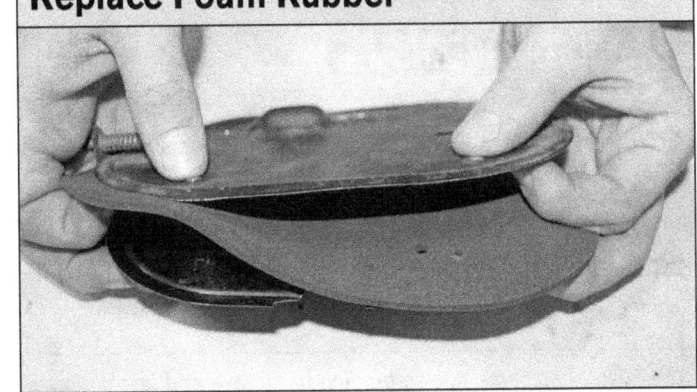

1 Aluminum rivets retain the two metal plates that sandwich the closed cell rubber foam comprising the cowl vent door. Use a 1/8-inch drill bit to drill out the rivet's head and replace the rubber foam. Coat the door surfaces with semi-flat black paint and install new rivets. Deteriorated rubber foam seals are commonly found on all Midyears.

Remove Screws

2 Four screws total typically retain this vent screen/cable mount. Many times one or two screws are installed leaving open screw holes for water to trickle in. Originally the lower and 3 o'clock screw holes are the same screw holes used for the kick panel. Many times in haste additional holes are drilled in addition to the correct holes.

Dash Assembly

If you plan on adding an aftermarket A/C system, it should be installed before the dash is assembled. You have A/C hoses, electrical wiring, and ductwork to integrate with the factory pieces. The factory or aftermarket A/C box is more easily installed on the firewall now. Likewise, Midyears with a heater only should have the heater core serviced before dash assembly takes place.

Assembly starts with installing the wiper motor on the firewall. The four 5/16-inch screws securing the wiper motor are easily accessed with the dash out of the way.

The dash is installed as an assembly, if it was removed. Proceed to the center of the dash, installing the speaker, radio, and defroster grille. I recommend installing the factory radio now. Once the dash has been completely assembled, A/C-equipped Midyear radios are really tough to install and work with. You can install an aftermarket radio in an installed dash with far less difficulty.

Next on the list is the gauge cluster and then the steering column.

The parking brake assembly is installed after the gauge cluster, to avoid cluster damage as the cluster is installed.

The glove box and door can then be installed to wrap up the dash assembly.

Once the dash assembly has been completed, make sure all the gauges operate and that the mechanical oil pressure gauge doesn't leak. Check the operation of the dash and exterior lights. Operate the radio and check the front speaker operation. If you are upgrading to multiple speakers, at the very least check for front speaker operation. Working behind the dash becomes difficult as the interior fills up, plus chances are good that something will get scratched or marked up as you fight a problem under the dash. Remember to install any sound system wiring before the insulation covers it up.

Install Dash Pad

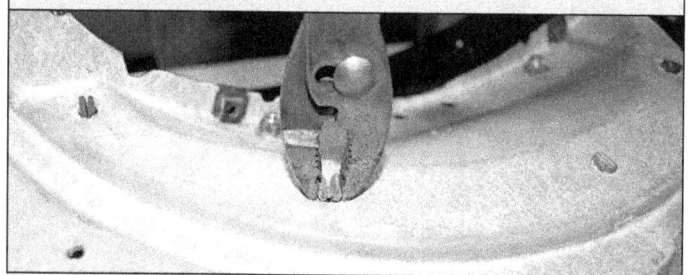

1 It takes some understanding to remove and install these dash pad retainers properly. First make sure the hole in the dash pad is ready. Cut away the vinyl material and be sure that there is no foam blocking the hole. Clips hold the Corvette America dash pad tightly against the center dash assembly. Then push each retaining clip downward and close fully with the pliers to grab the dash pad.

Install Gauge Cluster

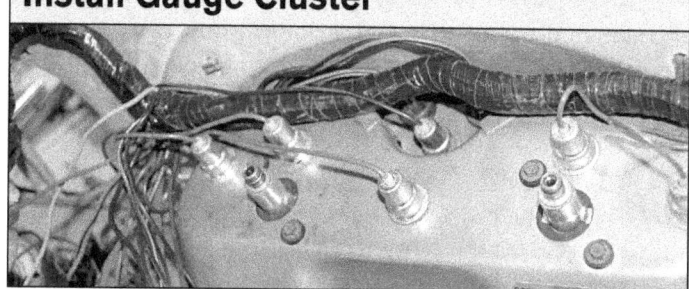

2 Install the dash as an assembly with the cluster as intact as possible. As you can see the wire harness fits tight against the dash assembly making it tough to correctly install the dash cluster later. All of the illumination bulbs have gray wires; watch carefully where you place them. Two bulbs are hidden by the harness: a pink-and-tan wired bulb socket for brake warning; a gray-and-black wired socket for headlamp warning.

Install Gauge Cluster Bulbs

3 This Corvette Instrument Service restored cluster and clock are just about wired up. Replace the original 2-candle-power dash illumination number-57 bulbs with part number 1816, which are 3-candlepower versions to brighten up the gauges. Bulbs are twist-lock like turn signal. Assembling the dash in this manner ensures correct wire harness placement and connection.

Route Wiper and Ignition Wires

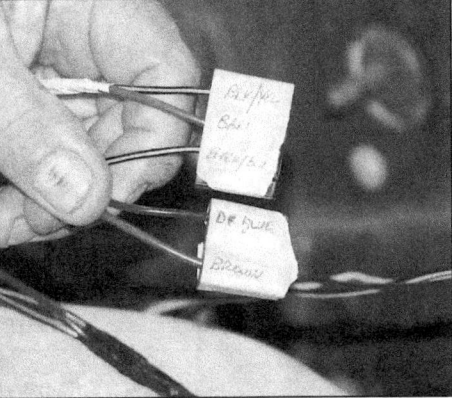

4 These five wiper wires and ignition wires (not shown) pass through the firewall sealed off with a grommet. This may seem simple, but it makes sense to remove the wiper motor electrical connector, rather than cutting the firewall grommet. Marking the connector makes the wire installation easy after the grommet is pushed over the wires.

Install Dash

5 Install the dash as an assembly after routing the main dash harness over the birdcage support bar. Route the tachometer and speedometer cables out the firewall as the dash is lowered into place. Be careful with wire harness placement near the center of the dash where it goes out the firewall. There are multiple pinch-points that can damage the harness.

Install Grommet in Dash

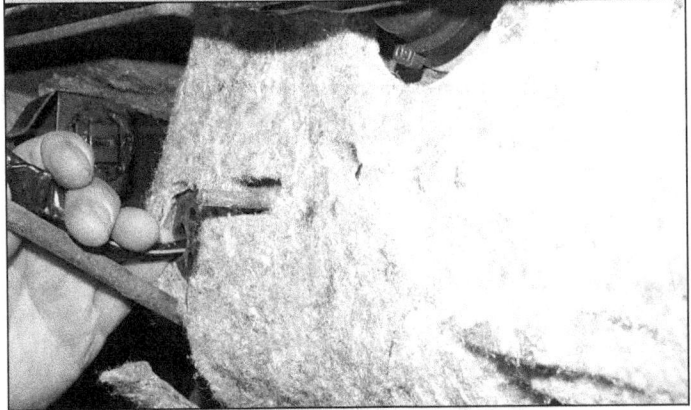

6 Install the four-hole grommet into the dash through the insulation. Super Lube works well for grommet installation. Work the grommet into one side of the firewall then push the other side in place. These grommets are often left out or the hardened original is left in place creating hot-air intrusion spots. Multiple air leaks due to missing grommets can cause A/C cases to sweat and let water accumulate on the carpeting.

Install Pedal Assembly

7 When you install the bolts that hold the pedal assembly to the dash support leave them loose until the brake booster or master cylinder is mounted and tightened onto the pedal assembly studs. The pedal assembly is held onto the firewall with studs that protrude through the firewall. Stud nuts retain the master cylinder or booster as an assembly to the pedal assembly. Once the booster or master cylinder is tightened the inside support bolts can be tightened. Check the brake master cylinder rod for proper clearance. There should be approximately 1/2-inch clearance between the master cylinder and brake booster pushrod.

CHAPTER 12

Attach Oil Pressure Line

8 You must connect and tighten this copper oil pressure line to the oil pressure gauge. You want to know this line is tight, dry, and leak-free before installing the insulation or carpet. At this point, the dash harness should be passed through the firewall and the ignition coil connected. Start the engine and check for leaks and proper gauge operation.

Carpet

Insulation and carpeting comes next with the trim being installed to hold all the carpeting pieces in place. I've found that the carpeting should be installed as soon as possible after the insulation is laid down, otherwise working around bare insulation usually results in torn areas, which defeats the purpose of putting a barrier between the floor and the carpet. I recommend and use the same Thermo-Tec sound deadening and heat insulation products under the carpet for the floorboards and transmission tunnel. Like the firewall, I prefer products that stick to the fiberglass well. Each piece is cut to fit, and I cover the entire floor and transmission tunnel. For the ultimate noise and heat control, I then use Corvette Central's ceramic heat barrier. The foil-covered ceramic cloth is laid on top of the stick-on insulation.

Any additional insulation must be carefully contoured to the floorboard or the carpet, otherwise interior panels do not fit properly. The stack up of additional materials must be considered, too, or you will be fighting every piece you install.

Carpet replacement begins with laying the carpet in the sun for as long as possible before installation. The heated carpet is more pliable and fits closer to the contours. Many carpet suppliers claim that cutting isn't required, which is somewhat true; however, I've found that all carpeting kits require some trimming, to avoid bunched-up areas. Too much carpeting around the center console plate can make a difficult-to-install console plate even more difficult, for instance.

Make sure the carpet lays flat and contours to the floorboard before any cutting begins. I also install the gas pedal and spacer assembly, which holds the carpeting in place, before beginning any trimming. Pay attention to the fit of the driver side carpet around the gas pedal's rubber wear guards.

Another good idea is to cut a small opening for each screw that passes through the carpeting. Sometimes a screw grabs the carpeting loops and pulls long strands out of the carpet. Just make sure the holes are not visible. Install the console plate and side panels to finish the carpet installation.

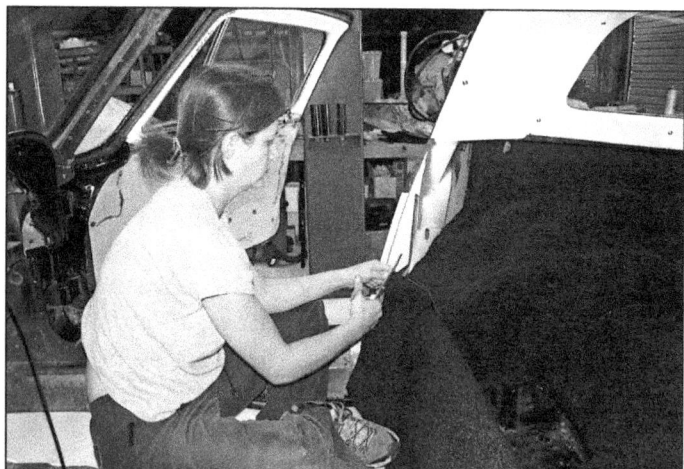

Trim the black 80/20 looped carpet carefully with scissors before the rear quarter trim is installed. Work at the rear compartment section first to avoid damage to the floorboard insulation.

Install each front floorboard carpet section after Thermo-Tec and jute insulation is installed. This is where you have to be extra careful and ensure the carpet is fully seated into the floorboard recesses. If the carpeting is not sitting tightly to the floorboard when trimming it can end up too short at the console.

INTERIOR

The retainers should be installed on top of the carpet; often they are installed with the carpet cut out just enough to fit over the retainer. When it comes time install the seat, the carpet and insulation make it very difficult to push the seat back far enough to start the front bolts easily. The wear plates under the carpet are an important part of preserving the fiberglass from seat frame damage. Once the plates and retainers are in place the seat track simply slides into the retainer and one bolt is installed on each seat track.

Window Trim

Midyear interiors have metal trim around the windshield, so there is no plastic to break or deteriorate and fall apart, as with the 1964–1967 rear window trim. The many years of paint can be stripped off the metal trim easily, making prep work go quickly. The plastic rear window trim must be handled carefully, since it can be easily broken, especially when cleaning or prepping for paint.

Priming is the first step to bring back the pieces, then paint them semi-flat black. Convertible Midyears have stainless-steel windshield trim that requires polishing. The upper stainless-steel windshield trim usually gets beat up from latching the top. In most cases, the trim can be smoothed and then polished by professionals.

You have to be careful during the installation of the trim pieces. If you aren't careful until all the screws are installed, trim pieces that lay on top of one another can scratch the paint. If you have some trepidation about how the pieces should be installed (which piece fits where), test-fit the pieces first, before painting them, then number them on the backside for easy installation.

Carefully tighten the rear window trim screws or you end up cracking the trim pieces around the screw holes. This is where a battery-powered screwdriver can prevent damage to fragile trim pieces.

Seats

Seat installation is simple, if the prep work was done during the body work phase. The most common installation mistake is leaving out the wear plates under the rear of the seat tracks. Wear plates are placed on top of the carpet and then the seat track retainers are bolted to the plates and floor. I don't cut the carpet out, but I place a flap of carpet over the front retaining bolts. The seat tracks are set on top of the carpet and the seats are bolted in place.

Door Panels

The door panels are last to install, to minimize the chance of damaging them while interior restoration work is performed. New door panels require some trimming or cutting for manual window cranks. The door panels have a plastic or fiber substrate that the vinyl is contoured to. Although it may seem smart to cut the panel's vinyl material to the edge of the substrate as General Motors did, you absolutely should not.

I install the door panel on the top of the door, then use the window regulator shaft as a guide and cut just enough to allow the shaft to come through the panel. Once the panel is fitted, I remove the panel to trim the opening further, to install the window trim pieces.

Convertible Top

Although the convertible top may be considered an exterior item, its composition is more interior-like. All the elements come into play: upholstery, exterior weatherstrip sealing, and metal work. Much like the seats, the top, or "skin" as it's called, installs similarly with staples.

The top material is stapled onto the tack strips; glue adheres the vertical sail panels to the top frame. The top frame's rear lower bow has two unique channels, one to capture the top material, and one to retain the rear deck weatherstrip. After the top material and weatherstrip are stuffed into place, a locking cord is installed to keep everything in place.

The installation of this door pull can try your patience. The screws go in at an angle to the front and down just a degree or so. To make things even more interesting the screws are machine thread so they must be started correctly, unlike a sheet-metal screw that can be close to being in the right direction. The best policy is to use a Phillips-head screwdriver. Another bit of advice is to start the screws without the handle in place. Once you understand the angle you are trying to place the screw at it goes easier with the handle in place.

CHAPTER 12

There are a couple of observations I have made concerning the best possible outcome of a convertible top installation. Many top frames have been tweaked over the years and necessitate careful fitting of the top frame. I always install all the weatherstrips that seal the top frame to the windows before installing the top.

Convertibles that have both a soft-top and hardtop should have the windows adjusted to the hardtop first, then the convertible top frame should be adjusted to fit the windows that were fitted to the hardtop. Installing the convertible top material before adjusting the top frame can be a real problem. If the top frame requires a major adjustment after the new material is installed, two problems can arise: the material may be too loose or worse, it may be extremely tight, requiring a new top.

While I am on the subject of loose or tight tops, I need to discuss the top material. All Midyear tops had date-coded, clear-vinyl rear windows. There were a few top color choices available: white, black, and tan. Al Knoch has cloth replacement tops available for Midyears. Although not correct for a numbers-matching Midyear, they certainly look good.

There are few things to consider concerning maintenance and the choice of top material. Vinyl tops shrink as they age making the outer edges of the top roll up, no matter how well you take care of it. Cloth tops go the other way and stretch, as they deal with wind blowing into the cockpit. Cloth tops are easier to install for the beginner, because they stretch during the installation.

No matter which top you choose, the rear window is clear plastic. Take care of the plastic, right from the beginning. It scratches easily, and many times scratches occur during top installation. Once the top is installed, make sure any dust or dirt is removed before folding the top. The folded material becomes easily damaged from dirt, and scratches occur at the rubbing folds.

Always store the car with the top up, to keep wrinkles to a minimum. Never drop the top in sub-freezing temperatures; I have seen the rear windows shatter as the driver attempted to fold the top. Also, make sure the rear window has a fold following the length of the window, as the top is lowered into position. Creased rear windows always retain the crease; top replacement is the only fix.

Like all the other areas of the project, the convertible top frame itself may require restoration. Top frame front bows often corrode badly, even on well-kept Midyears. The front bow has a fiber tack strip that absorbs any water that ends up under the front of the top. Rain finds its way under the front bow, taking a long time to dry out. The water-soaked tack strip fiber corrodes the underlying metal severely.

Fiber tack strips are used at each bow except the rear lower bow. Intermediate bows use the tack strips for bow pad retention. The upper rear bow tack strip holds the straps, top, and rear window panels. The hydem strip, which finishes off the seam where the two panels meet, also staples into the rear bow tack strip. There is a good chance that once the old top is stripped off, more metal and paint work will be required.

Corrosion damages many of the top frame screw threads and Heli-coils that are necessary. I Heli-coil all top frame threaded holes as a precaution, to allow for easy assembly. Many top frames also require hardware replacement. Thankfully, many suppliers have the hardware in kit form. Top frames almost always require some paint work, due to their high visibility from inside the car. By now, you should be well-versed in how to clean, repair, prep, and paint the frame. I apply a top coat of gloss black enamel paint to the entire frame.

Convertible Top Installation

This convertible top frame is in rough shape, and the convertible top needs replacement. When restoring a convertible top check the fit of the weatherstrip and the top frame before the top restoration begins. Make sure everything fits before the disassembly takes place. If you need to make frame alignment changes, do them before cleaning and painting the frame assembly.

INTERIOR

Adjust Pivots

1 Once the frame is ready for installation adjust these pivots for height and window fit. Be gentle with the 3/8 bolts when tightening them. The plates that they screw into are often stripped out and require a back-up nut. Using a back-up nut works but it is not easy to access the tight area. Replacing the plate is a major ordeal because it is riveted into a retaining pocket, which cannot be accessed for removal.

Center Bow Pins

2 The rear deck catches also have some play. They should be adjusted so the rear bow pins are centered. You need to have the frame fit properly now, not after the top material is installed. Adjust the release cables while you are in the area and make sure they open the catch fully.

Install Straps

3 Remove the rear bow off the top frame assembly once fitted to install the rear straps. Note the sewn seams where the material's folded edges meet. They need to be facing toward the outside of the frame. You do not want to see the edges from inside the car.

Install Weatherstrip

4 Stuff the rear bow weatherstrip into the channel after the top material is pushed into the bow's top material recess. The top material and weatherstrip are marked in the center to match to the bow center mark. Push the cord sticking out into the recess to lock the top material and weatherstrip in place just at the center.

Measure Welting Excess

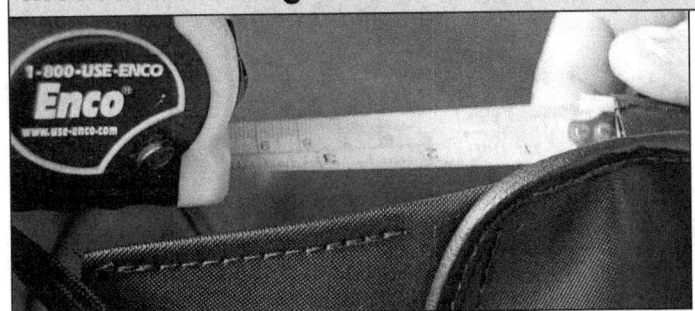

5 This measurement of the top material protruding past the end of the rear bow is not exact due to top variations. You can generally use 2½ inches from the outer welting that covers the top's outer edge as the outer point. The most important thing is that the measurement is equal to avoid wrinkles.

HOW TO RESTORE YOUR CORVETTE: 1963–1967

Lock Ends in Place

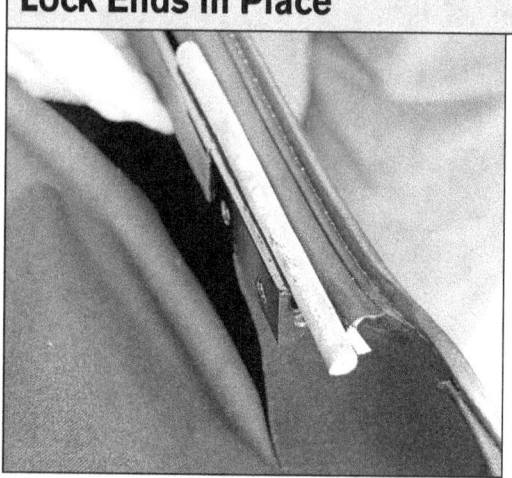

6 Once the measurement is established I use this piece of 8-mm ignition wire to lock the ends in place until the locking bead is in place.

Install Locking Cord

7 Installing the locking cord bead can be a challenge because it fits very tightly in place. I have seen smaller-diameter beads installed but they do come out over time. Installing this bead with the bow installed on the car is much tougher than on a table where you have control. Water does help ease the bead into place but don't slip out of the groove because top damage can result.

Remove Excess Weatherstrip

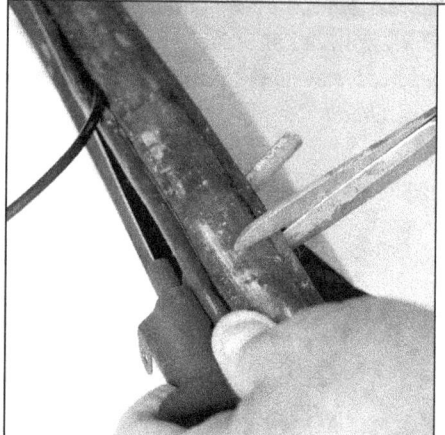

8 When the bead is close to the end measure and cut off the weatherstrip accordingly using the end weatherstrip piece as a guide. Cut the weatherstrip about 3/16 inch longer to keep the end piece tight against it.

Install Weatherstrip Ends

9 The rear bow is installed as an assembly using the 1/4-20 inch oval-head stainless-steel Phillips-head screws. There is a little 6-32 inch threaded screw that retains the weatherstrip end. Put that in now also to avoid real aggravation later. Installing the weatherstrip ends after the fact is a real pain in the backside.

Install Staples at Center Bows

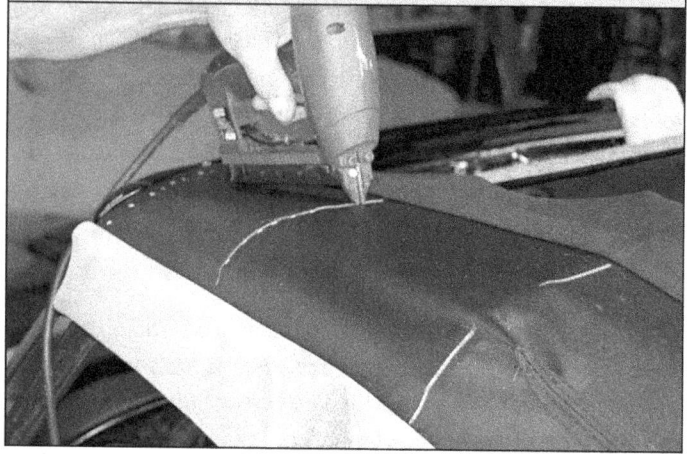

10 Line up marks with the center of each bow then staple with 3/16-inch-long Monel staples to prevent rusting. Stainless-steel staples work well; just watch the length. They do not hold the bow pad material tightly if they are too long.

Install Bow Pad and Strap

11 Strap installation length is marked for each Corvette top's generation by Al Knoch. Using their marks works almost every time, and only once in a while do you have to adjust longer or shorter for proper rear bow fit.

INTERIOR

Install Top Material

12 Glue the vertical top material in place with 3M weatherstrip adhesive with the weatherstrip installed. Use the convertible top's vertical weatherstrip to hold the top material on the frame as the adhesive dries. Installing the weatherstrip retaining nuts is much easier now also.

Close Top Rear Bow Seam

13 This is where having the trimmed Al Knoch top makes the difference. If the straps and bow pads are the correct length, the top material flap should be centered on the upper bow. Sometimes you have to stop and lengthen or shorten the rear straps to center the material. The material must be tight and centered on the upper bow or you get major wrinkles.

Add Hydem Welt

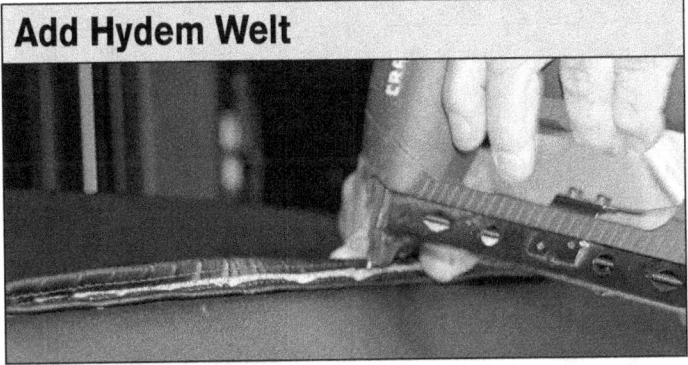

14 The Hydem welt goes on to finish the two cut edges and hide the staples. This is where you find out how well the job is going. As with the top material you want the welt to be centered on the upper bow. If any staples were installed outside of the welting cover area they show up now.

Locate Hydem Welt Cap

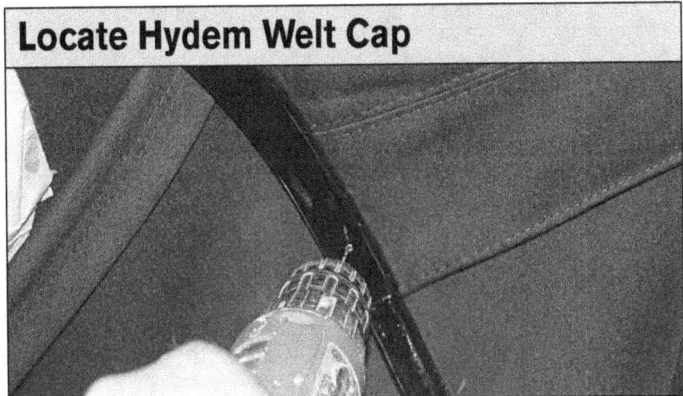

15 Use a small drill bit to drill through the new tack strip material and top material to locate the Hydem welt end cap. The end cap screw just slightly pierces the metal bow to make sure it stays in place.

Open Welt Cap Hole

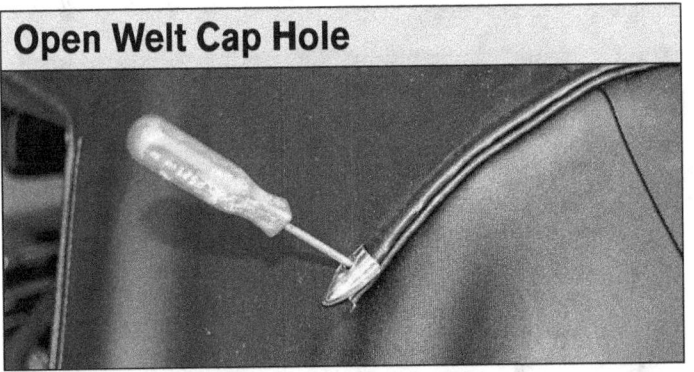

16 After the drill locates the bow's correct end cap hole use a pick to open up the hole in the welt and tack strip. Make sure you cut the welt off past the hole so the screw grabs it during installation.

Install Welting

17 After placing the front bow large welting bead in place the front bow gets this concealed staple trick. The welting bead has two flaps of material. One is tacked in place with the top material. After checking for correct positioning of the welting glue the second flap in place.

Glue Flap

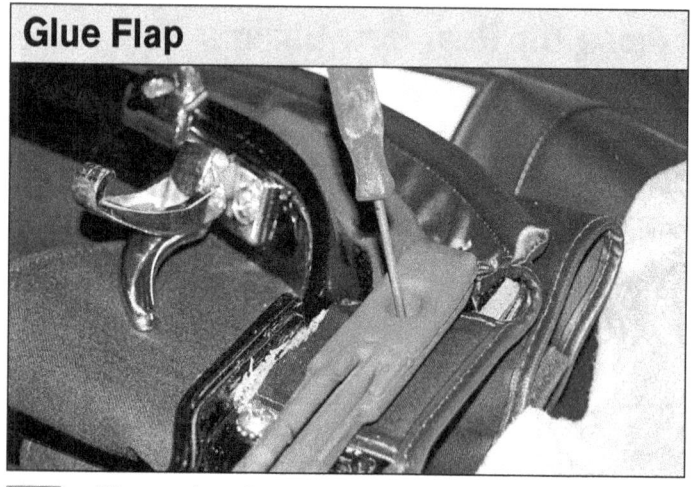

18 After you install the front weatherstrip, center the front top material and glue the flap under the weatherstrip into place. The large welting bead is right at the edge of top material. Always check the length and center the welting. Each top varies a bit in placement of the welting.

Remove Wrinkles

19 The pros at Al Knoch have this steamer to help ease out any wrinkles that may occur. Leaving your Midyear out in the sun for a day or two helps remove small wrinkles and flattens out the back window.

Hardtop

General Motors made a fiberglass hardtop with a Plexiglas rear window for the Midyear. In my opinion, the hardtop looks really good in place of the convertible top. Restoring the hardtop is a blend of interior, exterior, and mechanical work. Most restorers disassemble the entire top, including removing the weatherstrip retainers, before painting, then the assembly begins with the weatherstrip retainers and fitting the weatherstrips to the side windows before the headliner is installed and all trim pieces.

Many restorers leave the hardtop for the experts at Glassworks: The Hardtop Shop for an expert restoration. When you consider the cost of the pieces to restore the hardtop, Glassworks' services are very reasonable. Of course, no two tops are alike in condition. Each estimate they provide is based on the individual top's condition. They also sell hardtops for your convertible.

Glassworks: The Hardtop Shop has all the items you need for a complete hardtop restoration in one convenient kit. They know what you typically require for a top-notch restoration saving you from multiple orders and unintended downtime.

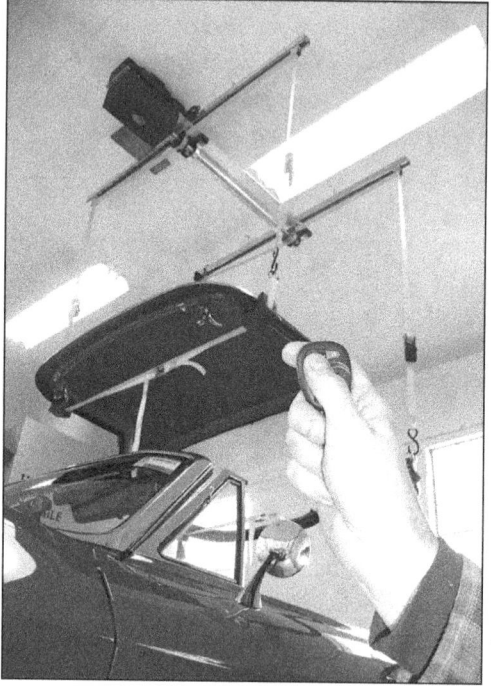

Now this is the way to store your Glassworks: The Hardtop Shop restored Midyear hardtop. The ultra-cool hardtop hoist makes owning a second top pleasurable. With it there are no concerns about tripping and scratching your finely finished, restored hardtop during installation.

Convertible Top Installation Techniques

The clean, painted, and adjusted convertible top frame is ready for the top material. Patience is definitely required to attempt the top installation. A few special tools make the job easier and are easy to justify. The tough part is making sure that the rear bow is placed correctly and that there are as few wrinkles as possible, once you are finished.

In my experience, Al Knoch tops fit well, right out of the box. The convertible top crew at Al Knoch denote where the bow pads and straps should be placed on the bows, which is very helpful for the first-time installer. They also keep the extra material to a minimum, in an effort to prevent improper installation. Some minor trimming is necessary; if you have too much material, something is wrong. Warm days with direct sunlight on the top also helps during top installation. This is especially true for the rear window; heat makes it lay flat to give you an idea whether the rear top material is correctly placed.

During top installation, remember to install the rear bow straps first. The rear bow top material and weatherstrip installation is tough, and forgetting the straps means starting all over. When I say the rear bow top material and weatherstrip installation is tough, I mean very tough. No embellishment here. The really difficult part is installing the cord that locks the pieces in place. After the rear bow is ready for installation, the rest is not so bad.

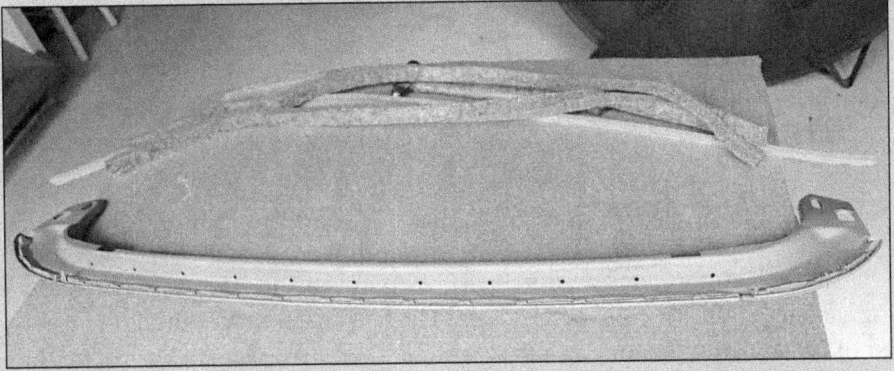

This is the 1966 convertible front bow after some intense therapy. I stripped the paint, bead-blasted the corroded areas, and applied urethane epoxy primer before installing the tack strip. I prefer to prime the bow then install the tack strips before the final coat of black acrylic enamel.

The window screen roller gets a workout when installing tops. I use the wooden handle roller to force the tack strip into place. Plastic rollers don't last long under this constant pressure. I also apply a bead of 3M weatherstrip adhesive under each tack strip to ensure it stays in place for the long term.

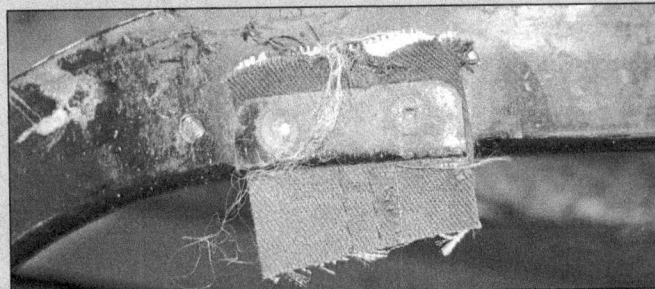

ARGH! This is all too common to see on convertible top bows. Years of water-soaked straps have destroyed these screws. When one screw breaks off, stop and drill the remaining screw out before breaking it off. The stripped-out screw head centers the drill bit easier than trying to find the center on the screw with the broken head.

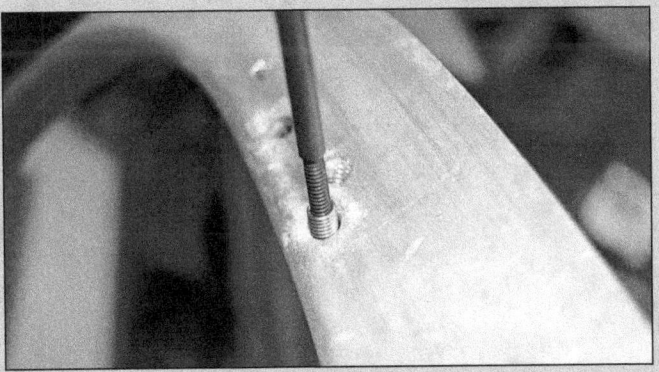

I make it a practice to drill, tap, and Heli-coil every threaded hole in the aluminum rear bow. After all, I may be the one that has to put a new top on in the future. Anti-seize should be applied to the screws going into stainless-steel Heli-coil inserts.

CHAPTER 13

OTHER COMPONENTS

We all enjoy amenities, and this chapter gives you some ideas about ones that you might incorporate into your new ride. Think carefully about these ancillary items, though because while they may make the ride enjoyable, if chosen or installed poorly, they can be aggravating. For example, if you choose an option like A/C, knowing that before you restore the interior helps save time and additional costs.

Midyear Corvettes did not have many options to check off during the ordering process. This 1966 convertible had two special boxes checked off: factory knock-off wheels and side-pipes. Then for whatever reason a Powerglide automatic transmission was chosen. It might have been one of those compromise Corvettes; you get the racy stuff and I will have the automatic transmission to ease around town. This chapter covers the ancillary components and options.

Other items, such as the cooling system, can be upgraded for better performance while maintaining original appearances.

Fuel System

General Motors used Carter WCFB carburetors on low-horsepower Midyears until 1965. Higher air flow Carter AFB carburetors were used on 350-hp versions, from 1963 to 1965. High-horsepower small-blocks and big-blocks received Holley carburetors, across the board. Three "deuce" big-block engines received three Holley 2-barrel carburetors.

Rebuilding any of these vintage carburetors at home produces minimal improvements, due to wear. Carburetor repair kits from your local auto parts store are very basic and are meant for internal cleaning, as opposed to remanufacturing. Carburetor throttle shafts and plates wear and cause vacuum leaks and poor idling. Warped throttle plate assemblies also cause vacuum leaks and rough idling. Corrosion plays a factor; many carburetors have internal damage, from years of water sitting in the bowl. The bottom line is that it's likely that you need professional help to properly restore an original carburetor.

A niche industry was born to restore vintage carburetors to like-new performance. Worn throttle plate and shafts receive bushings to eliminate vacuum leaks. Castings are checked for warpage, and if necessary, they're straightened or repaired. All of the carburetor's original coatings are restored, for that off-the-assembly-line look. Most importantly, internal pieces are checked for correctness.

HOW TO RESTORE YOUR CORVETTE: 1963–1967

Holley carburetors have a zinc wash on the carburetor main body and float bowls. The Quad Shop refinishes each carburetor with the correct casting coating for that original-equipment look. All pieces are checked for correctness, internally and externally. Each carburetor has been adjusted and is ready to be installed when it arrives. The Quad Shop tests each unit after restoration to ensure you have like-new engine performance.

Many early carburetors have been disassembled and reassembled numerous times, using whatever parts were available. Mismatched components cause a myriad of performance issues, such as poor idle quality, hesitations, and poor overall performance. Worn, incorrect carburetors make the most expensive, best assembled engine run poorly. Remanufacturing is the way to ensure you will enjoy all your hard work from the engine rebuild.

For owners who want to drive their numbers-matching Midyear, I recommend replacing the carburetor with a new assembly, which gives you that like-new engine performance. The original, numbers-matching carburetor can be put into storage for safe keeping. Spray the exterior with WD-40 or CRC to prevent corrosion during storage. If you decide that it is time to sell your Midyear, you have the original carburetor to enhance its value.

Those of you lucky enough to be working on a Tri-Power "deuce" 427-ci project have plenty of carburetor and tuning concerns. Adjusted properly, the three 2-barrel carburetors set you back in the seat upon acceleration. The sensation is similar to a supercharged engine when the additional four barrels come in.

A complete understanding of how the three carburetors work together is important. To begin with, the center carburetor is the master carburetor that controls idle air and primary fuel mixture. Jets control wide-open fuel flow through the center carburetor. The outer (or end) carburetors are for secondary use only. There are no jets in either of the end carbs; metering plates control fuel flow. The progressive linkage is not designed to open the outer carburetors. Instead, ported vacuum opens both of the outer carburetors when the progressive linkage is at wide-open throttle.

The Tri-Power's multiple fuel lines and fittings can be difficult to deal with. It is very easy to damage the inlet threads in the fuel bowls by over-tightening fittings. I ground a special wrench to be able to hold onto the inlet fittings. The fuel inlet must be held during fuel line tightening. Don't be surprised if you find one or two leaking connections. The myriad of lines and fittings tend to come loose and leak from engine vibrations. Original steel fuel lines are often replaced with stainless steel. They do look nice and stay that way longer, but the harder material makes them more difficult to seal.

Even if you have someone else restore your carburetors, you still need to understand a few basic adjustments. Holley carburetors have adjustable needles and seats for easy fuel level adjustment. I often find Holley fuel bowl needle and seat thread damage, which could be from cross threading or not properly loosening the needle and seat lock screw before turning the level adjusting nut. Corrosion damage also affects the needle and seat threads on the fuel bowls. Check the threads carefully, before spending a lot of time cleaning and prepping them for service or sending out for restoration.

No matter what carburetor you have in place, idle mixture must be adjusted. This is where I see the majority of wasted

Here is the big-dog 427-ci intake manifold with three new Holley deuces in-line. I replaced the entire fuel line assembly with Zip Products' stainless-steel pieces. I start all the lines into each fitting and then tighten them incrementally until they are all tight. Although difficult to get a wrench on, each carburetor's inlet fitting must be held while tightening the lines.

Use Teflon thread tape to help seal the end of the stainless-steel fuel lines. The tricky part is applying the thread tape right up to the edge of the inverted flare fitting. If any Teflon tape gets inside the line the sticking carburetor fuel flow control needles flood the engine.

fuel. For some reason, Corvette owners or tuners want a perfectly smooth idle, similar to what a Cadillac provides. I routinely find the idle mixture needles adjusted out too many turns, causing the engine to run way too rich at idle.

Positioning of the idle mixture screws reveals a lot about the carburetor's condition. When properly adjusted, the idle screws on Carter carburetors should be out about two turns from fully seated. Holley carburetors usually idle correctly at 3/4 to 1 turn out. Engine RPM should drop as the screws are turned in (clockwise) and, as they approach being fully seated, the engine should die. If there is no or minimal affect on the idle, the carburetor has an internal leak, which is allowing excess fuel to pass by. This can be due to the throttle plates being open too much. I always start my adjustment with the idle mixture screws turned out the prescribed number of turns before adjusting idle speed if the RPM is too high.

Sometimes, one idle mixture needle does not affect idle, and this means that the idle air bleeds are dirty. Fuel passes by the idle mixture screw and air is introduced on top of the column of fuel exiting the idle mixture screw. When idle air-bleed holes are dirty, fuel is not drawn out of the mixture screw properly. Often, the fix is easy, and with regular maintenance the dirty idle air-bleed problem never returns: simply spray carburetor cleaner into the carburetor inlet (airhorn) to wash out any build up of debris. The engine may stall as you spray the cleaner into the inlet, so do not rev up the engine. If a backfire occurs as the engine RPM is raised, the carb cleaner could catch on fire. If the engine stalls, let it sit for 10 to 15 minutes, then try starting it.

Today, we have ethanol blended fuels that can attack the castings and gaskets of early carburetors. Carburetor and fuel system preservation has come to the forefront because of this growing concern. You should consider using a fuel stabilizer in the fuel tank to prevent corrosion. The problem is, we really do not know what long-term effects these new blends have. Midyears that are driven daily have the fewest concerns because of the constant fuel flow.

I believe that Sta-Bil or another fuel preservative should be used often, especially when storing your car for the off season. But don't just dump a bottle in the tank when you come home from a drive. You need to let the stabilizer make its way through the fuel system, all the way to the carburetor fuel bowl.

Mechanical Fuel Injection

Rochester fuel injection systems made good power and looked awesome under the hood. That, of course, was for those who could live with its quirks. The real issue was fuel control under ever-changing atmospheric conditions. Today, computers compensate for changing conditions in nanoseconds, but it is difficult to tune the early fuelie system for optimal performance throughout the entire year.

Another concern was the fuel injection pressure pump was driven by the distributor. A large-diameter cable (similar to a speedometer cable) drove the fuel pump. Early fuelie owners usually had a spare fuelie drive unit cable in the glove box "just in case." With the typical driver expecting trouble-free driving, many of the fuelie units were actually dumped in favor of a carburetor.

Restoring an original fuelie Midyear is expensive, if the fuel injection pieces are gone. Used fuel injection units are available to restore, or it is possible to find complete ready-to-go assemblies. A select group of individuals, like Jack Podell, have dedicated their lives to these early fuelie units. Be prepared, though because the cost of the fuelie unit could easily exceed the cost of the engine rebuild. Podell's restoration service is flawless, from an aesthetic and performance standpoint. If you go this route, you need to become friends with your fuelie unit restorer, so he can help you through the installation and tuning process.

Holley carburetors have two adjustments that should always be checked after carburetor installation. The large brass plug above and to the left of the screwdriver is the float level sight plug. When the plug is removed fuel should be trickling out while the engine is running.

If necessary, loosen the large, slotted, flat-head screw counterclockwise while the 5/8 hex nut is held on top of the carburetor bowl for float adjustment. Rotate the 5/8 nut clockwise to lower the float and counterclockwise to raise the float. Use a screwdriver to adjust the fuel mixture on one side of the carburetor. Start with this screw one turn out clockwise from the seated position.

After the engine warms up turn this screw counterclockwise until the engine RPM stops rising. Then turn the screw back in again watching the RPM. When the engine RPM begins to drop, stop turning the screw. You want the idle mixture screw set where the engine RPM drops just slightly off the highest RPM you were able to achieve.

Many of the fuel injection wear items are available today, including pump overhaul kits. Rebuilding the fuel injection fuel meter pump is much like working on a carburetor. The trick is understanding how to make the adjustments, and how they react with your particular engine.

The 1963 Corvette service manual has the most fuel injection information for someone attempting to rebuild or adjust a fuelie system on their own. Fuel injection units usually run rich, so expect fouled spark plugs if you putt around or infrequently drive your Midyear. Long road trips at highway speeds are best for spark plug life and good overall performance. Frequently-fouled spark plugs also mean fuel-diluted engine oil, so check your oil level often and change it when it smells of fuel.

Fuel injection and carbureted engines use similar fuel pumps. Fuel injected engines use an engine-mounted fuel pump to lift fuel to the high-pressure pump. The 1963–1966 small-block fuel pumps are rebuildable. All big-block and 1967 fuel pumps are of a later design with a crimped lower cover. Fuel pump overhaul kits are available through Corvette Central. If you prefer, Corvette Central has a new, correct replacement fuel pump ready to go.

As with a carburetor, external refinishing is the issue for that correct look. Fuel pump overhaul kits include replacement check valves to control fuel flow, along with a diaphragm and the necessary hardware to make the fuel pump work like new. Debris in the fuel system affects both fuel pump and carburetor performance. Make sure the tank is clean, the fuel lines are clear, and that there is a new fuel filter in place before cranking the engine over.

If you go the route of a restored fuel pump and carburetor, do not attempt to return the assemblies to your restorer if contaminated fuel was used because they are acutely aware of the condition of vintage fuel systems.

Check the inside of your fuel lines and replace them if you find internal corrosion. Sometimes, the steel lines can fool you: the outside of the line may be fine despite nasty corrosion and debris inside.

Cooling System

Midyear cooling systems went through many changes in an attempt to cool the new-found horsepower and big-block engines.

Radiators

In an effort to cool engines with the highest horsepower of the era, General Motors used aluminum, cross-flow radiators. The new, cutting-edge radiator design did not allow for the typical brass/copper radiator service procedures. Instead, when the radiator required flushing, it was often time for replacement. Chemicals have to be used to clean any scale build-up, which (along with corrosion) was inevitable with cast-iron engine blocks and cylinder heads. Often, an original radiator needs to be replaced to restore proper flow. No one wants to overheat a new engine, so before you attempt to use the original or possibly a very dated aluminum radiator, have it flow checked by a radiator shop.

Today, radiator shops work mostly on plastic tank radiators with aluminum cores, so there's a good chance that they might be able to clean a vintage aluminum radiator. Today's cleaning chemicals are better, and technicians are well versed in their use. The most significant change has been the advent of flow checking capabilities. At the very least, you will know if the recommended amount of liquid flows through the radiator.

Keep in mind that the flow may be fair, even with scale coating the tubes. Scale acts like an insulator and prevents good convection, which traps heat in the radiator. Don't be surprised if the cleaned radiator does not provide adequate cooling. Cleaning may be worth a try, but my feeling is that 50-year-old radiators should be replaced.

Copper/brass replacements were popular to save money when an original aluminum radiator failed, but you can expect a 30-percent reduction in cooling system efficiency for the cost savings. Low-250- and 300-hp 327-ci engines

General Motors made quite a statement with this early fuelie unit. Jack Podell has completed many of these mechanically and aesthetically correct restorations. Knowing the ins and outs of each of these units takes years of experience. Having someone well versed to discuss the typical problems that occur is paramount for someone owning and driving a fuelie Midyear.

This fuel-filter installation is not NCRS-correct, but it sure can save the fuel pump and carburetor from debris in the fuel. Fuel pump check valves do not seal if any debris gets caught in the valves. It keeps the check valves open, which stops fuel flow.

This is a tale of two radiators. The copper/brass radiator on the left may look as efficient as the Dewitt's correct aluminum reproduction radiator on the right. I decided to use the Dewitt's radiator with high-performance cooling fan to keep the high-horsepower-output Midyear cool with the A/C on.

Be Cool radiators has a new line of radiators. At first glance you think this high-performing radiator is original equipment. The fit is factory-correct with all the fittings in the right location while providing more cooling-system capacity. It's the answer for high horsepower and large-cubic-inch engines with A/C.

might just squeak by if the engines are not run hard or lack the added load of A/C.

Dewitt's Radiators has a correct, number-matching, date-coded, aluminum radiator for your Midyear. This is the correct replacement radiator if you are looking to attain NCRS or Bloomington Gold Status. If you want to have a performance verification certificate, you should consider the Dewitt's replacement over a 50-year-old radiator.

Be Cool offers direct-fit, aluminum, replacement radiators for about $100.00 more than the copper/brass replacement. The tanks are welded, so they obviously are not original looking. If you plan on driving your Midyear, it makes sense to go this route.

Correct-numbered radiator and heater hoses are available from all of the major Corvette suppliers. I usually purchase my hoses from Corvette suppliers to ensure reliability.

Water Pumps

Water pump choice is about engine horsepower and use. A numbers-matching Midyear should have a correct water pump. Even if it does, I rebuild it. Again, make sure you have the correctly numbered, date-coded component before servicing it.

This aluminum water pump from Corvette Central flows better while helping to dissipate heat quicker. The pump must have an efficient design and properly fit impeller for maximum water flow. Look for cast-iron or brass impellers with 3/4-inch-diameter shaft bearings. This original fan clutch has a thermal spring on front that engages the fan blade as heat rises.

I found rust stains at the bottom of the heater core housing and deformed heater hose outlet and inlet tubes. I make a habit of pressure checking each new heater core before installing them. I apply low air pressure (no more than 15 psi) into the heater core. The core is then submerged in water to see if any bubbles come from the core.

OTHER COMPONENTS

Zip Products offers water pump rebuild kits. All you need is a hydraulic press for the service. Another source is O&G Water Pump Company. They restore all water pumps. O&G retrofits the latest components into a stock casting and provides a 24-month or 24,000-mile warranty.

I always upgrade to an aluminum pump for high-horsepower applications with A/C. If you opt for an aluminum pump, make sure the rotation is correct for your application.

Fans

Midyears have fan clutches to cycle the cooling fan when a thermal spring detects elevated heat. Horsepower and fuel mileage increases at highway speeds as the clutch releases. The idea is to utilize the cooling fan only when required. Many fan clutches are replaced because of an incorrect diagnosis. As the engine temperature rises, the fan clutch should engage.

A classic example of a failed clutch is a loose fan after engine temperature was above 180 degrees F. To test: after the engine has been idling at temperature, shut the engine down. The fan blade should stop almost immediately. If the fan spins freely, the clutch has failed. The other common failure is clutch lock-up. The cooling fan never cycles out, causing the fan to run at maximum speed at all times.

Heater Cores

I certainly need to mention the heater core, since it likely requires replacement. Non-A/C Midyears have coolant flowing through when the engine is running, keeping them fairly clean. The problem is that most Midyears sit for long periods of time.

Look over the heater core for green areas of corrosion. The copper/brass core corrodes, causing many small pin-hole leaks. Repairing a leaking heater core usually means fighting one battle after another. Once an area leaks, more leaks are sue to follow. Replacement of the core is the most logical fix.

Air Conditioning

Only about 3,700 Midyears were equipped with the factory RPO C60 A/C system, which was more than adequate to cool the small passenger area. Airflow was restricted by the small dash vents that kept you wanting just a little more airflow to be comfortable.

If you are one of the few Midyear owners with factory A/C, resealing the inside plenum assembly is smart. Kits are available with all the foam seals, gaskets, and rivets to attain maximum airflow; and you want that. Vacuum hose kits are also available to replace the deteriorated rubber hoses. Many pieces are available, in spite of the low number of cars produced with A/C.

The topic of R-12 usage in the original refrigerant system could be its own chapter, since R-12 and R-134a refrigerants work under different operating pressures.

Refrigerant operating pressures affect the temperature of air coming out of the A/C vents. High pressure equals high temperature. R134a must operate at lower pressures to attain the same level of cooling as R-12. Suffice it to say, R-134a is not as cool as R-12, unless the system pressures are reduced, which requires a more efficient compressor than the original A6. Additionally, the suction throttling valve (STV) operates at the R-12's required higher pressures. To make the system work at an optimum level with R134a, the STV should be replaced with an STV eliminator.

There are other refrigerants available to replace R-12, but most of them are blends of multiple refrigerants that could harm the internals of your system. I say if you must have the factory-correct look, bite the bullet and use the expensive R-12. If you choose the best possible cooling without worrying about the correct look, use the R-134a refrigerant, STV eliminator, and new-style compressor.

True gear heads would not hear of having the engine compartment filled up with fluff. They were interested in power under the hood, leaving the majority of Midyears without A/C. Because of this, I install more aftermarket Midyear A/C systems than any other Corvette generation.

The Vintage Air Sure-Fit R-134a compact, all-in-one system is an excellent upgrade. A/C, heat, and defroster come in one easy-to-install package. Vintage Air's use of late-model, fuel-efficient compressors requiring very little horsepower makes it a worthwhile investment for those who want to drive their Midyear. On top of that, the Vintage Air controls integrate with the original dash controls, making it look like an original install. I install the entire Vintage Air A/C system in a couple of days, in assembled Midyears. You can add A/C with the dash assembly to save even more time.

A/C compressor efficiency has come a long way since 1963. Classic Auto Air's S-6 replacement for the original A6 used from 1963 until the 1880s was designed for R134a refrigerant. The S-6 is a direct fit and no adapters are required for quick installation.

A/C Installation

Install A/C Condenser

1 Set the Vintage Air A/C condenser and drier assembly in place at the front of the radiator. Install a 1967 A/C radiator core support to radiator upper seal for better airflow through the radiator and A/C condenser.

Secure Air Evaporator

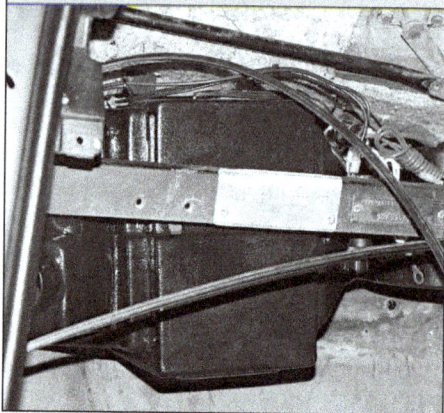

2 Set the evaporator housing into place then secure it with a couple of glove box hinge screws. The real plus to this system is the ongoing commitment by Vintage Air to make the most efficient and reliable A/C systems.

Install Plastic Cover

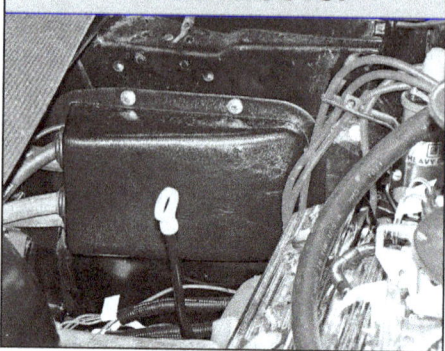

3 Install this plastic cover under the hood to seal up the firewall after evaporator installation. Route A/C and heater hoses out the cover along with the A/C compressor power lead. You need a helper to install the nuts from the inside while you hold onto the screws that hold the cover onto the firewall.

Sound System

Instead of calling it a sound system, it seems more plausible to say that, at best, there was some noise coming from the windshield area in Midyears. Radios and speakers of the era were not that great by today's standards. General Motors did offer FM, for the first time, along with signal-seeking AM for a short time, in 1963. Surprisingly, the majority of 1964–1967 Corvette purchasers went for the AM-FM option.

The unique, vertically-mounted radio was big and took up a lot of dash space. The speaker was also unique and required a voltage-limiting device to work with the Delco radio receiver. Replacing the speaker with a later style, without the limiting device, harms the radio and wiring.

It is best to send both the radio and speaker to an early Delco radio restoration specialist for repair. They repair the radio and check for the proper 1.5 volts at the speaker leads. The early radio parts are not available, as many have been stock piled. Repair specialists have spent many years at the swap meets picking out and saving as many pieces as possible. They can help you get the best possible sound out of the radio and speakers.

Another option is to use a new, electronic radio, converted to fit in the vertical opening. Replacement radios have a small chassis that makes installation much easier. There are no in-dash CD players available, due to space constraints.

My favorite aftermarket radio to consider is the AM/FM Slidebar stereo radio from Corvette Central. The face looks correct, while allowing for iPod or XM satellite inputs. Front speakers are available with dual voice coils or two separate 4-inch speakers. Zip Products has Ken Harrison Radios, which are very well made and reliable. It is just a matter of preference. Each of these radios makes a major difference in sound.

Remember to plan the wiring before the interior is installed. Install the speaker wiring now, even if you don't plan to install speakers until sometime in the future.

I am not, by any means, a sound system specialist; however, I do know that more watts equates to clearer sound. Original Midyear radios are lacking in wattage output, for sure, hindering sound quality. The best possible scenario is to check with an audio shop for input on the best pieces for any high-output system. They know the best location for tweeters, mid range, and woofers if you really want the best possible sound. If nothing else, have the wiring in place for them.

I love the sound of a big-block with side pipes, but you can only take that racket for so long. Quality sound with cool air blowing out the vents sure makes a long trip shorter.

Ignition Shielding

General Motors placed ignition shielding on its plug wires to avoid radio interference, but today's radios are not nearly as susceptible to radio interfer-

OTHER COMPONENTS

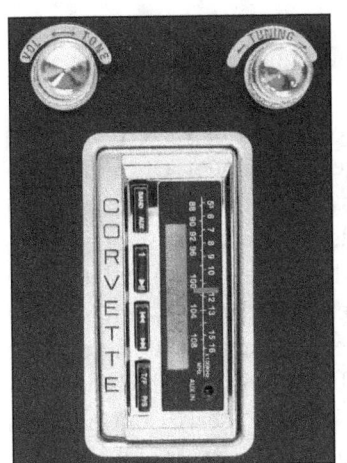

This reliable Ken Harrison 300 series radio has 200 watts of output power. RCA input and outputs are rear mounted for easy amplifier installations. There is also a provision to plug in your iPod for continuous sound on long trips.

Yes, this ignition shielding can be a pain to install. The trick is watching how the tabs are positioned on the exhaust manifolds. When the exhaust bolts are tightened the tabs tend to rotate with the bolt. Use a crescent wrench to hold the tab when tightening.

This is the transistorized ignition systems amplifier. The amplifier is found at the front of the radiator core support on the driver's side. Corvette Central has replacement amplifiers and amplifier circuit boards to repair an original unit. The replacement circuit boards have better circuitry for long, trouble-free life.

ence. The choice is yours whether you want to deal with the factory radio ignition shielding. Many restorers who are going for a show-car look eliminate the shielding, but Bloomington Gold or NCRS engines require the shielding. I recommend using the lower shields on the side of the engine, to keep heat off the wires. I also use the upper shielding for that "finished" look.

Speaking of heat, many exhaust manifold spark plug heat shields are left off. General Motors installed four shields: one at each group of two spark plugs. These are not for radio interference, but rather to prevent burned plug wire boots. If you are using stock exhaust manifolds, it is highly recommended that these shields be installed, even if no other shields are.

General Motors offered transistorized ignition under RPO code K66 for the 1964 Midyear. The 1965 L78 big-block Midyears had the K66 option as part of the package. Approximately 6,000 Midyears were equipped with the K66 option, for the years 1965–1967. Of the 74,000 plus Midyears sold in those years, only 12 percent had the option.

If you do find that you have the option, many replacement parts are available. The amplifier was the typical problem, though, over time. The distributor's stationary pole piece that supplied a signal to the amplifier magnet loses magnetism. Either problem causes hard or no-start conditions when the engine is hot.

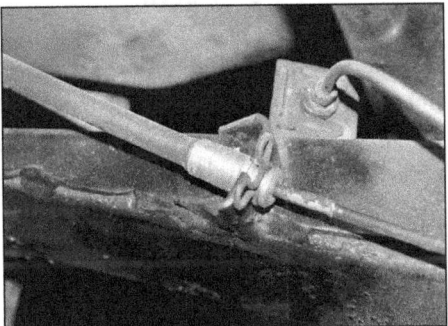

The key to adding that extra 1/2 inch of wheel backspacing is to move the parking brake cable mount from the side of the trailing arm to the top. We use a reciprocating saw and cut the mount off then weld it in place. The mount should be in-line with the brake hose retainer tab as shown. The best policy is to tack weld the mounts in place and check for proper cable length. If the cable is pulling on the parking brake lever when the cable is seated move the mount closer to the caliper vice-versa if the cable is too loose.

Wheels and Tires

Never in a million years would I recommend a particular style of wheel. With so many wheels on the market, I even have trouble deciding what I might like. Midyears had two factory wheels available: steel and then true aluminum knock-offs, beginning in 1964. By 1967, the true knock-off wheels were dropped,

The GM knock-off wheel look is classy, making any Midyear look period correct. There were a couple of Kelsey-Hayes versions like this 1965 reproduction available from Corvette Central. These beautiful reproduction wheels are available in true knock-off style or user-friendly bolt-on look-alikes.

in favor of look-alike bolt-on "knock-offs." Of course, both wheels had date coding and a manufacturer's stamp.

Knock-off wheels had a threaded adapter that bolted to the hub assembly. The adapters had five studs to locate and prevent wheel rotation on the hub. Factory wheels relied solely on a lead hammer to remove and tighten the wheels. Aftermarket knock-off wheels and adapter hubs were rifle drilled to allow the use of a locking pin. The use of a locking pin makes drivers feel more secure, knowing the wheels don't come off unintentionally. If the factory had used locking pins, the wheels would have met Federal safety concerns, which could have resulted in more knock-off wheels still being on the road.

Although pricy, the look of the Midyear knock-off wheel is timeless. Complete kits with wheels, center caps, hub adapters, and fasteners are available.

No matter what wheel you choose, there are a few hard and fast rules regarding sizing. Backspacing cannot exceed 4¼ inches, measuring from the wheel hub face inward toward the frame. It is possible to go as far as 4½ inches backspacing with modifications. I move the parking brake cable support from the side of the trailing arm to the top. Offset trailing arms are available that allow deeper backspacing, but then the tires rub the inner fenders. Eight-inch wheels with 4½-inch backspacing works on the rear, but you can expect fender rub up front with 8-inch-wide wheels.

I always make sure the aftermarket wheels I choose center on the hub, not the studs. Hub-centric wheels have less chance of vibration from being off center.

My last bit of wheel advice is to be conservative concerning the wheel diameter. Contemporary 18-inch-diameter wheels have a very short sidewall, which means more road variations are transmitted into the cockpit. The best Midyear wheel for all four corners is 17x7, if aftermarket wheels are your choice.

Just as there are too many wheels out there to recommend, there are also too many tire choices for me to recommend one. My favorite tire brand has been Michelin for many years. Excellent ride from the ultra smooth rolling tires is the reason all my vehicles have them. Many sets of the Michelin tires I have used end up being replaced due to age, not tread wear.

In my experience, new tires that require more than 2 ounces of weight during balancing will most likely vibrate. Tire suppliers don't like to hear this. I tell them that I want another tire if it requires more than 2 ounces to balance one. It is never a good idea to keep driving when a bad vibration exists. Shock absorbers, suspension, and steering components are subjected to rapid oscillations as the vibrations bounce the wheel/tire assembly.

Power Steering

In 1963, many thought power steering was for the weak and that it wasted valuable horsepower. Because of this, approximately only 25 percent of the Midyears were ordered with power steering. Today, few people consider buying a vehicle with manual steering. Maneuvering through a parking lot is probably the number-one reason. Spirited driving is another because it's tiring to have to put extra effort into steering while concentrating on where to point your car. Many Midyears have been converted to power steering to make them more fun to drive. You can easily convert your project or restore its power steering using kits with every needed piece in one package.

General Motors wanted the Midyear's power steering to be an assist, for the best road feel at speed. To accomplish that, they used an early design with a hydraulic cylinder attached to the steering center link. To actuate the cylinder, they placed a control valve that senses steering gear movement. Once the steering gear is actuated, pressure is applied to the cylinder to provide assist.

Two downsides to the system were its exposed cylinder rod and multiple hoses. The vulnerable cylinder could be damaged by road debris, which bends or scores the cylinder's seals. Control valves are also subjected to wear and anything the road throws at them.

The same Midyear power steering system was used until 1982 with very few modifications. Another industry was born to service these sought-after items. Today, you can buy new or remanufactured pieces for every power steering item you might need. If you have power steering, the best option is to replace both the control valve and cylinder with new units. I've found that the cost of restoring the cylinder and control valve often outweighs the cost of replacing the items.

Midyear steering columns came in two versions: standard, until 1965; then telescopic became available. Three steering wheels were available: black plastic for 1963; and teakwood and simulated wood for 1964–1967. The unique 1963 column has an externally-mounted, cable-operated turn signal switch. All other Midyears have traditional, internal turn signal switches.

Like all other components, the steering column has wear items. The lower column bearing takes the brunt of the abuse, from dirt and heat in the engine compartment.

Many aftermarket steering wheels are available. The original teakwood and simulated plastic steering wheels are also available. You can also have the teakwood wheels restored to original specs.

OTHER COMPONENTS

Power Steering Installation

Power steering pumps have an adapter fitting to connect the pressure hose to and prevent fluid loss. When the pressure hose is replaced this fitting often comes loose and requires the use of a large one inch wrench to hold the fitting during hose replacement. The best policy is to replace the rubber o-ring when this fitting is loose. Keep in mind that the o-ring must be placed in the groove shown or the pump will not work.

Install Shaft Key

2 Until 1974 early GM power steering pumps used shaft keyways and keys to keep the pulley tight on the shaft. This big-block power steering pulley does not require a specialized puller like the 1975-and-up pulleys for removal. You often need to use a small gear puller to break it loose if corrosion has made its way between the shaft and pulley.

Install Pressure Regulator Spring

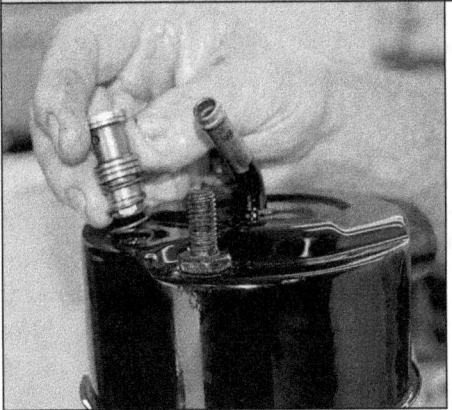

1 The fitting from the previous photo has this pressure regulator valve under it. The valve must be installed with the spring first and the valve in this position. When assembled in any other fashion you have no power steering assist.

Connect Hoses to Control Valve

3 Love 'em or hate 'em, this power steering control valve has multiple hoses to connect. Something to always remember is that the hoses must crisscross coming out of the control valve going to the cylinder. The 7/16-inch nylon lock nut centers the control valve. If the steering wheel is pulling to one side while standing still the nut is adjusted to unload the valve. Tighten the nut until the steering wheel just starts to move then back it off 1/2 turn.

Check Steering Coupler

4 This steering coupling absolutely amazes me. I hear complaints of loose steering all the time and typically find this steering box coupler completely trashed. Amazingly, I find couplers just like this with torn-out rubber discs cleaned and painted after a restoration. Thankfully there are safety pins to prevent total loss of steering.

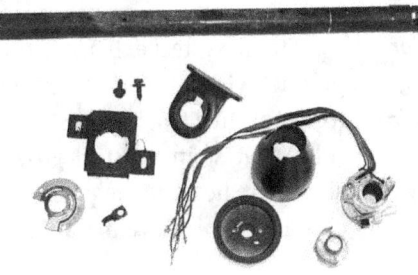

Midyear standard steering columns are simple, with very few pieces and all the typical wear items are available. The best policy is to replace the upper and lower steering column bearings. Telescopic columns have a few other pieces to be concerned about but they too are simple to restore.

CHAPTER 13

Power Windows

Power windows were available in all Midyears. Reliable ACDelco motors moved the glass up and down quickly. General Motors used a lift spring to assist the motor on the up travel. Missing or broken assist springs allow the window to move down rapidly, so quickly that you may think the glass will come out of the bottom of the door.

Install Roller on Stud

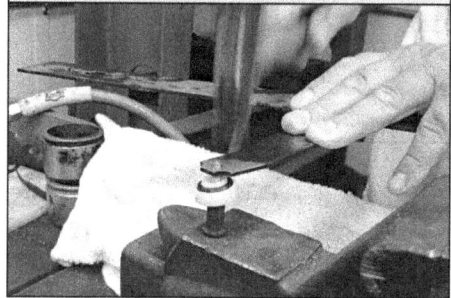

1 *Window regulator restoration components are available, including this roller from Long Island Corvette Supply. Use a back-up pin that fits inside the roller as an anvil to clinch the roller stud with a hammer. Be careful here; check the roller stud for a tight fit after just a few whacks. Too much hammering locks the roller on the stud.*

Install Spring Pin

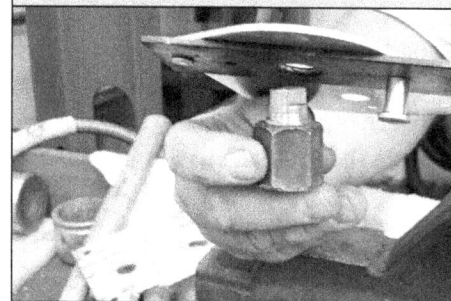

3 *This rear strut rod removal tool, or "strut rod knocker" as it is called, holds the spring pin well during installation. The spring pin and tool is set on the vise for more hammering to wedge the end into the regulator.*

Motor removal requires some thought, due to the regulator's assist spring. Window regulator restoration pieces are available, such as the regulator gear and rollers. Restoration makes sense if the lift arm pivot has minimal play. The pivot in question is for the lift arms with the rollers. Inspect the power window motor gear; the teeth wear and the clutch spring weakens. If the window regulator gear teeth are worn, most likely the motor's gear should be replaced. The same restoration procedure can be applied to a manual (non-power) window regulator.

Secure Rivets

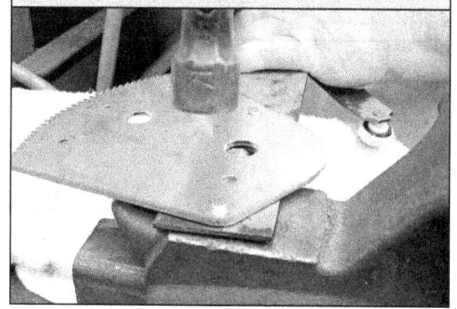

2 *This is where you can relieve some frustration on a Saturday afternoon. The supplied rivets are peened over with a few blows from the hammer to secure the new regulator gear to the lift arm. Keep an eye on the gear for centering on the spring pin to be installed next.*

Install Regulator

4 *The original regulator is ready for installation. Make sure the spring is installed and applies tension as the window is lifted. Note the bolt in the center of the regulator gear holding the assembly for installation of the window motor.*

Exhaust System

The following are a few simple tips that can make your exhaust restoration easier. General Motors never used exhaust gaskets for sealing; metal-to-metal was the plan. When you have your engine at the machine shop, have them surface the cylinder head side of the exhaust manifold for a good seal. While the manifolds are off, take some time and remove all the flange studs then sand blast the manifolds and apply a coat of CALYX exhaust coating on them with a cloth, and rub it in well. CALYX does a great job of looking like raw steel after repeated hot cold cycles. When the CALYX coating gets thin, spots can be touched up without recoating the entire manifold.

On this project, I chose Corvette Central's complete exhaust system package. The ready-to-go kit comes with ceramic-coated shorty headers and all the necessary exhaust pipes and mufflers. I could choose stock, GM-designed off-road, or Magnaflow mufflers. The only other required items are rear exhaust hangers. This proven system is easy to install that places the pipes in their stock location. No extra time was required to cut and fit the exhaust pipes to the shorty headers.

Exhaust pipes and mufflers come in various compositions: steel, stainless steel, and aluminized. Steel exhaust materials are rarely used today because of their short life span and how quickly they rust. Applying aluminized coating on steel exhaust pieces has become commonplace today. This was an excellent innovation that keeps rust at bay and extends the life of exhaust system products while keeping prices reasonable.

Stainless steel exhaust is the ultimate product, virtually indestructible and able to be polished to a high luster. The downside is tat stainless steel grows measurably as it heats up requiring additional clearance to prevent rattles. Another

Exhaust manifolds do warp in the center at the two ports in close proximately to each other. Use a precision straightedge to find out if the manifold has more than a .004-inch low area. Manifold machining is also required if the area is rough or warped.

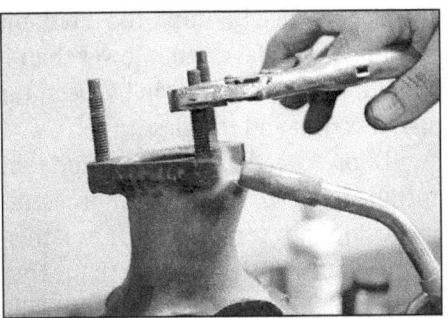

Heat is the best medicine when removing stubborn 40 year old studs from iron exhaust manifolds. Rust penetrant most times will not do the trick, but it certainly won't hurt to apply some long before any attempt is made to remove the studs. The trick is to heat just the iron surrounding the stud. If the stud becomes red hot it will twist off easily and you will have to drill out the broken piece.

major factor is cost. In most cases, plan on spending two thirds more on the stainless steel system over an aluminized system. A stainless steel undercar exhaust system on a Midyear requires plenty of extra work to keep the pipes off the transmission crossmember. GM uses two 3-7/8 inch passages in the transmission crossmember to route the exhaust pipes through. Keeping the O.E. 2-1/2 inch diameter pipes centered in the passages is tough with aluminized pipe; stainless steel is very difficult.

The choice is yours of course. Stainless steel makes sense on show cars that

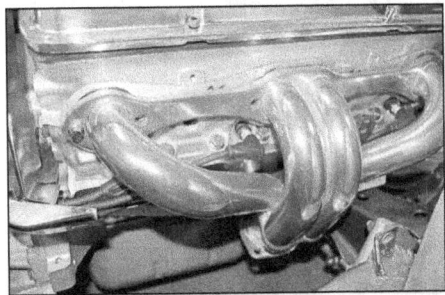

These coated Shortie headers are available from Corvette Central to replace tired cast-iron manifolds. These easy-to-install headers connect directly to Corvette Central exhaust system. No cutting or fitting required; all the pieces you need in one package.

are driven infrequently and aluminized makes sense on Midyears that will be driven. An alternative is using aluminized pipes with stainless steel mufflers. Midyear mufflers are somewhat visible from the back and stainless steel mufflers are a good way to go if you want some shine at the backside.

GM realized that the exhaust pipes would rattle as they passed through the transmission crossmember. They devised a hanger for both pipes that was sandwiched between the transmission and transmission mount. Specific hangers manufactured of steel were used at the rear crossmember that bolt directly to the mufflers. GM used guillotine-style exhaust pipe clamps that do an excellent job of clamping and sealing the pipes. Today all of the original clamps, hardware, and hangers are available to make exhaust installation easier.

Windshield and Glass

Windshield installation and trim can be challenging for the first timer. The windshield trim has clips all around the perimeter of the glass. Each clip grabs the edge of the trim. Careless removal can distort the trim, preventing the clips from grabbing properly. I check the fit and how well the trim secures to the clips before the glass is installed. The corners are especially tough areas to get the clips to grab the trim. Once the trim fits and is held securely in the clips, I can easily remove it for glass installation. Better to find out whether there is a problem with any of the clips before the glass is in place.

The glass is held in place with a rubber seal that sandwiches both the glass and the lip around the windshield opening. You either put the seal on the body's lip first, or on the glass, then pull the seal into place with a string that is placed in the cavity of the seal. As the string is pulled, the seal is pulled up and over the lip that retains the glass. Sealing the glass and body is not that easy without some type of pliable sealer. General Motors placed a bead of sealer around the entire circumference of the seal to ensure a weather-tight seal.

The problem is that, today, glass installers know little of this early technology. The correct glass sealer is comprised of rubber, not silicone or urethane, which are prevalent today. Urethane and silicone sealers dry without bonding to the rubber seal. You must use rubber-compatible sealer, or you end up with a water leak.

I found the correct windshield sealer at Lowe's home improvement stores, labeled as gutter seal. The butyl rubber gutter seal seals the glass and bonds to the rubber and fiberglass body. Butyl rubber sealer washes up with mineral spirits and stays pliable for many years. Squeeze a bead of sealer around the inside and outside of the windshield seal. Have at least a quart of mineral spirits available with plenty of cloths to wipe off the excess sealer, after the windshield is installed.

The 1963 split rear windows were held in with the same style seals as the front windshield. The 1964–1967 rear windows were held in place with a butyl rope seal. Federal regulations prevent the use of butyl rubber rope seals in late-model cars. Urethane sealer is used to increase the integrity of the glass installation. The sealer becomes part of the vehicle's overall crash integrity.

The downside to using the softer urethane sealer is that it lets the glass settle lower than the butyl rope does. I use rubber blocks to hold the glass at the correct height until the urethane sets up. If the glass settles lower than it should, there is a large gap between the stainless trim and the glass.

Door weatherstrips should be installed dry, to check their fit, especially around corners. Most weatherstrips are slightly shorter than they need to be, to avoid bunching up. Pulling the weatherstrip over the door at the corners stretches it, making it flatter. Pull the weatherstrip at the corner, then glue both sides so that it leaves the weatherstrip loose in the corner. After the sides dry, glue the corner of the weatherstrip.

Weatherstrip adhesive has a particular procedure required for proper adhesion. Apply the adhesive to the door weatherstrip area, then put the weatherstrip against the adhesive for transfer to the weatherstrip. Then wait until the glue has hazed over and apply the weatherstrip where it belongs. Be careful where you stick the glued weatherstrip. Once the glue dries, it should be stuck well enough to rip the rubber if you try to move it.

Windshield Installation

Install Windshield Trim Retainer

1 *This is where many mistakes are made concerning the Midyear windshield stainless trim installation. These upper corner trim retainers are often misshapen and should be replaced. Loose screws from stripped holes that hold these retainers can be trouble; usually the number-6 screws can be replaced with number-8 screws. Apply sealer to each retainer screw to keep water out of the passenger compartment.*

Fit Windshield Trim

2 *Install all the stainless trim to check fit before the glass goes in. If necessary, modify the trim retainer strips until the trim pieces line up. This is a trial-and-error procedure modifying the pieces in baby steps until they all fit in unison. Take your time here; if the trim pieces do not catch now into the retainers they definitely will not catch when the glass is in place.*

Add Windshield Sealer

3 *Although messy this butyl rubber sealant keeps water out of the passenger compartment. Apply a 3/16 bead of the sealer in the glass and body channels of the windshield rubber seal. Mineral spirits clean up any excess sealer. The sooner you remove this avoids extra work. This sealer does not affect the trim clips during installation due to its pliable nature.*

Install Windshield

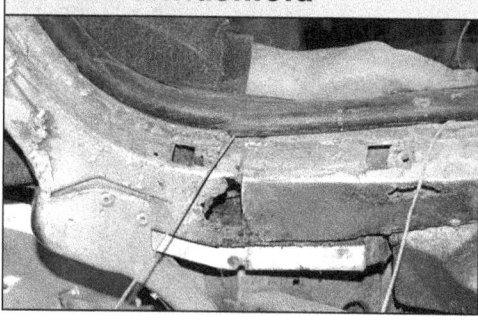

4 *Use a light string to pull the rubber seal over the windshield frame. Apply pressure on the outside of the glass as the string is pulled around the frame. The tough part is when the last foot or so of seal is pulled over the edge. We use a flat plastic blade to help the string ease the rubber seal over the edge at the very last few inches. Look over the seal to make sure the rubber is not bulging out on the inside or outside of the windshield frame. The rubber seal must lie flat around the entire windshield frame before attempting to install the windshield trim.*

SOURCE GUIDE

3M Products
www.3m.com

Al Knoch Interiors
9010 N Desert Blvd
Canutillo, TX 79835
www.alknochinteriors.com

Allstate Plastic Media Blasting
3101 Grays Ferry Ave
Philadelphia, PA 19146
215-462-1860

Apple Hydraulics
1610 Middle Rd
Calverton, NY 11933
800-882-7753
www.applehydraulics.com

Auto Custom Carpets
1429 Noble St
Anniston, AL 36201
800-352-8216
www.accmats.com

Auto Gear Equipment
530 State Fair Blvd
Syracuse, NY 13204
800-634-3001

AZ Speed
6313 W Commonwealth Pl, Unit 3
Chandler, AZ 85226
(480) 753-0208
www.azspeed-marine.com

Be Cool
310 Woodside Ave
Essexville, MI 48732
800-691-2667
www.becool.com

Bloomington Gold
705 E. Lincoln, Suite 201
Normal, Illinois 61761
309-888-4477
www.bloomingtongold.com

Blue Print Engines
800-483-4263
www.blueprintengines.com

Brad Penn
www.penngrade1.com

Chevrolet
P.O. Box 33170
Detroit, MI 48232
www.gm.com

Classic Auto Air
4901 Rio Vista Ave
Tampa, FL 33634
www.classicautoair.com

Comp Cams
3406 Democrat Rd.
Memphis, TN 38118
800-999-0853
www.compcams.com

Cool It/Thermo Tec
P.O. Box 96
Greenwich, Ohio 44837
800-274-8437
www.thermotec.com

Corvette America
100 Classic Car Dr
Reedsville, PA 17084
800-458-3475
www.corvetteamerica.com

Corvette Central
13550 Three Oaks Rd
Sawyer, MI. 49125
800-345-4122
www.corvettecentral.com

Corvette Instrument Service
9627 Begonia St
Palm Beach Gardens, FL 33410
561-627-9345
www.corvetteinstrumentservice.com

Crane Corvettes
4687 Chateau Place
San Diego, CA 92117
858-864-2883
www.cranescorvette.com

Dewitt's
1275 Grand Oaks Dr
Howell, MI 48843
517-548-0600
www.dewitts.com

East Willow Transmission Service
12665 Al Hwy 79
Scottsboro, AL 35768
256-259-3156

Eckler's Corvette
800-284-3906
www.ecklerscorvette.com

Ed Hartnett Standard Transmission Service
242 Pembroke Ave, #2
Lansdowne, PA 19050
610-623-9381

Evercoat
6600 Cornell Rd
Cincinnati, Ohio 45242
513-489-7600
www.evercoat.com

FAST
3400 Democrat Rd
Memphis, TN 38118
877-334-8355
www.fuelairspark.com

Fiberglass Coatings, Inc.
4301A 34th Street N.
St. Petersburg, FL 33714
727-327-8117
www.fgci.com

Glassworks: The Hardtop Shop
113 McGovern Blvd
Crescent, PA 15046
877-VET-TOPS
www.thehardtopshop.com

GM Performance Parts
www.gmperformanceparts.com

Harbor Freight
800-444-3353
www.harborfreight.com

Holley Performance Products
1801 Russellville Rd
Bowling Green, KY 42101
270-745-9547
www.holley.com

Home Depot
www.homedepot.com

Impact Restorations
5566 36th Street SE
Grand Rapids, MI 49512
616-954-9200
www.impactrestorations.com

Jack Podell
106 Wakewa
South Bend, IN 46617
574-232-6430
www.jackpodellfuelinjections.com

Masters City Classic Car Parts
3706 Merion Dr
Augusta, GA 30907
www.johnpirkle.com

K&C Harrison, Inc.
P.O. Box 1167
Mt. Vernon, TX 75457
www.oldcaraudio.net

Keisler Engineering
2250 Stock Creek Blvd
Rockford, TN 37853
888-609-0094
www.keislerauto.com

Long Island Corvette Supply
1445 Strong Ave
Copiague, NY 11726
800-466-6367
www.licorvette.com

Lucas Oil Products
www.lucasoil.com

Lucky's Customs
131 Teresa Dr
Madison, AL 35757

Market Street Performance
109 N Market St
Scottsboro, AL 35768
256-259-3058

Mid America Motorworks
17082 N US Highway 45
Effingham, IL 62401
866-350-4540
www.mamotorworks.com

Mobil 1
www.mobil1.com

Motive Products
5750 Obata Way, Unit G
Gilroy, CA 95020
www.motiveproducts.com

NAPA
www.napa.com

NCRS
6291 Day Rd
Cincinnati, OH 45252
513-385-8526

Paragon Corvette Reproductions
8040 S Jennings Rd
Swartz Creek, MI 48473
800-882-4688
www.paragoncorvette.com

Pertronix
440 E Arrow Highway
San Dimas, CA 91773
909-599-5955
www.pertronix.com

Petris Enterprises
809 West Willow St
Scottsboro, AL 35768
256-259-2400
www.petrisenterprises.com

Quanta Products
743 Telegraph Rd
Rising Sun, MD 21911
800-235-8788

RHS Racing Head Service
3416 Democrat Rd
Memphis, TN 38118
877-776-4323
www.racingheadservice.com

Richmond
1001 W. Exchange Ave
Chicago, IL 60609
864-843-1276
www.richmondgear.com

Sears
www.sears.com

Sermersheim's/Lee Bumb Composites
3817 N Saint Joseph Ave
Evansville, IN 47720
812-424-4701

SSBC Performance Brake Systems
11470 Main St
Clarence, NY 14031
800-448-7722
www.ssbrakes.com

The Quad Shop
5963 Linden Rd
Rockford, IL 61109
815-874-4884

V Tech Corvette/Performance
8245 N. Pheasant Tr
Stillman Valley, IL 61084
815-234-4340
815-262-1681
www.vtechcorvette.com

Valvoline
www.valvoline.com

Van Steel
12285 West Street
Clearwater, FL 33762
800-418-5397
www.vansteel.com

Vette Brakes and Products
7490 30th Ave N
St. Petersburg, FL 33710
800-237-9991
www.vbandp.com

Vintage Air
18865 Goll St
San Antonio, TX 78266
www.vintageair.com

Wilwood Engineering
4700 Calle Bolero
Camarillo, CA 93012
805-388-1188
www.wilwood.com

Zip Products
8067 Fast Lane
Mechanicsville, VA 23111
804-746-7043
www.zip-corvette.com

www.ingramcontent.com/pod-product-compliance
Lightning Source LLC
Chambersburg PA
CBHW081444070526
44586CB00019B/2228